FAMILIES ACROSS THE LIFE COURSE

JAMES M. WHITE
University of British Columbia

TODD F. MARTIN
Trinity Western University

SILVIA K. BARTOLIC
University of British Columbia

PEARSON

Toronto

Vice-President, Editorial Director: Gary Bennett
Editor-in-Chief: Michelle Sartor
Editor, Humanities and Social Sciences: Joel Gladstone
Marketing Manager: Lisa Gillis
Supervising Developmental Editor: Madhu Ranadive
Developmental Editor: Rebecca Ryoji
Project Manager: Richard di Santo
Manufacturing Coordinator: Susan Johnson
Production Editor: Susan Broadhurst
Copy Editor: Susan Broadhurst
Proofreader: Ruth Bradley-St-Cyr
Compositor: Cenveo Publisher Services
Permissions Researcher: Indu Arora
Art Director: Julia Hall
Interior and Cover Designer: Anthony Leung
Cover Image: Gettyimages

Credits and acknowledgments borrowed from other sources and reproduced, with permission, in this textbook appear on the appropriate page within the text, and on pages 368–370.

10 9 8 7 6 5 4 3   WC

Library and Archives Canada Cataloguing in Publication

White, James Martin
　　　Families across the life course / James M. White, Todd F. Martin, Silvia K. Bartolic.

Includes bibliographical references and index.
ISBN 978-0-13-214813-9

　　　1. Families. I. Martin, Todd, 1962– II. Bartolic, Silvia III. Title.

HQ503.W695 2012   306.85   C2011-907252-1

ISBN 978-0-13-214813-9

Brief Contents

Contents

Preface

Families Across the Life Course is intended to provide a comprehensive introduction to the study of marriage and the family. However, it is important to point out that while we state that we are studying "marriages" and "families," the actual subjects covered in this book are much broader and more diverse than would normally be encompassed by studying only those who are currently married and have children.

This book explores marriage and family through the theoretical approach of life course theory, which entails following individuals and social groups such as marriages or families through the life course. It may seem simple to follow individuals from birth to death but it is more difficult to conceptualize the birth of a marriage or a family social group. We trace these developing social relationships from early dating to later life and to the grief of losing a family member. No matter where you find yourself in this process, the life course approach affords retrospective explanations of how you arrived at this point and prospective analyses of the likely paths you might take in the future. This is a compelling approach for both students and teachers, since all are situated within the currents of time and events that make up our lives.

IMPORTANT THEMES

Some important themes permeate our study of the life course. Throughout the book, we have tried to acknowledge the **diversity** of paths that individuals and social groups traverse in the life course. This diversity has many sources, including ethnicity, gender, social class, Aboriginal status, immigration status, sexual orientation, and age. Diversity is not considered a negative component. Rather, diversity is considered both a difference and a force for social change. Indeed, it is through diversity that the world changes.

Another important theme is **social change**. As we examine how the dominant life course has changed across historical periods, such as wars and economic depressions, and across age cohorts, such as "baby boomers" and "Generation X," we can start to construct a larger picture of social change that encompasses both past generations and future generations. All of this is captured in the final chapter of the book, where we address questions such as "Is the institution of marriage dead?" and "What will the family of the future look like?"

DATA

Objectivity is an ideal state, rather than an actual state. When we say that we strive for objectivity, part of what we mean is that we try to ensure that researchers have not intentionally introduced bias into their research and that other researchers could use the same measures and replicate the research findings. Another important part of what we mean by objectivity is that the concepts that are used to understand and interpret findings are clearly defined so that measurement, whether qualitative or quantitative, is indeed possible. It must be remembered that "objectivity" is something we strive for, not a claim for privilege. There are many forms of knowledge, such as art, music, poetry, and science. This book is directed toward the last of these forms.

Canadian data are sometimes difficult to find. We rely on Statistics Canada for much of our population data, but Canadian researchers publish their studies in journals around the world. We have attempted to use Canadian data whenever possible. However, in some cases, such as with child development and family violence, findings come from all over the world. We have pursued a balanced approach of presenting Canadian findings but also situating the Canadian research in an international and global context.

ORGANIZATION OF THE BOOK

The book is organized in what we consider to be a logical progression. Chapter 1 addresses a basic question: "What are we going to study?" It may seem that a definition of "family" would be obvious to students, but once this concept is placed in different contexts, such as theory or cross-cultural research, it becomes more problematic. Therefore, we begin with a discussion of how to define the family.

Chapter 2 elucidates the life course theory. This approach guides and informs our interpretation of data and what we consider important. Chapter 2 introduces the broad array of theories used in the study of families and then concentrates on life course theory.

Chapters 3 through 10 approximate the chronological order of events that many of us experience in our lives: "First comes love, then comes marriage, then comes Suzy with a baby carriage." Beginning with dating and mate selection and traversing the topics of cohabitation, marriage, having a child, parenting, and eventually the aging family, these chapters contain a wealth of information about individual transitions and events as well as events and transitions for the social group. The order of these events and transitions in today's society is carefully examined.

Chapter 11 discusses the dark elements of the family: stress, conflict, and abuse. The family is a small, intimate social group that involves strong emotions; at times, violent behaviour is associated with these strong emotions.

Finally, Chapter 12 addresses the large number of ways in which the family and marriage are changing. This chapter reviews much of the research that has been presented throughout the book and challenges students to imagine future scenarios of what might happen within their lifetimes. New alternatives that might replace what we have known as marriage and family are emerging. This final chapter allows us to explore these possible futures.

TWO NOTES REGARDING PEDAGOGY

Two elements of our pedagogical approach need to be highlighted. The first is our **eclecticism**. Although the book is written from a largely sociological perspective, we have included research from many other fields, such as family studies, economics, political science, and demography. The study of the family is shared by a great many social sciences and we cannot afford to put on disciplinary blinders regarding this wealth of information and theory.

The second element is that we have sometimes included **old citations** that may seem to be "dated" or from a long time ago. These references are often the most important ones. In every area of study, there are seminal works that define and guide research for generations. Examples of such work include Gary S. Becker's work in the 1980s on the micro-economics of the family, Melvin Kohn's work on the transmission of social class in the 1960s, and Emile Durkheim's work on the functions of deviance in creating social change in the 1880s. Any citations that seem "old" should not be dismissed. These works have stood the test of time and have been well researched. The desire for current citations should not blind us to major leaps forward made in previous generations. We do not want to "reinvent the wheel" in each new generation.

We have enjoyed writing this book. As a group, we represent almost half a century of teaching and researching the topics discussed in this book. Every year, we see more students excited about and interested in the area that has occupied our interest and scholarly endeavours for so long. We welcome you to the study of one of the most vibrant areas of research in the social sciences, and to an area that is meaningful to us all.

James M. White
Todd F. Martin
Silvia K. Bartolic

SUPPLEMENTS

All of the following instructor supplements are also available for download from a password-protected section of Pearson Canada's online catalogue. Navigate to your book's catalogue page to view a list of the supplements that are available. See your local sales representative for details and access.

Instructor's Manual

The Instructor's Manual contains chapter overviews and outlines, a sample course syllabus, lecture suggestions, plus other useful resources to assist with teaching and student learning.

PowerPoint Slides

The PowerPoint Slides include up to 25 slides per chapter covering key concepts from each chapter, including selected figures and tables used in the text.

Test Item File

The Test Item File is available in Microsoft Word format. The test bank includes true–false, multiple choice, and short answer questions. Each question includes the correct answer; a page reference to the text where the answer can be found; a skill classification of Applied, Conceptual, or Factual; and a degree of difficulty of Easy, Moderate, or Challenging.

Companion Website with Grade Tracker

The Companion Website at **www.pearsoncanada.ca/white** is a handy reference for students. The site includes resources useful to both students and instructors. Students can also use the Companion Website's Grade Tracker function to record and review their progress on the self-graded multiple choice quizzes. Students can log on to the Companion Website using the Student Access Code that comes packaged with every copy of *Families Across the Life Course*.

CourseSmart for Instructors (ISBN 0132483416)

CourseSmart goes beyond traditional expectations—providing instant, online access to the textbooks and course materials you need at a lower cost for students. Even as students save money, you can save time and hassle with a digital eTextbook that allows you to search for the most relevant content at the very moment you need it. Whether it's evaluating textbooks or creating lecture notes to help students with difficult concepts, CourseSmart can make life a little easier. See how when you visit **www.coursesmart. com/instructors**.

CourseSmart for Students (ISBN 0132483416)

CourseSmart goes beyond traditional expectations—providing instant, online access to the textbooks and course materials you need at an average savings of 60 percent. With instant access from any computer and the ability to search your text, you'll find the content you need quickly, no matter where you are. And with online tools such as highlighting and note-taking, you can save time and study efficiently. See all of the benefits at **www.coursesmart.com/students**.

Technology Specialists

Pearson's Technology Specialists work with faculty and campus course designers to ensure that Pearson technology products, assessment tools, and online course materials are tailored to meet your specific needs. This highly qualified team is dedicated to helping schools take full advantage of a wide range of educational resources, by assisting in the integration of a variety of instructional materials and media formats. Your local Pearson sales representative can provide you with more details on this service program.

ACKNOWLEDGEMENTS

Pearson Canada would like to thank the following reviewers for their contributions: Andrew Buntin, George Brown College; Alana Butler, Ryerson University; Helene A. Cummins, Brescia University College; Wei Wei Da, Brescia University College; Jacqueline M. Quinless, Camosun College; Deb Wander, Selkirk College; and Weiguo Zhang, University of Toronto, Mississauga.

Chapter 1
Defining Family Across the Life Course

Learning Objectives

After reading this chapter, you should be able to:

1. Understand that definitions of family are important for making social, economic, and research decisions.
2. Acknowledge that there is no one correct definition of family.
3. Understand that research definitions of family involve measurement.
4. Understand that family definitions and terms are contained within the larger context of kinship organization.
5. Comprehend that kinship organization supplies a road map of social relationships, such as the "moral" or "right" way to select a mate and from whom one can expect inheritance.
6. Develop a working definition of the family.

Rapinda was elated. He had been distraught for more than a year about a decision made by Canada's immigration authorities. He had applied to be reunited with Amrita, his "wife," who is a citizen and resident of Canada. Canada allows immigrants to have special status as "family." Rapinda and Amrita had lived together in India but could not afford a wedding. In addition, they were from different castes and their parents did not approve of them marrying. The couple lived together for five years until Amrita's Canadian parents became sick and needed her help. Rapinda's original application to immigrate to Canada was filed in 2001; it was rejected because, at that time, the definition of conjugal partner was based on the federal convention of at least 12 months of cohabitation in the previous year. The problem was that the couple had been separated for some time by distance and immigration laws. In 2002, the Immigration and Refugee Protection Act was changed and the definition of conjugal partner was broadened beyond the previous understanding of common-law partner. *Finally,* Rapinda thought, *Amrita and I will be defined as "married" and we will be reunited in Canada.*

Definitions are important to our knowledge about families, and are also the key to understanding the various ways families are treated by health care providers, governments, and agencies. Formal definitions of family or marriage, such as those that appear in immigration acts or in health care or employment benefit policies, may have important implications for one's life. In the vignette above, the definitions in the Immigration and Refugee Protection Act (http://laws.justice.gc.ca/eng/acts/I-2.5/) affect not only Rapinda but also his wife and, in the long run, the nature of Canada as a country. Therefore, when definitions are formalized and codified into law, we can understand the importance of these definitions and how they may affect qualifying for or being denied access to employment and government benefits, for example.

Definitions are at the core of our knowledge. Imagine that your instructor asks you to spend the weekend observing "couples" in shopping centres and count how often they hold hands. You may want to be provided with a working definition for your observations. Is a couple only heterosexual or can it be same sex? Is a couple necessarily married, common law, or dating? Is the idea behind what we mean by a couple "romantic" or could a mother and her child, or two children playing together, also be a couple? All research begins with observation, but before it can begin, we must know what we are supposed to observe. Thus, the better our definition of what we are to observe is, the better our observation and knowledge will be. There is always the danger, of course, that when our definitions are too narrow we miss observations and that when they are too broad we include irrelevant observations along with the valid ones. Furthermore, we could imagine two separate research studies on, for example, handholding among couples conducted during the same time period and on the same sample but that reach different conclusions based on their use of different definitions of couple. Clearly, definitions are central to research and to the knowledge that results from research.

Definitions are social constructions that confer status and legitimacy for the group involved. Imagine that your friends find out that you have joined a sorority or fraternity. Your friends now define you as "one of them," meaning a member of the sorority or fraternity. Definitions may carry social legitimacy and social status. If all of your friends are yearning to be "one of them," your new definition as a member may confer status and an attribution of social success. On the other hand, among some people the effect could be the reverse.

What about "family"? Being defined as having a family often carries with it a status of normality. Being a mother or a father is a legitimate and normative status in most societies, and having a family carries distinct rights and responsibilities. For example, if you take your children to a public swimming pool, you would probably be allowed to pay the family rate. But, generally, the term *family* is not formally defined; instead, there is the common understanding of what is normally meant. In such cases, the definition resides in common use of the term with all of its normative biases, such as that families usually do not have multiple wives or husbands. This common normative meaning is even more evident in "family" functions. For example, if you are a father watching a girls' soccer match in a public park, you will be seen as legitimate; compare this to the reaction to a single, never-married male watching the same soccer match.

Data Box 1.1 demonstrates how important definitions are to our knowledge and to the way we construct our social world. Although Statistics Canada refers to the data as a "family portrait," there are clearly data about individuals (young adults), couples, marriages, and households. It is more or less left to the reader to determine whether a "marriage" is the same thing as a "family" and whether a "household" is the same as a "family." Clearly, a "one-person household" would not fit most people's definition of a "family." There is also an ideological component to definitions. For instance, defining same-sex couples as "families" is relatively new for Canada and even for the world. Indeed, only 10 countries have recognized same-sex marriages at this writing, so Canada is certainly a leader in this regard. Despite this fact, a substantial number of Canadians would disagree with this definition on moral or religious grounds. Definitions allow researchers not only to gather data but also to construct social legitimacy and tolerance.

This chapter is about definitions of family. We address many of the questions raised by the examples above. We first delineate some of the major ways in which family and marriage are defined. We then turn to a few different approaches to defining the definitions themselves. We discuss the different kinds of definitions of family, such as normative, legal, policy, and theoretical definitions. Finally, we discuss definitions of family in relation to dynamics across the life course so that we

Data Box 1.1

Portrait of Changing Families

Statistics Canada today releases a "family portrait" of Canadians using the third set of data from the 2006 Census. This release examines developments in families, marital status, households, and living arrangements in Canada between 2001 and 2006, and how children fit into these evolving family structures.

In addition, it provides information on the number of same-sex couples, both those living in a common-law union and, for the first time, those who are married.

In total, the census enumerated 8,896,840 census families in 2006, up 6.3% from 2001.

The census enumerated 6,105,910 married-couple families, an increase of only 3.5% from 2001. In contrast, the number of common-law-couple families surged 18.9% to 1,376,865, while the number of lone-parent families increased 7.8% to 1,414,060.

Consequently, married-couple families accounted for 68.6% of all census families in 2006, down from 70.5% five years earlier. The proportion of common-law-couple families rose from 13.8% to 15.5%, while the share of lone-parent families increased slightly from 15.7% to 15.9%.

Two decades ago, common-law-couple families accounted for only 7.2% of all census families. Married-couple families represented 80.2%, and lone-parent families, 12.7%.

In Quebec, where the prevalence of common-law-couple families has been one of the defining family patterns for years, the number of common-law-couple families increased 20.3% between 2001 and 2006 to 611,855. They accounted for 44.4% of the national total. Close to one-quarter (23.4%) of all common-law-couple families in Canada lived in the two census metropolitan areas of Montréal and Québec.

Among lone-parent families, growth between 2001 and 2006 was most rapid for families headed by men. Their number increased 14.6%, more than twice the rate of growth of 6.3% among those headed by women.

Same-Sex Married Couples Counted for the First Time

The number of same-sex couples surged 32.6% between 2001 and 2006, five times the pace of opposite-sex couples (+5.9%).

For the first time, the census counted same-sex married couples, reflecting the legalization of same-sex marriages for all of Canada as of July 2005. In total, the census enumerated 45,345 same-sex couples, of which 7,465, or 16.5%, were married couples.

Half of all same-sex couples in Canada lived in the three largest census metropolitan areas, Montréal, Toronto, and Vancouver, in 2006. Toronto accounted for 21.2% of all same-sex couples, Montréal, 18.4% and Vancouver, 10.3%.

In 2006, same-sex couples represented 0.6% of all couples in Canada. This is comparable to data from New Zealand (0.7%) and Australia (0.6%).

Over half (53.7%) of same-sex married spouses were men in 2006, compared with 46.3% who were women. Proportions were similar among same-sex common-law partners in both 2006 and 2001.

About 9.0% of persons in same-sex couples had children aged 24 years and under living in the home in 2006. This was more common for females (16.3%) than for males (2.9%) in same-sex couples.

Households: Large Increase in One-Person Households

Since 2001, there has been a large increase in one-person households.

During this time, the number of one-person households increased 11.8%, more than twice as fast as the 5.3% increase for the total population in private households. At the same time, the number of households consisting of couples without children aged 24 years and under increased 11.2% since 2001.

The households with the slowest growth between 2001 and 2006 were those comprised of couples with children aged 24 years and under; these households edged up only 0.4%.

Between 2001 and 2006, the number of private households increased 7.6%, while the population in private households rose 5.3%.

The census counted more than three times as many one-person households as households with five or more persons in 2006. Of the 12,437,470 private households, 26.8% were one-person households, while 8.7% were households of five or more persons.

More Young Adults Living with Their Parents

Over the last two decades, one of the trends for young adults has been their growing tendency to remain in, or return to, the parental home. This upward trend has continued over the past five years.

In 2006, 43.5% of the 4 million young adults aged 20 to 29 lived in the parental home, up from 41.1% in 2001. Twenty years ago, 32.1% of young adults lived with their parents.

Among individuals aged 20 to 24, 60.3% were in the parental home in 2006, up from 49.3% in 1986. Among those aged 25 to 29, 26.0% were in the parental home in 2006, up from 15.6% two decades earlier.

Saskatchewan (31.8%) and Alberta (31.7%) had the lowest proportions of young adults aged 20 to 29 living in the parental home in 2006. Among the other provinces, Newfoundland and Labrador (52.2%) and Ontario (51.5%) had the highest.

Among the census metropolitan areas, Toronto had the highest proportion of young adults who lived in their parents' home in 2006. Nearly 6 in 10 (57.9%) young adults aged 20 to 29 lived with their parents in Toronto, well above the national average (43.5%).

Unmarried People Outnumber Legally Married People for the First Time

For the first time, the census enumerated more unmarried people aged 15 and over than legally married people.

In 2006, more than one-half (51.5%) of the adult population were unmarried, that is, never married, divorced, separated or widowed, compared with 49.9% five years earlier. Conversely, only 48.5% of persons aged 15 and over were legally married in 2006, down from 50.1% in 2001.

Twenty years earlier, 38.6% of the population aged 15 and over were unmarried, while 61.4% were married.

Source: Statistics Canada (2007a).

are poised to move to Chapter 2 and the life course approach. The natural starting point for these discussions is the question "What is a definition?" which is addressed in Box 1.1.

EXAMPLES OF DEFINITIONS OF FAMILY AND MARRIAGE

Over centuries we have witnessed a great many definitions of the family. For example, the Bible reports that King Solomon's family included 700 wives and 300 concubines. It is interesting to compare this perspective on family with the current laws of many Western nations,

Box 1.1

What Is a Definition?

We can go back very far in human history and find heated discussions about definitions. For example, Plato's *Euthyphro* discusses the one stable characteristic that all things covered by a definition must have in common. Later, Aristotle argued that definitions capture the "essence" of what it is to be something; for example, to be human is to be a rational animal. Many distinctions can be made about definitions, such as whether they are intentional, extensional, vernacular, stipulative, and so on. We will not digress and discuss all of these, because to do so would take us very far away from our focus on the study of the family. Rather, we examine just two forms of definitions, Aristotelian and equivalence definitions, to give a taste of this complex terrain.

Aristotle's *Metaphysics* introduced what is now a standard form of definition, *genus and species definitions*. These definitions seek to establish the meaning of a word through two components. First, this type of definition establishes the genus of things that share similar properties. For example, horses share the category of "animal" with pigs and humans, for example. The second part of the definition states how the thing we are defining, horses, differs from other things in the genus, such as humans and pigs. So, for example, a horse is an animal that can whinny. Applying this logic to the family, we might argue that the family is a social group, similar to work groups, peer groups, or friendship groups. On the other hand, the family is the only form of social group whose membership is achieved through the *sexual bond* of same-generation adults (marriage) and *biological reproduction* (offspring).

Another way of defining things would be by *"equivalence" of meaning* (Hospers, 1967). This type of definition argues that each definition is simply a term to be defined that is then followed by several words or phrases that do the defining. Using the previous example, we would say that the term *horse* is equivalent to the phrase *an animal that whinnies*. The adequacy of this definition is then tested by the ability of the phrase to replace the word in a sentence without damaging the meaning or truth of the statement. For example, "Judy is riding the horse" could be replaced by "Judy is riding the animal that whinnies" and the meaning would remain the same. This type of definition provides more of a challenge for us than the genus and species definition since it must adequately replace all correct usages of the term *family*. Let's try our previous definition of a family as equivalent to "a social group containing sexually bonded adults and biological offspring" in the examples below:

Bill, Sue, and their children are a family.
Bill, Sue, and their children are a social group containing sexually bonded adults and biological offspring.

Or

Bill, Tom, and their children are a family.
Bill, Tom, and their children are a social group containing sexually bonded adults and biological offspring.

Or

Sheila belonged to the murderer Charles Manson's family.
Sheila belonged to the murderer Charles Manson's social group containing sexually bonded adults and biological offspring.

The first of these examples works well with the definition. However, the second and third including those of Israel, that largely ban polygamy and establish monogamy as the principal form of marriage.

Many dictionaries define the family as a fundamental social group for society or as a building block for society, but such general definitions don't really tell us what a family is so much as what its function is supposed to be. On the other hand, many dictionaries offer very specific definitions of the family, such as two opposite-sex adults and their biological or adopted offspring. The problem with such definitions is that they do not include same-sex couples and their children as families and they also exclude single-parent families. Furthermore, children raised by their grandparents would not be a family under such restrictive definitions. It is useful to examine briefly the major types of definitions of family and marriage and how they function.

TYPES OF DEFINITIONS OF FAMILY AND MARRIAGE

There are many types of definitions, each based on the context of the definition. Regardless of whether we use genus and species definitions or equivalence definitions, there are particular contexts in which those definitions must function. For the study of the family, we can identify *legal definitions*, where the context is enforceable legislated laws; *normative definitions*, where the context is the social norms in a society; *theoretical definitions*, where the context is the concepts and propositions of a social science theory; and *research definitions*, where the context is a specific research question.

Legal definitions of marriage and family may be definitions used in legislation, definitions used as common-law understandings, and definitions used in a court order. Usually when we find legal definitions relating to family law, they are about custody, maintenance, common-law relationships, and cohabitation, but not a definition of the family per se (e.g., www.publiclegalinfo.com/publications/Family%20Law%20Terms%20and%20Definitions%20second%20edition.pdf). However, other areas such as immigration law must define family relationships since one of the stated objectives of this legislation is "to see that families are reunited in Canada" (Immigration and Refugee Protection Act, 2001, section 3.1(d)). Such legal definitions are important to an individual's chances of claiming "family" reunification as a ground for admission to Canada. The Government of Canada, as well as each province and territory, has legislation about families. For example, Box 1.2 shows how Yukon extends federal legislation and defines a family member.

Legal definitions of marriage and family change from country to country around the world and often across political regions within a country. For example, in the United States, divorce laws are relatively liberal in Nevada and more conservative in Texas. Some of these differences are based on marriage legislation and it remains an interesting area of debate as to whether a same-sex couple that marries in Canada can get divorced if they reside in Texas, where no such union exists under Texas legislation. Regardless of the venue, we can see the power and importance of legal definitions and how they condone or restrict our intimate relationships.

Social constructions of family and *normative definitions* are those shared by the majority of people in a country or region. For example, the majority of Canadians accept that same-sex marriage is legitimate and constitutes an individual right under the equality section of the Charter of Rights and Freedoms. However, support varies by province and certainly by rural and urban regions. Nonetheless, Canadians as a majority support same-sex marriage and it can be considered "normative." In this case, normative means that a practice or action is regarded as socially legitimate and approved. When an act or practice is non-normative or deviant, there are often negative sanctions for the behaviour. For example, not more than 50 years ago divorce, though legal if there were grounds for it, was socially disapproved of and stigmatized.

Box 1.2

Definition of Family

Compassionate Care Leave—Definition of a Family Member

The federal government, in June 2006, announced an expanded definition of family for Compassionate Care leave under the Employment Insurance Act.

The Yukon Government has now mirrored the expanded definition of immediate family under the Employment Standards Act for Compassionate Care leave and consequently Bereavement leave.

Expanding the definition of family will provide more employees job protection while caring for a seriously ill family member, with a significant risk of death within a 26-week period, and allow job protection for a greater number of family members to attend a funeral for a family member.

This legislative amendment brings the Yukon in line with federal legislation.

Employees now covered under the Yukon's definition of a Family Member are:

- Spouse;
- Parent;
- Step-mother, step-father;
- Child, including a child to whom the employee stands in the place of parent;
- Brother, sister;
- Father of a spouse, mother of a spouse;
- Grandparent, grandchild;
- Son-in-law, daughter-in-law;
- any relative permanently residing in the employee's household or with whom the employee resides;
- Step-parent-in-law of the employee;
- uncle, aunt, niece or nephew of the employee or of the employee's spouse or common law partner;
- step-sibling of the employee;
- step-sibling-in-law of the employee;
- sibling-in-law or step-sibling-in-law of the employee;
- current or former foster parent, foster child, ward or guardian of the employee;
- spouse or common law partner of a child, grandparent, grandchild, uncle, aunt, niece, nephew, current or former guardian or current or former foster child of the employee;
- step-child-in-law of the employee;
- current or former foster parent or ward of the employee's spouse or common law partner;
- a person who considers the employee to be, or whom the employee considers to be, "like a close relative."

Source: http://www.community.gov.yk.ca/labour/deffamily.html

We sometimes find that legal definitions are out of sync with **social norms**. Sometimes this lack of consistency between our social norms and our legal definitions is the result of formal laws never being repealed or of interest groups advocating legislation that is not normative. Whatever the cause, it is important to note that social norms are not necessarily reflected in formal legislation and hence there may be a difference between a legal definition and a normative definition of the family or marriage. In addition, legal definitions only exist in those areas that require codification and formal sanctions, whereas much of our social life is governed by informal norms. For example, there is no formal law about queuing or politeness, but Canadians routinely line up, take turns, and say please and thank you.

Much of our social organization is tied to social norms, and normative definitions are inextricably linked to this social organization. Currently, most Canadians would say that a family is composed of two married, opposite-sex adults and their biological offspring. While this understanding may be central, Canadians also believe that the two adults may be of the same sex, that the children may be adopted, and that the adult relationship may be cohabiting and not formalized by marriage. Certainly, Canadians believe that a single mother and her child are also a family. Over the last 50 years, the normative definitions of family have broadened, and with multicultural and economic pressures, it is likely that they will continue to broaden.

It is interesting for each of us to ask which social groups we consider to be normative families and which we do not. For example, would a plural marriage of five adults with biological children be considered a family, or would a work group be considered a family? Is family normatively defined by the form of intimate relationships or by the roles and responsibilities that accompany those relationships? Is a father simply an older man who is supportive and warm with children or is he someone who bears responsibility for the nurturance, economic support, and behavioural outcomes of a child? Even though our particular religious or social group may construct "family" in a way that is different from the normative definition, social constructions of the family gain power only when adherents to a perspective increase in number. Eventually, this increase in the social construction would change the normative definition. This clearly has happened over the last 40 years by expanding the social construction of marriage to include gay and lesbian marriages.

Theoretical definitions of the family are those that use the concepts and propositions from a social science theory. A **concept** is an abstract set of things or ideas collected under one symbol or idea. For example, the concept of marriage contains all those things having a publicly recognized sexual bond between two people. Of course, societies may add dimensions such as consent, age of consent (adulthood), and voluntary versus involuntary to this simple definition. Definitions are the starting point for theory. We might develop theoretical propositions about what constitutes a happy marriage or a lasting marriage. These **propositions** are the backbone of a **theory** and are defined by any statement that relates one concept to another. Complex theories, such as those about families, are constructed by logically connecting many propositions about a specific phenomenon. For example, we have theories about mate selection, divorce, marital happiness, and marital stability, to name but a few in the academic study of family.

Many of the most useful of these theories share the assumptions of larger social theories (see White & Klein, 2008). For example, a theory about spousal exchanges may be rooted in the broader theoretical framework of social exchange or rational choice. A theory about the role of families in reproducing inequality may incorporate assumptions

Many Different Theories and Definitions

There are many theories in the social sciences, so there are also many ways of defining family. All of these various approaches are constrained by theoretical assumptions about the causal processes in the social world. For example, rational choice theories assume that the individual makes choices to optimize his or her profit in any situation. As such, the family is defined as that social group that over time optimizes the profit for each of its members. In this view, the family exists to optimize individual outcomes. Another theoretical definition is proposed by life course and developmental theory. Life course theory proposes that there are norms and expectations throughout the life cycle and that these norms create age-specific social roles. For example, a young mother of a newborn would be seen as meeting expectations and norms if she breast-feeds the infant, but a middle-aged mother would not be expected to breastfeed her adolescent. The life course definition of family focuses on the family as a temporal and normatively organized social group responsible for the nurturance and care of children. These two definitions are vastly different. The rational choice definition emphasizes individual profit and the life course definition emphasizes existing social norms and expectations.

from feminist theories or social conflict theories. Each of these major frameworks makes assumptions about the dimensions of study that are most important, and hence these assumptions guide these theories in constructing theoretical definitions. Examples of theoretically constructed definitions appear in Box 1.3.

Theoretical definitions are neither right nor wrong, but only consistent and coherent with the concepts and propositions in the associated theory. However, as we test competing theoretical hypotheses and find one theory superior at predicting and explaining forms of behaviour, we would consider the definitions within that theory useful. The problem with social science theories is that we want them to explain not only current family behaviours but also those of two centuries ago and those in other cultures. At present, we have many theories that supply some explanations but not others. In Chapter 2, we will cover some of the major forms of family theories.

Research definitions may be derived from a theory, from a social problem, or from a hunch. Although research definitions may come from diverse sources, they all have a common property in that they can be linked to measurement. **Measurement** is simply a way to assign numerals to a concept. For example, a ruler marked in centimetres is a measurement of the concept of length, but so is a ruler marked in inches. There are usually several ways to measure a concept. Every theory supplies conceptual hypotheses but those concepts must be tied to measurements for research to test predicted outcomes. We all may be concerned about social problems, such as the generally negative outcomes for children whose parents divorce, but we can neither mitigate negative affects nor successfully intervene without research. Social problem definitions for research would measure the concepts we use to formulate the social problem. For example, we may hypothesize that the negative outcomes usually linked to divorce are the result of a child's exposure to conflict in the marital relationship. Or, we may examine the post-divorce decline in resources for the child. Research questions may also be generated from gaps in our empirical knowledge or data. For instance, we may have good knowledge about single-parent families when mothers are the custodial parent but not when fathers are the custodial parent. Some research is driven by "what if" hunches. For example, a researcher might ask whether people who filed for divorce would have divorced if they had had free marital counselling available to them. Such "what if" questions also contain concepts that need to be measured, such as divorce rate and marital counselling. All of our concrete knowledge about families will depend on research definitions.

The family will be defined differently in different research contexts. For example, research on family structure must necessarily include single-parent families and extended families if the **variance** in family structures is to be examined. Indeed, if we have only one form of family structure, then we have nothing to research. On the other hand, if we want to research the effect of marital conflict on child outcomes, we would want to examine only intact families with children. The **variable** of interest would be the outcomes for children from low-conflict marriages versus high-conflict marriages. From these examples, it is clear that in order to understand research definitions of the family, we need to briefly examine the components and steps of the research process (see Box 1.4).

The initial step in the research process is to develop a research question. As discussed earlier, the research question can be derived from a theory, a social problem, a gap in existing data, or even a hunch. The research question can only orient a researcher. The reason for this is that the only way we can address a question is to answer it. However, our scientific research is more constrained and modest about what it can claim. Empirical research data cannot yield the answer to a question but only the probability that a statement is false. For example, imagine that we have the following research question: Does conflict in marriages affect children's academic performance? The long-term answer to this question will hinge on many research studies examining various forms and durations of marital conflict and various forms of academic achievement over time and at different ages. Any one research project will be able to formulate only a part of this research

Box 1.4

First Steps in the Research Process

1. The research question
2. The conceptual research hypothesis
3. Research definitions of concepts and relations
4. Identifying measures (operationalization)
5. Research design for measurement hypothesis

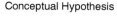

Conceptual Hypothesis

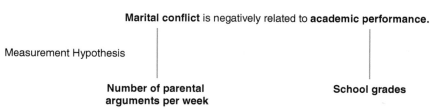

Marital conflict is negatively related to **academic performance.**

Measurement Hypothesis

**Number of parental
arguments per week**

School grades

Figure 1.1 Conceptual and Measurement Hypotheses

question, such as the short-term effects of marital conflict on children 11 and 12 years of age. Besides the fact that research scope is necessarily more focused than the research question, the most important difference is that we cannot examine questions but only statements. Scientific methods are founded on both logic and probability. A question cannot be true or false, but a declarative statement or proposition can be true or false. Therefore, every research question leads to a statement known as a conceptual hypothesis. A conceptual **hypothesis** is a statement that can have a truth value (true or false). For example, we might hypothesize that marital conflict is related to a child's academic performance. If we were to find that, according the bulk of probabilities, a conceptual hypothesis cannot be regarded as true, that does not mean we have a yes or no answer to the research question. Only many research findings on the question can lead us to a tentative answer to that question.

Figure 1.1 illustrates that there are actually two hypotheses in our research. One is the conceptual hypothesis, which is tied to theory, meaning, and interpretation of the research. The other is the measurement hypothesis, which is tied to the ways we measure our concepts. The only way we can address the conceptual hypothesis is to find reasonable and sound ways to measure the concepts (validity). Returning to the example of marital conflict and child academic performance, we would need measures of each of these concepts. For example, marital conflict might be measured simply by the number and intensity of disagreements a married couple has each week. Depending on the theory, it may or may not be important that the child is exposed to these conflicts. If the child's exposure is important, we may need to measure the child's reports of marital conflict. Indeed, some theorists would argue that the child's *perception* of conflict is more important than actual degree of marital conflict. For the outcome (dependent) variable, we might have several ways of measuring academic performance, including grades, standardized testing, and teacher reports. We would assume that these three ways of measuring a child's academic performance are consistent (reliability). Now that we have measures for our two concepts (marital conflict and child academic performance), we need to develop a measure for the relation between these two. Previously we stated the hypothesis that marital conflict *is related to* child academic performance, but now we need to specify what we mean and how we will measure the phrase *is related to*. First, there is some ambiguity in this phrase. For instance, it could be either a negative relation (as marital conflict increases, child

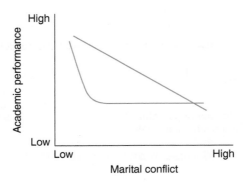

Figure 1.2 Two Patterns of Negative Relations

academic performance decreases) or a positive relation (as marital conflict increases, child academic performance increases). Assuming that we are hypothesizing a negative relation, we may want to specify further whether this relation is a straight line or a curve, as indicated in Figure 1.2.

In Figure 1.2, one pattern for a negative relation between marital conflict and child academic performance is a simple straight line that indicates a constant relationship whereby each measured unit increase of marital conflict is proportional to a unit decrease in child academic performance. The curve shows another possible relation where relatively modest levels of marital conflict lower child academic performance but then the effect remains stable for higher levels of conflict. If we are not guided by theory, the default relation for most hypotheses is the negative linear relation.

The research design involves complex questions about how we can isolate the effects of marital conflict from all other active variables such as parental income, the couple's time spent together, the child's school, and many others. If we were investigating rats, we could randomly assign them to high-parental-conflict and low-parental-conflict treatments and that would randomize any **extraneous factors**. However, in most social sciences, such experiments are either impossible or unethical, and while we may strive for the ideal of **random assignment,** we often cannot implement it in the real social world and use **random sampling** of a population instead. In the real social world, we usually conduct surveys and observations where all other explanatory variables are also present. Our research design attempts to give us the best chance of an accurate measure of the hypothesized relation. For instance, we would want to make sure that we have measured high and low levels of marital conflict in our study as well as high and low variability in child academic performance. Furthermore, if we know that we have major variables such as parental income that may offer a competing explanation, then we want to measure the variability in those competing variables.

Figure 1.3 shows a **correlational design** for our hypothesis. There are two control variables that we hypothesize have no effect on child academic performance. The only effect in Figure 1.3 is for level of marital conflict. We can change the value of the **dependent variable**, child academic performance, to reflect each **independent variable**. Indeed, this

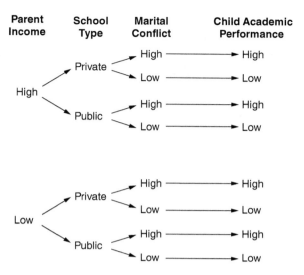

Parent Income	School Type	Marital Conflict	Child Academic Performance

Figure 1.3 Design for Three Independent Variable Effects on Child Academic Performance

would be a good exercise for researchers and students. For example, if parental income and not marital conflict accounts for child academic achievement being high or low, we would find that every time parental income is high child academic performance is also high, and whenever parental income is low so is child academic performance. Such a finding would also mean that we do not find an effect for marital conflict but only for parental income. Figure 1.3 guides us in our research design but the findings may be very different from our hypothesis and our design expectations.

Findings in the real social world have a nasty habit of being complex rather than simple. For the example we have been using, it would be very likely to find that all independent variables in the design contribute to child academic performance to various degrees. We may also find that certain combinations of variables work together (interaction effect) to create an even stronger outcome. For example, children with a combination of high parental income, private school, and low marital conflict may well have much higher academic performance than any other combination. That is called an interaction effect and we will see such effects in much of our research.

Regardless of design, sampling, and statistics, the final results and interpretations of research are only as clear and accurate as the definitions of the dependent variable (child academic performance) and the hypothesized independent variables. Therefore, research definitions must have characteristics we may not demand of other types of definitions. Research definitions must be clearly and precisely stated. Ambiguity and vagueness are simply the enemies of good research and accurate research definitions. In addition, we ask that research definitions be measurable. It is extremely important that research definitions be tied to measures, since without this we would be incapable of doing research. Finally, we need to measure (operationalize) the definition of the dependent variable so its components are logically independent of other variables; that is, they cannot be used to measure any other definition or variable included in our research. This is required because before we do the research we must believe that all variables in our research may vary independently of one another. Our research attempts to show that there is a relation between these variables but we do not want to begin with that relation being true by definition. For example, if our definition of child academic performance includes a measure such as internet access and having one's own computer, we would immediately notice that parental income allows for these resources and therefore these variables may not be independent. However, if we were to operationalize child academic performance as the results on a knowledge test, it would be easier to see that it is independent of parental income. These three characteristics (precision, measurement, and independence) are critical for good research definitions and distinguish research definitions from other forms of definitions.

DEFINITIONS AND DYNAMICS

All of the forms of definitions we discussed above (legal, normative, theoretical, and research) seem to be relatively straightforward. Indeed, they are straightforward until confronted by time and change. Laws change in response to changing societies, and new legal definitions are required as old definitions become useless or even laughable (e.g., the law that requires one to clean up after one's horse within the city limits of Vancouver and Toronto). When societies change their norms, social expectations change as well. Fifty years ago, it was considered bad manners to talk during a movie but now it is bad manners to leave your cellphone on during a movie. As societies and social norms change, new research and theory may be required.

It is critical to understand that much of the information you receive is limited by the particular point in time at which that information is produced and then received. As such, much of our information is somewhat static in nature. The information does not look at the processes of change but simply is a product of these processes. Dynamic theory and research focuses on the processes that assist us in understanding how the pieces of information fit in the larger picture of social change. As discussed in Box 1.5, understanding dynamics and change is essential for you and for understanding our world today.

Envisioning individuals and families over the life course is a dynamic way of looking at and exploring both individuals and families. You are of course an individual. If you compare a picture of yourself at age 5 to a recent picture, you will notice definite change. You have grown and matured physically, emotionally, and socially. You have experienced events that the 5-year-old neither envisioned nor comprehended yet you undoubtedly identify the person in both pictures as the same individual. What does this mean? What is the same about you then and now? We can see a host of differences but most of you would maintain that there must be some sameness upon which your identity over the life course is constructed. Likewise, most of you have family photos. You say, "Here is a picture of my family when I was small and here is one now." Yet some people may have exited your family through death or divorce and others may have

Box 1.5

Dynamics and You

Change is inevitable. Your parents and grandparents can perhaps see the effects of change more clearly, because in order to observe or measure change we need the passage of time. At any one point in time, everything looks fairly stable. Over longer periods, however, change becomes increasingly observable and real to us.

Some argue that social change is speeding up for today's students. This is a difficult claim to make since it must compare identical time frames, such as years, decade, or centuries. A grandfather of one of the authors of this textbook rode on the last real cattle drive, drove the first automobile in his town, lived through two world wars and the Cold War, and witnessed the beginning of space travel and the first manned landing on the moon. He experienced changes from horse-drawn transport to space travel. It is difficult to say whether the current cohort of students will experience such profound changes or if change will occur at a faster rate.

What is certain is that you will experience change in your lifetime. For example, it is commonly argued that the amount of information available increases exponentially every year. Indeed, there is an information "clock" online that effectively demonstrates this point (www.emc.com/leadership/digital-universe/expanding-digital-universe.htm). However, information may be relevant to change only if we lack knowledge. Knowledge is composed of the theories and concepts we use to organize and classify the mass of information we receive. If we learn only information and fail to recognize that theories and concepts are what allow us understanding and a sense of structure and control, then change will seem to be very rapid indeed.

One reason why university education is so important is that many of you will learn the theories and concepts that help to turn bits and bytes of information into knowledge. The fact that female singing artist A breaks up with male movie star B is information, but it is far from knowledge. Knowledge allows us to classify and eventually understand events. You will feel swamped and confused by information only if you lack knowledge. In your lives, family and work events will prove to be central for most of you, and this book intends to give you essential knowledge in this area so you can handle the information you will receive over your lifetime.

been added through birth or marriage. What, then, is the foundation for saying "this is my family" in both instances? These are thorny questions and immediate answers are often unsatisfactory. Let us return to some definitions, but this time in the context of the ongoing dynamic processes.

Defining Families over the Life Course

Families change and shift over the life course yet we believe that they have an identity just as individuals do. Imagine being born into the Jones family. Your experience of the family begins with your birth but this experience may have been preceded by the birth of an older sibling and the wedding of your parents. Therefore, the Jones family has an identity separate from you. Indeed, if you had not been born, they would still be the Jones family.

What is a family? "A family is an intergenerational social group organized and governed by social norms regarding descent, and affinity, reproduction and the nurturant socialization of the young" (White, 1991, p. 37). This statement is very complex and it requires a little "unpacking" for us to understand all that is entailed here. The idea that a family is intergenerational means that the basic unit required for a group to be a family is the adult–child relationship. However, in retrospect, families may begin with a dating couple as long as over time a parent–child bond is developed. Therefore, dating may be part of the history of a family, but not all dating couples form families. When a dating couple does form a family later in the life course, we find that they develop internal social norms and are constrained by external social norms (the institution of the family). Both sources of social norms develop the organization of the family in terms of who is related to whom, who is allowed to marry whom, and how a child will be socialized and raised. Indeed, the child or children supply a goal for the family: the successful raising of children.

These ideas may still be a bit fuzzy. A number of diagramming approaches can make this clearer. For example, we could use genogram analysis (McGoldrick & Gerson, 1985) or kinship analysis (Schusky, 1965), but both of these offer more complexity than we need for this example. Figure 1.4 shows a modified kinship approach to diagramming commonly used by life course scholars to diagram families over time (for other examples see Rodgers & White, 1993; White, 1991).

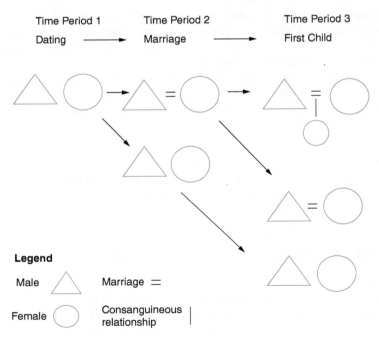

Figure 1.4 Dating to First Child Transitions

Figure 1.4 shows that we begin with Time Period 1 and a dating couple (which just as easily could be an arranged marriage) followed by Time Period 2, when the couple may get married or may continue dating. This is followed by Time Period 3, when the couple may have a child, may get married if they were not married at Time Period 2, or may continue dating. This branching process clearly shows that in terms of analysis of families, we would study only those that form an intergenerational or consanguineous bond. However, once the family exists we may analyze its history and future.

Historical Families and Kinship Systems

Kinship systems represent basic assumptions about how we should behave (norms) and to whom we are related. Kinship is dynamic in that it allows us to trace families over larger periods such as centuries and even millennia. The study of a family's kin is just a particular expression of how the kinship structure works. Kinship always involves the analysis of kinship structures and of the norms regulating behaviour and hence creating those structures from generation to generation.

In general, the structural analysis of families may be across time, as in Figure 1.4, or at one point in time. Family scholars are often interested in descriptions at one point in time, such as how many single-parent families there are in Canada. These cross-sectional or point-in-time descriptions, though not dynamic, nonetheless convey important information about a society and its families. However, it should be clear that if we know how many married couples there are in Canada, that point-in-time information does not tell us how many of those couples will become parents in the future.

Definitions are essential in kinship systems. Most basic is that an individual usually has two families. The family one is born into is called the *family of orientation*. As you enter adulthood, you form a second family, your *family of procreation*. As an individual, some of your relationships will be lifelong, such as with your siblings in your family of orientation and with your spouse in your family of procreation. Some relationships extend into the future, such as with your children, and some reach back in history, such as with your grandparents. Figure 1.5 shows a conventional kinship diagram that captures some of these many relationships. In Figure 1.5, *ego* (darkened circle) is that place or location where you can figure out the other relationships. We have filled in only a few of these; as an exercise, you could try to diagram your own family.

Kinship diagrams such as the one shown in Figure 1.5 can tell us many things about our families. For example, if we can name relatives on our father's side back only one generation but can name our mother's relatives back many generations, we might suspect either geographic closeness or a kinship system that was matrilineal and in which descent was reckoned through female relatives on the mother's side. Many societies reckon their kin through only one side or the other; these are systems of unilineal descent. The two major forms of unilineal descent are matrilineal and patrilineal. Alternately, bilateral systems of descent use both the mother's and father's sides of the family to reckon descent.

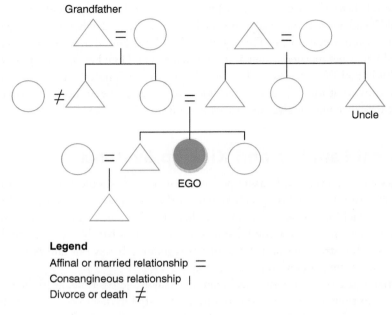

Legend
Affinal or married relationship $=$
Consangineous relationship $|$
Divorce or death $\neq$

Figure 1.5 Abbreviated Kinship Diagram

Kinship systems are not just systems for organizing descent; they preceded govern-ments and laws and were the original sources for social organization. As such, kinship sys-tems organized marriage, social status, inheritance, and property. Who a person married was not just an individual concern but also a kinship concern because it involved the kin group's property, status, and transmission to successive generations. Arranged marriages were important because of what was at stake for the kin group. However, as we globalize and modernize and inheritance changes from the family estate or farm (physical capital) to the parent-sponsored education of children (human capital), the kin investment in marriage is lessened and individual romantic choice is more likely.

The structure of kinship is maintained across successive generations by the norms and social rules governing areas such as **marriage** (monogamy or polygamy), **authority** (patriarchal or matriarchal), **residence** (matrilocality, patrilocality, or neolocality), and **descent** (matrilineal or patrilineal). There are almost 300 diverse societies in the world and some of these practise unique variants of kinship systems. For example, rules or norms of marriage may dictate that you should marry your fraternal cousin or the sister of your wife if the sister is widowed. Despite all of the variations, most cultures and societies see their kinship system as the correct and moral way of forming families and reckoning kin.

Today, when we discuss kinship systems many people feel that our system is "nuclear" and that kinship systems have little or no meaning. Kinship, however, still provides a road map for most families, and this road map is accompanied by moral

judgments and sanctions. The most basic example is incest. Most families would be appalled if a brother and sister wanted to marry, and this is illegal in our society (see Box 1.6). Many support their disapproval of incest by pointing to shared genetic material and the dangers of recessive genes. This same taboo, however, is applied to stepsibling relationships. In the past, many provinces outlined prohibited degrees of consanguinity for marriage, and among these prohibitions was "not to marry your dead sister's husband or wife." Note that there is no shared genetic material in these cases. In general, then, outside of the nuclear family, most of our incest taboos are a matter of control over mating. For example, would you marry your first cousin? It is not prohibited, and among many families worldwide, first-cousin mating is preferred. In general, most social scientists view incest, especially once it is defined for persons outside the nuclear family, as largely serving social rather than biological functions. After all, if we are that concerned about recessive genes, genetic testing can determine the risk for each couple.

No one seriously doubts the revulsion people feel regarding incest. It is part of the road map inherent to kinship systems. The problem is that this revulsion may be felt even when totemic clans such as Bear and Eagle mate, even though this is forbidden and it is considered incest for a Bear woman to marry an Eagle man. This mating is considered unnatural. If we extend this argument, we see that many kinship systems contain emotionally charged judgments, such as about whom we marry, where a newly married couple lives, and who controls decision making in the family.

Canada is a multicultural country. It is also a country composed of immigrants. It has people from polygamous families and monogamous families. It has people who

MARRIAGE (PROHIBITED DEGREES) ACT 1990, C. 46

[Assented to December 17th, 1990]
An Act respecting the laws prohibiting marriage between related persons

Her Majesty, by and with the advice and consent of the Senate and House of Commons of Canada, enacts as follows:

Short title

1. This Act may be cited as the *Marriage (Prohibited Degrees) Act.*

No prohibition

2. (1) Subject to subsection (2), persons related by consanguinity, affinity or adoption are not prohibited from marrying each other by reason only of their relationship.

Prohibition

(2) No person shall marry another person if they are related lineally, or as brother or sister or half-brother or half-sister, including by adoption. 1990, c. 46, s. 2; 2005, c. 33, s. 13.

Marriage not invalid

3. (1) Subject to subsection (2), a marriage between persons related by consanguinity, affinity or adoption is not invalid by reason only of their relationship.

Marriage void

(2) A marriage between persons who are related in the manner described in subsection 2(2) is void. 1990, c. 46, s. 3; 2005, c. 33, s. 14.

Complete code

4. This Act contains all of the prohibitions in law in Canada against marriage by reason of the parties being related.

5. [Repeal]

Commencement

*6. This Act shall come into force on the day that is one year after the day it is assented to, or on such earlier day in any province as may be fixed by order of the Governor in Council at the request of that province.

*[Note: Act in force December 17, 1991.]

Source: http://laws.justice.gc.ca/en/M-2.1/index.html

are matrilineal, including some of Canada's indigenous peoples. It has people who are matrilocal and patrilocal. The diversity of Canada means that as students mature into professionals in health care, education, and business, we expect that in these capacities you will be able to use your education and sensitivity to understand and recognize the various kinship road maps in our diverse culture (see Career Box 1.1).

So, kinship offers a specific type of dynamic definition of the family based on linking families across generations. This is only one form of dynamic definition since we can also examine families historically or across the life course. Dynamic approaches focus our attention on changes over time. This, in turn, focuses family researchers on concepts such as stages, transitions, and events in the life course. As we will see in the following chapter, these ideas guide much of the analyses in this book.

Sensitivity and Professional Conduct

Sharon just came home from teaching in an elementary school. As soon as she came through the door, Bill could see she was upset.

He asked, "What happened?"

Sharon explained that she has a boy in her grade 3 class that is doing very poorly in reading and she has tried several times to arrange a meeting with his parents. A meeting was finally organized but the parents didn't show up. Instead, the boy's uncle came to the meeting. Sharon said, "Can you imagine that the parents wouldn't even show up for this meeting . . . These folks don't seem to care how far their son falls behind."

Bill asked if the boy was a member of the Gitxsan First Nation, a Northwest Coast Aboriginal group.

Sharon replied, "Yes, how did you guess that?"

Bill explained that the group is matrilineal and that in many matrilineal societies the mother's brother is often the head of the family. Indeed, in this case the family may have considered this meeting so important that the head of the family decided to come rather than the parents. Bill said, "Sharon, you had the most important decision maker there but you mistook this as an affront and as proof that the parents didn't care, when it was the opposite."

CONCLUSION

One would perhaps think that defining the family would not be so complicated as to require an entire chapter. Indeed, from any one perspective, defining the family may be seen as relatively simple as long as we stay in the legal world or in the world of the researcher. The purpose of this chapter, however, is to portray the variety and diversity of approaches to the family.

We first established that there is not simply one understanding of what exactly a definition is. We covered two types of definitional forms: equivalence of meaning and differentiating genus and species. There is no one correct form, and we may find that some of our definitions of the family do a poor job of meeting the criteria of one form while doing a good job with another. The important point is to realize that when we say "this is a good definition," we should also specify what we mean by "definition."

When we turned to types of family definitions, we found that each type—legal, normative, theoretical, and research—has its own forms of language and systems of relevance. Certainly there is some overlap between all of these, but the overlap is not sufficient for us to say that one definition of family will serve all of these sectors. Furthermore, our discussion was not exhaustive since there are other types of definitions of the family, such as religious and economic, that were not addressed.

Finally, we discussed moving to definitions of the family that are more dynamic. Dynamic definitions are those that allow us to incorporate time and change in the meaning of family. Kinship system definitions of the family focus on the intergenerational bond that can be traced forward and backward over time, measured in generations. Life course definitions focus on the parent–child bond and tracing the development and denouement of this family unit. Family historians may also use time and define families across generations. These dynamic approaches—kinship, history, and life course—share a common concern with generations, normative change, and group change. The dynamic perspective suggests that a starting point for a dynamic study of the family would be the following definition:

> A family is an intergenerational social group organized and governed by social norms regarding descent, and affinity, reproduction and the nurturant socialization of the young. (White, 1991, p. 37)

In the chapters that follow, we will examine the institutional and interpersonal aspects of this definition. We will examine the events such as marriage and divorce that serve as transition points for individuals and families over time. Over the course of your reading and study of the family using a life course perspective, you will gain understanding of the terrain you have already traversed and that which is yet to come.

SUMMARY OF KEY POINTS

- Definitions are important because they construct our laws and social expectations and guide our research and knowledge.
- Defining exactly what a definition is has always been challenging (see Box 1.1).
- The 2006 census identifies several ways in which the family is changing:
  - There are fewer married-couple families (down to 68.6 percent from 70.5 percent in 2001).
  - Same-sex couples are increasing at a faster rate than opposite-sex couples (32.6 percent compared to 5.9 percent).
  - Single-person households are increasing.
  - More young adults aged 20 to 29 live with their parents.
  - For the first time in Canadian history, unmarried people outnumber married people.
- Research definitions of the family are always tied to a research question and to measurements.
- Much of our data (e.g., census data) captures only one point in time and does not trace the major transitions that individuals and families experience. Life course analysis (dynamics) focuses on changes, transitions, and flows of people over time.
- Kinship systems organize consanguineous descent and affinity in all societies.
- Understanding kinship differences between cultural groups is important in a multi-cultural society.
- A family is an intergenerational social group organized and governed by social norms regarding descent, affinity, reproduction, and the nurturant socialization of the young.

Critical Thinking Questions

1. If you ask for a family rate at your local swimming pool or community centre, what do you think is the defining property to be considered a family?

2. Research questions use particular definitions to study aspects of families. What aspects would be the focus of a study of child welfare? Do they include adult children?

3. The dynamic nature of families means that our families are always changing. How is it possible to study or define something such as family that is always changing?

Glossary

authority patterns Social norms establish who is expected to make decisions in the family. In patriarchal systems, the husband or father is expected to be the head of the household. In matriarchal systems, the wife or mother is the head of the household. In egalitarian systems, both spouses share equally in decision making.

concept An abstract set of things or ideas collected under one symbol or idea.

correlational design Field studies conducted using sampling procedures and that examine the covariation of two or more variables. It is in contrast to experimental design.

dependent variable The outcome variable, the variable to be explained, or the effect variable. It is in contrast to the independent variable.

descent systems Patterns of descent are how we reckon our lineage. In unilineal systems, we would reckon kin on only the mother's side (matrilineal) or the father's side (patrilineal). Most North American families reckon kin on both sides of the family (bilateral system).

extraneous factors Variables that may influence a dependent variable and should be added as control variables in correlational design.

hypothesis A statement that can be either true or false. A conceptual or theoretical hypothesis is a statement about how one concept is related to another. A measurement hypothesis is a statement about how one set of measures (independent variable) is related to another set of measures (dependent variable).

independent variable The causal variable or the variable that predicts or explains an outcome. It is in contrast to the dependent variable.

marriage type Monogamy and polygamy are the two major marriage types. Monogamy refers to having only one mate and polygamy refers to having multiple mates at the same time.

measurement Assigning a numeral or position to a case based on an underlying dimension such as length, belief, attitude, practice, etc. In the social sciences, many measurements are quantitative, such as "do you agree fully, somewhat, or not at all," or qualitative, such as divorced (1) or not divorced (0).

proposition A statement that relates one concept to another concept.

random assignment The practice of randomly assigning each experimental subject to a treatment or control group in an experiment.

random sampling A practice used for surveys and correlational design. This type of sampling involves the selection of individuals so that each individual in the population has the same chance of being chosen for inclusion in the sample.

residence patterns The generally expected patterns for living arrangements when a couple marries. In matrilocal residence, the new couple would reside with the bride's family. In patrilocal residence, the new couple would reside with the groom's family. In North America, the expectation is that the couple will practise neolocal residence and set up a new household.

social norms A norm or social rule followed by most people in a group (frequency) and that is sufficiently common to be an expectation (social psychological).

theory Composed of at least two logically related propositions.

variable The name for one set of scores of the same measure for different people. If we ask people if they would like a chocolate bar, some will say "yes" and some will say "no." The variable is "wants a candy bar" and the values of the variable are "yes" and "no."

variance The variability on any set of measures. All social sciences study variance. For example, we want to know why one person has high social status and another has low social status. If everyone scored the same on a variable such as social status, we would have a constant and therefore nothing to study.

Connections

www.community.gov.yk.ca/labour/deffamily.html
http://laws-lois.justice.gc.ca/eng/
http://laws.justice.gc.ca/en/M-2.1/index.html
www.emc.com/leadership/digital-universe/expanding-digital-universe.htm
http://anthro.palomar.edu/kinship/kinship_2.htm

Remember to log on to the Companion Website at **www.pearsoncanada.ca/white** to find self-graded quizzes and useful resource tools for further study. You can log on to the Companion Website using the Student Access Code that comes packaged with your copy of *Families Across the Life Course*.

Chapter 2
Life Course Analysis

Learning Objectives

After reading this chapter, you should be able to:

1. Understand that there are many theories about the family.

2. Acknowledge that all theories make assumptions, such as whether causes are based on individual motive, or social norms, or macroscopic global forces.

3. Understand that life course theory examines pathways that family groups and individuals follow through time.

4. Use levels of analysis to explain the difference between individual properties such as having a child and population phenomena such as Canada's fertility rate.

5. Acknowledge that individual agency and family life course can be modified and changed by macroscopic forces such as war and economic depression.

Bob just didn't understand. Emily had been out late again and he'd had to get the kids supper and put them to bed without their mother being around. Bob wanted to be supportive of Emily's interest in oil painting but he thought it was starting to be detrimental to their family life and unfairly affect the workload around the house. He finally decided to confront Emily.

"I think that being at the studio every night until midnight or later is cutting into our being a family," said Bob.

Emily looked hurt and defensive. She replied, "I am working on a picture and it will be finished soon. Then I will be home more regularly."

Bob quickly responded, "Oh, right, until the next project. You know when we decided to have a family we took it on as a joint effort, not solo!"

Emily paused, breathed out an exasperated sigh, and then said, "That was before I became consumed by art. When I started the art courses, I didn't know how all consuming this would be. Finally I have found a deep passion in my life and there is no way I can give it up. I would hope you'd understand."

With a hint of anger, Bob replied, "I wish you would stick to your commitments."

Emily hastily shot back: "Bob, our lives take all sorts of twists and turns and marriage is about helping the other person be the kind of person they want to be, and for me, that is my art."

"And for me," Bob added, "that is our kids and family!"

Do people change? Certainly, in the case of Bob and Emily, that seems to be part of what has happened. But that is not the complete story. They are also experiencing changes in fairness, division of labour, time spent with their children, and expectations about the mother–child and father–child relationships. These issues are not just individual ones but involve relationships and family organization. The question we ask in this chapter is how to analyze such complex family and individual changes over time. We will argue that life course theory is the best way to analyze family and individual change, but first we must ask, What do we mean by analysis?

THE NATURE OF ANALYSIS

Analysis involves trying to understand a phenomenon or event by breaking it into its parts and seeing how they fit together and are organized. In doing this, we get an explanation of *how* something has happened. An important component of how things happen is *why* an event or phenomenon occurred. In general, "how" explanations tend to examine the mechanisms at work whereas "why" explanations tend to identify causes. Often these two types of explanations are the same. For example, explaining both how ocean tides work and why ocean tides work involves lunar gravitational pull on large bodies of water. In this case, there may be little difference in the two types of explanations. On the other hand, when we analyze people, we often assume that people cause themselves to do things through self-motivation. For instance, imagine that you are sitting in a classroom. How you got there and into your seat is one type of analysis, but why you are in the classroom is a matter of your motivation for formal educational training. With regards to human behaviour, motivation is often seen as the cause of behaviour or why people act as they do. So, analysis involves identifying both how and why events occur.

In the social sciences, the principal way we answer "how" and "why" questions is through theoretical analysis. Returning to our example, we might argue that the goals held by Bob and Emily have changed. We could argue that they have grown in different directions, with Bob becoming more family oriented and Emily becoming more extra-familial because of her interest in art. Even such a simplistic analysis makes some fairly far-reaching *theoretical assumptions*. For example, can we conclude that people whose goals become more similar over time have happier marriages or a more equitable division of household labour? Indeed, the assumption that growing in different directions is a problem clearly depends on the issues and the situation in which a couple finds themselves. The important point here is that all analyses and all theories make theoretical assumptions in order to explain things.

Theoretical Assumptions

There are a great many ways to explain any phenomenon in the social sciences. That is, we have many theories that could compete to explain the same phenomenon. This richness of explanatory theories is one of the great strengths of the social sciences. After all, when we test competing theories, we find out which ones can predict and explain and which cannot. The richness of concepts and theories gives us alternative ways of viewing any one phenomenon.

There are too many theories about families to detail all of them here (see White & Klein, 2008). What we *can* do is summarize the major sets of assumptions that exist (see Box 2.1). Although various authors have detailed the general forms of social science theories (e.g., White, 2004), we will abbreviate these to just three sets of assumptions: motivational theories, normative theories, and macro-historical theories.

Motivational theories assume that you choose or determine why and how you do something. Most of us like to think that we determine our actions. If someone offers you a choice between a chocolate bar and a package of gum, you will choose whichever one brings you the greatest rewards. Indeed, **rational choice theory** (Coleman, 1990) and much of micro-economics (Becker, 1981) are founded on such an assumption. Critics point out that what something is worth to you depends on the situation and the norms in the society. If chewing gum is viewed as perverse whereas having chocolate is perceived favourably, the value of a reward is set not by you but by society. There are other problems with a purely motivational approach, such as the argument that your choices are conditioned genetically and you are in fact determined to act in a certain way even though you may perceive choice. Finally, some notable critics argue that there is little logic in our choices since we cannot compute the costs and rewards of any action in a rational way (Tversky & Kahneman, 1988).

Box 2.1

Major Theoretical Frameworks for Studying Families

Functional theories. This school of thought maintains that the family is a normative institution in all societies and that the family is central in all societies to perform the functions of reproduction, control of sexuality, and socialization of children. It emphasizes the maintenance of functional institutions and therefore tends to see social change as a threat to society's institutional functional relations.

Conflict theories. This framework tends to think of the family as a social group that mirrors and is affected by large-scale forces such as historical dialectical materialism (Marx & Engels, 1965/1865) or a clash of cultures (Huntington, 1996). It often sees family as expressing the larger forces in society, as in the argument by Straus and Donnelly (2001) that family violence is related to social and cultural values about violence such as those favourable toward guns and spanking.

Feminist theories. This complex framework encompasses many distinct schools of thought such as cultural feminism, critical race feminism, and liberal feminism. This diversity of thought is unified by the common perception that women are subjugated and oppressed by patriarchy. The family is most often seen as the central institution that reproduces the social roles and mechanisms that maintain patriarchal oppression.

Systems theories. This group of theories focuses on the notion that all elements of a system affect each other and that to understand a family system, scholars must examine it holistically. Its major concepts are feedback and equilibrium. Families have members that affect both one another and the balance of the entire family system. When the system is thrown out of equilibrium or balance, members try to correct the dysfunction by recalibrating means and goals or by changing inputs and outputs. This approach to the family has the dubious credential of having produced such concepts as the double bind hypothesis, the dysfunctional family, and the refrigerator mother. All of these have been shown to have little empirical utility for social science researchers, though a few therapists may continue to use them.

Rational choice and social exchange theories. This framework is based on individuals having the rational capacity to choose those actions deemed to produce the greatest rewards relative to costs. Over time, individuals engage in relationships such as marriage that bring, on average, more rewards than costs; as a result, these social relationships become valued exchange relationships in themselves and individuals maintain and continue them. Certainly, this microeconomic theoretical framework is one of the most popular perspectives in sociology, economics, and social psychology, in part because it strongly supports individual actors having "agency" and choice.

Symbolic interaction theories. This framework focuses on individuals being constructed by their society. Society precedes the individual. When individuals arrive in the world, they learn signs and symbols so that they can express and negotiate meanings in the social world. Some variants of symbolic interaction see the individual as being strongly determined by the existing meanings and roles in society whereas others emphasize individuals' ability to negotiate and reorganize their social relationships. The central concept used in the study of families is social roles and how much these are socialized or negotiated. For example, when you marry, do you assume a well-determined role of husband or wife or do you negotiate the role expectations with your spouse?

Bioecological theories. This broad framework encompasses the interplay of our biological and evolutionary selves with our social selves. Early proponents focused on the concept of inclusive fitness, whereby individuals act to maximize the survival of their genes from one generation to the next. Because this process was viewed as common to our species, it failed to explain why some mothers murder their children while others are excellent parents. In the last two decades, researchers have focused on such areas as hormonal linkages between married partners, cortisol levels (stress hormones) in family interactions, and the biosocial effects of breastfeeding on a mother's attachment to her child.

Developmental and life course theories. This framework focuses on the concepts of stages and transitions. Individuals, relationships, and families are all conceptualized as traversing stages of development. As we traverse the life course of a family or individual or relationship, significant events propel a transition to another stage. For example, a dating couple may have sexual intercourse and that may propel them to a more serious relationship. This framework is clearly concerned with multiple levels of analysis (individual, relationship, and family) and multiple determinants of transitions across time. It easily integrates many of the other theoretical approaches by using concepts and social mechanisms as they pertain to transitions and stages. Both agency and choice are included, as is social structure. It is the major theoretical framework used in this book.

Normative theories assume that social norms predict behaviour and action. A **social norm** is a rule about our conduct that is held and followed by most people in a society. Because the rule is held and followed by so many people, it becomes the basis for social **expectations**. When we approach a stop sign, we expect people to stop because of the shared rule. Social norms are commonly divided into **formal norms**, such as laws or rules established by an authority such as a teacher, and **informal norms**, which are not codified or written down but are shared by many people. For example, your employer may formally demand that you show up at work at a certain time, but the pace and speed of work may be set by more informal norms held by the workers. Thus, two identical workplaces may have very different productivity rates because of the different informal norms about the pace of work.

Life course theory is largely a normative theory. It takes the perspective that all societies need to organize people across their life courses. The norms that organize individual and family change are related to our ages and stages of life. For example, you cannot be a lifeguard until you are at least 16 years old. This is an **age-graded norm** that is codified. Stage-graded norms refer to stages of life, such as the expectation (norm) that you should not have children until you are married. Thus, the stage of life (married) sets the normative expectation for having children. There are many stage-graded norms, such as finishing your education before you marry and launching your children before you retire.

The major criticism of normative theories is that they fail to explain how norms are formed and how they develop. Many rational choice theorists argue that the development of norms is dependent on the rational choices of individuals. The problem is that the norms are very different from society to society, even though we are all rational human beings. Another take on the development of norms comes from evolutionary social theory, which argues that norms are based on our biological nature. Here again, most human beings have the same biological nature but societies are very different.

For example, in Korea it is the norm that people walk on the left side rather than on the right side, as is the norm North America. Differences in norms cannot be accounted for by assuming that one group is not rational or by assuming biological differences. Nonetheless, the thorny problem of how norms arise is one that plagues normative theories and, more particularly, must be addressed by life course theorists.

Macro-historical theories assume that forces beyond the individual or society create change. These forces may be historical (Marx & Engels, 1965/1865) or even evolutionary (van den Berghe, 1979). This perspective argues that individuals are "blown like leaves" by the winds of historical change. In other words, our behaviour is determined neither by us nor by particular social norms but by macroscopic forces such as **historical dialectics** and **evolution**. For example, if a mother is walking between her house and her sister's house and both houses simultaneously catch fire, which burning house will she run to first to save the children? Evolutionary theory argues that she will run to her own house to save her own children because they have more of her genetic material than her sister's children have. Thus, her behaviour is "explained" by the general proposition that everyone seeks to maximize the reproduction of his or her own genetic material.

The major problem with macro-historical theories is explaining variation in human responses. If historical and evolutionary forces are everywhere, why is there variation between individuals, social groups, and societies? For example, some individuals are willing to give up their lives for their country but others are not. Some societies have capital punishment but others do not. Clearly, the great variation in human response to the same stimuli provides difficulties for macro-level theories. At a minimum, macro-level theories need to identify processes other than macro-level forces to explain individual variation.

These three major sets of assumptions offer very different perspectives on what causes our behaviour: individual choice, social norms, or macro-level forces (see White, 2004). Although many explanations in the social sciences can be placed in one of these three broad categories, there are specific theories that are not so easily pigeonholed. Furthermore, many students have already been exposed to theories such as symbolic interaction, exchange, developmental, and conflict (see White & Klein, 2008) and will have trouble characterizing these specific theories in such broad terms. It is important to recall that the categories we developed above refer to broad theoretical assumptions rather than to any specific theory. As we shall see, today's life course theory has developed by borrowing aspects from each of these categories to address the particular problems that arise with theories that are dynamic or apply over time.

LIFE COURSE THEORY

We introduced life course analysis in Chapter 1 (see Box 1.5 and Figure 1.4) and in the discussion of normative theories above. Thus far, the references to life course theory have been relatively unsystematic. The discussion that follows is much more detailed and systematic. The concepts and propositions we discuss in this section are essential in gaining a comprehensive and integrative understanding of your life course and the

life course of families. Because this is necessarily abstract and "heady" material, you may find that some time is required to absorb the information before it all falls into place. For many of you, these ideas will become clear only when you see them applied in later chapters to topics such as dating or aging.

This section is organized into three subsections. The first subsection gives a general overview of social dynamics and why we want to move toward a dynamic approach to social and family changes. The second subsection deals with four basic concepts: events, stages, transitions, and pathways. The final subsection deals with advanced concepts such as levels of analysis.

Social Dynamics

As we pointed out in Chapter 1, change is everywhere. When change is slow, we perceive it as stability. When it is rapid, we perceive it as cataclysmic change. The basic question that any theory of society must address is this: How does the theory incorporate change? Change can be measured only across points in time. We know that change takes place when Family A at Time Point 2 is not the same as Family A at Time Point 1. Thus, questions of identity (same across time points) and change (different across time points) are central to developing a dynamic theory.

In Chapter 1, we raised one difficult question regarding the study of change: If everything is changing, how is it possible to have a unit to study that can be considered stable? If the Lee family has one child and then adds a second child, the family structure and interaction patterns change. How can we say that the Lee family is the same family? We resolved this problem by stating that a family exists when there is at least one intergenerational bond and this social group is recognized and governed by social norms. When the Lees have a child and there are social norms that establish relationship expectations such as nurturance and financial support, that is a family. The important point, though, is to recognize that families have histories and futures that can be analyzed. When the Lees were dating they were not a family, but their dating is part of the Lee family's history. When both parents die and only the sibling relationships remain, that is not a family but it is part of the Lee family's history.

This perspective on family and change further suggests that we can analyze changes over time. One issue in this regard is determining important changes and distinguishing them from less important ones. This is largely a matter of theoretical assumptions. Because we would like our analysis to be generalizable and to study the important changes experienced by the great majority of families and individuals, idiosyncratic or unique events and changes are useless. An example of such an idiosyncratic or unique event is when a person watches a boa constrictor eat a mouse and finds this a major turning point; others, however, may not be equally affected.

On the other hand, there are events that necessarily affect all families. Figure 1.4 in Chapter 1 suggested that structural changes are important to families. Returning to our example of the Lee family, when they have a second child this change in structure is accompanied by changes in relationships, such as the addition of the sibling relationship. Besides births, other structural changes include divorce or separation, leaving home, death, remarriage, and becoming a step-parent. All of these changes in structure necessitate qualitative changes in the relationships with the group. This would be equally true for a family in Greece or Singapore as it is for one in Canada.

But what if the Lee family were unusual? What if the spouses live in different countries due to work and education, and the oldest child attends residential private school in yet another country, and the new baby resides with the maternal grandparents? It may be overstating things to say that the relationships change with the addition of the new child. Indeed, a hidden assumption in the structural approach to change is the notion that family members share a common household or domicile. Social interactions in such households would naturally affect family members. Likewise, concepts such as "separation" and "leaving home" take for granted the idea that families share a common household.

Figure 2.1 illustrates a family moving through structural transitions. This example of adding one child is not problematic. The importance of the household becomes clear as

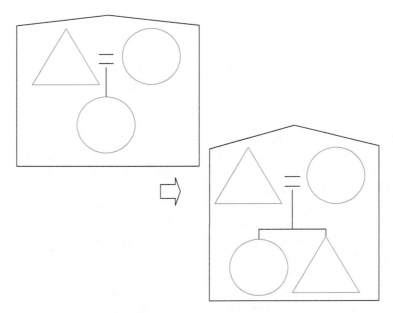

Figure 2.1 Family and Household: Adding a Child

we think about an eldest child leaving home or a divorce and remarriage. Indeed, North American families may have several members living outside the household at any point in time. These diagrams will become indispensable when we discuss divorce and stepfamilies.

Another tacit or hidden dimension of social dynamics is the biological constraints on individuals and groups. The single most significant biological constraint is aging. All individuals and groups are aging. This implies that the mere passage of time has effects on both individuals and social groups. Somewhat better nomenclature than calling this an "aging" effect might be to call it a "duration" effect. Indeed, as we move across different units (e.g., individuals, sibling relationships, families), all of these can be said to be affected by the duration of time since the date of inception as well as the duration of time exposed to any factor. For example, your duration of time since inception would be your age but your exposure to the influence of your younger sibling would be a shorter period.

Many biological conditions are associated with age but are not lifelong factors. For example, your fertility begins only with completion of puberty and, if you are female, stops with menopause. Thus, some biological parameters require a duration until onset and another duration until closure. As we shall see in the next subsection, this characteristic is commonly referred to as a stage.

Basic Concepts

Events Our lives are experienced as **events** such as birth, graduation, wedding, and death. Our lives are measured by events but so are many other phenomena, such as diseases (onset, presentation of a symptom, fever, etc.). When someone asks you how your life has changed, you may recount events such as your father dying or your mother remarrying. These events are meaningful to people and even though they have chronological dates, it would be meaningless to say August 20, 2001, rather than "when my father died." The date itself does not carry the same critical information about our lives that the event does.

An event is relatively instantaneous in time. If an event has a long duration, it becomes a stage (as defined below). An event is experienced by the individual but is also a shared understanding that can be communicated to others. An event such as "a death in the family" can be readily communicated and understood by others in the same society. Certainly, there are idiosyncratic events such as "watching the boa constrictor eat a mouse," but these are not commonly understood as turning points in life and they would require significant effort to explain how they affected you.

One reason that most life events are readily understood is that they are "normative." Even though we may not like to think of events such as death as normative, death is nonetheless expected and there are a host of social and cultural practices surrounding it. We may talk about premature death as shocking but overall death, like birth, is a major life event for everyone.

Stages The life course is often conceptualized as moving from one stage to another. A **stage** is a duration of time characterized by a particular property not present before the stage and not present after the stage. The stage during which a couple becomes new parents offers a good example. When a couple has a child, the structure of the household changes from two to three members and the couple's interaction also changes. When the couple has a second child, the addition of a sibling relationship—with its fighting and friendship—changes the family once again. Each of these is a stage and the duration of the stage is marked by properties of interaction that are qualitatively distinct from prior stages and successive stages.

Stages are used to describe the life course of individuals, with terms such as *infancy*, *childhood*, *adolescence*, *middle age*, and so on. We can also use stages to describe small social groups such as the family or a work group. Furthermore, stages can be used to discuss the development of social organizations such as Apple and IBM. Finally, stages are often used to describe the development of nations and cultures, such as with *Third World development*.

The fact that stages are used with such a variety of units of analysis (individuals, groups, nations, etc.) should not disguise the common elements in these diverse analyses. Indeed, stages are characterized by three defining elements. First, all stages have a beginning point that is marked by an event. Because it marks a move from one stage to another, the event is called a **transition event**. Second, an ending or exit event marks the end of the duration of the stage. Third, for its duration, the stage is marked by a particular property that the stages before the transition event did not have and the stages after the exit event will not have. For example, the larval stage of most insects is marked by a lack of exoskeleton and a voracious appetite. When the insect transitions to the pupal stage, it usually has a cocoon or some form of exoskeleton for protection and will not feed as it did during the larval stage. Likewise, when a young married couple has their first child, interactions change from romantic dinners to caring for the newborn. Interactions change again with the birth of a second child, when sibling interactions supplant some of the previous parent–child interactions and add a new dimension of sibling play and conflict.

Transitions Every organism and social organization experiences transitions. In some ways, age and duration alone will account for changes. However, when those changes are described as stages, it becomes clear that events mark the transitions.

We can use the now familiar example of the transition to parenthood. The transition events of the first birth and the second birth provide markers that are relatively instantaneous transition points. Duration then becomes a characteristic of the stage and not of the transition event. As essential as this perspective of instantaneous transition points is for analysis, it may conceal the fact that many transitions have a period during which a great number of changes and adaptations occur with some rapidity. For instance, the marker of birth is accompanied by pregnancy, baby showers, prenatal classes, and other such preparations for the transition. Obviously, if the birth does not occur (as with stillborn infants), the transition to parenthood does not occur regardless of the preparation.

Transitions can be studied more or less independently of stages. We may want to study the transition to adulthood, the transition to old age, the transition to marriage, the transition to parenthood, or the transition to the empty nest. All of these transitions contain intense adjustments and, as Holmes and Rahe (1967) point out, relatively high stress loads.

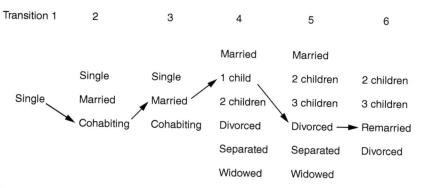

Figure 2.2 Family Stages Pathway Through Six Transitions

Pathways At any point in the life course of an organism, an individual person, or a family, there is always the possibility of a stage transition. For example, a young, newly-wed may experience a heart attack and die, leaving his wife a widow. Though this is both improbable and unexpected, it is nonetheless possible. The life course can be conceptualized as a pathway through a maze of possibilities. Figure 2.2 shows one example through six transitions.

In Figure 2.2 we can see that there are three options for moving from the starting stage of single, never married: stay single, get married, or cohabit. If all three of these possibilities were equally likely, there would be a 1 in 3 chance for any to occur. This, however, is not the case. In Canada, about 60 percent of young people in their twenties will cohabit before they marry. For this age group, then, premarital cohabitation is more likely than marriage. The probability of a transition depends on the stage you are currently occupying, how long you have been in that stage, and the social norms favouring one type of transition over another. Someone who has been single, never married for 40 years is unlikely to get married since he or she has been exposed to the risk of marriage for a long time. On the other hand, a young couple in the early years of marriage is very likely to have a first child since most first births occur within a couple of years of marriage. The important point is that at any specific time the alternatives for transition are not equally likely.

As we think about pathways, many of us may conclude that the "cause" of transitions is really the choices we make. Certainly, rational choice theory would like to think this is so. However, do we choose for a spouse to die or choose to divorce? Many historical and random factors arise to change or modify our pathways. For example, wars, economic depressions, and even hurricanes may have major effects on our life course. The life course perspective acknowledges that individual choices are made but also that, for the most part, these choices are driven by the norms of the society and many other factors. For example, Aboriginal peoples have choices that other Canadians do not have, associated with treaty status and "Indian" status, but these institutional statuses also constrain the choices available to Aboriginal peoples by making them "different" and distinct from other Canadians. This perspective will become increasingly clear as we discuss the advanced concepts in life course analysis.

Advanced Concepts

Levels of Analysis Thus far, our discussion has wandered across diverse levels of analysis. We have discussed families, individuals, institutions, organizations, and relationships without acknowledging that we are shifting levels of analysis. This carelessness creates two problems for analyses. First, it makes it seem as if the processes of change, transitions, and stages are the same at all levels of analysis. This certainly is not the case. Second, this sloppiness makes it difficult to understand how levels of analysis influence one another. For example, institutional norms influence relationships differently when premarital cohabitation is normative rather than proscribed or viewed as deviant. As we discuss the idea of levels of analysis, both of these problems will become more apparent.

When we do research, we may sample different units such as schools or marriages or students. The sampling unit is not the same thing as a level of analysis. A level of analysis is the theoretical and conceptual level on which we are conducting our analysis or explanation. In general, the major levels of analysis are as follows: the individual, the two-person relationship, the social group (family), and the institution (norms). The processes and stages are different for each of these, as shown in Table 2.1.

In Table 2.1 we can see that an individual may experience a need for perceptions and ideas about the world to be relatively consistent. In psychological studies these processes have variously been discussed as psychological balance and cognitive dissonance. When we move to a two-person relationship, individuals may still want consistency but there is a new process that can occur only with two people: agreement or disagreement. Indeed, conflict is a process that begins only in two-person relationships. Once a couple has a child and becomes a family (three-person group), another new process is added. A three-person family can have coalitions of two against one, especially in democratic families. Coalitions are not possible in two-person relationships. Finally, every normative institution (e.g., family, education, work) has norms that organize our society. When most people conform to these norms, either willingly or because of coercion, the resulting stage for the institution is one in which the frequency of the behaviour is highly uniform or, to use a statistical term, **leptokurtotic**.

Table 2.1 Levels of Analysis

Level of Analysis	Example of Process	Example of Stage
Individual	Cognitive consistency	Single
Relationship	Agreement	Cohabiting
Family	Coalitions	Married with children
Institution	Conformity	Norm leptokurtosis

The stages and transitions an individual is experiencing will undoubtedly affect the relationships that person has with other people. If a person's marital relationship is not going well, that will affect the family. Disruptions in marriage and family will affect conformity to social norms. Thus, all levels of analysis are capable of interacting. For instance, a lack of conformity in social norms about fathers in society may be experienced by the individual as a lack of clarity and an ambiguity about the bread-winner role.

Institutional Norms Every family develops its own internal norms for bedtime, hygiene, division of labour, and so on. These internal family-specific norms are idiosyncratic and are developed by the group and its organizational leadership, such as the mother or father. These internal norms, however, should not be confused with the broader society's institutional norms. Institutional norms are those social rules agreed upon by most members of a society. Some institutional norms are codified as formal norms in legislation while others are more informal. For example, the marriage contract (licence) is a formal norm that publicly acknowledges a monogamous relationship between two adults. When a couple enters into such a contract, other legislation such as matrimonial property acts and medical acts become relevant. On the other hand, some institutional norms are informal and consensual, such as the idea that one should get married before having children. These informal norms may have informal sanctions such as shaming tied to them, but they do not have formal sanctions that the courts would enforce (as with matrimonial property acts).

It is essential that institutional norms be looked at in two very dissimilar ways (Durkheim, 1893/1984). On one hand, it is essential for every society to have a considerable degree of conformity to institutional norms, whether they relate to the family, politics, work, education, or religion. These norms organize and stabilize all societies. They allow us to develop expectations about the actions of others and hence to predict our world. On the other hand, social change comes about mainly by normative change. For example, in the 1950s, cohabitation among the middle class was almost unknown but now it is the most popular stage before marriage. Norms that favour cohabitation rather than condemn it represent a huge social and institutional change. This change started as deviance. Indeed, most social change begins with deviance. Not all forms of deviance are successful and become institutional in nature, but most social change is rooted in deviance at some historical point. Thus, while we all like social order, change is also important in helping us adapt to a changing world.

Among all of the informal norms about the life course is a subset of norms that are consensual agreements about the timing of events and stages as well as the sequencing of events. For example, "one should get a driver's licence or an education while one is a young adult" is a **timing norm** or **age-graded norm**. On the other hand, "one should get married before having a first child" is an example of a **sequencing norm**. Sequencing norms suggest the order in which one should experience stages or events. Although such statements may appear in isolation, we can see that when they appear in conjunction, much of the early life course is full of social expectations (norms). For instance, when conjoined, "don't get married until you complete your education" and "get married before your first child" suggest that you should finish your education, then get married, and then have your first child. Although this sequence seems obvious to most North Americans, there are societies in which the norm is that a woman should first have a child to prove her fertility before she is considered "marriageable." The fact that these informal norms organize many of our expectations for the life course should not blind us to the fact that other ways of organizing these events and stages are possible.

Off Time and Out of Sequence The fact that social norms organize societies is important. When social norms start to break down, individuals do not know what is expected of them nor can they anticipate what others will do. Organizations do not know how to plan facilities and offer incentives to motivate workers. Indeed, when social norms break down, social expectations and an orderly society no longer exist.

The biological nature of humans means that we age. Every society must organize around the basic needs and abilities tied to infancy, adulthood, and old age. Some of these age-graded norms are formalized in laws, such as those governing the drinking age or the age at which you can get a driver's licence. Other age-graded norms are more informal, such as the age at which you should be married or the age at which you should finish your schooling. However, even the informal norms have social sanctions; for example, if you are not married by a certain age, you may be called an "old maid." Indeed, when you are **off time** with the commonly agreed upon age-graded norms, there are usually sanctions or consequences, such as people saying you are "too old" for a certain task or experience.

An important complement to age-graded norms is sequencing norms. Whereas age-graded norms have expectations about how old you should be when an event is experienced (learning to drive, drinking alcohol, marriage), sequencing norms are social norms about the expected sequence of events. For instance, one sequencing norm is that you finish your education before starting a full-time job and that you get your career (job) started before you marry and that you marry before having a child.

What happens when you don't follow these sequencing norms? Hogan (1978), and later White (1991), demonstrated that getting out of sequence early in life is associated with later life disruptions such as interrupted labour force participation and divorce. That is, once sequencing is thrown off in one area, it tends to pile up in other areas and have consequences. A straightforward example of this is teen pregnancy. When a teenager has a baby, she might take time off from school. Upon returning to school, she is with a younger cohort and her experiences of childbirth and motherhood may further separate her from her fellow students. Thus, what may seem as just being out of sequence has significant ramifications for timing of labour force entry and post-secondary attendance.

It may not be obvious, but there is a strong association between being off time and being out of sequence. Since sequences are largely constructed from age-graded events or stages, being out of sequence is necessarily tied to being off time with certain events. Thus, we usually talk about being both off time and out of sequence.

Family Stages By now you should have some idea of the intimate relationship between life events and stages of your life. Events are age graded and subject to sequencing norms. However, since a stage is defined as the period of time between two events, there is necessarily a connection between events and stages. We can see this in Figure 2.3.

The necessary connection shown in Figure 2.3 ignores an important defining element of stages: that a stage must represent a qualitatively different period of interaction or family life from the stages occurring before and after. Thus, "married" must be qualitatively distinct from both "cohabiting" and "family with one child." There are three major ways in which life course theory deals with this qualitative dimension of stages: defining stages by family structure, defining stages by normative structure, and defining stages by developmental tasks.

Stages of family development can easily be defined as structure. Family structures are composed of the basic relationships and members we covered in our discussion of kinship (see Chapter 1). Members are designated by sex and by three relationships: inside or outside the household, affinal relationship, and consanguineous relationship. These structures are shown in Figure 2.1. The qualitative structural difference between "cohabitating" and "married" is that cohabitants live in the same household but are not married (=). The difference between "married" and "family with one child" is the addition of the child to the household and the consanguineous relationship.

In many ways, the normative definitions of stage resemble the structural definitions. With normative definitions, we identify the particular norms that are different for each stage. Thus, the norms for cohabitation, such as division of labour and power, are different from the norms for marriage, which has more defined expectations for husband and wife roles. Likewise, the norms for the parent role in a family with one child are distinct from the norms for marriage.

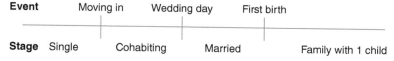

Figure 2.3 Stages and Events

Developmental tasks were first discussed by Havighurst (1948) and later added to life course theory by Hill and Rodgers (1964) and most recently by Aldous (1999). A developmental task is a task that must be completed or achieved before a successful transition to a next stage can be made. For example, you must be able to master counting before you can master subtraction. With regards to stages, we talk about cohabitation as concerned with developing commitment, maturity in living with another person, and the ability to handle conflict within a relationship. We can talk about the developmental tasks in marriage as developing accurate communication, task coordination, and division of labour before a couple can successfully move to having a child. The idea behind developmental tasks is that if you are not successful in meeting a developmental task, then your transition to the next stage also will not be successful.

Developmental tasks may be an attractive idea to some, but the research to support the idea of developmental tasks is lacking. It can be argued that normative and structural definitions are more useful for predicting behaviour. Norms supply age-specific expectations while structure supplies the group context. Nonetheless, the idea of developmental tasks supplies a useful metaphor for this interaction of norms and structure.

Duration and Transitions Timing and sequencing norms construct expected durations for each stage before making a transition. For example, if you are engaged to be married, how long do you expect the engagement stage to last? Would six months be as appropriate as six years? If Jill gets married for the first time, how long do you think it will be before she has children? Would you expect it to be within 2 years or 20 years? As we think about timing of events, we cannot help but think about durations in each stage.

In general, the probability of a transition from one life course stage to another is a curve. Figure 2.4 graphically represents the relationship between first birth and duration of marriage. It shows that the transition from the early marriage stage to the family with one child stage is not a straight line but curvilinear. As we think about the many transitions in our lives, we find that most of our expectations have an implicit duration attached to them. This implied expectation is the result of the conjunction of age-graded timing and sequencing norms. For example, if we are dating someone seriously, there comes a time when we ask what the next step is for the relationship. We generally do

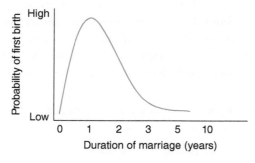

Figure 2.4 Probability of First Birth and Duration of First Marriage

not intend to be 70 years old and still dating the same person. Instead, many of us would expect transitions to other relationship stages and to family.

Age, Period, and Cohort Normative expectations depend on your age, the historical time period, and the birth cohort into which you were born. Age is very simply your chronological age. It is also used to suggest your maturity level and the kinds of individual stages you have experienced. For example, we do not expect a mid-life crisis for a 20-year-old but one may be more expected for a 40-year-old. The historical period in which you live is a factor in the choices and social norms that surround you. For example, living at the time of the Great Depression (1929–1938) would reduce your choices for jobs and education. Finally, the birth cohort into which you are born shares experiences and is raised with similar norms and understandings. For instance, "baby boomers," who entered adulthood in the late 1960s and early 1970s, clearly shared common understandings and norms that make up what is commonly called the baby boom generation.

Whenever we examine life course behaviour, we have to ask if the behaviour is best predicted by one of these three factors (age, historical period, birth cohort). For example, if we assume that a mid-life crisis is determined by the age of the individual, we would not expect to find it related to birth cohort or historical period. Let's imagine that we can measure mid-life crisis in males as the time when they drive a convertible sports car while wearing a tweed golf hat. We assume that this behaviour is related only to turning a certain age, such as 40, and does not exist before or after that time. We can show what these data would look like in an age, period, and cohort matrix (Table 2.2).

The arrow in Table 2.2 represents when we expect to observe sports car–driving males wearing tweed hats, if that is a valid measure of mid-life crisis. If this behaviour is truly determined by age alone rather than by advertising (historical period) or birth cohort norms (the tweed generation), we would expect to observe it only along this diagonal line. This matrix assists us in deriving theoretical expectations for an individual's development (age) rather than historical events (war, depression) or social norms tied to a birth cohort. If mid-life crisis is a phenomenon seen only among 40-year-olds in the baby boom generation, we would expect to observe it only among those born in the 1950s and it would occur in 1990s (see bolded 40 in Table 2.2). This combination of age and birth cohort was well documented in

Table 2.2 Age, Period, and Cohort Matrix

Birth Cohort	Historical Period					
	1960	1970	1980	1990	2000	2010
1920	40	50	60	70	80	90
1930	30	40	50	60	70	80
1940	20	30	40	50	60	70
1950	10	20	30	**40**	50	60
1960	0	10	20	30	40	50

Elder's (1974) work *Children of the Great Depression*, in which he demonstrated that those who experienced the Great Depression (historical period) in their youth (birth cohort) developed a lifelong concern with being frugal. Indeed, there are many places in this book where we will examine the interactions of age, birth cohort, and historical period, such as in our discussion of cohabitation and dating patterns.

Other Socio-Cultural Factors It would be naive to believe that our lives and the life course of our families are determined simply by social norms about the family. Many other influences need to be considered. For instance, there are the norms for other social institutions such as work and education. If educational norms suggest that we all complete university, that normative change in education will have ramifications for starting a first job and getting married. In other words, a change in the norms and expectations for one institution (education) means that there will be consequent adaptations in the norms of other institutions (work, family). Other institutional norms need to be considered as factors of social change.

Another set of important factors influencing the life course is individual factors surrounding individual choices and the ease with which individuals can negotiate changes. There is little doubt that **anticipatory socialization** accounts for much of our ability to adapt to change. A child who grows up taking care of younger siblings will have socialization and experience that will make the transition to family much easier than that same transition for, say, an only child. Even babysitting and being a camp counsellor can be considered anticipatory experience for the parental role. The choices an individual makes are undoubtedly determined by macroscopic factors and by the more microscopic factors of individual values and preparation. Box 2.2 gives us an idea of how these many variables can be incorporated in research.

Box 2.2

What Does Life Course Research Look Like?

THE EFFECTS OF SINGLEHOOD AND COHABITATION ON THE TRANSITION TO PARENTHOOD IN THE NETHERLANDS

by Clara H. Mulder

University of Amsterdam

Abstract

Previous research has shown that singlehood and cohabitation are associated with postponement of parenthood. This study examines whether this association extends to the long term, potentially leading to a higher likelihood of ultimate childlessness among those with singlehood or cohabitation experience. Results from analyses of retrospective life course data from a sample of people born since 1935 and living in the Netherlands show that experience with nonmarital living arrangements has a long-term impact on the transition to parenthood. This impact is greater for females than for males and is partly caused by the higher likelihood among cohabitors to end their partnerships.

Source: Mulder (2003).

CONCLUSION

We have covered a lot of conceptual material in a fairly condensed form. How will we use these ideas to examine families across the life course? Certainly, all of the ideas discussed in this chapter will be useful in understanding our own and our family's life course. However, some central concepts will prove most useful.

Stage of the life course or family stage is a central concept. Within each stage, there is maturation and development until a transition is made to the next stage. Humans in any stage of development continue to learn and change within that stage. In the language of life course theory, the individual or family adapts to the norms of the stage and meets developmental tasks so that a transition to a next stage is possible.

Transitions from one stage to another are central to the life course perspective. Most importantly, transitions can be seen as the most important events in our life course. Birth, graduation, first job, marriage, birth of children, and retirement are all significant turning points in our lives and the lives of families. A second dimension of transition is also important: the adaptation to the stresses of moving from one stage to another. Indeed, transitions represent stressful points in our lives that may become the focus of study.

Time is incredibly important in understanding change and development. Time has several dimensions regarding the life course. The duration of time spent in any one stage helps to predict transitions to another stage. We have seen that the duration of time spent within a stage changes the probability for certain transitions (see Figure 2.4) in nonlinear ways. Furthermore, time and duration can be further broken down by age, birth cohort, and historical period. Every stage we experience is affected by these dimensions of time such that the duration of time we spend in a stage is also tied to the age at which we enter the stage and the norms of the birth cohort and the historical period. In one birth cohort and historical period, a woman may be considered an "old maid" when not married by age 24; in another birth cohort and historical period, she may not transition to marriage until age 30.

At each point in the life course, you are faced with choices (agency). Your choices will certainly be determined by your values but also by how those values are "contextualized" by historical period, stages already traversed, your age, and the duration spent in the current stage. Whereas rational choice theories may emphasize your choices, life course theory sees these choices as being constrained by experience, current stage, time, and aging. Furthermore, life course theory views your values as being determined by factors such as historical period, birth cohort, and age. So while personal agency is possible, it is the social construction of choices and constraints that interests life course theorists.

The macroscopic theorist often wants to know how life course theory deals with war, pestilence, revolution, and other major events in history. Life course analysis conceptualizes these as historical period effects that affect family, relationship, and individual trajectories. For example, if you were a 20-year-old male at the start of World War II (1939), you may have enlisted in the army. If you survived the war, you would be 26 years old at its end. You likely would perceive that you are *off time* because, by your age, your parents had completed their education, had completed having children, had bought a house, and were raising school-aged children. The historical period effect of the war altered your life course timing.

This is not to say that life course analysis does not explain macroscopic historical events; it does so, but in a complex way. All social institutions have timing and sequencing norms to stay organized and keep stress levels for individuals manageable. One does not experience having a first child, marrying, finishing school, starting a first job, and buying a house all at once. Each institution has sequencing and age-graded norms. These norms, however, change over time. For example, in the 1970s, women's labour force participation soared. To get good jobs, more women enrolled in post-secondary education programs. Marriage was delayed because these women were in school. The delay in marriage to the late twenties instead of the early twenties was a major factor in reducing fertility in Canada. This reduction in fertility created labour force shortages that can be solved only by immigration. As we look at how changes in timing in one institutional area (such as labour force and work) leads to accommodations in other institutional areas (such as marriage and family size), we see that our normative institutions are always changing and adapting to each other and to the changes in timing and sequencing norms. This is a more nuanced and subtle view of social change than the cataclysmic period effects of war and economic depression. As we shall see in later chapters, this more subtle view used in life course analysis explains some of the major trends in our society such as cohabitation, lowered fertility, and increasing immigration.

SUMMARY OF KEY POINTS

- The social sciences attempt to answer "why" and "how" questions about social behaviour.
- "How" and "why" questions are usually addressed by theories that cite causes or the social mechanisms involved in producing a phenomenon.
- The major theoretical assumptions used to explain social behaviour are:
  - Theories that cite individual motivation as a cause
  - Theories that cite people following social norms as a cause
  - Theories that cite macro-historical factors as a cause (economic depression, war).
- There are eight major schools of thought or theoretical frameworks used to study families (see Box 2.1).
- Life course analysis integrates many of the concepts and social mechanisms from other social science theories, including agency and social structure.
- Life course analysis examines the pathways that individuals, relationships, and families take as they transition from one stage to another.
- The level of analysis refers to any of the following units of study: the individual, a particular dyadic relationship (e.g., husband and wife, father and daughter), the family group, or the normative institution (family, education, religion, polity, etc.).
- Institutional norms that are followed by the majority of people (high conformity) show a leptokurtotic pattern, whereas norms that are weak and followed by fewer people (low conformity) show a platykurtic pattern (see glossary definition of *leptokurtotic*).

- Timing norms may be either age-graded norms (you cannot be a lifeguard until you are 16 years old) or sequencing norms (finish your education before you get married).

- Development depends on duration. This means that the length of time determining a transition is not linear but curvilinear (think about the probability of having a first child depending on how many years a couple has been married).

- Development at any level of analysis (as measured by age or duration of a unit) can be confounded with birth cohort or historical period (see Table 2.2).

- Macro-historical forces such as economic depression and war (historical period effects) will always affect life course trajectories. At the same time, institutional changes in timing and sequencing norms and cross-institutional accommodations explain any social change in our world.

Critical Thinking Questions

1. As an individual, can you identify stages in your life? Are these stages—such as infancy, childhood, and adolescence—the same ones that would be identified by researchers?

2. Throughout your life and the life course of your family, there will be many important events. Which events qualify as transition events? Are there uniform transition events across different kinds of families and in different cultures?

3. If there were a contagious outbreak of a deadly virus in your city, would you expect health officials to respond at the population level of analysis or at the individual level? What happens to individual rights and liberties when a population response is chosen?

Glossary

age-graded norm A social norm that refers to the age or timing of a particular event or stage. When people say, "Oh, you're too old for that," they are expressing an age-graded norm expectation. See also *timing norm*.

anticipatory socialization This refers to training, skill acquisition, and knowledge gathered for a future anticipated social role such as spouse or parent.

developmental tasks Tasks that are expected in a given stage. The successful transition to a next stage depends on the completion of these tasks. For example, newlyweds should learn to coordinate tasks before they become parents.

expectations Social expectations are a corollary to social norms. If we have social rules about behaviour, we can form expectations about how people will behave. For example, when we get on a bus, we expect the driver to ask for some form of ticket or payment.

event Any occurrence or experience that can be pinpointed to a relatively instantaneous time. For example, pregnancy is a stage or period of time, but finding out one is pregnant is an event.

evolution Any process determined by a consistent set of rules or principles that explain and predict the continuity of change. For example, Darwinian evolution predicts change as a result of natural selection.

formal norms Social rules that are codified or written down in legislation or institutional documents such as contracts.

historical dialectics A dialectical process moves from thesis to antithesis to synthesis. Historical dialectics is the interpretation of historical events as representing thesis → antithesis → synthesis. The most cited examples of this are the works of Marx and Hegel.

informal norms Social rules shared by people in a society but not written down as laws or contracts. For example, the expectation that students study is an informal norm. Schools, however, only measure and record test scores.

leptokurtotic This term refers to a type of frequency distribution in which all cases tend toward the central values. Therefore, this type of distribution suggests high conformity of behaviour. This can be compared to a platykurtic distribution, which is spread out and suggests less behavioural conformity.

off time *On time* and *off time* refer to whether your age at an event or the duration in a stage matches the age or duration expectation. For example, the expectation is that you will be in your late twenties or early thirties when you have your first child.

rational choice theory This theory proposes that individuals choose events, people, and things based on the principle of maximum profit (rewards versus costs). Some rational choice theories, such as those of Coleman (1990), derive social norms and social organizations from the individual's profit-seeking calculations and behaviour.

sequencing norms Norms about the expected sequence or order of life events (normative pathway).

social norms Norms or social rules followed by most people in a group (frequency) and that are sufficiently common as to be expected (social psychological).

stage A duration of time characterized by a particular property or form of interaction or structure that is qualitatively different from that found in the preceding stage and not present in the subsequent stage.

transition event An event that is considered relatively instantaneous in time and that divides the previous stage from the next stage in a life course.

timing norm A norm that suggests at what age you are expected to experience a stage or event. See also *age-graded norm*.

Connections

http://en.wikipedia.org/wiki/Life_course_theory
http://en.wikipedia.org/wiki/Holmes_and_Rahe_stress_scale
http://ezinearticles.com/?Negotiating-Difficult-Life-Transitions&id=9419
http://www.digitalhistory.uh.edu/learning_history/children_depression/depression_children_menu.cfm

---

Remember to log on to the Companion Website at **www.pearsoncanada.ca/white** to find self-graded quizzes and useful resource tools for further study. You can log on to the Companion Website using the Student Access Code that comes packaged with your copy of *Families Across the Life Course*.

Chapter 3
Dating and Mate Selection

Learning Objectives

After reading this chapter, you should be able to:

1. Outline the functions of dating, both historically and today.

2. Compare and contrast theories of attraction and identify factors related to who we find attractive.

3. Examine what should be included in the term *sexual coercion*.

4. Describe factors that are influential in mate selection.

5. Summarize the difference between dating and mate selection.

Fatinah didn't know what to do. She had to find a way to make Simon understand, but it was hard. She really liked him, but if she didn't put a stop to their friendship there would be serious trouble for her. How could she explain that she wasn't allowed to date? That even being seen alone together was inappropriate? That her life depended on him staying away from her? Everyone around her was dating or "hanging out." It was so frustrating to live in Canada but to have to follow her parents' Muslim rules. Her dad's warning was serious, though. She had to stay away from Simon. She could not bring shame to the family or there could be deadly consequences.

As discussed in Chapter 2, life course theory states that we go through several transitions from one stage to another over our life course. The goal of this chapter is to discuss transitions that tend to occur during young adulthood as a first step toward family formation: dating and mate selection. With the increasing diversity in Canada, we need to be aware, as the opening vignette suggests, that not all individuals date prior to marriage. In addition, keep in mind that dating and mate selection can occur at any age and may be repeated several times throughout the life course, but they are most prevalent in young adulthood. This chapter will explore the goal of finding someone to share one's life with for short-term or longer-term experiences. We begin by discussing what it means to date and then discuss mate selection strategies that may lead to cohabitation, marriage, or remarriage. Since research on same-sex coupling is rare, this chapter primarily deals with heterosexual coupling strategies. Future research is required to determine whether the same processes exist for same-sex couples as exist for opposite-sex couples.

DATING: NOW AND IN THE PAST

We tend to believe that the way we have been socialized to do things is the way it has always been done. This is not the case with dating rituals. Prior to the 1920s, dating activities were closely regulated by parents or other family members (chaperones) and often occurred in the home of the female. Dating during this time was considered serious and an indication of commitment to marriage (White, Larson, Goltz, & Munro, 2005). Thus, the dating individuals did not spend time alone together and dating was done for the purposes of showing commitment to the intent of marriage, not for fun.

The period between 1920 and 1960 was the "golden age of courtship" (Langhamer, 2007). After World War I, dating was less supervised. Courtship then became an important rite of passage (Langhamer, 2007) through which young adults could refine gender roles, status, and identity. Dating generally followed four stages: casual dating, steady dating, engagement, and marriage (Nett, 1988). Employment opportunities and available earnings during this period made long courtships unnecessary. Thus, there was a high rate of marriage and a decrease in age at marriage. Members of the working class were especially likely to marry young, as they tended to finish their education sooner than members of the middle class. "Where marriage remained a woman's primary goal, courtship was less tied to a particular individual and instead became a state of being" (Langhamer, 2007, p. 181). Therefore, at least for women, dating was an essential stage of life with the main goal of attaining a husband.

Beginning in the 1960s, dating practices changed dramatically. As women gained more freedom, dating practices shifted. While traditionally men were the initiators, planners, and payers for dates, today women have more of a direct role in these processes (although Laner and Ventrone [1998] have found that gender roles with respect to the early stages of dating have not shifted that much since men still tend to plan and pay for dates—at least the ones they initiate). Dating has become much less formal, with spur-of-the-moment activities more and more likely. Group activities or "hanging out" has become commonplace, allowing individuals the chance to meet and develop friendships or intimate relationships. Technology has also become a source for meeting individuals through internet dating, social networking websites, chat rooms, and even reality TV shows. The goal of dating, it seems, has shifted to that of having fun and meeting new people.

Traditionally, dating followed a basic script. A man asked a woman out a few days before the event would take place. He planned the activities they would do, picked her up, and brought her home, and, since he was responsible for initiating and planning the date, paid for the date's expenses (Bailey, 1988). Murstein (1980) was one of the first scholars to ask, is dating dying? Today, rather than dating, a more common practice on college and university campuses is "**hooking up**" (Bogle, 2007). Glenn and Marquardt (2001, p. 4) define this as "when a girl and a guy get together for a physical encounter and don't necessarily expect anything further." In other words, the hookup is a physical encounter without any expectation of a relationship to follow. According to their research, approximately 40 percent of the women sampled stated they had engaged in a hookup sometime during their college or university experience. Studying a sample of teenagers, Manning, Giordano, and Longmore (2006) found that (at least for teens) the hookup partner was usually a friend or an ex-boyfriend or ex-girlfriend. However, one third of those hooking up hoped that it would lead to a more conventional dating relationship. Thus, the purpose of hooking up may be to initiate dating. Hooking up is most common among college and university students.

When young adults talk about **dating** today, they generally are referring to a man and a woman who attend functions together (Bogle, 2007). Dating differs from mate selection in that the purpose of dating is entertainment only, not choosing a life partner. However, dating can be a source of pressure, as it is often linked to social status (Bibby, 2002). If you don't have someone to date, you may be seen as lower in status (value) than someone who has many people interested in dating him or her.

It is important to keep in mind that the extent of dating that occurs depends somewhat on the subculture to which a person belongs. For example, dating is strongly encouraged in the Mormon community. An individual is supposed to date many people before getting married, to find the right mate (note, though, that in this context "dating" is really

Box 3.1

Arranged Marriage

Arranged marriage is the practice of having someone other than the individual who will be married select the marriage partner, avoiding (or at least shortening) the practice of dating. The marriage partner can be chosen by parents and extended family, matchmakers, or religious leaders. The purpose of the marriage is to have a family. Love is expected to develop as the marriage progresses due to similarities in socio-economic status and cultural background between the two individuals. It is believed that parents and matchmakers have practical knowledge and experience with regards to partner selection, while young adults choosing partners based on emotion (love) may make avoidable mistakes.

The following common misconceptions exist about arranged marriages:

- *Individuals do not get to choose their marriage partners*. In modern arranged marriages, the individuals do get to decide if the selected "match" is suitable to them. Often, the individuals have the final say in whether a marriage will occur (Ternikar, 2004).

- *Arranged marriages are forced marriages*. In fact, this is not the case in most cultures that practise arranged marriage. In some cultures, the individuals are even encouraged to date their potential match to get to know each other better.

- *Individuals are unhappy and "stuck" in their arranged marriage*. There is some evidence that the divorce rate is lower among arranged marriages compared to love marriages. However, we must keep in mind that this may be due to either the quality of the marriage itself or a more traditional culture that frowns on divorce (and thus people stay in their marriages and make the best of it).

Source: http://www.professorshouse.com/Relationships/
Marriage-Advice/Articles/Arranged-Marriage-Facts/

mate selection and does not involve sexual encounters). In the South Asian culture, dating is discouraged (especially for women). Women are to remain virgins until they marry, so dating "for fun" is seen as risky. The practice of arranged marriage also interferes with the idea of dating someone who is not chosen by one's family. Box 3.1 discusses some common misconceptions around the practice of arranged marriage.

According to King and Harris (2007), immigrant youth tend to date less than their Canadian-born peers. This can occur for a number of reasons. Parenting style, for example, can have an influence on dating opportunities. Immigrant families may restrict opportunities by trying to foster cultural identity in their children through organized cultural events (both at home and in the community). King and Harris (2007) found that parents who try to control their children's social lives are at risk for dating rebellion, as the children in their study were found to engage in unwanted romantic relationships (that is, unwanted by the parents). Immigrant teens may also have fewer opportunities to date since they must take on more responsibilities in the family (e.g., translate for their parents). Interracial dating, however, is on the rise. Tucker and Mitchell-Kernan (1995) found interracial dating among more than 50 percent of the African-American,

Latino, and white participants in their study. Although interracial dating is increasing, interracial marriages are quite rare—3.2 percent of marriages in 2001 (Statistics Canada, 2006a).

There is little research on same-sex dating to provide an accurate picture of this process. However, Elze (2002) suggests it may be a more difficult process for gay and lesbian teens and young adults because they may have a harder time recognizing potential partners and do not have access to enough potential partners to find a suitable match until they have established larger social networks. Comparison with opposite-sex dating is also lacking in the research and would be a fruitful area for future research.

The Functions of Dating

As suggested above, the dating process can occur for a variety of reasons. Dating can establish short-term sexual encounters and relationships, mate selection, cohabitation for practical purposes and to avoid being alone (e.g., to share bills), cohabitation as a trial or precursor to marriage, and cohabitation as a substitute to marriage. Cohabitation and marriage will be explored more fully in subsequent chapters. We focus on dating for short-term relationships and mate selection in this chapter.

Skipper and Nass (1968) identified four main functions of dating: gaining status, socialization, recreation, and mate selection. Dating someone who is considered highly desirable (popular) can increase a person's status within his or her social group. You must be a "worthy" individual if an attractive or popular person wants to date you. In fact, for men, dating an attractive female will cause others to believe that they have some highly desirable attributes (this is called the **radiating effect of beauty**). In this way, your partner's attractiveness can improve the way people perceive you. Dating is also a great arena for socialization. It allows men and women to learn how to behave and adjust to others in an intimate context. Often, dating allows a person to get an "outsider's view" on his or her personality and character, which can lead to self-improvement. Dating also provides opportunities for recreation. You can have fun with another person who may make you try something new. Finally, dating can lead to mate selection by allowing you to determine whether a particular person would make a good life partner for you. Box 3.2 provides a brief look at the use of non-verbal behaviours during the courtship process.

Dating and Sex

Castells (2004) argues that sex has been "de-linked" from marriage and family (where, historically, sex was supposed to occur in the context of marriage only). Reiss (1967) states that there are four general premarital sexual standards in which individuals believe today. **Abstinence** is a belief that sex should occur only in the context of marriage (not during dating). **Permissiveness with affection** is a belief that sex is considered okay if the two people are not married but in love. **Permissiveness without affection** is a belief

Box 3.2

Who Initiates? Non-Verbal Courtship Behaviours

Moore (2010) reviewed research conducted on non-verbal flirting (courting) behaviour. The first descriptions of human non-verbal courtship behaviours were recorded in 1965 by psychiatrist Albert Scheflen, who wrote about some of the flirting behaviours displayed between clients and therapists in psychotherapy sessions. Both therapists and clients exhibited these flirting behaviours. Scheflen (1965) categorized them into four types of courtship behaviours: (1) courtship readiness cues (e.g., presenting muscle tone), (2) preening behaviours (e.g., stroking one's hair, fixing makeup), (3) positional cues (e.g., leaning toward the target), and (4) actions of appeal or invitation (e.g., palming or displaying an open wrist or hand, gazing, rolling the pelvis).

Further research into non-verbal courting conducted by Cary (1976) proposed that women hold the power in initiating conversations both in the laboratory and in bar settings. Conversations started only after the woman looked at a man more than once. Similarly, Moore and Butler (1989) found that a trained observer could predict, with high accuracy, the outcomes of interactions based on female courtship behaviours. Signalling was more important than attractiveness, as men were more likely to strike up a conversation with an average-looking woman who signalled interest than with a beautiful woman who did not signal. Moore and Butler (1989) also compiled a list of rejecting behaviours that seemed to be the opposite of flirting (e.g., leaning away and crossing one's arms over one's chest, frowning, picking at teeth or nails). In terms of sexual initiation, non-verbal strategies (e.g., touching, kissing) were used by both men and women 70 percent of the time (Jesser, 1978). Although women seemed more likely to elicit initial interaction, men were more likely to make non-verbal gestures to elicit sex.

that love does not have to exist for a person to have premarital sex. Finally, the **double standard** occurs when there is a belief that women should practise permissiveness with affection but it is considered okay for men to practise permissiveness without affection. Although attitudes toward premarital sex have become more permissive, it is still socially regulated (e.g., you cannot have sex with certain family members or in public places) (Eshleman & Wilson, 2001). Bibby (2001) found that 82 percent of teens believe that sex before marriage is fine if the two people are in love (permissiveness with affection). Approval rates for permissiveness without affection (okay if the two people only like each other) drop to 48 percent for females and 68 percent for males. Rotermann (2008) found that, in 2005, 33 percent of Canadians aged 15 to 17 years and 66 percent of Canadians aged 18 or 19 years had had sex. A study of university students in British Columbia found that 71 percent of non-Asian males and 76 percent of non-Asian females had had intercourse. The rates for Asian males and Asian females were 63 percent and 52 percent, respectively (Meston, Trapnell, & Gorzalka, 1996). Thus, premarital sex is occurring but at different rates depending on age, gender, and ethnicity.

ATTRACTION: THE FIRST STEP TOWARD DATING

Many theories of attraction have been developed to explain why we are attracted to some individuals but not to others. This section describes several theories of attraction that have been proposed in the literature.

Propinquity Theory

The first perspective is proximity or **propinquity theory**. This perspective simply states that we are attracted to those individuals who are around us. In other words, to be attracted to someone we must first be able to meet him or her! Repeated contact (or familiarity) causes us to like an individual (Zajonc, 2001). A classic study by Festinger, Schachter, and Back (1950) looked at individuals living in a series of apartment buildings. People who lived close to each other were much more likely to become friends than those who lived farther away. It has been suggested that if you want to make personal connections at work, you should try to get an office or cubicle by either the bathroom or the water cooler, as you will run into more fellow employees that way. Keep in mind that familiarity can work in reverse, too. If you are disliked by someone, repeatedly encountering him or her will only heighten that person's dislike for you (Ebbesen, Kjos, & Konecini, 1976).

Historically, this perspective made sense. An individual could meet only those in his or her immediate surroundings. Thus, the choice of partners in small towns, for example, may be limited. However, with the advent of new technologies, virtual spaces are now

Box 3.3

Finding a Date Through Advertisements

Today, finding a date is much easier than it was in the past. One way individuals are finding dates is by using advertisements. This is not a new idea, as people have been placing personal ads in newspapers for decades. With advances in technology and the widespread availability of internet service, however, online ads on dating websites are becoming a common method used to find dates. Many dating sites are available, from free sites such as Plenty of Fish to paid sites such as eHarmony. There are sites for pet lovers (e.g., Love Me Love My Pets), sites geared toward specific religious groups (e.g., Catholic Singles), and sites specifically for the elderly (e.g., Senior People Meet). What exactly are we buying or selling in these ads?

An article by Elizabeth Jagger (1998) examined the content of 1094 dating advertisements placed in local newspapers. She wanted to see if traditional mate selection strategies were still the norm. In other words, she expected that men would "sell" their financial and occupational status and "buy" (look for) physical attractiveness in a potential partner. Women would "sell" their attractiveness and "buy" status and resource attributes. Interestingly, Jagger found that lifestyle choices were becoming more important than resources for women, as women were marketing traditionally masculine attributes (e.g., "I'm athletic," "I like to golf") and looking for men who had some traditionally feminine attributes (e.g., emotionally supportive, sensitive men). Note that ideas about what is "masculine" and what is "feminine" are socially

constructed and can change over time. Body characteristics continued to be important for both men and women. Specifically, when placing ads, men were most likely to describe their body, personality, resources, and lifestyle interests. Women were most likely to describe their body, personality, lifestyle interests, and attractiveness. When asked what they wanted in a prospective partner (what they were looking for), men reported the important attributes to be personality, body, attractiveness, and lifestyle factors while women reported looking for personality, body, resources, and non-smokers.

Ellison, Heino, and Gibbs (2006) looked at the self-presentation strategies of online dating participants. They found that small cues became very important in the online context. For example, writing ability, such as spelling and grammar, was perceived as an indication of intelligence level. Writing too much in an email response was thought to show desperation or lack of friends. Participants also focused on the timing of the message—when it was sent. One participant learned that he was being perceived as a night owl (seen as a negative trait) due to his late-night emails. Honesty was a theme explored in this study. Participants found a way to be honest yet also attractive to a potential partner by describing their ideal self instead of their real self. For example, a man may state in his ad that he likes hiking even though, in reality, he hikes only once a year. In this way, he is being honest but also identifying what he perceives to be attractive to a potential dating partner.

available where individuals can "meet" in a virtual sense. It is now possible to meet someone halfway around the globe through an online dating site such as Match.com or Lavalife. In fact, dating sites of all kinds exist. If you are an animal lover, you can meet someone on the website Love Me Love My Pets. Sites such as Lavalife allow you to choose the type of connection you want to make: sexual encounter, just for fun, or committed relationship. There are even dating sites specific to certain groups (e.g., seniors, religious groups). Box 3.3 describes strategies used to attract a date and attributes looked for when trying to find a date using advertisements (both in print and online).

Similarity Theory

Similarity theory states that "birds of a feather flock together" or that "like attracts like." We generally like those who are similar to us (McPherson, Smith-Lovin, & Cook, 2001). Similarity allows people to have shared experiences, helps to strengthen relational identity, and lowers the risk of breakup (Kalmijn, 2005). **Assortative mating** occurs when we chose partners based on certain traits. **Homogamy** means that we choose individuals with traits similar to ours. Demographic similarity is important. We tend to like people who are close to us in age, education level and social class (Nelson & Robinson, 2002), ethnicity (McClintock, 2010), and religion. Religious homogamy is more important to some groups, such as Jews, Sikhs, Hindus, and Muslims, than to Christian groups such as Protestants and Catholics (Statistics Canada, 2006a). We also are attracted to people with similar attitudes; we like people who think the way we do. We even choose people with the same moods (Locke & Horowitz, 1990). For example, non-depressed people are attracted to other non-depressed people. Homogamy may be less important to same-sex couples, however (Jepsen & Jepsen, 2002); often, gays and lesbians are more open to dating a wider variety of individuals. Initially, similarity leads to attraction; later, similarity can help to strengthen our attachment to someone.

Complementary Theory

Complementary theory relates to the notion that "opposites attract." For example, a person who hates cooking will be attracted to someone who loves to cook. There is little evidence to support the idea that complementary personalities cause attraction. However, we do find complementary behaviours and interests attractive (Aron, Steele, Kashdan, & Perez, 2006) and often will exchange beauty for resources (Mathes & Kozak, 2008). If we have evidence that people who are similar are attracted to one another and that people who are different are attracted to one another, how do we reconcile these findings? How do these two theories work together? What we have learned is that similarity provides the context for the relationship in which different skills and interests become complementary (Aron et al., 2006). For example, since professor A is a sociologist, people may think that the best match for professor A is another sociologist (they would likely have similar attitudes toward social issues or, at minimum, have similar work schedules). However, dating someone in the same department would likely be problematic. They would be in constant competition. Who would be the better academic? Perhaps, then, a person with similar attitudes toward social issues and a similar work schedule would be attractive as long as that person worked in a different department or position. Then they could both be experts in their own areas and not be in competition with one another. People who have different interests allow us the opportunity to try to learn about new things we wouldn't normally (opportunities for self-expansion) and this can be gratifying.

Stimulus-Value-Role Theory

Murstein (1986, 1987) proposed stimulus-value-role (SVR) theory in an effort to merge these ideas. According to SVR theory, we are initially attracted to external attributes (the stimulus stage). Approval by the partner is the primary reward in first encounters (e.g., if they validate our beliefs, we feel accepted). During the stimulus stage, we focus on choosing someone who is attainable, not necessarily someone who is our ideal (e.g., we may choose someone with a similar level of attractiveness as we have, not the most attractive person we know). The second stage is the value stage. Here, we get to know each other to see if our attitudes, interests, and beliefs match. Over time, we disclose information about ourselves to our partner. The pace of this disclosure is important. If you reveal too much information too soon, you may scare your date away (Buck & Plant, 2008). If you reveal too little information, you may frustrate your partner. In the value stage, we focus on gathering information through verbal interaction. We may even set up little "tests" to check for attitude similarity. For example, if you want to see if your partner likes children, you may take him or her to a playground or invite him or her over when your niece or nephew or baby sister or brother is there, and then see how he or she responds. During the value stage, you are in essence determining whether a long-term relationship is possible. The final stage in SVR theory is the role stage. A role is a set of behaviours that are expected of a person who occupies a specific position in a group. During this stage, we evaluate a mate on two dimensions: (1) how we actually function in the relationship compared to how we expected we would function in the relationship, and (2) how our partner functions in the relationship compared to how we expected him or her to function. We are evaluating not only how well our partner meets our expectations but also how we are behaving as a result of this relationship. Sometimes a relationship ends because we do not like who we become when we are with a particular person. Thus, according to SVR theory, successful performance of our respective roles will lead to commitment.

Psychological Reactance

The theory of **psychological reactance** states that we like people we cannot have (Brehm & Brehm, 1981). This is due to both internal and external barriers. A person is more desirable if he or she plays hard to get (internal barriers). However, if he or she plays *too* hard to get, that person may be seen as not worth the trouble. So, it may be important to be seen as selectively hard to get. External barriers may also increase psychological reactance. For example, if a parent disapproves of a particular partner, this may in fact enhance one's feelings for the partner (especially among teenagers). Sometimes geographical distance or closing time at a bar can act as an external barrier as well.

THE DARK SIDE OF DATING
Getting a Date

With the advent of new technologies, it is becoming easier to find a date. Individuals can now connect through social networking sites such as Facebook, join online dating sites such as Plenty of Fish, and even "meet" through avatars on virtual reality sites such as Second Life, in addition to meeting face to face at school or at work. For those who are technologically inclined, "sites" to meet abound. However, especially among younger and older groups, there may still be some stigma attached to using online dating sites to meet someone special. Younger individuals may believe that they should be able to meet someone in person (e.g., at school) rather than go online to date. Older individuals may not be technologically savvy enough to use online sites. However, these sites allow individuals who are normally shy the opportunity to "talk" at their own pace (and with as many re-writes as needed before pressing send) (Baker & Oswald, 2008). Due to the visual nature of these sites (most sites allow you to upload pictures), there are still some disadvantages for individuals who do not fit the norm for attractiveness. It is also possible to be dishonest in the online context, and individuals often lie about their age, weight, and relationship status (i.e., married or single) (Ellison et al., 2006).

Interference

Although most Canadians (with the exception of some ethnic subgroups) practise free choice dating, our family and friends can have a large influence on who we ultimately choose. It is not uncommon to "check in" with our friends and family to see if they approve of our dating partners. Many individuals will consider ending a relationship if their friends and family disapprove. Sprecher and Felmlee (1992) found that people were more satisfied with a relationship if it was approved of by their social network. Zhang (2009) conducted a cross-cultural study examining the influence of network members on commitment to a relationship and marriage intentions in China and the United States. Network influence predicted Chinese relationship commitment and marital intentions. For U.S. participants, the length of the relationship and feelings about support and care as well as network influence predicted relationship commitment and marital intentions. Thus, in both countries, research indicates that our family and friends have an impact on our choices but the amount of influence may vary by culture.

Violence and Coercion

Hartwick, Desmarais, and Hennig (2007) examined **sexual coercion** among undergraduate students at a Canadian university. They used a definition of sexual coercion proposed by Struckman-Johnson and Struckman-Johnson (1994, p. 96): "an experience of being pressured or forced by another person to have contact which involved touching of sexual parts or sexual intercourse—oral, anal, or vaginal."

Research has shown that females who are coerced have had a greater number of sexual partners. Some evidence for low self-esteem and low assertiveness has also been found (Testa & Dermen, 1999). Research on male characteristics associated with being coerced is rare. Craig (1990) and Loh and Gidycz (2006) performed reviews on sexual coercion and found that initiators and victims (both male and female) are more likely to have had more sexual partners and a history of childhood victimization than those who are not coerced or coercing. The authors found that an almost equivalent number

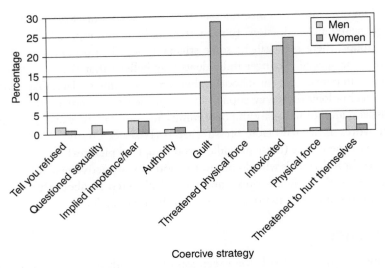

Figure 3.1 Prevalence of Men's and Women's Experiences with Sexual Coercion Strategies

Source: Hartwick et al. (2007).

of males (24.4 percent) and females (23.3 percent) reported some form of sexual coercion before age 14. Overall, 47.9 percent of female participants and 38.8 percent of male participants in the study reported being victims. Guilt and intoxication were the most common strategies used to coerce another (see Figure 3.1).

We must keep in mind, however, that sometimes studies on unwanted sexual activity equate unwanted activity and coerced activity. O'Sullivan and Allgeier (1998) show in their study of heterosexual dating relationships that often college students have unwanted sex that is consensual. In other words, you can feel no drive to have sex but still accept a partner's invitation for sex. In their study, 38 percent of the participants reported having unwanted sex during a two-week period. Motivations for doing so include satisfying a partner, avoiding relationship tension, promoting intimacy, feeling obligated because of past experiences with a partner, and feeling unable to refuse.

Muehlenhard and Linton (1987) found that, in their sample, 77.6 percent of the women and 57.3 percent of the men had experienced sexual aggression in their relationship and that 14.7 percent of the woman and 7.1 percent of the men had had unwanted sexual intercourse. Risk factors include men's acceptance of traditional sex roles, men's initiating and paying for a date, miscommunication about sex, alcohol and drug use, and adversarial attitudes about relationships. Length of time in the relationship was not related to risk for sexual aggression.

In response to the issue of sexual coercion and violence on its campus, Antioch College proposed a set of rules in an attempt to decrease and ultimately eliminate sexual aggression on campus (see Box 3.4). Should your campus community enforce such rules?

Box 3.4

Date Rape and Antioch College

Most studies of date rape have been conducted on college and university students. Estimates of date rape range widely from 15 to 78 percent. It is difficult to get accurate statistics because of the ambiguity of the term *rape*. Stets (1992) proposes that date rape and dating violence occur because the individual is unable to take the role of the other—that is, to see the situation from the other person's point of view. Antioch College, in Ohio, found this to be such an important issue that it proposed the following rules on its campus.

The Antioch College Sexual Offense Prevention Policy

In 1991, a group of Antioch students began to create a policy in an attempt to end sexual coercion and violence on campus and foster a culture of consensual sexuality. Individuals who attend, work at, or visit Antioch College must now be familiar with and follow the following rules.

Consent *Consent* is defined as the act of willingly and verbally agreeing to engage in specific sexual conduct. Previously agreed-upon forms of non-verbal communication are not appropriate methods for expressing consent. In order for consent to be valid, all parties must have unimpaired judgment and a shared understanding of the nature of the act to which they are consenting, including safer-sex practices. The person who initiates sexual conduct is responsible for verbally asking for the consent of the individuals involved. Consent must be obtained with each new level of sexual conduct. The person with whom sexual conduct is initiated must verbally express consent or lack of consent. Silence conveys a lack of consent. If at any time consent is withdrawn, the conduct must stop immediately.

Offences Defined Any non-consensual sexual conduct is an offence under this policy. Examples of offences include but are not limited to the following.

Sexual assault is a non-consensual sexual act including but not limited to vaginal penetration, anal penetration, and oral sex. Penetration, however slight, includes the insertion of objects or body parts.

Sexual imposition is non-consensual sexual touching.

Sexual harassment is any unwanted sexual attention, including but not limited to sexually threatening or offensive behaviour.

Source: Adapted from Antioch College (2005).

Honour Killings

Honour killings are not the same as murder in a domestic violence scenario. According to Welden (2010, p. 380), an **honour killing** is "the death of a female family member who is murdered by one or more male family members, sometimes with the active assistance of other women related to the victim. In 'honor' murder, a female family member is deemed by her male relatives to have transgressed the family's 'honor.'" These killings are planned and, as the vignette at the beginning of this chapter suggests, the victim is often threatened beforehand.

It is difficult to determine the prevalence of honour killings, as they are under-reported. Since the victim brought shame to the family (or so is believed by the family members), these deaths are not often reported. As suggested by White and Mick (2007), these murders are rare in Canada. The United Nations General Assembly (2006) stated that about 5000 women per year are killed in this manner.

In situations where an honour killing occurs, the patriarch or dominant male in the family is considered responsible for the actions of his family members and must restore his honour by killing the offender. Inappropriate actions by a female family member can include failing to cover her face, hair, or body; choosing to wear Western clothes or makeup; dating those not approved of by the family; attending higher education; marrying someone not chosen by the family; divorcing; and acting autonomously (e.g., driving by herself) (Chesler, 2009).

As reported in the *Vancouver Sun* and on CBC News (Hildebrandt, 2009), Aqsa Parvez, a 16-year-old girl from Pakistan, was strangled by her father and brother in Mississauga, Ontario, in December 2007. She had wanted to wear Western clothes and get a part-time job. A year earlier, Muhammad Shafia; his second wife, Tooba Muhammad Yahya; and his son Hamed Shafia were charged with first-degree murder for killing Muhammad Shafia's first wife and three daughters. They were found submerged in a vehicle in a canal in Kingston, Ontario. It is not known how many other such cases exist in Canada.

THE DIFFERENCE BETWEEN DATING AND MATE SELECTION

In everyday language, we use the term *dating* to mean both dating for fun and mate selection. From a research standpoint, we need to make the distinction between these two terms clear. As stated earlier in the chapter, the purpose of dating is simply to have fun with another person we are interested in romantically. **Mate selection** is the term used by social scientists to refer to the time when people are actively looking to find a life partner. "Dating" in this sense becomes a quest for "the one." Dating tends to focus on choosing people we like and find attractive. In mate selection, other attributes may become more important (e.g., potential stability, love). Mate selection is supposed to lead to marriage or marriage-like cohabitation (i.e., with the intention of permanence).

Historically, marriage fulfilled economic, status, and kinship needs (Ackerman, 1994). You did not necessarily need to love your partner but he or she had to have status, wealth, or a political alliance of some kind. Love was expected to develop after marriage (if at all). Modern ideas about marriage and marriage-like cohabitation insist that we love our partners (at least at the time we marry) (Simpson, Campbell, & Berscheid, 1986).

Several theories classify types of love. One such classification was developed by Lee (1988), who proposed six styles of loving. **Eros** is a type of love that has an intense, physical component. People focus on the attractiveness of their partner. **Ludus** is playful love or game-playing love (e.g., "playing the field") in which a person may try to juggle several dating partners at one time. **Storge** is love based on friendship that grows to lasting

commitment. **Mania** is obsessive, possessive love where a person feels out of control. **Agape** is altruistic and selfless love. Finally, **pragma** is practical love in which a person carefully considers a person's vital attributes (e.g., education level, age) to find the best match. Men generally score higher on ludus love than women do, while women are more likely to score high on storge and pragma love (Hendrick & Hendrick, 2003).

DeMunck, Korotayev, deMunck, and Khaltourina (2011) conducted a cross-cultural study on the meaning of love using American, Russian, and Lithuanian samples. They found that all three groups agreed that love included intrusive thinking, happiness, passion, altruism, and increased well-being. However, comfort and friendship were critical to the U.S. sample but were irrelevant to the Russian and Lithuanian samples. These latter two groups also perceived love as fleeting and unreal.

THEORIES OF MATE SELECTION

Biosocial Theory

Buss (1989, 2003) and Kenrik, Trost, and Kelley (1987) propose a biosocial theory of mate selection. This theory is based on an evolutionary perspective in which choosing a sexual partner is related to genetically adaptive procreation. According to this perspective, since a woman gives birth, she is certain the child is her offspring. Men, on the other hand, cannot be sure if a child is theirs (except, of course, through DNA testing, which was not available until recently). Women must bear the brunt of raising their children and, since they have higher parental investment, will be more selective in their choice of sex partner and mate, favouring someone who shows willingness to contribute time and resources to potential offspring. Men are less selective since it is to their advantage (genetically speaking) to have as many children as possible; thus, they favour choosing someone for a sexual encounter rather than as a long-term mate.

Due to differences in parental investment, men and women find different traits attractive. Women are attracted to men who look strong and dominant (Rhodes, 2006), especially when the women are ovulating (Puts, 2005), as these men presumably have better genetics that can be passed on to offspring. If you look at the animal kingdom, the strongest male will win fights over fertile females and will subsequently mate while the male who lost must find another partner.

Men are attracted to women who outwardly exhibit health and the potential to bear offspring successfully. In other words, men are attracted to women who are young (Buss, 2003) and have an hourglass figure (birthing hips). In fact, research has shown that a waist-to-hip ratio of 0.7 is most attractive across many cultures (Singh, 2004) (see Figure 3.2). (To calculate your waist-to-hip ratio, measure your waist and divide this by the measure of your hips.) Interestingly, the actual size of the woman is less important than the ratio. So, a woman could be a size 2 or a size 22 and still have a 0.7 waist-to-hip

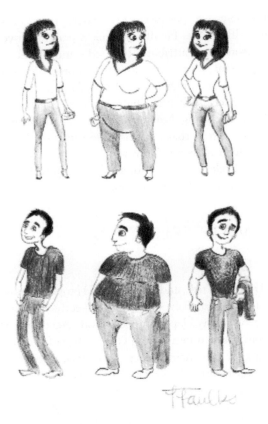

Figure 3.2 Which Body Type Do You Prefer?

Source: Adapted from Miller and Perlman (2009). Illustrated by Tara Faulks.

The Wedding Ring Effect

The **wedding ring effect** is scientifically known as mate choice copying. This is the idea that (among humans) married or unavailable men are more desirable to women than single or available men. This idea stems from the animal kingdom, where among certain species (e.g., guppies, a type of fish) the female will choose a male that is already taken even though there may be a "better" (e.g., bigger, brighter coloured) available male present. The wedding ring is said to signal that a man has valuable attributes (e.g., he must be rich or kind) as well as that he is willing to commit to a long-term relationship. However, some stigma is associated with starting a relationship with a man who is otherwise taken. Uller and Johansson (2003) decided to test this theory using engaged versus single men. The study was done in a laboratory setting and each male confederate was both "engaged" and "single" in various conditions. The researchers found that the effect did not hold. The women in the study were not more attracted to the "engaged" men. The authors suggest that this effect may work for unattractive men but it offers no additional benefit to men who are already attractive—an idea that needs to be tested further.

ratio that is considered attractive. Of course, higher weight is an indicator of poor health, so often heavier women are seen as less attractive (Swami, Greven, & Furnham, 2007).

Today, as status and wealth are often achieved through intelligence rather than brawn, what is attractive to women is shifting. An intelligent, successful, and wealthy male may be the "winner" in the mating competition over strong, dominant men. Stereotypes about muscular men have turned negative, as extremely muscular men may be viewed as self-absorbed and unintelligent. Note that studies have shown that, while ovulating, women prefer a dominant, muscular man, whereas during the rest of their cycle they prefer a committed man (Puts, 2005). From an evolutionary perspective, this makes sense. When the chance of pregnancy is high (during ovulation), mating with a dominant male may provide the best genetics to one's offspring. But highly attractive, dominant men may have many opportunities to mate and thus may be less committed to one partner. Thus, when not ovulating, a committed male is preferred, as he is more likely to stay and provide resources for the child, which will enable survival. Box 3.5 explores whether unavailable men (i.e., married men) are perceived as more attractive than available men.

Social Exchange Theory

Exchange and investment theories are often used to explain mate selection. Exchange theory is an economic model of human behaviour developed by Thibaut and Kelley (1959). The focus of this theory is motivation. To understand a person's behaviour, we need to understand his or her motivations. A central assumption of the theory is that people are motivated by self-interest to maximize their profit and minimize their loss. In other words, we are selfish and will do what is best for us when we can. Another assumption of the theory is that we are rational—that is, we have the ability to make the best choice based on an assessment of the costs and benefits of each alternative. Nye (1979, p. 1) states:

> Humans avoid costly behavior and seek rewarding statuses, relationships, interaction, and feeling states to the end that their profits are maximized. In seeking rewards they voluntarily accept some costs; likewise in avoiding costs, some rewards are forgone, but the person, group, or organization will choose the best outcome available, based on his/her/its perception of rewards and costs.

Rewards are things a person likes, while costs are things a person dislikes. Professors can reward you in two ways: (1) they can give you something pleasant (e.g., an A in the course), or (2) they can take away something unpleasant (e.g., your need to write the final exam). Costs also work in two ways: (1) they can give you something unpleasant (e.g., an extra assignment), or (2) they can take away something you like (e.g., your formula sheet for a statistics exam). Costs can also include rewards forgone. For example, if you decide to go to graduate school, you must give up benefits that go along with your other options, such as getting a paid job in the workforce. In this case, you give up the benefits of having a salary to continue with your education. *Profit* is the term used to describe our calculation of the rewards minus the costs of a choice.

There are two other concepts we need to discuss in relation to exchange theory. Comparison level (CL) "is a standard by which the person evaluates the rewards and costs of a given relationship in terms of what he feels he deserves" (Thibaut & Kelley, 1959, p. 21). We can measure CL in several ways. We can compare what we have now to our ideal or to what we had in the past. For example, how does your new girlfriend or boyfriend compare to what you had in the past? If your new partner is better than your old partner, you will be satisfied. However, if your new partner is worse than your old partner, you will not be very satisfied. Thus, CL is a measure associated with satisfaction (Miller & Perlman, 2009). Comparison level of alternatives (Clalt) is "the lowest level of outcomes a [person] will accept in the light of alternative opportunities" (Thibaut & Kelley, 1959, p. 21). Our Clalt is the measure of our options. If you have many options, you will be less dependent on the one that you have chosen. If you have few options, you will be more dependent on the one you have chosen. Thus, Clalt is a measure that relates to our dependency level (Ellis, Simpson, & Campbell, 2002).

Another concept we must consider is salience. In our assessment of rewards and costs, some factors may be more important than others and thus have greater weight in our decision making. Finally, we need to take time into consideration. Life isn't static, so we must consider how our decisions will pan out in both the short term and the long term.

The formal propositions for exchange theory are as follows (Nye, 1979, p. 6):

1. Individuals choose alternatives from which they expect the most profit.
2. Costs being equal, they choose alternatives from which they anticipate the greatest rewards.

3. Rewards being equal, they choose alternatives from which they anticipate fewest costs.

4. Immediate outcomes being equal, they choose alternatives that promise better long-term outcomes.

5. Long-term outcomes being equal, they choose alternatives that provide better immediate outcomes.

Let's look at these propositions in the context of dating. Let's say, for the sake of this example, that you are a heterosexual female, two men want to date you, and you must choose one of them. You have created the following cost–benefit list:

Person A	Person B
Funny	Smart
Confident	Attractive
Wealthy	Polite
Smelly	Pessimistic
Flirty	Cheap
Immature	Dishonest

To this list, you add the relative salience of each trait. Positive traits are rated on a scale from 1 to 10, with 10 being the best; negative traits are rated on a scale from −1 to −10, with −10 being the worst.

Person A		Person B	
Funny	9	Smart	7
Confident	8	Attractive	10
Wealthy	10	Polite	4
Smelly	−4	Pessimistic	−6
Flirty	−7	Cheap	−8
Immature	−5	Dishonest	−10
Total	11		−3

If we calculate the overall scores, we see that Person A would be the "rational" choice for a dating partner. We have listed positive traits (rewards), negative traits (costs), and calculated profit (rewards minus costs) for each alternative. We have also incorporated the concept of salience by giving the traits weights to indicate which are more or less important to the decision. Now we must add the time component. Let's say that both Person A and Person B are college students and that their calculated profits are equal (i.e., short-term profits are equal). However, Person A wants to be a "bum" (live off his partner) when he graduates while Person B wants to be a manager. According to

Proposition 4 above, you would rationally choose Person B to be your partner, since in the long run this person will be the more profitable choice. Now let's say that Person A and Person B both want to be managers when they graduate (i.e., long-term profit is equal). Rationally, according to Proposition 5 above, you would choose Person A for your partner since he has the better profit outcome in the short term.

Equity Theory

Equity theory is another interdependence theory that is similar to exchange theory. Like exchange theory, equity theory states that people will try to maximize their outcomes (rewards minus costs) when making a choice. Additional propositions include the following (Walster, Walster, & Berscheid, 1978, p. 6):

1. Groups will generally reward members who treat others equally and generally punish (increase costs) members who treat others inequitably.

2. When individuals find themselves participating in inequitable relationships, they will become distressed. The more inequitable the relationship, the more distress individuals will feel.

3. Individuals who discover they are in an inequitable relationship will attempt to eliminate their distress by restoring equity. The greater the inequity that exists, the more distress they will feel, and the harder they will try to restore equity.

Once again, the assumption of this theory is that people are selfish. However, we learn quickly that for society to exist (and work fairly smoothly), it is more profitable to behave equitably than inequitably. Thus, in the first proposition listed above, people will punish members of society who do not follow this rule. More important for mate selection purposes are propositions 2 and 3 above. We want our relationships to be equitable. In other words (Miller & Perlman, 2009, p. 201):

$$\frac{\text{Your outcomes}}{\text{Your contributions}} = \frac{\text{Your partner's outcomes}}{\text{Your partner's contributions}}$$

According to the principle of equity, the more a person contributes to a relationship, the more he or she should gain from it. For example, if you increase your contributions, to have an equitable relationship your partner should increase his or her contributions in turn. This may be something you want to try in your own relationship. Spend at least a few weeks doing more nice things for your partner and see if he or she will reciprocate in kind. If a relationship is not equitable, this theory suggests that we will feel distress. The person whose ratio is smaller (who is not getting as much as he or she should) is called the underbenefitter, while the person whose ratio is larger (who is getting too much) is called the overbenefitter. The underbenefitter will feel unappreciated and used, while the overbenefitter will feel guilty (note that *both* feel distress, just in different ways) (Hatfield, 1983). According to Proposition 3 above, a person will try to alleviate the stress by (1) restoring actual equity (making changes in real life) (Canary & Stafford, 2001),

(2) restoring equity psychologically (believing that the relationship is equitable), or (3) leaving the relationship.

We must keep in mind one final idea. The egocentric bias suggests that people tend to overestimate the amount they contribute to a relationship and underestimate the contributions of other people. Therefore, they will tend to feel they are giving more rewards than they are receiving—not a good outcome according to equity theory! Floyd and Wasner (1994) have shown that the equity balance is predictive of relationship satisfaction (the more equitable, the more satisfied). Satisfaction with the relationship in turn predicts commitment to the relationship.

Filter Model of Mate Selection

Several theories, such as Murstein's SVR theory, show that the process of mate selection occurs over time. Another process theory is called the filter model of mate selection (see Figure 3.3), which was introduced by Kerckhoff and Davis (1962). This model incorporates both personal and societal factors related to our choice of mate and shows how our choice of mate is filtered along several dimensions. Through a process of filtering, we narrow the total number of people who are available or in the "mating market" to a small group.

We first divide the pool of eligible people by roughly half simply by filtering out those who are not of the gender we prefer or are attracted to. We then tend to narrow our search to those who are in close proximity to us (recall propinquity theory, explained above). Even with the advent of new technologies, we still tend to prefer dating face to face, so individuals near us are kept in the pool of eligibles while those who are not near us are filtered out (Sahlstein, 2006).

The sex ratio of a given area can have an impact on our pool of eligibles and how we behave in the mating game. A **sex ratio** is defined as the number of men per 100 women in a given population. When the sex ratio is high, there are more men than women in a population; when the sex ratio is low, there are more women than men. Trovato (1988) found that when the sex ratio is high (more men), the rate of marriage increases. In fact, when there is a high sex ratio, societies tend to be more traditional.

Think about the following example: Say that we have a heterosexual society made up of 10 men and 5 women, all of whom want to get married and migration is not possible. Five of the men (under monogamous rules) will not be able to marry, as not enough women are available. Therefore, the men will have to compete with each other to "gain" a wife. Thus, it is likely that the men with the highest resources (recall exchange theory)

Pool of eligibles → Gender preference → Propinquity and sex ratio → Endogamy/exogamy → Homogamy → Value and role similarity → Cohabitation or engagement

Figure 3.3 Filter Model of Mate Selection

Source: White et al. (2005).

will win a mate while those with lower resources will lose the competition. To keep a mate, it would also make sense to isolate the women from the single men. In a traditional society, men are breadwinners (have resources) while women are homemakers (depend on resources and are not in the workforce where they can easily associate with other men). Now assume that our society has 10 women and 5 men. In this case, five of the women will not be able to marry. Therefore, they will have to enter the workforce to support themselves. Here, a traditional system no longer works, as five women would have no male "breadwinners" to support them. In this case, society tends to become more modern. Of course, this is a simplistic example but it should help to explain how sex ratios can influence the modernity of a society. Figure 3.4 shows the number of men and women (by age) in Canada in 2010. Notice that overall (total) there are more women than men in Canada. However, most of this difference occurs in later life, when there are higher numbers of females than males in the same age groups. Data Box 3.1 discusses the role of sex ratios on mate preferences.

As you can see, an imbalance in sex ratio can reduce marriage for one group or the other. This is called a **marriage squeeze**, where marriage is reduced for a given group due to lack of available partners. Social norms can also cause specific groups to be squeezed out of marriage. For example, women who are very successful (i.e., have high status and resources) as well as men at the bottom of a social class (i.e., those with few resources and low status) are often squeezed out of marriage. Since it is normative for women to marry up in status, there are few available men with equally high or similarly high status and resources to those of very successful women. Thus, very successful women often choose not to partner and instead rely on family and friends as sources of social support. Similarly, men with few resources to offer a potential mate will be squeezed out, as there will be fewer available women for them. This is due to the **mating gradient**, where women seek men of similar or higher status and men seek women of similar or lower status (Mitchell, 2006).

The next filter is whether your mate must be within or outside of your social group. **Exogamy** is marriage outside a social group. For example, cross-cultural marriages are exogamous. **Endogamy** is marriage inside one's group. For example, two Muslims getting married is endogamous. In Canada, for the most part we will select a mate who is homogamous to ourselves. **Homogamy** is the tendency to select a partner with similar social and personal characteristics. **Heterogamy** occurs when we choose an individual who is not like ourselves. We tend to be homogamous in terms of age, education, socio-economic status, race and ethnicity, and religion (McClintock, 2010; Nelson & Robinson, 2002). This is called assortive mating—that is, people choose mates "like themselves."

At this point in the filtering process, you can see that many of the available people have now been selected out, leaving us with a much smaller pool of eligibles. The next filter fits with Murstein's SVR theory. Among our narrow pool, we now look for individuals who fit with our value system and are compatible with our role expectations (see

	Canada	Male	Female	Canada	Male	Female
Age group	Persons (thousands)			% of total of each group		
Total	34 108.8	16 917.3	17 191.5	100.0	100.0	100.0
0 to 4	1878.2	963.4	914.7	5.5	5.7	5.3
5 to 9	1803.3	928.4	874.9	5.3	5.5	5.1
10 to 14	1935.2	992.1	943.2	5.7	5.9	5.5
15 to 19	2226.8	1140.1	1086.8	6.5	6.7	6.3
20 to 24	2364.9	1214.8	1150.1	6.9	7.2	6.7
25 to 29	2394.5	1212.1	1182.4	7.0	7.2	6.9
30 to 34	2301.4	1150.7	1150.7	6.7	6.8	6.7
35 to 39	2294.7	1153.1	1141.6	6.7	6.8	6.6
40 to 44	2421.0	1219.6	1201.4	7.1	7.2	7.0
45 to 49	2793.4	1405.3	1388.1	8.2	8.3	8.1
50 to 54	2618.8	1306.5	1312.2	7.7	7.7	7.6
55 to 59	2288.3	1128.2	1160.1	6.7	6.7	6.7
60 to 64	1968.7	965.0	1003.7	5.8	5.7	5.8
65 to 69	1468.9	712.6	756.4	4.3	4.2	4.4
70 to 74	1104.6	519.5	585.0	3.2	3.1	3.4
75 to 79	912.4	412.1	500.2	2.7	2.4	2.9
80 to 84	688.2	283.8	404.3	2.0	1.7	2.4
85 to 89	427.5	150.6	276.8	1.3	0.9	1.6
90 and older	218.1	59.4	158.8	0.6	0.4	0.9

Figure 3.4 Population by Sex and Age Group, Canada, 2010

Note: Population as of July 1.

Source: Statistics Canada CANSIM database http://cansim2.statcan.gc.ca, table 051-001, April 5, 2011.

Data Box 3.1

Mate Preference and Sex Ratio

Stone, Shackelford, and Buss (2007) wanted to see if sex ratios had an effect on mate preferences. They specifically wanted to test two hypotheses: (1) the *classical sex ratio mate preference shifts hypothesis*, which states that "in imbalanced sex ratio societies, the more numerous sex will lower their standards, to facilitate acquisition of a partner of the less numerous sex" (p. 288), and (2) the *alternative sex ratio mate preference shifts hypothesis*, which states that "in lower sex ratio societies, men will lower their standards to secure more short-term matings, whereas women will raise their standards to avoid deception by men seeking short-term relationships" (p. 288).

In this study, sex ratio was defined by the number of men per 100 reproductive-aged women within a society. Table 3.1 provides sex ratios by country or culture.

The findings suggest that in a lower sex ratio society (i.e., more women than men), men will raise their standards when choosing a long-term mate. This is consistent with the classical hypothesis. Women's mate preference ratings supported the alternative hypothesis. In a low sex ratio society, although competing for men, women also increase their mate preference standards. The alternative hypothesis suggests that this is to avoid being deceived by men seeking short-term relationships. The authors conclude that "women who maintained more stringent mate preference standards and successfully avoided being deceived by short-term relationship seeking men in lower sex ratio contexts might have experienced relatively greater reproductive success over human evolutionary history" (p. 294).

Source: Stone et al. (2007).

Table 3.1 Sex Ratio by Country or Culture

Country or Culture	Sex Ratio
Australia	103.23
Belgium	103.38
Brazil	99.26
Bulgaria	101.61
Canada	102.60
China	108.30
Colombia	98.19
Estonia	99.47
Finland	104.47
France	102.30
Germany	104.55
Great Britain	102.18
Greece	100.08
Hawaii	100.60
India	108.26
Indonesia	100.81
Iran	102.42
Ireland	104.00
Israel (Jews)	101.03
Israel (Palestinians)	101.03
Italy	100.41
Japan	101.52
Netherlands	104.76
New Zealand	100.72
Nigeria	100.15
Norway	105.23
Poland	101.95
South Africa	100.15
Spain	101.33
Sweden	104.55
Taiwan	108.62
United States (contiguous)	100.60
Venezuela	102.24
Yugoslavia	102.75
Zambia	98.51
Zulu	86.79

Source: Adapted from Stone et al. (2007, p. 293).

Box 3.6

Making a Choice

Kamal's parents insisted it was time for him to get married and wanted to pursue an arranged marriage for him. Given that he grew up in Canada, they thought it would be fair if they first let him try to choose a mate on his own: a love match. If he was unsuccessful, they would arrange a suitable match through their family and friends.

Kamal was sensitive to both his South Asian heritage and his Canadian upbringing. He decided that since he was in his early thirties and, despite having dated several nice women, had not yet found a suitable partner, he would like to have a "modern" arranged marriage in which he would have the final say in the choice of mate. His extended family began setting up formal meetings with potential mates. Kamal, however, did not know how to choose. He did want to have a

successful marriage but he did not know how to ensure this for his future.

While reading a textbook for his university course in family sociology, Kamal learned that people generally choose individuals similar to themselves. This seems to reduce the number of areas of potential conflict in a marriage. He also learned that having an equitable relationship would help keep both members of the relationship happy. Finally, he learned that having similar values and role expectations was important. With this information in hand, he used exchange theory to make a list of benefits and costs of each potential partner and then discussed it with his parents. In the end, Kamal realized that a long-time friend had all of the qualities he was looking for in a mate. He wasn't sure she would agree to marriage at this stage in their relationship, so instead he asked her out on a date.

the discussion of SVR theory earlier in this chapter). Kerckhoff and Davis (1962) state that for a relationship to become more permanent, it depends on shared beliefs (similarity or homogamy filter) but also role expectations needed to be complementary. Once we find this lucky person, we then choose whether we want to cohabit with them (as a precursor to marriage or as an alternative to marriage) or to marry them. As you can see, filter theory incorporates a wide range of factors that influence the formation and continuation of a relationship. Box 3.6 provides an example of how some of the theories discussed in this chapter can be used in the process of choosing a marriage partner.

CONCLUSION

This chapter explored the first steps to family formation: dating and mate selection. The road to family formation is diverse. Some individuals date or hook up for fun and socialization. Others date for status or as a means of mate selection, while others still have their mates chosen for them (e.g., arranged marriage). Dating today often involves sex but does not necessarily have to. Getting a date has become easier with technological advances such as the internet. Several theories of attraction have been proposed, such as propinquity, similarity, and complementary theories. We can be influenced in our dating choice by our family and friends. Often sexual coercion or aggression occurs, although most research is limited to studies of college students. Today, for the majority of Canadians, love is paired with mate selection. Exchange and equity theories as well as filter theories are useful in explaining our choice of mate.

SUMMARY OF KEY POINTS

■ Dating is considered the first step toward family formation. Not all individuals date prior to marriage. In addition, dating and mate selection is not restricted to the young and can occur at any age.

■ Historically, dating was regulated by parents or other chaperones. Dating generally followed four stages: casual dating, steady dating, engagement, and marriage (Nett, 1988). Dating today has become less formal, often with group activities involved.

■ Hooking up is a physical encounter without any expectation of a relationship to follow. According to Glenn and Marquardt (2001), approximately 40 percent of the women sampled stated that they had had a hookup sometime during their college or university experience.

■ Arranged marriage is the practice of having someone other than the individuals to be married select the marriage partners, avoiding (or at least shortening) the practice of dating. There are several common misconceptions about arranged marriage.

■ Reiss (1967) states that there are four general premarital sexual standards in which individuals believe: abstinence, permissiveness with affection, permissiveness without affection, and the double standard. Rotermann (2008) found that, in 2005, 33 percent of Canadians aged 15 to 17 years and 66 percent aged 18 or 19 years had had sex.

■ There are several theories of attraction. Propinquity theory states that we are attracted to those individuals who are around us. With the advent of new technologies, virtual spaces are now available where individuals can "meet" in a virtual sense, so propinquity is becoming less important. Similarity theory states that "birds of a feather flock together" or "like attracts like." We generally like those who are similar to us. Complementary theory relates to the notion that "opposites attract." Murstein (1986, 1987) proposed stimulus-value-role (SVR) theory in an effort to merge these ideas. The theory of psychological reactance states that we like people we cannot have.

■ Although most Canadians (with the exception of some ethnic subgroups) practise free choice dating and mating, our family and friends can have a large influence on who we ultimately choose.

- Craig (1990) and Loh and Gidycz (2006) found that an almost equivalent number of males (24.4 percent) and females (23.3 percent) reported some form of sexual coercion before age 14. Overall, 47.9 percent of female participants and 38.8 percent of male participants reported being victims. O'Sullivan and Allgeier (1998) show in their study of heterosexual dating relationships that college students often have unwanted sex that is consensual.

- Estimates of date rape range widely from 15 to 78 percent. It is difficult to get accurate statistics because of the ambiguity of the term *rape*. Stets (1992) proposes that date rape and dating violence occur because the individual is unable to take the role of the other—that is, to see the situation from the other person's point of view.

- According to Welden (2010, p. 380), an honour killing is "the death of a female family member who is murdered by one or more male family members, sometimes with the active assistance of other women related to the victim." As suggested by White and Mick (2007), in Canada these murders are rare. The United Nations General Assembly (2006) stated that about 5000 women per year are killed in this manner.

- Lee (1988) proposed six styles of love: eros, ludus, storge, mania, agape, and pragma. Men generally score higher on ludus love than women do, while women are more likely to score high on storge and pragma love (Hendrick & Hendrick, 2003).

- Economic theories of mate selection include exchange theory and equity theory.

- Buss (1989) and Kenrik, Trost, and Kelley (1987) propose a biosocial theory of mate selection. This is based on an evolutionary perspective in which choosing a sexual partner is related to genetically adaptive procreation.

- Kerckhoff and Davis (1962) introduced the filter model of mate selection. This model shows how our choice of mate is filtered along several dimensions. Through a process of filtering, we narrow the total number of people who are available or in the "mating market" to a small group.

Critical Thinking Questions

1. Parental image theory (based on Freud's Oedipus complex) states that we will be attracted to a partner who is similar (e.g., in personality, looks) to our opposite-sex parent. Think about the people you have been attracted to in the past. Have you been attracted to someone who was similar to your opposite-sex parent? Do you think this similarity played a role in your attraction?

2. How do you know if your partner is dating you or in the process of selecting a mate?

3. What do you believe is the most influential factor in the process of mate selection? Why?

4. If you had to have an arranged marriage, who would you want your matchmaker to be? Why?

5. What would you write in an online dating ad in order to find a date? Find a mate? How would these differ?

Glossary

abstinence A belief that sex should occur only in the context of marriage (not during dating).

agape Altruistic and selfless love.

arranged marriage The practice of having someone other than the individuals to be married select the marriage partners.

assortative mating Occurs when we chose a partner based on certain traits.

complementary theory Opposites attract.

dating Nowadays refers to a man and a woman who are *already a couple* attending functions together.

double standard A belief that women should only practise permissiveness with affection while it is okay for men to practise permissiveness without affection.

endogamy Marriage inside of a social group.

eros A type of love that has an intense, physical component.

exogamy Marriage outside of a social group.

heterogamy We choose a mate with traits different from our own.

homogamy We choose a mate with traits similar to our own.

honour killing "The death of a female family member who is murdered by one or more male family members, sometimes with the active assistance of other women related to the victim" (Welden, 2010, p. 380).

hooking up A physical (sexual) encounter without any expectation of a relationship to follow.

ludus Playful love or game-playing love.

mania Obsessive, possessive love.

marriage squeeze Occurs when marriage is reduced for a given group due to lack of available partners.

mate selection Choosing a life partner.

mating gradient Occurs when women seek men of similar or higher status, while men seek women of similar or lower status.

permissiveness with affection A belief that sex outside of marriage is appropriate if the two people are in love.

permissiveness without affection A belief that love does not have to exist for a person to have premarital sex.

pragma Practical love where a person carefully considers a person's vital attributes.

propinquity theory We are attracted to those individuals who are around us.

psychological reactance We like people we cannot have.

radiating effect of beauty When you are dating someone attractive, people believe you must have some positive traits that make you a desirable partner.

sex ratio The number of men per 100 women in a given population.

sexual coercion "An experience of being pressured or forced by another person to have contact which involved touching of sexual parts or sexual intercourse—oral, anal, or vaginal" (Struckman-Johnson & Struckman-Johnson, 1994, p. 96).

similarity theory We like those who are similar to us.

storge Love based on friendship.

wedding ring effect The idea that (in humans) married or unavailable men are more desirable to women than single or available men.

Connections

www.professorshouse.com/Relationships/Marriage-Advice/Articles/Arranged-Marriage-Facts/
www.cbc.ca/news/canada/story/2009/07/24/f-honour-killings.html
www.vancouversun.com/life/Honour+killings+rise+Canada+Expert/3165638/story.html
http://secondlife.com/
www.dosomething.org/whatsyourthing/Violence+And+Bullying

Remember to log on to the Companion Website at **www.pearsoncanada.ca/white** to find self-graded quizzes and useful resource tools for further study. You can log on to the Companion Website using the Student Access Code that comes packaged with your copy of *Families Across the Life Course*.

Chapter 4
Cohabitation

Learning Objectives

After reading this chapter, you should be able to:

1. Understand the recent historical development of both the rise and the prevalence of cohabitation.

2. Develop an awareness of the international differences in the practice of cohabitation to better appreciate the diverse social influences that affect cohabitation patterns and outcomes.

3. Understand the legislative influences affecting union formation patterns from one national context to another.

4. Discuss the key variables associated with cohabitation research as well as the major typologies used to understand cohabitation in relation to other union statuses.

5. Discuss the effects of cohabitation on later relationship stability and child outcomes, and the effects when cohabitation is practised among the elderly.

The small neighbourhood restaurant was unusually busy for a Monday evening, but this was Valentine's Day and virtually every table was occupied by a couple. Mary and John were out for a romantic dinner to celebrate the three-month anniversary of their relationship. As the couple ate their meal, John's mind was on popping the question: Should we move in together? Mary's thoughts were slightly different. She was wondering if John was the type of man who could commit to a long-term, meaningful relationship and care for her daughter.

At the next table, another couple was talking about whether they really wanted to spend a lot of money on a wedding or use that money to buy new furniture and make their condominium look more inviting. Meanwhile, the table in the corner was occupied by a sad-looking couple. Their conversation revolved around their relationship as well. They had been living together for more than a year yet they kept coming back to the same nagging question: How did this happen? How did we end up living together without a plan of where the relationship was going to go next?

Harriet and Marv, an older couple, were discussing their banking excursion earlier that day. They talked about how much easier things would be if they had joint accounts and didn't have to placate their 50-year-old children. They would have married if they hadn't gotten so much flak about inheritance complications. Harriet and Marv both lost their lifelong spouses more than a decade ago and live comfortably together, yet for the sake of the children they keep their substantial assets separate.

Late adolescence and early adulthood bring increased responsibilities and opportunities. Most often, the two are connected. One of the most anticipated desires and yet a feared opportunity at this stage of life is of forming an intimate relationship outside your kinship structure. Early crushes turn into first dates, then progress to going steady, and eventually lead to a completely new realm of physical and emotional experiences and feelings. Since most individuals find these new feelings enjoyable, there is a desire to increase their frequency or at least create a more stable environment in which these experiences can continue. Historically, marriage was the next step, but this is not so in the twenty-first century. The rise of **non-marital cohabitation** is one of the most important recent trends in the study of the life course of the family. The combination of earlier and important life course decisions being made in late adolescence and early adulthood creates outcomes that often guide a person's pathway for the rest of his or her life (Barber, Axinn, & Thornton, 2002). As acceptance of and participation in non-marital cohabitation continue to rise, changes in cohorts will also continue. The type of person who cohabited and the reason for cohabiting in the 1960s are quite different from those of the cohorts in the twenty-first century. Of particular interest to researchers is the influence that various types of union formation patterns will have on later outcomes such as **relationship stability**, financial solvency, and child adjustment.

This chapter explores cohabitation across the life course. It begins by setting the historical context needed to understand the importance of the rise in cohabitation. This is followed by a cross-national comparison of cohabitation patterns. Next, we explore the varied approaches to cohabiting, especially in relation to marriage. For example, will the prevalence of cohabitation establish it as a new life stage leading to marriage? What differences might social stratification and ethnic variability have on cohabitation patterns? This section also includes a focus on the controversial issues of commitment differences between cohabiting and married couples as well as cohabitation's impact on later relationship stability. Next, a section is dedicated to the changing legal landscape surrounding the increased prevalence of cohabitation, addressing issues such as child custody and personal property. Finally, we address the growing trend of cohabitation among older adults.

THE RISE IN NON-MARITAL COHABITATION

Over the past 40 years, cohabitation has moved from being viewed as a deviant form of union formation to the preferred social norm that precedes marriage, acting for many as a trial marriage. The dramatic change in the number of cohabitors over just a few decades bears this out. About 10 percent of marriages between 1965 and 1974 included cohabitation as a transition state. By the early 1990s, 55 percent of U.S. marriages were preceded by cohabitation (Bumpass & Lu, 2000). Internationally, the developed world shows an even a greater adoption of cohabitation. For example, 77 percent of married couples in Australia cohabit before marriage (Australian Bureau of Statistics, 2008). In Norway, approximately 80 percent of individuals cohabit before their first marriage (Wiik, 2008). At the turn of the twenty-first century, Canada mirrored France, New Zealand, Mexico, and Finland with approximately 16 to 18 percent of all unions taking the form of non-marital cohabitation. Canada illustrates the diverse regional patterns of cohabitation in the difference between rates in Quebec and the rest of the country. In 2001, non-marital unions in Quebec represented 29.8 percent of all unions, compared to 11.7 percent for the rest of the country (Ambert, 2005). A concern for cohabitation research has been the heterogeneity of cohabiting couples. Union formation pathways are diverging from historical normative patterns and the question is whether the life course is becoming too de-standardized to be of empirical value. Previous research pointing to the diverse and disordered nature of family-related transitions gives some support to these concerns (Hogan & Astone, 1986). This rise in divergent life course pathways involving cohabitation has led to increased research on the impact that premarital cohabitation has on later marital stability.

COHABITATION IN CONTEXT

Historical Context

Intimate union formation has been the centrepiece of human behaviour over time. Without some form of intimacy, humanity would not reproduce itself. Customs, patterns, and traditions regarding union formation have varied over time and across cultures. For most of the last two millennia, Western civilization has given preference to monogamous, heterosexual relationships legitimized by religious edicts or state laws in the form of marriage. The social customs surrounding marriage—the arranging of marriage partners, traditions surrounding the ceremony, who pays, what people wear, how long the wedding ceremony lasts, what the couple do and where they live after the wedding—are just a taste of the myriad wedding variables. In light of this diverse yet enduring social pattern the events over the past 50 years gain significance.

The latter half of the twentieth century has seen a variety of prominent social changes that have affected the pattern and sequence of an individual's life events. The rise in the prevalence and acceptance of non-marital cohabitation is one such change. How millennia of tradition can be reversed in just a few decades is the type of social phenomenon that social scientists find fascinating research material. Historically, marriage as a significant life event has gained privileged status over other forms of union formation. Thornton, Axinn, and Xie (2007) link the change in the establishment of unions with other social institutional changes that have affected the life course, such as changes in labour markets, educational norms, and welfare state policies. The secularization of society, the feminist movement, availability of reliable birth control, the sexual revolution, female labour force participation, and the rapid rise in the divorce rate have all been cited as additional factors connected to the change in union formation patterns over the life course.

Historically, marriage is an institution that formed out of economic necessity. Men and women have always been attracted to each other, but attraction alone has seldom provided a solid rationale for establishing a permanent relationship. In contrast to the

highly sensual and emotional appeal that often characterizes the modern idea of marriage, survival and function have driven most people to marry. Women relied on men to provide protection and provisions for themselves and their children, while men relied on women for child care and meal preparation. Both men and women relied on children as economic assets who could provide additional labour to meet household needs. Today, in most of Western culture, women no longer need men to provide for them or to protect them and their children, and men no longer see the need for women as economic partners. Children are viewed as economic liabilities and—because of longer life expectancy and greatly reduced infant mortality—few children are born. The Industrial Revolution ushered in the daily geographic segregation of the family as an economic unit by removing the father from the household while the mother adapted to an ever-growing middle-class lifestyle focused on domestic responsibilities. The Industrial Revolution cracked and eventually broke the economic dependency that men and women had with marriage.

Further individuation of family structures led to the decline of marriage as a marker of one's transition to adulthood. **Social norms** regarding sexuality began to adjust to the rapidly changing culture created by changes such as universal education for children and adolescents, not to mention technological changes such as the automobile, the telephone, and eventually the internet and cellphones.

Technological Context

What the automobile was in the 1920s, the cellphone may be in the 2010s. The automobile played an important part in changing the way young people courted one another. No longer was sitting in the parlour sipping tea or sitting on the front-porch swing with a glass of lemonade the only way for a potential suitor to spend time with his object of interest. The automobile provided freedom and autonomy from watchful guardians. Peter Ling (1989) argues that the "devil's wagon" and "brothel on wheels" shouldn't get all of the credit for planting the seeds of the sexual revolution since it was only "one of the changes in social and group relationships that made easier the pursuit of carnal desire" (p. 18). In addition to social media sites, the introduction of low-cost cellphones marketed to children has provided greater autonomy and freedom from parental monitoring almost 100 years after the automobile was introduced. This freedom has implications, however (see Box 4.1). There was a time when each household had one phone attached to the wall by a cord. Everyone knew which family member was called and who was on the other end. Today, with individual phones capable of text and video messaging, the ability to send sexual content directly to another person has created an entirely new level of personal communication. *Sexting* is the term used to describe text messaging of sexual content via cellphones and is growing in prevalence (see Box 4.2).

Technological advancements, including easy access to reliable birth control, greatly influenced the dating and sexual patterns of young adults. All of this newfound independence and freedom facilitated greater sexual exploration and expression outside adult supervision. Thornton et al. (2007) see this trend as contributing to the rise of sexuality

Box 4.1

Reiss's Theory of Autonomy

There is presumptive evidence for assuming a general tension between a courtship sub-culture which furthers a high emphasis on the rewards of sexuality and a family sub-culture which stresses the risks of sexuality. . . . If youth culture stresses the rewards of sexuality, then to the extent young people are free from the constraints of the family and other adult type institutions, they will be able to develop their own emphasis on sexuality. The physical and psychic pleasures connected to human sexuality are rewards basically to the participants and not to their parents. . . . Thus, the autonomy of young people is the key variable in determining how sexually permissive one will be (Reiss & Miller, 1979).

Source: Ishwaran (1983, p. 137).

Box 4.2

Sexting

Today, many teens seem to engage in "sexting." One survey, conducted on behalf of both CosmoGirl.com and the National Campaign to Prevent Teen and Unplanned Pregnancy, found that 20 percent of the 653 teenagers surveyed had engaged in sexting.

Source: National Campaign to Prevent Teen and Unplanned Pregnancy (2008).

as a recreational activity in contrast to an activity within a relationship. Easier access to consenting sexual partners combined with the decline in social stigma for those sexually active outside of marriage appealed to some and but not others. Conservative social groups decried the new liberal attitudes toward sexual expression. Even some feminists generally supportive of the sexual revolution saw this trend toward sexual freedom as removing some of the influence that women had over men to commit to marriage. With ample willing partners available and little perceived social cost to being sexually active, why engage in marriage just for sex?

The National Marriage Project at Rutgers University in New Jersey (Whitehead & Popeno, 2000) conducted a study of twentysomething males and females regarding their views on and experiences with dating and mating. This study is interesting for a variety of reasons, but one important reason is that it relied on a sample of non-college-educated young adults, a group often neglected in social research because of the ease of accessing college-educated respondents. The young men and women in this study indicated that marriage was a desirable goal and that they expected marriage to last for a lifetime. Unfortunately, the goal of finding one's soulmate was viewed with skepticism, especially by the females. This group represents a generation jaded by divorce and lack of committed relationship templates in their lives. The National Marriage Project found that this group of young people was not interested in marriage during their twenties, nor did they see their twenties as a time to focus on romantic relationships. Instead, as labelled by the researchers, it was a time for sex without strings and relationships without rings. The word *love* was seldom used by the respondents. Instead, the focus was on sex and relationships, the distinction being that the latter requires some level of commitment and investment of time and money. Sex, on the other hand, is fun and requires no ethical obligation other than mutual consent. Males and female agreed that in casual sexual encounters, people will lie about their sexual histories. The best advice for those looking for casual sexual hookups is to "trust no one." The club scene is a frequent destination of young, working twentysomethings, but not to find a mate. Clubs are viewed as a place to drink, have fun, and look for casual sexual hookups. One young male put it bluntly when he referred to the calibre of females he thinks frequent clubs: "Club girls are trash." Females have just as low an opinion of the male club clientele, which they describe as liars who are only looking for sex. The option for a regular sexual partner without the commitment connected to marriage made cohabitation a nice fit for this cohort.

The rapid change in norms and values surrounding non-marital sexuality and the resultant rise in cohabitation led to a serious generation gap between cohabitation's early adherents and their parents. That gap may be diminishing, as current cohorts of parents grew up in a time when cohabitation and sexual freedom were more normative than when *their* parents grew up.

International Context

Cohabitation patterns have been shown to be highly influenced by contextual factors. Early research almost universally showed negative consequences in regards to later marital stability. As cohabitation becomes more **normative**, that connection has become less consistent. Teachman (2003) and Smock (2000) found little or no negative impact of cohabitation on later marital stability. Research in Australia (De Vaus, Qu, & Weston, 2005) and Canada (White, 1987) show support for positive marital stability. These divergent findings reflect not only the moving target that is both marriage and cohabitation but also the varied context in which union formation patterns take place. Not only is there diversity among nationalities regarding union formation patterns and later outcomes, there are variations among nations as well. Canada provides an excellent example of the cultural context regarding the study of cohabitation. Canada is officially a multicultural country with a general tolerance for diverse ethnic traditions and customs. The most distinct cultural differences are found between the two charter language peoples: the French and the English. The province of Quebec has a distinct culture and language as well as distinct attitudes and behaviours regarding cohabitation. Cohabitation is much more socially acceptable in Quebec and as a result is more prevalent there than in other parts of Canada. That prevalence translates into cohabiting unions that last longer and are more likely to have children present. Quebec tends to resemble some of the European countries in this regard rather than the rest of Canada and North America.

International differences in cohabitation practices also reflect this diversity. Heuveline and Timberlake (2004) and Liefbroer and Dourleijn (2006) studied cohabitation from a comparative perspective. Both sets of authors make arguments regarding the normativeness of cohabitation affecting a variety of family transitional events such as fertility, stability, and formation patterns.

Heuveline and Timberlake (2004) see the increase in fertility among cohabiting couples as a major contributor to the general interest in the topic. Non-marital cohabitation has existed through time, but the connection of births to unmarried mothers has attracted the attention of the public. They cite Ventura and Bachrach (2000) to indicate that non-marital births have grown from 4 percent in 1950 to 33 percent in 1999. Research has consistently pointed to the statistically significant negative effects on children who grow up in single-parent households. The place of fertility in the study of cohabitation is important. The more cohabitation is accompanied by fertility, the more it will resemble and compete with marriage as a preferred form of family union.

Heuveline and Timberlake (2004) use fertility patterns to establish six typologies of cohabitation (listed later in Table 4.5) that examine the social context of the acceptance of cohabitation alongside the empirical indicators and predicted outcomes on the participating adults and affected children when present. Their findings show clusters among the 17 included nations. Countries with a low incidence of cohabitation included Italy, Poland, and Spain. Belgium, Czech Republic, Hungary, and Switzerland were clustered in the prelude to marriage typology. This group is characterized by a higher incidence of cohabitations that last for a shorter time, end in marriage, and precede the birth of children. The countries grouped together in the stage in marriage process treat cohabitation as a transition stage that tends to last longer. This group is more likely to have children in the union, but marriage follows shortly after their birth. This cluster included Austria, Finland, Germany, Latvia, and Slovenia. The United States and New Zealand represent the alternative to being single typology characterized by cohabiting unions that are brief, non-reproductive, and end in separation rather than marriage. The alternative to marriage typology is defined by cohabiting couples who remain in their relationships for longer periods, are less likely to get married, and expose children to the cohabiting union for longer periods. This cluster contained Canada and France. The last typology had Sweden alone and is described as indistinguishable from marriage. This final group is similar to the alternative to marriage group in that there is a higher incidence of cohabitation lasting for longer periods. Children are frequently exposed to their parents' cohabitation in this group but for a shorter time, because parents do not view cohabitation as an alternative to marriage and are ambivalent about the difference. Heuveline and Timberlake (2004) see these couples as entering marriage for pragmatic reasons rather than avoiding it on principle.

Heuveline and Timberlake (2004) make some important summary points regarding the regional findings of their research. They note that the three non-European countries in the study—Canada, New Zealand, and the United States—were difficult to categorize because of the heterogeneity of the population. Canada has two official languages and all

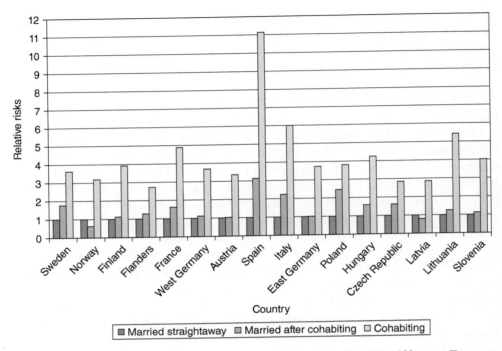

Figure 4.1 Relative Risk of Union Dissolution for Women in Different Types of Union, by Country

three countries are ethnically diverse. The authors caution against making overgeneralizations about these populations' cohabiting patterns. What should be taken from these findings is the importance of contextual factors that influence the union formation patterns of adults across the life course and the diverse ways in which children are influenced as a result.

The second important cross-cultural study on cohabitation also focuses on the local context's impact on union formation patterns. Liefbroer and Dourleijn (2006) studied 16 European nations in their research on the role of diffusion in explaining the differentiating patterns of marital stability outcomes for those who previously have cohabited. Figure 4.1 shows the relative risk of union dissolution for women married with prior cohabitation and women cohabiting outside of marriage compared to women going straight to marriage. Values above 1 indicate a higher risk of dissolution compared to women who go straight to marriage, while values below 1 imply lower risks.

The results indicate that women in cohabiting relationships are much more likely to face a union breakup than women who married right away. Most countries show a risk of 3 to 4 times that of the risk for those who marry right away, with Spain showing an increased risk of 11 times. Those who cohabit prior to marriage fare much better. In some cases, the data indicate that an improvement in risk is created after cohabiting, as in Norway. For half of the countries, no statistical difference in risk was seen between

Table 4.1 Cohabitors as a Percentage of All Couples

	1990s		2000s		% Change
Australia	1996	10.1	2006	15.0	48.5
Canada	1995	13.9	2006	18.4	32.4
Denmark	1995	24.7	2006	24.4	−1.2
France	1995	13.6	2001	17.2	26.5
Germany	1995	8.2	2005	11.2	36.6
Italy	1995	3.1	2003	3.8	22.6
Netherlands	1995	13.1	2004	13.3	1.5
New Zealand	1996	14.9	2006	23.7	59.1
Norway	2001	20.3	2007	21.8	7.4
Spain			2002	2.7	NA
Sweden	1995	23.0	2005	28.4	23.5
United Kingdom	1995	10.1	2004	15.4	52.5
U.S.	1995	5.1	2005	7.6	49.0

France, Germany, Italy, Netherlands and Spain generated from United Nations Economic Commission for Europe (UNECE), Statistical Database, Gender Statistics (http://w3.uncce.org/pxweb/Dialog/Default.asp).

Australia: Statistics Australia Census Tables, Australian Bureau of Statistics, Cat. No. 2914 (2006) and No. 4102 (1996).

Canada: Statistics Canada 2007, Legal Marital Status, Common-law Status, Age Groups & Sex.

Denmark: United Nations Economic Commission for Europe (1995) & Statistics Denmark (2006).

New Zealand: Statistics New Zealand, Census of Families and Households & 2006 Table Builder, Marital Status.

Norway: Statistics Norway, Population & Historical Census, Table 24 and Statistical Data Bank.

Sweden: For 1995, all couples from United Nations Economic Commission for Europe data less married women from Statistics Sweden. For 2005, Population Table 28 and Statistics Sweden Statistical Database.

Great Britain: Focus on Families & Focus on Families National Statistics.

United States: America's Families and Living Arrangements, 1995 & 2005 (rate is based on self-identified unmarried cohabitors not POSSLQ (Persons of the Opposite Sex Sharing Living Quarters).

Source: Popenoe (2009, p. 431).

those who went straight to marriage and those who cohabited before marriage. As in the previous cross-cultural study, this research focused on the role of changing norms regarding the social acceptance of cohabitation as a stage of marriage or a marriage alternative. Diffusion as an explanation for national differences of subsequent negative marital outcomes for cohabitors is based on the idea that innovation is usually adopted among a smaller group before spreading to the general population (Jaakkola, Aromaa, & Cantell, 1984). Schoen's (1992) test on cohort data in the United States supports the hypothesis that as cohabitation becomes more common (see Table 4.1), the distinctions between those who cohabit before marriage and those who do not will diminish.

Liefbroer and Dourleijn (2006) present the argument that, with diffusion, you will have both early adopters and late adopters (or "laggards"), with the general population fitting between these extremes. In the area of cohabitation studies, religiosity has been identified as a barrier to acceptance and participation in cohabitation. This is illustrative of those labelled as late adopters. The authors use this line of reasoning to show that the selection hypothesis (people with fewer relationship skills or less relationship commitment tend to be more likely to cohabit) explains later marital instability. Marital instability will be most prevalent when cohabitation occurs in a social context in which just earlier adopters or late adopters dominate the landscape. They state, "If the proportion of cohabitors and noncohabitors is more or less in equilibrium, selection processes might still be operative, but certainly to a lesser extent than when the proportion of cohabitors is either very high or very low" (p. 206).

Using data from Kiernan (2002), Liefbroer and Dourleijn hypothesize that the variation in observed post-cohabitation marital stability in Europe will be a result of diffusion difference in those countries studied. Specifically stated, they expect the relationship to be curvilinear. Differences should be higher when only a small portion of the population is either choosing to cohabit or choosing not to cohabit. When about half of the population has experienced non-marital cohabitation, they would expect to see the least amount of difference in later martial stability compared to those who go straight to marriage without cohabitation.

Liefbroer and Dourleijn (2006) include a number of variables known to influence cohabitation in an attempt to control for their effect. These covariates included birth cohort, parental divorce, place of residence during childhood, age at the start of the union, educational attainment, activity status, and parenthood. Figure 4.2 shows that union dissolution does explain at least part of the variation in post-cohabitors' marital stability across Europe. As the populations of countries approach equilibrium of those who have and have not cohabited prior to marriage, the difference in marital stability outcomes decreases. The authors caution that the findings explain only a part of the mechanisms at work and point to other institutional factors, such as religion and legislative regulations, that may be at work. They conclude by emphasizing that the selection effect continues to operate across all scenarios and that the important question continues to be this: What makes the marriages of people who reject unmarried cohabitation so stable?

Variations beyond the European Family Cohabitation as a union formation practice has been extensively researched in the context of the European family. Therborn (2004) states that although Eastern Europe has begun to see a rise in cohabitation, the practice is still rare. In most of Asia and North Africa, cohabitation is not often practiced, and if practiced, is done in a clandestine manner. He cites 1997 data from Japan showing that among those aged 30 to 34, only 8 percent report sexually cohabiting; among those aged 25 to 29, that number drops to 5 percent. China had less than 1 percent cohabiting in 1989 (Ruan, 1991). Post-Soviet central Russia reported only a few percent practising informal sexual unions, and limited South Asian data showed the Philippines as having

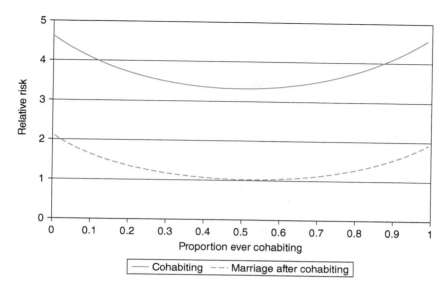

Figure 4.2 Relative Risk of Union Dissolution of Cohabitors and Former Cohabitors Compared with Women Who Marry without Prior Cohabitation, by Incidence of Unmarried Cohabitation

Source: Liefbroer, A. C., & Dourleijn, E. (2006). Unmarried cohabitation and union stability: Testing the role of diffusion using data from 16 European countries. *Demography, 43*, 203–221. Figure 1 page 213, Figure 2 page 217. Reprinted with permission.

adopted cohabitation at a modest level with only 8 percent of women aged 20 to 29 indicating they had done so (Therborn, 2004).

Brazil provides a good illustration of how cohabitation has been practised in the Latin American culture. Over a period of 50 years, religious marriages dropped from 20 percent of all sexual unions to 4 percent in 2000. On the other hand, consensual unions rose from 7 percent to 28 percent over the same period (Therborn, 2004). The Caribbean picture shows an even stronger adoption rate. Widespread poverty is a known structural factor influencing the adoption of non-marital cohabitation (Ortmayr, 1997). Therborn cites Tremblay and Capon (1988) in stating that two thirds of the sexual unions are unmarried in Haiti and more than 50 percent are unmarried in the Dominican Republic, with Jamaica and Central American countries in the range of 40 to 50 percent.

Adoption rates in African countries vary. These variations can be attributed to the structural influences of religion, socio-economic status, and the unique socio-historical cultures of the represented groups. Cohabitation represents a majority of sexual unions in Mozambique and Gabon among women aged 20 to 24 and one third of unions in Uganda, Ivory Coast, and Ghana among the same age group and sex (Therborn, 2004). The African countries that have significant Muslim and Christian populations have much lower levels of cohabitation.

Diversity of cohabitation patterns is found within the Canadian context as well. Clear differences between the country's two charter groups is evident, as Quebec's cohabitating and married couples have similar child-rearing, child-bearing, and union stability patterns (La Bourdais & Lapierre-Adamcyk, 2004). Aboriginal and indigenous groups have much higher adoption of non-marital unions. The immigrant population's adoption rate resembles the patterns in their countries of origin, whereas the Aboriginal population's high adoption rate represents a life course that varies from that of the general population in the late adolescent and early adult period (Table 4.2). Aboriginal youth finish their education and leave their parents' home at a much younger age. As a result, they are more likely to form a union and have a child. Beaujot and Kerr (2007) report that by age 20, 20.6 percent of Aboriginal youth report cohabiting or being married, compared to 8.8 percent of the general population and 6.3 percent of immigrants.

Cross-National Government Policies Regarding Cohabitation Different countries have different approaches to legislation regarding cohabitation. In an additional examination of cross-national cohabitation patterns, Popenoe (2009) found that almost all nations have **domestic partnership** or **registered partnership** legislation that provides marriage-equivalent status and protections. Popenoe notes that only France, the Netherlands, and Belgium make this status available to same-sex couples. Divorce laws for these partnerships mirror those for their marriage counterparts. Additional benefits extended to cohabitating couples, such as partner coverage in health insurance and the transfer of a partner's property upon death, vary considerably depending on the location. What constitutes a couple officially cohabiting also varies considerably and relies on diverse criteria such as ongoing sexual relations, duration of cohabitation, and holding a joint residence. Each country may be marked by heterogeneity when applying these criteria. Australia, Canada, and the United States illustrate this point, as each province or state differs from the next in applying such criteria. Citing research from Waaldijk (2004), Popenoe states that non-marital cohabitation remains distinctive, where it is found, in that no specific procedures exist for getting into it or getting out of it.

DEFINITIONS AND LEGAL ISSUES

The rapid rise in cohabitation around the world has not been accompanied by a systematic legal structure. Bowman (2007, p. 38) writes: "Many people in the United States mistakenly believe that the law in fact does protect them after a certain period of cohabitation, although common law marriage is recognized in only a handful of states." She goes on to show that even though common-law marriage was abolished in the United Kingdom in 1753, a large-scale survey indicated that a majority of people thought that after a certain period of residence (six months to six years) cohabitants were granted the same rights as married couples. Cohabitation is not synonymous with **common-law marriage**, although the terms are often used interchangeably. Common-law marriage is typically defined as the union of a couple who consider

Table 4.2 Percentage of Women Married or Cohabiting and Percentage with At Least One Child Aged 5 or Under, Canada

Percentage Who Are Married or Cohabitating

Age	All Canadians	Immigrants	Aboriginal Identity
15	0.1	0.3	0.4
16	0.3	0.5	1.5
17	0.8	0.9	3.0
18	2.1	1.4	6.7
19	4.7	4.2	11.2
20	8.8	6.3	20.6
21	13.5	9.0	23.3
22	18.6	15.3	29.3
23	25.7	20.5	35.8
24	32.4	28.1	42.3
25	39.2	36.1	46.4
26	45.2	39.1	45.7
27	51.8	49.5	52.2
28	55.9	54.0	53.6
29	60.5	60.0	57.0

Percentage of Women with at Least One Child Aged Five or Under

Age	All Canadians	Immigrants	Aboriginal Identity
15	0.3	0.3	1.1
16	0.3	0.3	3.0
17	1.0	0.9	5.6
18	1.9	1.5	9.5
19	3.5	2.6	18.5
20	5.8	3.9	27.1
21	8.3	6.6	33.9
22	10.5	8.3	32.6
23	15.6	13.2	38.1
24	20.2	18.9	40.6
25	23.1	22.2	41.5
26	26.3	24.1	33.6
27	30.2	30.4	36.5
28	33.3	32.5	35.6
29	35.4	36.6	37.5

Source: Statistics Canada, Public Use Files, Canadian Census, 1991, 2001.

themselves to be husband and wife but who have not solemnized the relationship with a formal ceremony. Common-law marriage has its roots in medieval Europe, where partners were able to marry formally without any witnesses. Later, religious and constitutional bodies began to demand that marriages be performed by a representative of the church or state and witnessed by additional parties.

Do Legal Incentives Help?

One important area of interest for social policy-makers is the implication of legislation on the choices couples make with regard to union formation. A brief summary of historical and recent legislative attempts to alter marriage adoption patterns reveals the resiliency of marriage as an institution. A well-documented attempt to alter marriage laws is found in the Bolshevik family law reforms. Bowman (2007) interprets Wardle's (2004) work to show that despite attempts to reduce the distinction between marriage and cohabitation, there is no evidence to support the idea that the institution of marriage was harmed. In 1980, the marriage rates in the former Soviet bloc nations of Belarus (10.1 percent), Russia (10.6 percent), and Ukraine (9.3 percent) exceeded those in the United Kingdom (7.4 percent) and Italy (5.7 percent) and were on par with those in the United States (10.5 percent). Only after the fall of the Soviet Union did marriage rates in these former Soviet bloc countries begin to fall to the levels in other Western nations. In 2001, the marriage rates in Belarus (6.9 percent), Russia (6.9 percent), and Ukraine (5.6 percent) were much lower than they had been under Bolshevik family law. The development and evolution of family policy and its effects are more complex (see Waters [1995] for a more detailed analysis of Bolshevik family law) than simple attempts to destroy the family for state purposes, yet they do present a compelling glimpse at a modern attempt to legislate family change through marriage and divorce law.

The impact of legislation on union formation can also be seen by looking at current protections offered to cohabitants in various countries. Bowman (2007), for example, shows that even though extensive legal protections are offered to cohabitants in the Netherlands, Sweden, and France, the rate of cohabitation is not necessarily different from that in countries without the same protection. In the Netherlands, the legal protection offered to cohabitors means that no distinction exists between them and those who marry, yet the cohabitation-to-marriage ratio of 25 percent is the same as in the United Kingdom, where legal protection is denied cohabitants. Citing data from Sweden, France, and the United States, Bowman (2007) concludes that offering legal recognition and support for cohabitation does not discourage marriage but may in fact encourage it. In Sweden, where cohabitation has a long history of favourable treatment, 61.2 percent of cohabitants eventually marry their partner, compared to 48 percent in the United States. Other researchers do not see the same neutrality of the legislation. Popenoe (2009) argues that although the Nordic nations have high levels of cohabitation, they also attach the most legal consequences to it; Germany, which has a low level of cohabitation, attaches the least legal consequences to it. Popenoe feels that legislation is written after the widespread acceptance of cohabitation and therefore puts a stamp of approval on the practice. Popenoe concludes by arguing that this trend weakens the distinctive cultural and legal status of marriage.

Property and Child Custody

The lack of standardized legal treatment of cohabitation leaves the distribution of assets and assignment of child custody to local magistrates, should the union cease. Because cohabitation is often not a structured event, the ending of the union faces the same lack of clarity. This affects the legal rights one may have to property and possessions acquired during the union and the custodial rights of parents, especially if children are brought into the union. Legal professionals advise clients who cohabit to establish legal agreements regarding significant assets such as a home. Without specific laws in place to ensure the equitable distribution of assets, one party may be at a disadvantage when the union dissolves. This disadvantage is usually the woman's.

Asset Protection Approaches to the legal rights regarding both property rights of individuals and child custody rights are divided into two categories: proactive and reactive. Proactive approaches include those strategies that an individual may take advantage of prior to dissolving the union. Reactive strategies are those strategies available to individuals after they have ended the union.

With regard to asset protection and estate planning, a cohabiting couple must realize their rights as a couple apart from marriage law. This may include special state or provincial protections for registered partnerships or for couples who meet the types of criteria associated with a recognized cohabiting union. In the United States, the **Defense of Marriage Act (DOMA)** was passed by Congress in 1996 to establish the definition of marriage as the legal union of a man and a woman. Primarily introduced to prevent states from having to recognize same-sex couples married in other states, the law also established who was entitled to federal spousal and tax benefits.

Because each legal jurisdiction may have its own laws concerning cohabitation, it is difficult to summarize them. A few key concepts are **cohabitation agreements, civil unions**, and domestic partnerships. These are not identical concepts and they do not provide the same rights as marriage. Many jurisdictions do not recognize cohabitation agreements, since they attempt to circumvent laws (such as DOMA) designed to protect the distinctiveness of marriage. Domestic partnerships have more legal recognition but that recognition is not universal across the United States. In the states, cities, and counties in which they are recognized, domestic partnerships tend to follow a standard definition containing the following elements: (1) partners are at least 18 years old, (2) neither partner is related by blood closer than what is permitted by state law for marriage, (3) the partners share a committed exclusive relationship; and (4) the partners are financially interdependent. Currently, only the District of Columbia, California, Hawaii, Maine, Maryland, New Jersey, Oregon, and Washington offer some form of domestic partnership (Hickey, 2009).

The legal tools available to non-married couples are diverse and generally mirror the tools for non-residential partnerships. Hickey (2009) recommends cohabitation agreements if the long list of criteria needed to make them binding are met. She also suggests that other estate planning tools be put in place as well as items such as power of attorney, living wills, and health permission release forms (so medical professionals can talk about a patient to non-kin). In addition to what is needed during the lives of the partners, there is the matter of dealing with the transfer of assets upon the death of one of the partners. Without formal arrangements, the assets will not automatically go to the surviving partner. Designating one's partner in a will makes it easier to transfer assets, but it is also possible to look at specific financial accounts and designate a beneficiary who is different from that in the will and will actually supersede what is in the will. Financial assets such as life insurance, retirement accounts, bank accounts, annuities, and trust accounts can all be designated to one's partner rather than to a legally recognized family member.

Child Custody Child custody issues are another concern for couples who do not have legislative protection. Custodial concerns for cohabiting couples do not focus on children born within the union, for which both parents would be legally granted parental rights, but on a non-biological partner's rights to parental authority and visitation. This is relevant not only in the context of an intact relationship (e.g., the issue of medical decisions) but also to clarify the rights and responsibilities of each partner if the union dissolves. Kunin and Davis (2009) define the importance of the latter scenario using five facts: (1) the couple has resided together for a significant period of time, (2) a parental relationship has been established between the child and the individual with no parental rights, (3) the parties have ended the relationship, (4) there is no traditional second legal parent, and (5) the parent without parental rights has been alienated from the child. The authors explain that these criteria would apply to both heterosexual and homosexual unions in locations where both types of union are recognized.

Proactive strategies include second-parent adoption, co-guardianship, and a cohabitation agreement. **Second-parent adoption** suffers from limited availability. In the United States, most states have laws that allow single adults or married couples to adopt; the idea of second-parent adoption is limited to only a few states. Co-guardianship is another option when second-parent adoption is not available. It ensures that all responsibilities of a legal parent, such as making medical decisions for a child, would remain in place upon dissolution of the union unless a partner petitions to have these responsibilities removed and provides reasons why this would be in the best interests of the child. Cohabitation agreements suffer from the limitations discussed in section above on asset protection. They are recognized in only a few locations and, in the case of the United States, may be void because of being superseded by DOMA.

The only proposed reactive strategy to child custody issues for cohabitants is to petition for third-party visitation rights. This strategy is a long shot since, in a best-case

Table 4.3 Similarities and Differences between Married and Unmarried Couples in Canada

	Married	Common Law
Equalization payment upon separation	Yes	No, but may be claim for unjust enrichment
Possession of the matrimonial home upon separation	Yes	No
Special treatment of matrimonial home in dividing property	Yes	No
Spousal support	Yes	Yes, if lived together for 3 years or are in a relationship of some permanence and have children
Time limit to apply for spousal support	No	Yes in several provinces
Order restraining depletion of property	Yes	No, but can use Rules of Civil Procedure for similar sorts of orders
Child support	Yes	Yes
Child custody	Yes	Yes
Succession rights if partner dies intestate	Yes	No, but may be claim for unjust enrichment
Dependant's relief on death of partner	Yes	Yes
Equalization payment on death	Yes	No, but may be claim for unjust enrichment
Possession of matrimonial home on death	Yes	No, but may be able to claim as an incident of support

Source: www.common-law-separation-canada.com

scenario, it only begins to approach the rights of a non-custodial parent and requires proof that the legal parent is unfit in some capacity. Child custody options for non-biological partners in cohabitation reveal the uncertainty surrounding future parental rights.

Internationally, conditions similar to those in the United States exist. Countries with greater legal protections for cohabitation will have laws that more closely resemble those governing marriage. In most cases, there are regional differences within a country. Table 4.3 provides a general outline of the similarities and differences between married and unmarried couples in Canada, Box 4.3 highlights how these two relationships differ when they end, and Box 4.4 discusses how these relationships are taxed.

Box 4.3

The Main Differences upon Separation between Being Married and Being in a Common-Law Relationship

In William Shakespeare's play *All's Well That Ends Well*, a French orphan named Helena attempts to win the love of Count Bertram. Unfortunately, despite Helena's beauty, the social class differences between the couple make the match seem impossible. Through a series of events involving the timely administration of the healing arts that Helena learned from her physician father, she is able to save the king; as a reward, she is given the hand of any man in the realm, and of course she chooses Bertram. The wedding takes place and then the relationship goes poorly very soon thereafter. Bertram is appalled by the match, flees the country, and refuses to honour his wedding vows unless Helena can get his family ring from his finger and become pregnant with his child. Helena's wisdom exceeds her beauty and she is able to use Bertram's attempts to seduce a young virgin to trick him into giving her the ring and getting her pregnant. *All's Well That Ends Well* is the story of a relationship with twists and turns including fighting over family possessions, relationship legitimacy, and relationship stress and breakdown. As in Shakespeare's play, relationships don't always work out as planned. How they end and what happens to a couple's possessions after a relationship breaks down depends a great deal on how the relationship is defined.

There is often confusion and misunderstanding regarding the legal rights and responsibilities that common-law partners have to one another when a relationship breaks down. This confusion frequently results from differing definitions and legislation regarding couples living together. The key areas to consider include the following.

Division of Property

The equalization of net family property occurs when a person's net worth (assets minus debts) at the date of relationship separation is compared to his or her net worth (assets minus debts) at the date of marriage. The net change in each person's worth at the date of separation is the net family property. The partner with the larger growth in net worth is ordered to pay half of the difference between the two net worth amounts as an equalization payment. In common-law relationships, a problem occurs in that this equalization of net family property is required only by those who meet the definition of being legally married. This law has been challenged, but the Supreme Court of Canada has stated that the difference is not discriminatory, insisting that people's choice to marry or not is a personal one and that marriage and cohabitation are not the same.

The Matrimonial Home

When a marriage ends, generally there is an automatic right to stay in the matrimonial home, even if it is not in one's name. In Ontario, however, this is not the case. If you are not married and your name is not on the home, you have no legal claim to it. A distinction also exists in how the matrimonial home's value is divided upon its sale. Unlike the division of other assets, which are subject to the formula discussed above, the value of a matrimonial home is automatically divided between the spouses. However, this is not the case for couples in a common-law relationship.

Spousal Support

Married couples have automatic responsibilities to receive or pay spousal support. There is also no time limitation to make a claim for spousal support. This is not the case for common-law relationships in parts of Canada. In Ontario, for example, a couple must meet the stricter criteria of having lived together for three years or having had a child together. As well, a claim for support must be made within two years of separation.

Protection Against the Depletion of Property

If you are concerned that your partner may go on a spending spree to deplete his or her assets before having to divide them, then being married will protect you but being in a common-law relationship will not. Common-law partners cannot obtain a court order to prevent the partners from depleting assets, but married partners can.

Inheritance

If you are married, you are automatically entitled to receive a share of your partner's estate, even if he or she dies without a will. If the will seems to provide an unfair settlement, married partners can seek an equalization payment to compensate for this. Those in a common-law relationship do not enjoy these same rights; instead, the surviving partner must bring a claim for unjust enrichment against the deceased partner's estate.

FACTORS INFLUENCING COHABITATION

Intergenerational Cohabitation

Early research on the subject of cohabitation identified the importance of parental influence on the union formation patterns of their offspring. Axinn and Thornton (1992) found that children's non-marital cohabitation patterns were correlated to mothers' attitudes toward cohabitation. Their more recent work (Thornton et al., 2007) outlines numerous intergenerational influences on union formation patterns extending back as much as two generations (see Table 4.4). Manning, Cohen, and Smock (2011) examine

Table 4.4 Intergenerational Factors Affecting Cohabitation

1. Parental Factors during Childhood and Adolescence
   a. Influences of Parental Youth Factors before Birth of Study Child
      i. Family immigration
      ii. Farm background
      iii. Parental SES [socio-economic status] at time of birth—1962
      iv. Maternal marital experience
      v. Parental childbearing
      vi. Grandmother's religiosity
      vii. Maternal religious affiliation and participation
      viii. Family closeness and sex role attitudes
   b. Influence of Parental Factors during Childhood and Adolescence of the Child
      i. Updated parental information from 1962–1977
2. Parental and Child Factors during the Children's Young Adulthood
   a. Courtship Process and Union Formation
      i. Age at first date, age at first steady, age at first intercourse
   b. Religious Affiliation and Commitment
      i. Maternal and paternal religious attendance—1962/1977
      ii. Maternal religious attendance/belief/importance—1980
      iii. Child's religious attendance/belief/importance—1980
   c. The Influence of Attitudes, Values and Beliefs
      i. Mother's attitude toward premarital sex/cohabitation
      ii. Mother's preferred age at marriage and family size for child
      iii. Mother's educational expectations for child
      iv. Child's attitude toward premarital sex/cohabitation/being single/abortion/ toward career & sex roles
      v. Child's preferred age at marriage and family size
      vi. Child's educational expectations
   d. Educational Influences
      i. Educational expectations
      ii. School grades, enjoyment, years accumulated
   e. Work, Earnings Potential, and Career Aspiration
      i. Recent work and earning history
      ii. Current work history and earnings
      iii. Near future work and earning history
      iv. Past earnings
      iv. Lifetime earning

Source: Thornton, A., Axinn, W. G., & Xie, Y. (2007). *Marriage and cohabitation*. Chicago: The University of Chicago Press. Reprinted with permission.

the influence of parents and peers on emerging adults' decisions to cohabit. They put forth the idea that emerging adulthood may be more sensitive to social context than adolescence because of the developing and changing dynamic with romantic partners, family, and peers during this period of development.

Data on the intergenerational influences of parents on their children's relationship pathways demonstrate that they do influence their children's decisions, whether in the form of an arranged marriage or some other form of socialization. Marriage formation and stability have been linked to a number of parental attributes such as religiosity, education, socio-economic status as well as to the family structure and the parents' marriage stability. Children of divorced parents are less likely to marry and, when they do, their marriages do not last as long as those raised in two-parent, intact homes (Cherlin, 2009). Although much work has been done on the influence of parents in guiding and influencing their children's marriage selection, timing, and stability, the intergenerational effects of cohabitation are just now reaching the forefront of social research. Twenty-first-century young adults (particularly those in North America) are the first generation to grow up in a society in which cohabitation was socially acceptable for their parents and a modal state for their peers. As would be expected from learning theory and parental socialization, early research shows that adolescents who grew up in a cohabiting-parent family are more likely to expect to cohabit than adolescents who were not part of a cohabiting parental environment (Manning, Longmore, & Giordano, 2007). In addition, young adults whose parents cohabited were more likely to have cohabited than their counterparts (Lonardo, Giordano, Longmore, & Manning, 2009; Sassler, Cunningham, & Lichter, 2009).

Religion is another mechanism through which the intergenerational influence on cohabitation is transmitted. Religion and religious traditions encourage family values that emphasize the importance of one's relationship to parents and the centrality of marriage (Goldscheider & Goldscheider, 1999). Together, religion and family form a strong influence in establishing and maintaining the importance of the family and, by extension, marriage. Cohabitation patterns have been shown to correlate to one's religious orientation (Lehrer, 2000). Religious individuals are less tolerant of sexual expression outside of marriage and therefore do not look favourably on cohabitation as a legitimate form of committed relationship, although general acceptance and practice has been increasing among religious adherents concurrently with the general population. As mentioned earlier, the influence of parents and peers on one's religious beliefs and practices is clearly documented. As parents socialize their children in religious traditions and beliefs, they are also influencing the likelihood of marriage instead of cohabitation. Manning et al. (2011) suggest that religious beliefs affect a couple's decision to cohabit when one or both partners do not want to go against what they have been taught to believe from their parents regarding the acceptability of cohabitation. Not wanting to disappoint extended family may also play a part in the couple's choice.

Marie Cornwall's (1989) channelling hypothesis would apply in the area of cohabitation acceptance. Parents who desire to steer their children toward certain beliefs and behaviours often will channel their children into supporting socialization opportunities such as parochial schools and carefully control the child's peer network. This process can be seen to influence the intergenerational transfer of cohabitation beliefs and practices. Manning et al. (2011) recognize the role and importance of adolescent peer socialization in forming attitudes and behaviours regarding the opposite sex. They cite a variety of authors (Brown, 1999; Cavanagh, 2007; Collins, Hennighausen, Schmit, & Sroufe, 1997; Connolly, Furman, & Konarski, 2000; Hartup, French, Laursen, Johnston, & Ogawa, 1993) who support the influence of adolescent peers but state that limited research is available for emerging adults and conclude the following: "Past theoretical and substantive findings have suggested that peers should have some influence on the nature and course of romantic relationships in early adulthood" (Manning et al., 2011, p. 122). They also provide support for peer influence through modelling. Using research from Japan (Rindfuss, Choe, Bumpass, & Tsuya, 2004) and Germany (Nazio & Blossfeld, 2003), they show that emerging adults look to the patterns and experiences of their peers as a guide to their own cohabitation behaviour. In addition, Arnett (2004) states that emerging adults look to peers' marriage experiences as a guide to their own opportunities. It would then be expected that they also look to their peers for direction in cohabitation choices.

Traditionally, marriage has a played an important social role in the transition to adulthood (Goldscheider & Goldscheider, 1999). In some societies, it was the only legitimate transition out of single status. Marriage also legitimized childbirth and, as a result, established kinship connections that had enduring impact in the form of

inheritance and social identity. As cohabitation becomes more normative, some of the distinctions between marriage and cohabitation are being removed. Marriage no longer serves as the sole means to legitimize a committed relationship and non-marital fertility is rising among both cohabitors and non-cohabitors. The lack of social clarity surrounding cohabitation has led to divergent relationship pathways of those embracing it. Motivations for cohabitation are often diverse, serving different purposes for different groups (Guzzo, 2008). This fact is true with racial and ethnic differences (Manning, 1993; Manning & Smock, 2002), gender and life course stage (Oppenheimer, 2003), age (Moustgaard & Martikainen, 2009), economic status (Carlson, McLanahan, & England, 2004), and historical periods (Schoen, 1992).

Transition to Adulthood

Age-graded institutions such as education, workplaces, and marriage laws give structure and regularity to the life course (Hogan & Astone, 1986). These regularities change over historical periods and cohorts and, as a result, change the way in which transitions from adolescence to adulthood vary. For example, more males and females are continuing their education for longer periods than in previous generations since workplaces require greater and greater training. As a result, young adults are delaying marriage and choosing to cohabit instead (Thornton et al., 2007). Passage to adulthood has typically been associated with five major events: leaving home, finishing one's education, getting a job, marrying, and having children. Because of extended education, all of these events have been delayed compared to previous cohorts (Beaujot & Kerr, 2007). Not only has the transition to adulthood been delayed, but it seems less permanent and is non-linear and subject to reversals (Mitchell, 2006).

In a recent analysis of Canadian census data, Clark (2007) showed that over a period of 30 years (1971 to 2001) the number of transitions made by age of young adults continued to decline. In 2001, the typical 25-year-old had gone through the same number of transitions as a 22-year-old in 1971. In comparison, a 25-year-old in 1971 parallels a 30-year-old today. Studies over longer periods indicate that during the two world wars the time of transition in these five areas was compressed, but after World War II until the present that the transitions have gradually extended into later ages.

COURTSHIP PATTERNS AND PATHWAYS

Ever since early moral philosophers and social scientists such as Bertrand Russell and Margaret Mead advocated cohabitation as a precursor to marriage, a diversity of pathways into and out of a cohabiting relationship has been travelled. This section briefly discusses the deliberateness of entering a cohabitating relationship in contrast to drifting into one in a social context that does not sanction it. After this overview, three different typologies of cohabitors will be presented in Table 4.5 to provide you with a glimpse of the heterogeneity that exists in the conceptualization and study of cohabitation. How couples

Table 4.5 Typologies of Cohabitation in Relation to Marriage and Being Single

Thornton, Axinn, and Xie (2007)

1. Being single and cohabiting as equivalent contrasts to marriage
2. Marriage and cohabitation as equivalent contrasts to marriage
3. Marriage and cohabitation as independent alternatives to being single
4. Marriage and cohabitation as a choice conditional on the decision to form a union
5. Cohabitation as part of the marriage process

Casper and Bianchi (2002)

1. Substitute for marriage
2. Precursor to marriage
3. Trial marriage
4. Co-residential dating

Heuveline and Timberlake (2004)

1. Marginal
2. Prelude to marriage
3. Stage in marriage process
4. Alternative to being single
5. Alternative to marriage
6. Indistinguishable from marriage

approach cohabitation and how they see its role in future relationship status changes are quite important in predicting the length of cohabitation and whether children will be brought into the union (see Table 4.6).

More attention is being paid to the deliberateness of a couple's entry into cohabitating relationships as a possible clue to a negative correlation to marital outcomes. This is especially important for those who see cohabitation as a screening process that weeds out potentially unsuccessful relationships before marriage. Stanley, Rhoades, and Markman (2006) describe the gradual steps that culminate in a non-residential intimate relationship as *sliding* (see Box 4.5). They note that Manning and Smock (2005) found that many, if not most, couples slide from non-cohabitation to cohabitation before fully realizing what is happening. This supports earlier work by Lindsay (2000) that concluded from a study of Australian focus groups that most couples say that cohabitation "just happened," indicating a lack of formal decision making about the transition to cohabitation. This "decisionless" union formation is associated with lengthier periods of cohabitation regardless of whether the cohabitation becomes a pathway to marriage or is dissolved. This relates to the fact that length of cohabitation has been shown to have important

Table 4.6 Ideal–Typical Roles of Cohabitation, Descriptions of Types, and Empirical Indicators and Predictions

| | | Empirical Indicators and Predictions | | | | | |
| | | Adults | | | Children | | |
Role	Description	Incidence of Own Cohabitation	Median Duration	% Ending in Marriage	Exposure to Parental Cohabitation	Median Duration	% Ending in Marriage
A. Marginal	Cohabitation is not prevalent and is likely discouraged by public attitudes and policies.	Lower	Shorter	Higher	Lower	Shorter	Higher
B. Prelude to marriage	Exists as a prereproductive phase for adults. Unions tend to be brief and nonreproductive, but end in marriage.	Higher	Shorter	Higher	Lower	Shorter	Higher
C. Stage in marriage process	Exists as a transitory phase in reproduction. Unions tend to be longer, and children are more likely to be born into a cohabitation than in (B), but with short duration of exposure.	Higher	Shorter	Higher	Higher	Shorter	Higher
D. Alternative to single	Cohabitation primarily for brief, nonreproductive unions that end in separation instead of marriage.	Higher	Shorter	Lower	Lower	Shorter	Lower
E. Alternative to marriage	Is a discrete family component. Adulthood cohabitation prevalent, and for longer duration than in (C). Low proportion leading to marriage, more exposure to cohabitation during childhood than in (C), and for longer duration.	Higher	Longer	Lower	Higher	Longer	Lower
F. Indistinguishable from marriage	Little social distinction between cohabitation and marriage. Children more likely than in (E) to experience the marriage of parents because cohabitation not seen as an alternative to marriage.	Higher	Longer	Lower	Higher	Longer	Higher

Source: Heuveline and Timberlake (2004, p. 1219).

Sliding or Deciding?

After a few months of dating, Lee and Sasha decided that with school ending, moving in together for the summer seemed like the financially smart thing to do. Before they knew it, they had a shared cellphone plan, had co-signed for a used car loan, and had spent more than a few dollars at IKEA outfitting their new place. Summer came and went—three times!

Lee and Sasha were comfortable together and enjoyed each other's company, but where was this relationship going? One day, Sasha broached the topic and Lee got prickly. He did not want to talk about it. Even though they had seemed compatible and enjoyed each other intimately, the thought of greater commitment made Lee uneasy. Sasha decided to try another strategy. She told Lee that a recent study (Barg & Beblo, 2007) showed that men who married made over 13 percent more than those who stayed single. Lee responded by saying that he had read the study as well and that those who lived with a partner saw an almost 7 percent increase in wages over those who remained single, and he didn't think the other 6 percent was really worth it. As Sasha reflected on the ambiguity of it all, Lee grabbed the TV remote and hit play.

implications for later marriage outcomes. Earlier research showed that relationship risk for couples who cohabited for short periods (less than six months) prior to marriage did not differ from those who took a direct pathway to marriage (Teachman & Polonko, 1990). The authors concluded that this is probably the result of engaged couples moving in together prior to their imminent wedding. Yet De Vaus, Qu, and Weston (2005) found that, after controlling for selection effects, those who cohabitated for longer than three years prior to marriage had a separation rate significantly lower than those who went directly to marriage.

Transition rates across the life course have been found to be important in the attempts to disentangle the cohabitation effect. The importance of frequent transitions across the life course is often missed because of focusing on only one aspect of the life course such as labour force attainment, family formation, housing, or parenthood. Life course trajectories are seldom linear and often involve "U-turns, detours and yo-yo movements in and out of statuses" (Martin, Schoon, & Ross, 2008, p. 180). Specific to cohabitation periods, Lichter and Qian (2008) found that female serial cohabitors (defined as cohabiting two or more times) who eventually married increased their odds of divorce by 141 percent, or almost one and a half times, compared to those who cohabited only with their future husband, even after controlling for past fertility and socio-economic characteristics. Complex life courses differ in outcome from those life courses that are more stable (Stanley, Rhoades, Amato, Markman, & Johnson, 2010; Teachman, 2008).

Stanley et al. (2006) summarize the reasons why, after several decades of research, they believe the academic community is still unable to answer the "why" question regarding the negative influence of premarital cohabitation on later marital quality and stability.

> Although there have been notable advances in knowledge, we know far less than we would like about why, and under what circumstances, the cohabitation effect occurs. This is in part because of limitations in the existing literature, the three greatest being (a) a lack of theory, (b) a general dearth of longitudinal methods with sufficient sensitivity and quality of measurement, and (c) the fact that a vast number of studies published on the cohabitation effect are from a single, now aging data set (the National Survey of Families and Households). (pp. 499–500)

EFFECTS OF COHABITATION

Cohabitation and Later Effect on Children

Parental cohabitation and its impact on children across the life course has been gaining interest as a research focus. The complexity of the issues influencing child outcomes is being understood more fully. Early research predicted that cohabitation would have negative outcomes on child development. Several explanations were put forth by Bulanda and Manning (2008). The instability of cohabitation in comparison to marriage was identified as one potential problem since parental instability has been shown to lead to negative child outcomes. Lower educational level of cohabiting couples was another potential problem put forth. A third was that a selection effect was at work. By **selection effect**, the authors are referring to the idea that mothers with children who have behaviour problems may be less attractive marital partners and therefore choose cohabitation instead of remaining single. Parents with weaker parenting abilities may be more highly represented among those who cohabit. This last explanation ties in to the lack of legal and social benefits to which married parents have access. Without clear social or legal definitions of responsibility, non-biological parents in particular may be a poor influence on a child's behaviour.

A recent project in Britain based on the Millennium Cohort Study showed less positive outcomes among young children in a cohabiting home than those in a home in which the parents were married (see Figure 4.3). The study looked at almost 19 000 new births across the United Kingdom around the turn of the millennium. The children were visited at ages 9 months, 3 years, and 5 years for assessment of developmental measures. The study found that, on average, children born to cohabiting parents scored lower than those born to married parents on social and emotional development (as measured by the Strengths and Difficulties Questionnaire [SDQ]) and cognitive development (captured by the British Ability Scales [BAS] vocabulary element). It is important to note that although children born to cohabiting parents scored lower than those born to married parents, the differences were not as large as socio-economic factors such as parental education, family income, and occupational measures (see Figures 4.4 and 4.5).

Research has focused not only on outcomes of young children but also on outcomes of adolescents. By looking at adolescent outcomes, the research is able to take more of the family

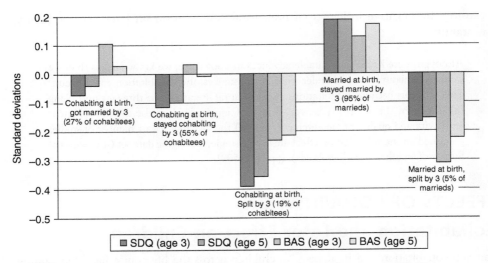

Figure 4.3 Differences in Social and Emotional Development (SDQ) and Cognitive Development (BAS) between Children Born to Married and Cohabiting Couples, at Ages 3 and 5

Source: Data from the Millennium Cohort Study.

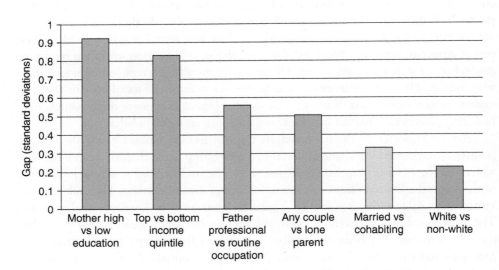

Figure 4.4 Differences in Social and Emotional Development between Children of Married and Cohabiting Couples in Context (Age 3)

Source: Data from the Millennium Cohort Study.

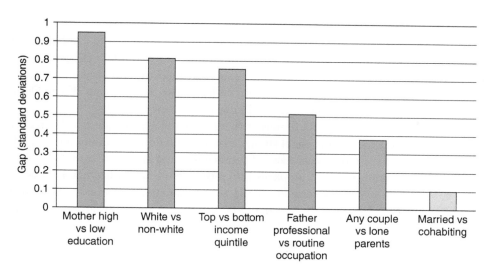

Figure 4.5 Differences in Cognitive Development between Children of Married and Cohabiting Couples in Context (Age 3)

Source: Data from the Millennium Cohort Study.

life history into consideration. Bulanda and Manning (2008) found that living with cohabiting parents is correlated to earlier sexual initiation, a greater likelihood of teen pregnancy, and lower rates of high school graduation compared to those adolescents who grew up in a married-parent household. However, their study found that the simple explanation of parental union instability was insufficient to explain why the negative adolescent outcomes existed. One explanation presented involved the idea of more parental monitoring being associated with later sexual initiation and later teenage pregnancy. The authors contemplated the idea that cohabiting parents may invest less in their parental relationships, leading to the adolescent outcomes that do not differ from those associated with single-parent families.

Cohabitation and Later Marital Quality

Research on premarital cohabitation has consistently shown a negative impact on later marital stability and quality (DeMaris & Rao, 1992; Hall & Zhao, 1995; Lichter, Qian, & Mellott, 2006; Liefbroer & Dourleijn, 2006; Lillard, Brien, & Waite, 1995; Sassler, 2004; Teachman & Polonko, 1990). Researchers are divided on the explanation for this persistent correlation. Early research in the area suggested that *selectivity* (Lillard et al., 1995; Phillips & Sweeney, 2005; Smock, 2000) may be the cause of this negative impact. Other researchers (Axinn & Barber, 1997; Axinn & Thornton, 1992; Brown, Sanchez, Nock, & Wright, 2006; DeMaris & Rao, 1992; Hall & Zhao, 1995) suggested that the actual *experience* of cohabitation was the precursor to the poorer outcomes. Another group of researchers see this effect as an inaccurate conclusion based on analysis of earlier cohorts of cohabitors who cohabited when this was not considered a normative pathway to marriage. These researchers point to more recent cohort studies that do not reflect the earlier findings (Brown, Lee, & Bulanda, 2006; De Vaus et al., 2005; Hewitt & De Vaus, 2009; Hewitt, Western, & Baxter, 2006; Schoen, 1992; Seltzer, 2004). However, other current literature does seem to support the earlier conclusions regarding the negative impact of premarital cohabitation on later marriage outcomes (Kamp Dush, Cohan, & Amato, 2003; Kline et al., 2004; Phillips & Sweeney, 2005).

Smock, Casper, and Wyse (2008) suggest that part of the explanation may lie in conclusions based on the use of older **panel studies** that do not reflect the current understanding and meaning of the term *cohabitation*. Measurement issues may be at work because of definitions, timing ambiguity, and problems with retrospective data collection. Discussion of the cohabitation effect has centred on the two explanations previously mentioned (Axinn & Thornton, 1992; Smock, 2000): *selection*, or the pre-existing characteristics and life course patterns of people who cohabit, and *experience*, or the explanation that there is something about cohabitation itself that increases the risk for relationship distress, divorce, or both. Selection variables typically have been related to socio-demographic factors such as religiosity, number of previous marriages, education level, income, presence of children, and age. Identifying selection effect variables is viewed as a means to predict more accurately who will cohabit, who will marry, and the various combinations and timing of each alternative. Some studies have shown that selection accounts for a portion of the cohabitation effect (Lillard, Brien, & Waite, 1995; Woods & Emery, 2002). A number of studies highlight that selection does not fully account for the cohabitation effect (Kamp Dush et al., 2003; Stafford, Kline, & Rankin, 2004; Stanley et al., 2006). Those who began cohabiting prior to a formal engagement were found to have more negative interactions, lower levels of interpersonal commitment to their partners, lower relationship quality, and lower levels of confidence in their relationships compared to those who cohabited only after engagement or not at all before marriage. After controlling for socio-economic factors and other previously identified influential variables such as ethnicity, education, income, length of relationship, religiosity, and duration of premarital cohabitation, the effect remained (Kline et al., 2004). These studies suggest that something about the experience of cohabitation may be associated with risk in later marriage.

Some of the strongest evidence for the experience perspective is attributed to Axinn and his associates. Axinn and Barber (1997) demonstrated that frequency of cohabitation and length of cohabitation are important in explaining the diminished value of marriage and child rearing over time. The experience of cohabitation may erode the motivation for and commitment to marriage. Axinn and Thornton (1992) found that the experience of cohabitation was associated with increased acceptance of divorce, which may help to explain cohabitation's links with actual divorce.

Some researchers (Schoen, 1992; Teachman, 2003) predict that, based on life course theory, as cohabitation becomes more normative, the negative outcomes on later marriage will begin to subside and these unions will show outcomes consistent with more traditional forms of union formation. While there is some limited evidence that the effect of premarital cohabitation on the risk of marital dissolution may have reduced for more recent birth cohorts (Brown et al., 2006; De Vaus et al., 2005, Hewitt et al., 2006; Hewitt & De Vaus, 2009; Schoen, 1992; Seltzer, 2004), other recent research suggests that this is not the case (Kamp Dush et al., 2003, Kline et al., 2004). Jose, O'Leary, and Moyer's (2010) recent meta-analysis of 26 studies of cohabitation effects on marital stability and marital quality, collected from diverse journals, reiterates that premarital cohabitation continues to be associated with negative marital outcomes.

COHABITATION AMONG THE ELDERLY

Cohabitation as a union formation alternative has been growing in popularity over the last 50 years among all age groups. Although often associated with the young adulthood stage of the life course, the fastest-growing age segment regarding cohabitation is the elderly. According to Brown et al. (2006), 10 percent of cohabitants are over the age of 50 and that number is expected to continue to grow as the baby boom generation, which made cohabiting as young adults popular, begins to enter old age. The rise in older couples experiencing cohabitation has not been matched by a similar increase in research on this age group. With few exceptions—most notably Brown et al. (2006), Brown & Kawamura (2010), Hatch (1995), and King and Scott (2005)—research on elderly cohabitants generally has been ignored. Brown et al. (2006) gathered evidence to show that remarriage is distinctive for older adults because their personal economic resources may decrease the attractiveness of marriage, especially for women. Brown et al. (2006) also feel that cohabitation may play a unique role in the life course of older adults. Citing Bulcroft and Bulcroft (1991) and other related research, Brown et al. argue that older adults have been found to have fewer incentives to remarry. As a result, the explanation often cited for why young adults choose to cohabit may be quite different for older adults. The elderly have a distinct set of issues they must navigate regarding union formation, such as retirement income restrictions based on marital status as well as adult offspring's concerns regarding asset preservation and inheritance protection.

Older adults have a different orientation to cohabitation because their characteristics germane to cohabitation are different. Brown et al. (2006) highlight four distinctions between younger and older potential cohabitors: demographic characteristics, economic resources, physical health, and social relationships. The elderly population has a unique sex ratio, with many more women than men. Men tend to partner with younger women. Older cohabitors are disproportionately men, who make up 25 percent of the elderly unmarried population but account for 60 percent of the cohabitors over age 60 (Chevan, 1996). Typically, cohabitation is more strongly correlated with partners who have fewer economic resources and lower education levels, but there has been a narrowing of the gap between those with more human capital in recent years. These data reflect a younger population and there is a less clear correlation between education and cohabitation in older adults. Hatch (1995) looked at 1980 U.S. census data and concluded that older men are less likely to be working and bring home less income than married men when they are working. Brown et al. (2006) point out that cohabitors report poorer physical health and as a result may be less attractive as potential spouses. This selection process means that less healthy people may end up cohabiting rather than marrying because cohabitation is understood to have less commitment from their partner than marriage. Lastly, Brown et al. (2006) see a variety of factors at work regarding social capital. One study shows that greater social connections among the elderly are associated with increased dating patterns (Bulcroft & Bulcroft, 1991). This increase in social dating increases the likelihood of friendships developing into intimate relationships in the form of marriage or cohabitation. The research concludes that there are moderate differences between cohabiting elderly adults and married or unpartnered elderly adults. A gendered image appears that negatively affects women more than men. Male cohabitors are more likely than their unpartnered counterparts to own their own homes. There is little difference between these groups among females. Women cohabitors are three times more likely to be without health insurance than remarried or unpartnered women, while males show no significant difference in this area. Income also differs among these groups. Remarried and cohabiting men have similarly higher incomes than unpartnered men, whereas cohabiting women report incomes of about two thirds that of remarried women. Full-time employment is expectantly much higher among cohabiting women, although no difference was found between remarried and cohabiting men. Brown et al. (2006) make it clear that to understand the role cohabitation plays in older adults as distinct from younger adults, we need to assess the motivation behind why the elderly choose to cohabit. This information is less well known and needs to be the focus of future research. For example, do older cohabitors divide responsibilities and resources in a way that is similar to younger cohabitors or older remarried partners?

Brown's recent research (Brown & Kawamura, 2010) on relationship quality among older married and cohabiting adults continues to examine the motivational factors influencing older adults to cohabit and their distinction from motivations for young adults. Data from the 2005–2006 National Social Life, Health, and Aging Project (NSHAP) provide a more contemporary look at the issues surrounding older adult cohabitation. The more recent data build on earlier findings that point to detrimental outcomes and poorer relational environments for cohabitors in general compared to married couples. King and Scott (2005) report higher levels of relationship quality among older (i.e., over age 50) cohabiting couples than among younger cohabiting couples. Relationship stability is also higher among older couples (nearly five years versus two years). They also find that older couples plan to marry less frequently than younger couples. Brown and Kawamura (2010) conclude from King and Scott (2005) that, based on the interaction between age and marriage plans, as age increases, the positive effect of plans to marry decreases. This seems to indicate that cohabitation plays a different role for older couples than it does for younger couples. Whereas younger couples may see cohabitation as a step to marriage, older couples may view cohabitations as a long-term alternative to marriage.

The current research on cohabitation later in life can be summed up by noting that motivations such as compatibility, independence, sexual satisfaction, and commitment do not vary by age (King & Scott, 2005). However, the research also demonstrates that the outcomes do differ by age. Younger cohabitors report less relationship quality than younger married couples (Brown, 2003; Nock, 1995) and less stability, which points to a distinct function that cohabitation serves older adults when compared to younger couples. There is a need for more research in this area. It may be that older cohabitors have greater selectivity (they know what they are getting into), exhibit more emotional maturity, and as a result have more stable relationships. It is also possible that older adults are less likely to be attracted to alternate relationships since they view time as a rapidly diminishing commodity. Regardless, the study of older cohabitors will continue to grow in importance as our population continues to age and as cohabitation becomes more commonly practised.

CONCLUSION

Traditional patterns and pathways of forming intimate relationships no longer dominate in most Western cultures. Non-marital cohabitation has existed through history yet only recently has gained social acceptance across all age groups. A majority of young adults will experience some form of cohabitation and older adults continue to adopt the practice in record numbers, both for a divergent number of reasons. The diversity of cohabitation experiences will be a major research challenge going forward. No longer will all cohabitors be painted with the same brush. Different typologies reveal different strategies and goals of cohabitors. These varied experiences are bound to have different effects on both the partners and the children born into or brought into these unions. A complex set of social and institutional contexts also leaves its fingerprint on the cohabitation experience. Legislative, legal, and social bodies continue to interact as they attempt to keep in step with the changing nature of couples and families created by the rise in cohabitation. Whether cohabitation becomes a solidified stage of the marriage process, establishes itself as an alternative to marriage, or some combination of the two will be played out in current and future age cohorts. Along the way, researchers will continue to be interested in the positive and negative effects cohabitation has on both the union and the children affected by the union.

SUMMARY OF KEY POINTS

- The rise in non-marital cohabitation is one of the most important recent trends in the study of the life course of the family.

- At the turn of this century, Canada mirrored France, New Zealand, Mexico, and Finland with approximately 16 to 18 percent of all current unions taking the form of non-marital cohabitation.

- Early research almost universally showed negative consequences with regard to later marital stability. As cohabitation becomes more normative, that connection has become less consistent.

- The more that cohabitation is accompanied by fertility, the more it will resemble and compete with marriage as a preferred form of family formation.

- Marriage no longer serves as the sole means to legitimize a committed relationship and non-marital fertility is rising among both cohabitors and non-cohabitors.

- Beaujot and Kerr (2007) report that, by age 20, 20.6 percent of Aboriginal youth report cohabiting or being married compared to 8.8 percent of the general population and 6.3 percent of immigrants.

- Cohabitation is not synonymous with common-law marriages, although the terms are often used interchangeably.

- The legal implications of cohabitation with regard to property rights and child custody are often misunderstood by the partners involved.

- The entrance to a cohabiting relationship has been dichotomized by some researchers as sliding or deciding. Manning and Smock (2005) found that many, if not most, couples slide from non-cohabitation to cohabitation before fully realizing what is happening.

- Research on cohabitation struggles with the varied approaches to the types and patterns of cohabitation.

- A recent project in Britain based on the Millennium Cohort Study showed less positive outcomes for young children in a cohabiting home than for those in a home in which the parents are married.

- Selection effects and experience explanations are two competing ideas used to explain the continued negative impact that cohabitation has on later marital stability.

- Cohabitation as a union formation option has been gaining popularity among the elderly, who may have fewer incentives to remarry.

- King and Scott (2005) reported higher levels of relationship quality among older cohabiting couples (i.e. over 50) than among younger cohabiting couples.

Critical Thinking Questions

1. Will the level of cohabitation continue to rise? If so, when will it stop, and why?

2. If early cohabitants were considered deviant because of their non-normative behaviour, will those who choose to marry without cohabitation be at a disadvantage in terms of relationship stability if current trends continue?

3. As cohabitation continues to become more normative, what will take its place as legislative changes make cohabitation indistinguishable from marriage?

Glossary

civil union The relationship status granted to same-sex couples when same-sex marriages are not legal in a jurisdiction. The purpose is to grant the couple the same legal rights as married couples but without married status.

cohabitation agreements Legal agreements drawn up between cohabiting couples to define the limitations and boundaries of responsibilities to one another should the cohabiting union dissolve. Property rights, pension distribution, and child support are some of the relevant areas usually contained in an agreement. Family relationships are not established by cohabitation agreements.

common-law marriage The union of a couple who considers themselves to be husband and wife but has not solemnized the relationship with a formal ceremony.

Defense of Marriage Act (DOMA) A law passed in 1996 in the United States to define marriage as a union between one man and one woman.

domestic partnership; registered partnership Terms used to apply to couples sharing a common domestic life without marital or civil union status. These terms may be used for same-sex unions in some jurisdictions, but can also be applied to heterosexual couples. The partnerships are formalized by law.

non-marital cohabitation An inclusive term used to describe cohabiting unions outside of marriage.

normative The most frequent occurrence of an event or stage in reference to life course pathways.

panel studies Research studies that use longitudinal data and incorporate the dimensions of time and change into their designs. They incorporate repeated measures of the samples involved.

relationship stability A term used to define whether a union is still intact or not.

second-parent adoption A legal process in which a non-biological parent seeks to adopt his or her partner's biological or adopted child without terminating the parental rights of the partner.

selection effect The explanation of cohabitation's negative effect on subsequent marital stability that states that people who choose to cohabit possess personality or character deficiencies that make them more prone to relationship instability and hence will have higher divorce rates whether they cohabit before marriage or not.

social norms Societal-level views regarding the acceptance of social behaviours and rules.

Connections

www.virginia.edu/marriageproject/
www.common-law-separation-canada.com/
www.ifs.org.uk/comms/comm114.pdf
www.cra-arc.gc.ca/tx/ndvdls/tpcs/ncm-tx/rtrn/cmpltng/prsnl-nf/mrtl-eng.html
www.TheNationalCampaign.org/sextech

Remember to log on to the Companion Website at **www.pearsoncanada.ca/white** to find self-graded quizzes and useful resource tools for further study. You can log on to the Companion Website using the Student Access Code that comes packaged with your copy of *Families Across the Life Course*.

Chapter 5
Marriage

Learning Objectives

After reading this chapter, you should be able to:

1. Understand the reasons why people marry.

2. Describe today's marriage trends (based on current statistics).

3. Outline the key tasks required in the transition to marriage.

4. Identify under which conditions marriage is good for one's health.

5. Describe the influences on marital satisfaction and success.

Leslie's wedding date was in two weeks but she wasn't as excited as she thought she would be. She was happy to be marrying Paul, but the wedding planning was a nightmare. Their families couldn't agree on anything and since both sets of parents were paying for the wedding, there wasn't much she or Paul could do to stop the arguments. The whole event was getting out of hand. Leslie's friends weren't supportive because they thought she was crazy to be getting married so young. "Don't you know how high the divorce rate is?" they asked her. "Don't you want to have a life before you get tied down?" Leslie thought she *was* going to have a life: one with her partner. Most of her parents' friends had married even younger—at age 18!—and their marriages had lasted, so why couldn't hers? Maybe her friends were right . . . maybe she really didn't know what she was getting into.

Chantal was tired of the dating scene. Now age 29, she thought she would have been married by now. Most of her friends were already married or engaged, or at least happily cohabiting. She couldn't seem to find the "right" guy. Everyone keeps asking her when she is going to "settle down." Settle down with whom? It's not as if she wasn't trying to meet someone. She was starting to feel a sense of panic. She needed to find someone soon or she'd never get married and have children.

Dave was tired of talking about it. Why was it so important to his parents that he get married? He was happy with the way things were. He had a great girlfriend and a great job and a lot of free time to hang out with his friends. What more could he want? How was marriage going to make his life better? Besides, he knew if he got married, the nagging wouldn't stop. His parents would then start pressuring him to have children. He wasn't sure he wanted any . . . at least not now.

WHY DO WE MARRY?

Marriage is one possible outcome following the selection of a life partner or mate. As discussed in Chapter 4, many individuals choose to cohabitate rather than get married. Some individuals never marry, some transition from cohabitation to marriage, and others marry prior to living together (or at least get engaged before setting up a household together). But why get married? As you can imagine, the answer to this question will be different for each individual who makes that choice. Matouschek and Rasul (2008) suggest three hypotheses as to why people choose to marry rather than cohabitate. First, the couple may receive some exogenous payoff by marrying. By following socially normative customs, they are rewarded by society. Marriage may serve as a rite of passage into adulthood and social approval of the couple. Second, marriage may act as a commitment device. Since it is still harder to end a marriage than to end a cohabiting union, getting married may promote relationship-specific investments such as purchasing a home or having children together. Finally, marriage may be used as a signalling device to state very publicly the extent of one's love for the partner. Marriage may seem a stronger signal of love ("I want to marry you") than cohabitation ("I want to move in with you"). Matouschek and Rasul (2008) found that the majority of the couples in their study got married because it served as a commitment device.

Historically, people didn't marry for love but rather for political or economic reasons (Morton, 1992). Marriage was important in terms of creating family alliances. Love was expected to occur after the marriage, if at all. Today, reasons for marriage vary. Often, people marry for religious reasons. Marriage is seen as an important part of serving a higher power. Some individuals get married for emotional security. Their partner provides them with a shoulder to lean on when it is needed or with a "soft place to fall." Other individuals marry for companionship. They enjoy spending time with their partner (who is often their best friend) and want to spend life's day-to-day moments with that person. Still others report wanting to get married before they start a family. It is important to them to be married before children are brought into the relationship.

Additional reasons for marriage include getting married because of intense physical attraction to a person or because the partner provides economic security (e.g., individuals believe that the partner can rescue them from economic disparity). Others marry because they are pressured into it by family or religious leaders, perhaps due to an unplanned pregnancy or by being told that they are "getting old." Others still get married to escape the parental home, to rebel against parental control, to rebound from a previous relationship, or to be "rescued" from an unsatisfying life (McGoldrick, 1999).

Marriage Rates

Whatever the reason for marriage, many Canadians are still making this choice. According to the Vanier Institute of the Family (2010), 58.4 percent of Canadians in 2006 were in a conjugal union and, of those, 80 percent were married. As you can see in Figure 5.1, the rate of married couples with children has been decreasing while the rate of cohabiting couples has been increasing. Canadians are still coupling at a fairly high rate but are simply changing the way they do so.

The marriage rate can be measured in two ways: The **crude marriage rate** estimates the number of marriages for every 1000 people in a given year. The problem with this measure, however, is that the denominator in this equation includes unmarriageable people such as children and therefore is not a good indicator of the likelihood of marriage. Using the general marriage rate gets around this problem. The **general marriage rate** estimates the number of people in a population eligible for marriage and restricts the denominator to unmarried women age 15 and older. This eliminates children from the equation. Figure 5.2 shows the conjugal status of Canadians aged 15 years and older in 2006. Notice that the largest group is made up of married couples (47.9 percent), with those never legally married representing the second-largest group (27.6 percent) (Statistics Canada, 2006c). Of the 45 300 same-sex couples recorded on the 2006 Census, 16.5 percent were married (Vanier Institute of the Family, 2010).

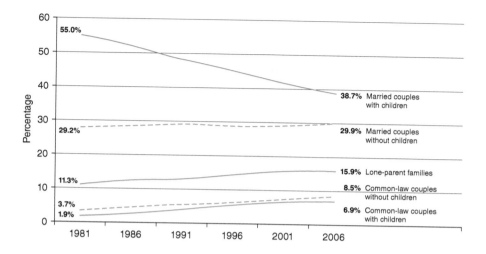

Figure 5.1 Percentage Distribution of Census Families by Type, Canada, 1961 to 2006

Source: Statistics Canada, 2006 Census of Population, Catalogue no. 97-554-XCB2006011.

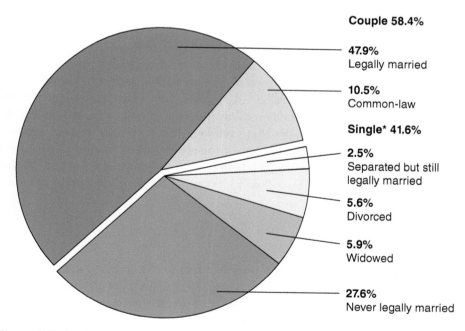

Figure 5.2 Conjugal Status of Canadian Population Aged 15 Years and Older, 2006

*Not in marital or common-law relationship.

Source: Statistics Canada, 2006 Census of Canada, Catalogue no. 97-552-XCB2006007.

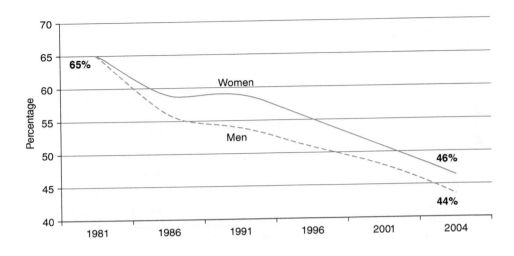

Figure 5.3 Total First Marriage Rate: Percentage Who Can Expect to Legally Marry Before Age 50, 1981 to 2004

Source: Statistics Canada (2010).

Figure 5.3 shows the change in total first marriage rate from 1981 to 2004. *Total first marriage rate* is the percentage of individuals who can expect to marry before age 50. In 1981, 65 percent of both men and women could expect to marry at least once before age 50 (Statistics Canada, 2010). In 2004, this had decreased to 46 percent for women and 44 percent for men. Not all marriages are first marriages, however. In 2003, 66.2 percent of the marriages that year were first marriages for both spouses, 18.4 percent were marriages in which one of the spouses was getting remarried, and 15.5 percent involved marriages in which both spouses were getting remarried (Vanier Institute of the Family, 2010). Data Box 5.1 examines the marriage rate by province or territory in 2005.

Age at Marriage

The age at which people marry is increasing (see Figure 5.5). In 2004, the median age of marriage was 30.5 years for men and 28.5 years for women. In comparison, the average age of marriage for men in 1970 was 25.0 years and the average age for women in 1960 was 22.6 years. The median age for all marriages (first and subsequent) in 2004 was 34.9 years for men and 32.4 years for women. Same-sex couples tend to marry somewhat later, with the median being 42.7 years for men in same-sex marriages and 42.1 years for women in same-sex marriages (Vanier Institute of the Family, 2010). We generally marry someone who is close to us in age (**age homogamy**), with husbands being slightly

If You Want to Get Married, Does It Matter Where You Live?

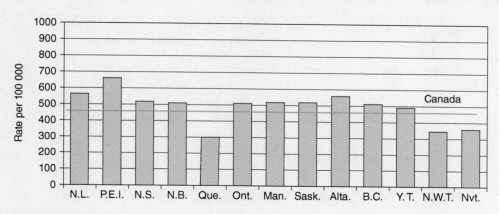

Figure 5.4 Marriage Rate, 2005, Canada, Provinces, and Territories

Source: Statistics Canada, Annual Demographic Statistics, 91-213-XIB2005000, April 2006; http://www.statcan.gc.ca/bsolc/olc-cel/olc-cel?catno=91-213-XIB&lang=eng#olcinfopanel and the Statistics Canada CANSIM database http://cansim2.statcan.gc.ca, Figure 5.2, April 5, 2011.

Figure 5.4 displays the marriage rate in each of Canada's provinces and territories. Prince Edward Island has the highest rate of marriage, while Quebec has the lowest rate. Why do you think this is the case?

older (by about 2 years) than wives, especially when we are young (Mitchell, 2009). As we get older, the age gap between spouses increases. This can lead to a marriage squeeze (discussed in Chapter 3) where mid-life and older women commonly are squeezed out of opportunities to marry. This occurs because, normatively speaking, men marry younger women. As people age, it is not uncommon for a middle-aged man to marry someone much younger than himself. The same is not true for middle-aged women. Exchange theory would suggest that the man is trading wealth and status for the younger woman's beauty (therefore, men with higher status and more resources will be more successful in marrying much younger women than men with lower status and fewer resources). Accordingly, the number of eligible men in a woman's age group decreases as the woman ages, since she must compete with younger women. In addition, as we move into later life, women outlive men (Chappell, McDonald, & Stones, 2008); therefore, there are even fewer eligible men in the elderly age group.

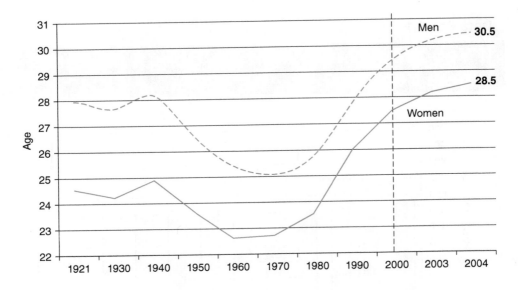

Figure 5.5 Average Age at First Marriage, Canada, 1921 to 2004

Source: Statistics Canada, CANSIM table 101-1002.

DEFINING MARRIAGE

Traditionally, marriage was defined as *the voluntary union for life of one man to one woman to the exclusion of all others*. Note that this implies a lifelong commitment to another person and also that the marriage is heterosexual and monogamous. Because of this definition, gay and lesbian couples were not able to marry or divorce until recently. On July 20, 2005, the Civil Marriage Act legalized same-sex marriage across Canada (see Box 5.1). Research on same-sex marriage is extremely limited, so this chapter will focus on heterosexual marriage for the most part. It is anticipated that we will gain more knowledge in this area in the future.

Box 5.1

The First Same-Sex Divorce in Canada

The first same-sex divorce in Canada was granted on September 13, 2004, to "M. M." and "J. H." in Ontario. The couple married on June 18, 2003 (the Ontario Court of Appeal had legalized same-sex marriage in Ontario one week prior to this date). The problem with the couple's divorce application was that, according to the Divorce Act at the time, the term *spouse* was defined as "either of a man or a woman who are married to each other." Thus, the couple was not eligible for divorce since they did not fit the definition of spouses to each other. The Ontario Superior Court of Justice ruled that this definition of *spouse* was unconstitutional and thereby granted the divorce.

Source: CBC News (2004).

In Canada, only monogamy is legal. **Monogamy** is the marriage of one person to another at one time. We often practise serial monogamy, which means that a person can have more than one marriage partner in his or her lifetime but must have these partners one at a time (in other words, he or she must get divorced and then remarry).

Some areas of the country practise **polygamy**, or marriage to several individuals at the same time. It is believed that this practice is supported by the values of both genders and is often linked to religious beliefs. The most common form of polygamy worldwide is **polygyny**, in which one man has several wives. **Polyandry**, the marital practice in which one woman has multiple husbands, is rare but is practised in parts of Africa and Southeast Asia. This practice occurs in conditions of extreme poverty and can be a way to keep the population from growing too large (Harris, 1997). (A woman can have only one child every nine months, while a man can have as many children as he has partners; therefore, if a woman has several husbands, the number of children born is significantly reduced). According to Beeby (2006), new policy and laws around polygamy are being considered as some refugees and immigrants come to Canada with foreign polygamous marriages, as well as because of the open practice of some polygamous groups in Canada, such as those in Bountiful, British Columbia (see Box 5.2).

Traditionally, marriage was a sacred phenomenon maintained by a higher power and socially maintained by religious institutions. Religious teachings provided the guidelines for conduct. Marriage was also a social obligation (to create and nurture new members of the society) and was maintained by the community. Guidelines for conduct were maintained by conformity to social norms. Modern ideas about marriage revolve around the notion that marriage is for individual growth and well-being. The goal is to increase individual happiness. Often, guidelines for conduct are found in self-help books (hopefully ones based on scientific research on relationships!). With knowledge of high divorce

Two religious leaders of a faction of the Fundamentalist Church of Jesus Christ of Latter-Day Saints, Winston Blackmore and James Oler, were charged with one count each of breaching Section 293 of the Criminal Code, which bans polygamy in Canada, because they entered into a conjugal relationship with more than one individual at a time. In fact, Blackmore (who is 52 years old) is married to 19 women while Oler (age 44) is married to 3 women at the time of this writing.

British Columbia Supreme Court Judge Sunni Stromberg-Stein dropped the charges against the men, as there is question about whether the ban on polygamy is unconstitutional since it violates religious freedoms.

Source: CBC News (2009).

rates, some individuals may consider signing a prenuptial agreement (see Box 5.3) before they marry, as it can facilitate clear communication before marriage and help avoid unnecessary conflict if the marriage dissolves.

A fairly novel way to be married today is **living apart together**, or **LAT marriages** (formerly called commuter marriages), where the individuals in the marriage live in separate homes, usually in separate cities, often in separate countries, and at times in separate houses in the same neighbourhood (Borell & Karlsson, 2002). Sometimes this is a short-term arrangement, while for others this can be a lifelong living arrangement. Typically, the main reason for a LAT marriage is the career advancement of one or both spouses forcing them to live apart (Levin, 2004). Sometimes one partner becomes the "trailing spouse" who relocates several times to "follow" the other partner, having to restart his or her own career in each new location. For example, a married graduate student may have to move three times before he or she gets a career off the ground: once to attend graduate school, a second time to take on post-doctoral training, and a third time to begin his or her first academic job. If he or she is married, the spouse may have to move each time as well.

THE TRANSITION TO MARRIAGE

The transition to marriage is the time when a newly married couple must learn to integrate with each other and with their extended families. This transition requires the couple to negotiate their roles as a married couple (McGoldrick, 1999). People often spend a lot of time planning their wedding ceremony and reception but give little thought to how the marriage will function *after* the wedding. People have expectations about their own role and their partner's role in the marriage but often these are *assumed* and not discussed. What happens on the day after the wedding, and on all the days that

Box 5.3

Should You Have a Pre-Nup?

Marston (1997) challenges the assumption that only the rich, selfish, or greedy benefit from having a **prenuptial agreement**. This type of agreement is a legal document that specifies how premarital assets will be divided if the marriage were to end.

Marston points out that the vilification of pre-nups seems irrational given that the document simply helps to enforce how assets will be divided should the marriage fail and that drafting one can potentially improve communication between engaged partners on important topics (e.g., personal finances, provision of care for children and stepchildren) that should be discussed prior to the marriage. For the prenuptial to be fair, Marston suggests that each party consult with an independent lawyer to ensure that each person is aware of his or her rights prior to signing the contract.

Source: Marston (1997).

follow? This section outlines a few common marital "tasks" that must be negotiated by the newly married couple.

The first task is to determine how the couple will present themselves to the larger society. Although we don't often think in these terms, this task is akin to developing a marital "theme" or image. Are we going to be the "fun, party couple," the "renovators," the "money machines," or the "black sheep"? The couple must find their unique place or identity within their extended family network that they then present outwardly through their social interactions. They also have to negotiate the meaning of their own new identities as spouses in this relationship. Does this mean that the wife takes her husband's surname, or does she keep her own name? Note that, in Quebec, women generally do not change their names when they marry and this choice is becoming more common among women who have established their careers before marriage.

A second task is to negotiate marital boundaries. What should be the extent of connection within the marriage and between family members and friends? Now that the couple is married, how much leisure time should be devoted to "couple time" versus "time with friends and family"? Is it okay for a wife to go out dancing with her friends on a Friday night without her husband? Is it okay for a husband to have a few drinks with the guys at the local pub without his wife? Or, does the couple have to go to these events together? Must they go together always or only some of the time? How much time should the couple spend with their respective parents? How close should this bond be now? Is it okay to share every detail of their married life: the latest fight, their plans to buy a house, or their plans to have a baby? Should they talk to or visit their respective parents every day? What information is private and what is not private? Can the parents drop by at will? Do they get a key? Do they have to call first? Does the couple have to attend regular family dinners? Or, do they have to live with one set of parents, as is the custom in some cultures? You may have some strong feelings associated with these questions, but there is no correct option. All of these boundaries must be negotiated between the newlyweds and their families, and sometimes must be renegotiated over time.

A more commonly anticipated task is determining how the household will be managed. Does the couple join their bank accounts or keep separate accounts? Or, should they have a combination of these? Who pays the bills and is in charge of the finances? How will major purchase decisions be made? How much is too much to spend before you have to let your spouse know? Becker (1981) discusses investments in marriage. The more investments you make, the harder it is to dissolve the marriage. In a sense, you are creating barriers to leaving. Joining bank accounts and funds is one such investment. Having separate accounts may feel less constraining but it is also linked to higher risk for divorce (Blumstein & Swartz, 1983). Another area of household management is the division of labour within the household. Will household labour be divided along traditional gender lines, where the husband takes care of the yard and car and the wife takes care of the household tasks? Or, do we divide them by talent, ability, expertise, or simply who is willing to scrub toilets? Or, is this division determined by who holds the power in the relationship?

Finally, the "emotional climate" of the marriage must be negotiated. How will conflicts be resolved? Does the couple stay up as long as needed to resolve a conflict, or do they go to bed angry and try to resolve it the following day? Is yelling okay, or must you remain calm at all times? This may sound strange as you are reading it but think about the conflict resolution style used in your own family. Does everyone remain calm, or is there a lot of yelling? Can you imagine entering a room full of strangers (e.g., your in-laws) who are in the middle of a fight and yelling very loudly (or, alternately, who are very quiet and reserved), when you are used to the opposite? At best, it would seem strange; at worst, it would be terrifying! Keep in mind that we often "learn to fight" from our family of origin. If our family is loud, speaks their mind, and then lets the conflict blow over quickly, that is how we will approach conflicts in our new marriage. Your partner, on the other hand, may have been socialized into a very different style of conflict resolution. Once again, there is no right approach. A couple must negotiate what is and is not allowed in their own marriage. They also will negotiate a "sexual script." Although this doesn't sound very romantic, it must be negotiated as a married couple. Perhaps you expect to have sex every day (perhaps this was the pattern you established while you were dating, so why would it change now?). Your partner, on the other hand, may have other ideas (more or less frequent sex). With challenging work demands, deadlines, and setting up a new household, a couple may find their real sex life does not match their ideal sex life. They may need to set up "appointments" (formally or informally). Finally, a couple needs to negotiate how best to provide emotional support to each other. If your spouse wants to talk about a problem, do you try to solve it for him or her? Or, do you simply provide a sounding board and let him or her vent frustrations? As you can imagine, the transition to marriage is often bumpy, but this should not be cause for immediate alarm. Over time, these transitional tasks are resolved and a husband and wife learn how to be a married couple.

MARRIAGE AND HEALTH

It is generally believed that marriage is good for one's health. Marriage has been linked to a number of health benefits such as decreased mortality, increased cardiovascular health, increased immune system functioning (Kiecolt-Glaser & Newton, 2001), and increased psychological health. There are three common perspectives that explain the link between marriage and health: selection, protection, and marital quality hypotheses. We discuss each in turn.

Selection

The **selection hypothesis** states that it is not marriage per se that is responsible for the link between marriage and health. Rather, healthier people tend to marry each other and unhealthy people have a harder time finding and keeping a mate. Getting married is associated with the availability of suitable partners (who is available) and the desirability of our own traits (how desirable we are to potential mates) (Fu & Goldman, 1996). People with poor past health or those who show evidence of poor future health have lower rates of marriage. This is explained by exchange theory and the **assortative mating principle**. People pair up with individuals much like themselves and search for the best possible match they can get in exchange for the resources they have to offer. Exchange theory suggests that people with desired attributes will be the winners in the mating game. They will be selected as the best option in a set of available options. Thus healthy people tend to marry each other and unhealthy people are left to marry similarly unhealthy people or do not marry at all (i.e., they get squeezed out of marriage). In this sense, marriage does not *cause* better health. Research that has tested the selection hypothesis has found limited support for it. That is, despite this matching process in mate selection, marriage *does* seem to provide health benefits beyond the selection effect (Friedman, 1991).

Protection

The **protection hypothesis** states that marriage provides social and economic supports that are linked with improved health (Whitson & El-Sheikh, 2003). For example, marriage improves physical health by improving emotional health. Emotional health and physical health are linked. You can make yourself sick (e.g., give yourself a stomach ache) by feeling nervous. Marriage also reduces risk-taking behaviour. The fact that you are now responsible for another person (your spouse would be greatly affected by your illness or death) makes you cut back or eliminate risky behaviour. Finally, marriage can help in the early detection of an illness so that treatment can be sought in time for it to be effective. For example, you may have the beginnings of skin cancer on your back due to sun damage. Since you are not able to view your back easily, you may not notice or may ignore the fact that a mole is changing shape and size. Your partner, however, can easily see your back and may alert you to this problem in time for you to have the mole removed before it becomes life-threatening.

Ross, Mirowsky, and Goldsteen (1990) propose the **social support hypothesis** as an explanation for the link between marriage and health. Marriage allows us opportunities for social engagement and companionship. Through marriage, we extend our social networks to include those of the spouse. This offers us many opportunities to interact with others. The development of these friendships can provide meaning in our lives. Regular contact with other individuals promotes well-being. We feel loved and valued by our family and friends. Individuals who report having positive relationships throughout their life also report fewer physiological problems later in life. Therefore, having a social network can improve your health (Ryff & Singer, 2005).

Marriage can also affect our behaviour. It can change our moods and influence our health habits (Robles & Kiecolt-Glaser, 2003). Married couples often begin diet and exercise programs together. Or, one spouse will insist that the other quit his or her drinking or smoking habit.

Marriage may also provide financial security. Married individuals are generally more financially secure than the non-married. It is less expensive for two people to live together than for two people to live alone. For example, a couple pays only one rent or mortgage payment, heating bill, cable bill, and utility bill. Also, as part of a married couple, you have a backup; knowing that you are not solely responsible for paying all of the bills can provide a huge psychological benefit. If you were to lose your job, both you and your spouse could find a way to pay the household expenses. Mortality and morbidity are reduced for those who have financial resources. If you become ill and need special treatment, you can afford to pay for that treatment and recover.

However, marriage is more protective of men's health than of women's health (Gove, 1984). This may be because women tend to have more intimate sources of social support than men do. When women need someone to listen to their problems, they often call friends who provide them with moral support. Sometimes they leave their husbands completely out of the loop, as men often tend to try to "fix" issues when women simply want someone to listen to them! Men, on the other hand, are likely to seek emotional support from their wives. It is less common for a man to call up a friend to talk about his problems. Male friends are people to do activities with and thus men tend to have fewer people who they can intimately connect with in times of emotional upset. Men are also more likely to engage in risky behaviours prior to marriage than women are (Umberson, 1987). Therefore, after getting married they may alter their behaviour significantly, thereby improving their chances for a long and healthy life. For example, they may regularly drive too fast, skydive, eat fatty foods, and drink a lot of alcohol before marriage and then, once married, significantly cut back on these behaviours. Women already engage in fewer risky behaviours and thus do not benefit as much from a reduction in such behaviours once they are married.

Marital Quality

The quality of one's marriage can greatly affect the link between marriage and health. The **stress buffering hypothesis** states: "the negative consequences of stress are *diminished* by the presence of social support . . . [thus] the *quality* of the marriage impacts the effectiveness of the protective function of marriage" (Riessman & Gerstel, 1985, p. 288). In other words, the protection hypothesis works only if the marriage is good, because a quality relationship will help to eliminate stress. Not only do good marriages protect one's health, but bad marriages can further reduce health. The **social strain hypothesis** states: "not only do unfulfilling marriages fail to protect the individuals involved but [they] can also impede the well-being of the marriage partners" (Riessman & Gerstel, 1985, p. 288). Positive relationship quality (e.g., marital harmony and marital satisfaction) is associated with higher levels of well-being across the life course. For men, this reduces their risky behaviours. Positive quality is also related to physiological responses to stress (we adapt and cope better with stress when in a happy marriage). Negative quality (e.g., conflict), in contrast, is associated with poor physical and psychological health. It increases depression and bad health behaviours, which in turn decreases physiological mechanisms such as cardiovascular, endocrine, and immune functioning (Kiecolt-Glaser & Newton, 2001). Unfortunately, negative quality has a greater impact on health than positive quality does, especially for women (Kiecolt-Glaser et al., 1993), as women have traditionally been socialized to focus on their relationships. Thus, a failed marriage may be viewed as more of a detriment to women than to men.

MARRIAGE AND HAPPINESS

Research on happiness in marriage has been vast. Several terms (with minor differences in meaning) have been used interchangeably in the literature: *marital happiness*, *marital adjustment*, and *marital satisfaction*. All of these terms are used to ask the question: How happy, satisfied, or well adjusted are you in your marriage?

The majority of research on marital satisfaction over the life course has shown that happiness in marriage takes the form of a U-shaped curve (see Figure 5.6). People are happiest (most satisfied with their marriage) on the day they get married. Then, over time, marital satisfaction declines to its lowest point during mid-life or when children hit their teenage years. (Think back: Were you an easy teenager to live with?) Marital satisfaction then begins to increase slowly as people move through retirement and later life, but it never reaches the same level of satisfaction as when first married. Interestingly,

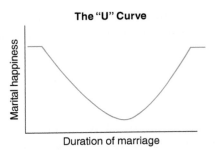

The "U" Curve

Marital happiness

Duration of marriage

Figure 5.6 Marital Satisfaction over the Life Course

even childless couples experience this U-shaped curve over the life of their marriage, although the decrease in happiness is not as drastic as for couples with children (therefore, we cannot blame all of the decline on the kids!). In fact, Twenge, Campbell, and Foster (2003) conducted a meta-analysis of studies linking parenthood and marital satisfaction. They found that parents report lower marital satisfaction than non-parents. The number of children influences satisfaction, with more children causing less satisfaction with the marriage. The authors suggest that decreases in marital satisfaction after the birth of a child are due to conflict over roles and the decrease in freedom parents have when caring for young children.

Many other factors have been found to be associated with marital satisfaction. Amato, Johnson, Booth, and Rogers (2003) found that declines in marital quality were associated with premarital cohabitation, job demands, and extended work hours of the

wife, while increases in marital quality were associated with increased economic resources, equalitarian attitudes, and support for the idea of lifelong marriage. Increases in the husbands' share of housework made the husbands feel worse about their marriages but made the wives feel better!

Schoen, Rogers, and Amato (2006) examined the links between wives' employment and marital satisfaction. Using two waves of the National Survey of Families and Households data set, the authors found that unhappy wives were more likely to move from part-time to full-time employment over the two waves. However, contrary to predictions made by economic theories (such as social exchange theory), the full-time employment status of wives was related to increases in marital stability (but not necessarily to satisfaction). It appears that working wives may make the marriage more stable but less satisfying.

Plagnol and Easterlin (2008) examined changes in life satisfaction over the life course. They found that women tend to have higher well-being early in life while men tend to have higher well-being later in life. The authors explain that women tend to fulfill their material and family goals early in life (e.g., they buy a house and car, travel, and have children). Men tend to be more satisfied with their financial and family lives later in life (e.g., the house is paid off, they have adequate retirement funds, and child rearing is over for the most part). The authors suggest that an underlying factor that influences these outcomes is the shift in the proportion of men and women in marital and non-marital unions over the life course (recall our discussion of sex ratios in Chapter 3). Women tend to marry at higher proportions when they are young, but because of differences in longevity and the mating gradient (men marrying younger women), men in later life are proportionally higher in marital status than women.

Marital satisfaction does not always lead to marital stability. Can you think of a couple you know who seem to be very unhappy yet have been together for years, or even decades? Can you also think of a couple who seemed to be very happy yet broke up anyway? Lewis and Spanier (1979) proposed four types of marriage based on level of marital satisfaction and marital stability. One type of couple is happy and stable, with a high level of marital quality and a high level of marital stability, thus their risk of separation or divorce is very low. This type of couple intuitively makes sense. If a couple is happy, they should be likely to stay together. Another type of couple is unhappy and unstable (they have a low level of marital quality and a low level of stability). This type also makes intuitive sense: If a couple is unhappy, their risk of breaking up should be higher (they are unstable). We also know that there are couples who are unhappy yet stay together for a variety of reasons, such as for the sake of their children. These are unhappy and stable couples who have a low level of marital quality and a high level of stability. The type of marriage that initially was most puzzling to researchers occurs when a couple is happy yet unstable (they have a high level of marital quality but a low level of marital stability). Why would someone leave a satisfying relationship?

Figure 5.7 Levinger's Attraction-Barrier Model of Marital Cohesiveness

Source: Adapted from Levinger (1999).

Levinger (1965, 1976, 1999) proposed an attraction-barrier model of couple commitment that can explain these relationship types (see Figure 5.7). The model attempts to predict the level of commitment an individual has to his or her relationship. Levinger states that in order to predict a person's level of commitment, we need to take into account all of the attractions to the relationship, all of the barriers to leaving the relationship, alternative attractions that are present, as well as any barriers to leaving a particular alternative. **Attractions** in this model are the net attractions to the marriage (rewarding aspects minus negative aspects) (e.g., love for one's partner). These keep an individual invested in the relationship. **Barriers** are restraining forces (both internal and external) that make a person feel that he or she must stay in the relationship (e.g., religious beliefs or children). **Alternative attractions** are the individual's net attractions to the most salient alternative to the relationship (e.g., the sum of all feelings for another partner or for single life), and these act as forces that pull the individual out of the relationship. **Alternative barriers** refer to the strength of the barriers around leaving the alternative (e.g., the mistress gets pregnant, your job requires you to move and your family doesn't want to come along). Thus, commitment to a relationship depends on the level of attractions to the relationship, plus the level of barriers to leaving the relationship, minus the alternative attractions net of barriers around leaving the alternative.

Based on this model, we can explain why happy couples may still be unstable. A person may have a high level of marital attractions (high satisfaction with the marriage) but at the same time may have low barriers (few things keeping him or her in the marriage) and have several or at least one strong alternative. He or she may also have alternative barriers and thus the combination of factors would make the individual choose to leave despite having high satisfaction. Let's look at an example: Matt is happy as Jill's husband. They share similar values, enjoy many of the same activities, and hardly ever fight (high level of attractions). However, Matt and Jill have no family living nearby and have no children of their own (low barriers). Matt was recently told by his boss that he is being promoted and must move to Europe (alternative); if he chooses not to go, the company will have to let him go as there is no longer a need for his position where he currently resides (alternative barrier). Jill has her own thriving career and would not have the same opportunities in Europe. Matt decides that it is better to end the relationship than to try to make a go of it long distance.

Premarital factors and interaction patterns can also have an effect on marital satisfaction (and subsequent stability). Caughlin and Huston (2006) proposed several models of marital change that illustrate how these patterns can affect satisfaction and stability over time. The emergent distress model assumes that when people get married, they begin their marriage feeling positive about it (e.g., high levels of love and affection, trust, and intimacy). Over time, however, negative factors (such as negative interaction patterns) start to chip away at the positive aspects of marriage. Gottman and Levinson (1992) propose four common interaction patterns that are very destructive to a relationship: contempt, criticism, defensiveness, and stonewalling. From the emergent distress perspective, a person may say, "You aren't as nice as you used to be."

The disillusionment model also assumes that all marriages begin with high levels of positive factors. However, some people idealize their partners and ignore or fail to see their partners' negative traits. Over time, the "rose-coloured glasses" come off (people cannot maintain the idealization and continue to ignore the negatives), which then leads to declines in satisfaction. Disillusioned individuals may say, "You aren't the person I thought I married."

The enduring dynamics model states that people begin their marriages with a realistic view of their partners (are aware of both positive and negative aspects of their partners). The pattern of interaction established while dating continues into married life. If, for example, you had a rocky relationship with many dramatic ups and downs while dating, you will have the same rocky relationship in marriage. The relationship doesn't necessarily change or get better after marriage! However, as we become older and busier with day-to-day responsibilities, this drama may not be as enticing as it once was, which then leads to dissatisfaction.

Caughlin and Huston (2006) thus propose that we can identify four types of marriage based on levels of positive and negative marital quality. They use the dimensions of affection and antagonism (see Figure 5.8). Couples high in affection and low in antagonism are

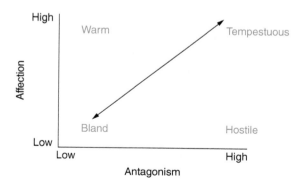

Figure 5.8 The Two Sides of Satisfaction

Source: Adapted from Caughlin and Huston (2006, p. 132).

labelled *warm* couples. On the opposite end of the spectrum, if there is high antagonism (conflict) in the marriage and low levels of affection, couples are labelled *hostile*. Couples with high levels of both affection and antagonism are *tempestuous* (dramatic) while those with low levels of both affection and antagonism are *bland*, or boring.

MARITAL INTERACTION

As discussed, marital interaction patterns can greatly affect the quality of a marriage. Gottman, Coan, Carrère, and Swanson (1998), through observations of couples, found that there seems to be a 5:1 ratio of positive to negative interactions necessary to maintain satisfaction in a given relationship. In other words, if you say or do something negative, you had better be prepared to say or do five nice things to even out the score. This is because we tend to focus more on the negative aspects of our partner and relationship than we do on the positive aspects. Therefore, it takes many more positive interactions to make up for the one negative interaction that occurred. Depending on the severity of the negative, you may need many more than five positives (five was the average). For example, you could spend several decades happily married and generally enjoying life together and all of that could be ruined by one serious negative act: you are unfaithful. In some cases, no amount of positives can ever make up for that one negative behaviour. Box 5.4 discusses some of the common mistakes in communication made by relationship partners.

Peterson (2002) proposes four common types of relational conflict. **Criticism** occurs when a person makes verbal or non-verbal demeaning acts. For example, you may call your partner demeaning names, which generally leads to or escalates conflict. **Illegitimate demands** are another common source of conflict. This occurs when you ask your partner to do unjust things for you (e.g., lie to, trick, or deceive a family member). **Cumulative annoyances** are repetitive behaviours your partner does that become extremely frustrating over time (e.g., continuously clearing his or her throat, leaving dirty socks on the floor). Finally, **rebuffs** occur when you fail to act on a demand (e.g., your partner asks you for a glass of water and you do not bring it to him or her).

Research on attributions in conflict (cognitive thought processes related to how we view ourselves and others) has shown that during conflict we are generally more motivated to look for reasons for our own and our partner's behaviour (we want to understand why we did what we did and why they did what they did) than at any other time. Unfortunately, we tend to view the causes of our behaviour as innocent but will attribute evil motives to our partner's behaviour. Thus, we get into disagreements about motives (e.g., "You did that on purpose"; "No, I didn't") that are impossible to solve. We try to convince the other person that our view of why they behaved the way they did is correct and that their own understanding of their own behaviour is incorrect. You can see how this will never get resolved! Unhappy couples tend to attribute their partners' negative behaviour to internal ("Your personality makes you an inconsiderate person"), stable ("You are always inconsiderate"), and global ("You are inconsiderate to everyone") causes. They also attribute positive behaviour to external ("Your mom told you to bring me a gift"), unstable ("You bring

Box 5.4

Improving Your Communication

All relationships have conflict. Conflict is inevitable. Unless we are married to ourselves, we are going to encounter differences in opinion at some point in our relationship. However, some married couples do a better job than others of communicating through conflict. The following are some common mistakes made during conflict that only end up making things worse:

- Focusing on the negative and continuing to make negative statements.

- **Cross-complaining** occurs when a person answers a complaint with a complaint of his or her own instead of listening to the partner's point of view. For example, the partner says, "You need to put your dirty laundry in the hamper." Instead of listening to the request for help with domestic chores, a partner who cross-complains responds with something like: "Well, you need to iron my shirts!"

- Offering **counter-proposals** occurs when instead of listening to and accepting a valid solution offered by the partner, an individual comes up with a counter-proposal—not because it is a better idea, but rather to *not* do what the partner suggested.

- **Mindreading** occurs in two ways: (1) an individual expects the partner to be able to read his or her mind (e.g., "If you cared, you would *know* what I want"), and (2) an individual decides in his or her mind what the partner's intentions were (e.g., "You did that just to get me back!").

- **Self-summarizing** occurs when an individual continues to repeat his or her points ad nauseam until the partner stops trying to make arguments of his or her own (in other words, the individual doesn't listen to what the partner is saying but rather keeps repeating him- or herself until the partner gives up).

- **Kitchen-sinking** occurs when every argument or infraction that has occurred in the past is brought into the current argument instead of the partners focusing on the *current* issue.

Source: Adapted from Miller, R., & Perlman, D. (2009). *Intimate Relationships*, 5e, McGraw-Hill Ryerson. Reprinted with permission.

me a gift only when you want something"), and specific ("You only neglect me") causes. Happy couples think in the opposite way (Fincham, Harold, & Gano-Phillips, 2000). You can now see how thought processes affect how we view our partners' behaviour and how they subsequently affect our satisfaction with the relationship.

There are five ways in which a conflict can end (Peterson, 2002): (1) **separation** or withdrawal of at least one partner without any resolution to the conflict; (2) **domination**, where one person continues to pursue his or her goal until the other partner gives in; (3) **compromise**, where both partners reduce their expectations and find a mutually acceptable alternative (a problem with compromise, however, is that neither partner is completely satisfied and may still tend to focus on what they had to give up in the compromise); (4) **integrative agreement**, where both people have their goals satisfied (this can be difficult to achieve in most situations); or (5) **structural improvement**, where a positive change is made in the relationship (e.g., negative attributions are changed, trust is developed, and hope is increased). Conflict *can* increase intimacy and satisfaction *if* done fairly! If there is a lot of conflict, however, our commitment to the marriage may begin to suffer.

MARITAL COMMITMENT

Johnson (1999) developed a model of commitment that distinguished between three types of commitment to a relationship: personal commitment, moral commitment, and structural commitment (see Figure 5.9). **Personal commitment** refers to being dedicated to continue with a course of action. It consists of three components with respect to marital commitment: (1) attraction to one's partner, (2) attraction to the relationship, and (3) definition of the self in terms of the relationship. Personal commitment relates to the phrase *I want to stay*. We generally want to stay in a relationship because we like who our partner is as a person (attraction to partner). We also may want to stay in a relationship because we like the relationship itself (attraction to the relationship)—it functions well and makes us happy. We also may want to stay in a relationship because part of our identity is wrapped up in that relationship. Who would we be if we weren't "Mrs. Smith" or "Jane's husband"? We like the identity associated with the role of spouse. All of these factors give us a sense of personal commitment, or wanting to stay.

Moral commitment refers to feelings of obligation to maintain the relationship. Here, we feel we *ought* to stay. The feeling of obligation comes from both a sense of social duty ("I can't leave him now after all of these years. What would people think of me leaving him alone as an old man?") and personal feelings of obligation to the spouse ("I can't leave her now after all that she has done for me"). We may also believe we are the type of person who honours their commitments ("I always do what I promised to do") (general consistency values) and thus feel obligated to stay.

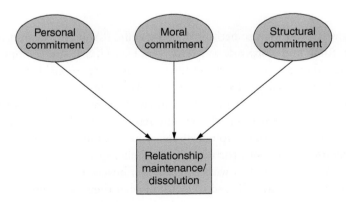

Figure 5.9 Johnson's Commitment Model

Source: Adapted from Johnson (1999, p. 77).

The third category of commitment in this model is **structural commitment**, or conditions that cause a person to continue on a course of action once he or she has initiated that course of action regardless of whether he or she is personally committed to it. This speaks to social factors that may increase commitment. Here, the phrase *I have to stay* fits well. This category is composed of four parts: (1) irretrievable investments, (2) termination procedures, (3) social pressure, and (4) attractiveness of available alternatives. Irretrievable investments are investments made in the relationship that you cannot get back once it has ended. Time, for example, is an irretrievable investment. You can never regain the years spent with an individual. Children and assets such as a home are also considered irretrievable investments. Even though you may not completely lose your children or the money invested in the home, you never get *all* of them or it back. For example, you may have to share custody of your children, so you do not get to spend all of your free time with them. You also may split the proceeds of the house, so you cannot buy the same amount of house after doing so. Of course, there are exceptions to this, but the underlying point should be apparent. How difficult, expensive, or time consuming termination procedures are can also cause you to feel as if you have to stay. If you cannot afford to get divorced and do not have the time or energy to deal with the process, you may decide it is not worth leaving the relationship. Social pressure can also make you more committed to your existing relationship. This is not because your friends or family will make you like your partner more, but rather that they may pressure you to stay in the relationship for their own benefit (even though they may phrase it as being beneficial to you). They may talk about social stigma associated with divorce ("People will think something is wrong with you") or about damage you may cause your children, or about how divorce may affect your friendship ("We won't be able to hang out anymore if you break up"—although this may not be stated directly). Finally, attractiveness of available alternatives may also play a role in your level of structural commitment. If you have no other options (other than being alone) or if the options are not very appealing, you may decide to stay with your spouse.

As you can see, marital satisfaction and marital commitment are not the same thing. You can be unhappy in your marriage yet still feel obligated to (moral commitment) or stuck in (structural commitment) the relationship.

Covenant marriages have come about to try to make it more difficult to end a marriage. Nock, Sanchez, and Wright (2008) wrote a book about covenant marriage. Over the past few decades, political and religious leaders have promoted marriage as a solution to many of our long-standing social problems (e.g., increase in divorce rates, increase in cohabitation rates, increase in single motherhood). Covenant marriage laws require a couple to choose between a covenant marriage and a conventional marriage. Covenant marriage makes it harder to dissolve the marital relationship. It often requires premarital counselling and proof of fault (e.g., adultery or abuse), or at minimum requires long waiting periods before a divorce will be granted. A person entering into a covenant marriage must sign an agreement to abide by the covenant rules

Protections in Marriage

Emily and Alex decided it was time to get married. They wanted to have children and both believed they should do so in the context of marriage. Both Emily and Alex were deeply committed and wanted to make sure their marriage would work. Emily decided to look into premarital counselling and workshops that she and Alex could attend. She believed that this would force them to have some "hard discussions" that they seemed to be avoiding, such as disclosing their personal financial assets and liabilities as well as discussing their ideas about parenting. Emily specifically wanted to discuss which religion they would follow and teach to their children.

Alex had other ideas. He didn't think counselling was necessary. He believed that they were reasonable adults and could "work things out" as issues arose. It didn't seem important to decide on religion and delve into finances now. Alex wanted to plan a fun wedding and a great honeymoon, not spend time attending marriage preparation classes. He thought they should have a covenant marriage. Then they wouldn't be able to break up on a whim, so there would be less risk of divorce.

With whom do you agree: Emily or Alex?

(meaning that they agree that if they choose to divorce, they will have to prove fault and attend premarital counselling before it will be granted). This is in stark contrast to the no-fault divorce requirements associated with conventional marriage. Career Box 5.1 illustrates two very different ways to attempt to "protect" one's marriage from dissolution.

CONCLUSION

Marriage is only one possible outcome following the selection of a mate. The reasons for marrying vary from person to person. Most Canadians will partner at some point in their lives, but the way in which we do so is changing. Fewer individuals are choosing to marry and cohabitation is becoming a popular alternative to marriage. Age at marriage is increasing, with same-sex couples marrying at older ages than opposite-sex couples. The transition to marriage involves several tasks that the couple must negotiate (e.g., household division of labour). Generally, marriage has been found to be good for our health—especially for men's health. However, marital satisfaction tends to decline for most couples, leading to instability for approximately one third of couples who marry for the first time. Interaction patterns that we develop in marriage, including conflict and communication styles, can help to stabilize marriages, as can having a strong commitment to marriage.

SUMMARY OF KEY POINTS

- Matouschek and Rasul (2008) provide three reasons why people choose to marry: (1) marriage may serve as a rite of passage into adulthood, (2) marriage may act as a commitment device, and (3) marriage may be used as a signalling device.

- Historically, people did not get married for love, but rather for political or economic reasons. Love was expected to occur after the marriage, if at all. Today, reasons for marriage vary.

- According to the Vanier Institute of the Family (2010), 58.4 percent of individuals in 2006 were in a conjugal union and, of those, 80 percent were married.

- Of the 45 300 same-sex couples recorded on the 2006 Census, 16.5 percent were married (Vanier Institute of the Family, 2010).

- In 2003, 66.2 percent of the marriages that year were first marriages for both spouses, 18.4 percent were marriages in which one spouse was getting remarried, and 15.5 percent involved marriages in which both spouses were getting remarried (Vanier Institute of the Family, 2010).

- In 2004, the median age of marriage for men was 30.5 years and for women was 28.5 years. The median age for all marriages (first and subsequent) was 34.9 years for men and 32.4 years for women. Same-sex couples tend to marry somewhat later, with the median being 42.7 years for men and 42.1 years for women (Vanier Institute of the Family, 2010).

- We generally marry someone who is close to us in age (age homogamy), with husbands being slightly older than wives, especially during young adulthood.

- Monogamy is the only legal form of marriage in Canada. This is the marriage of one person to another at one time. Polygamy, or marriage to several individuals at the same time, is practised (but is not legal) in parts of Canada.

- The transition to marriage is the time when a newly married couple must learn to integrate with each other and with their extended families. Several tasks must be negotiated, such as determining their marital identity, negotiating the meaning of their own new identities as spouse in the relationship, negotiating marital boundaries, determining how the household will be managed, and negotiating the "emotional climate" of the marriage.

- It is generally believed that marriage is good for one's health. Marriage has been linked to decreased mortality rates, increased cardiovascular health, increased immune system functioning, decreased functional disability, and increased psychological health. There are three common perspectives that explain the link between marriage and health: selection, protection, and marital quality hypotheses. Marriage is more protective of men's health than of women's health.

- The majority of research on marital satisfaction over the life course has shown that happiness in marriage takes the form of a U-shaped curve. We begin our married lives happy, experience a decline in happiness at mid-life, and then return to higher levels of happiness in later life.

- Lewis and Spanier (1979) proposed four types of marriage based on level of marital satisfaction and marital stability: (1) happy-stable, (2) unhappy-unstable, (3) unhappy-stable, and (4) happy-unstable.

- Levinger (1965, 1976, 1999) proposed an attraction-barrier model of marital commitment. To predict the level of commitment to marriage, we need to take into account attractions to the relationship, barriers to leaving, alternative attractions, and any barriers to leaving a particular alternative.

- Premarital factors and interaction patterns can have an effect on marital satisfaction and subsequent stability. Caughlin and Huston (2006) proposed several models of marital change that illustrate how these patterns can affect satisfaction and stability over time: the emergent distress model, the disillusionment model, and the enduring dynamics model.

- Gottman et al. (1998), through observations of couples, found that there seems to be a 5:1 ratio of positive to negative interactions necessary to maintain satisfaction in a given relationship.

- Peterson (2002) proposes four common types of relational conflict: criticism, illegitimate demands, cumulative annoyances, and rebuffs.

- There are five ways in which a conflict can end: (1) separation or withdrawal of at least one partner, (2) domination, (3) compromise, (4) an integrative agreement, and (5) a structural improvement.

- Johnson (1999) developed a model that distinguished between three types of commitment to a relationship: personal commitment, moral commitment, and structural commitment.

- Covenant marriage makes it harder to dissolve a marital relationship, often requiring premarital counselling and proof of fault or at minimum requiring a long waiting period before a divorce is granted.

Critical Thinking Questions

1. Under what circumstances would you ask your future marriage partner to sign a pre-nuptial agreement? How would you approach him or her with this request?

2. You are considering marriage but are concerned about making this commitment because of the high divorce rate. You have seen the damage that divorce has caused among your friends and family members. What would you do to try to "divorce-proof" your relationship before you marry?

3. You have just gotten married and your spouse wants to set up a joint bank account and close your individual accounts. Your spouse also wants to give his or her parents a key to your new place. How do you respond? What kinds of issues should you discuss?

Glossary

age homogamy Marrying someone who is close to us in age.

alternative attractions Alternatives to a marriage (e.g., another partner or single life). These act as forces that pull a person out of a marriage.

alternative barriers Barriers around leaving an alternative to a marriage.

assortative mating principle People choose mates who are much like themselves.

attractions Positive aspects of a marriage and partner (net attractions to the marriage equal rewarding aspects minus negative aspects).

barriers Restraining forces (both internal and external) that make a person feel that he or she must stay in a relationship.

compromise Both partners reduce their expectations and find a mutually acceptable alternative in a conflict.

counter-proposal This occurs when instead of listening to and accepting a valid solution offered by the partner, an individual comes up with a different proposal instead.

covenant marriage A marriage contract in which the individuals agree to terms that make it harder to dissolve the marital relationship (should they want to divorce). It often requires premarital counselling and proof of fault (e.g., adultery, abuse) or at minimum requires a long waiting period before a divorce is granted.

criticism Occurs when a person makes verbal or non-verbal demeaning acts.

cross-complaining Occurs when a person answers a complaint with a complaint of his or her own instead of listening to the partner's point of view.

crude marriage rate The number of marriages for every 1000 people in a given year.

cumulative annoyances Repetitive behaviours a partner does that over time become extremely frustrating.

domination Occurs when one person continues to pursue his or her goal until the partner gives in during a conflict.

general marriage rate The number of people in a population eligible for marriage, restricting the denominator to unmarried women age 15 years and older.

illegitimate demands Occur when you ask your partner to do unjust things for you.

integrative agreement Occurs when both people have their goals satisfied in a conflict.

kitchen-sinking Occurs when every argument or infraction from the past is brought into the current argument instead of focusing on the current issue.

LAT marriages (living apart together) Marriages in which the spouses live in separate homes.

mindreading Occurs when you expect your partner to be able to read your mind or when you decide in your own mind what your partner's intentions were.

monogamy The marriage of only one person to another at one time.

moral commitment Feelings of obligation to maintain a relationship.

personal commitment Dedication to continuing a course of action (Johnson, 1999).

polyandry The marital practice in which one female has multiple husbands.

polygamy Marriage to several individuals at the same time.

polygyny The marital practice in which one man has multiple wives.

prenuptial agreement A legal document that specifies how premarital assets will be divided if the marriage were to end.

protection hypothesis States that marriage provides social and economic supports linked with improved health.

rebuffs Occur when you fail to act on a demand.

selection hypothesis States that it is not marriage per se that is responsible for the link between marriage and health, but rather that healthier people tend to marry each other and unhealthy people have a harder time finding and keeping a mate.

self-summarizing Occurs when an individual continues to repeat points in an argument until the partner stops trying to make arguments of his or her own.

separation Withdrawal of at least one partner without any resolution to a conflict.

social strain hypothesis States that marriages with high levels of negativity do not protect individuals but actually can decrease their well-being.

social support hypothesis An explanation for the link between marriage and health. Marriage allows opportunities for social engagement and companionship that improve our well-being.

stress buffering hypothesis The negative effects of stress are reduced by the presence of social support.

structural commitment Conditions that cause a person to continue on a course of action once he or she has initiated that course of action, regardless of whether he or she is personally committed to it (Johnson, 1999).

structural improvement Occurs when a positive change is made in a relationship following a conflict.

Connections

www.samesexmarriage.ca
www.cbc.ca/canada/british-columbia/story/2009/09/23/bc-polygamy-charges-blackmore-oler-bountiful.html
www.lovemore.com
www.todaysfamilynews.ca/tfn/family/articles/Together_forever.htm
www.datehookup.com/content-the-wowing-world-wedding-traditions-guide.htm
www.iaml.org/iaml_law_journal/back_issues/volume_1/an_overview_of_pre_nuptial_agreements_in_
    canada/index.html
www.cbc.ca/news/background/samesexrights/samesexdivorce.html

Remember to log on to the Companion Website at **www.pearsoncanada.ca/white** to find self-graded quizzes and useful resource tools for further study. You can log on to the Companion Website using the Student Access Code that comes packaged with your copy of *Families Across the Life Course*.

Chapter 6
Fertility and Having a Child

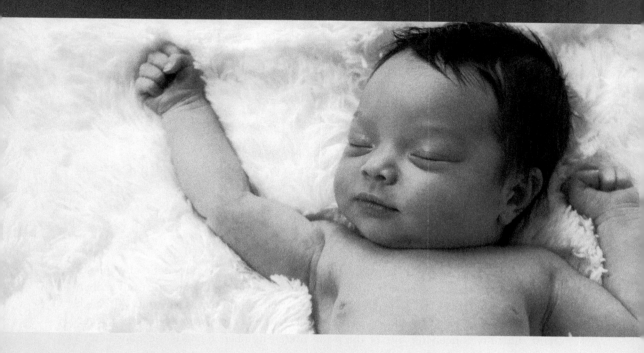

Learning Objectives

After reading this chapter, you should be able to:

1. Distinguish between the levels of analysis used in the study of fertility.

2. Understand the difference between actual and desired fertility.

3. Analyze the consequences of 30 years of low fertility in Canada.

4. Understand the transition to parenthood and its effects on marriage.

5. Analyze the many ways in which parental roles are "gendered" and non-egalitarian.

"Mr. Li, your wife is going to need your help having this baby!" the obstetrics nurse said. "The reason you are here at this prenatal class is that childbirth involves both parents and the father or partner is coach and helper in the process. In a few minutes we will take a look at a birth video but, first, are there any questions?"

William Li raised his hand hesitantly. "When my parents were having their children, the dads never went into the delivery room. That was something for women. How did we get to the point that men rather than nurses are in there?"

The nurse drew a long breath and replied, "Nurses are needed to help with many of the technical medical parts of childbirth, including checking for dilation of the cervix. You, as husband, will be responsible for helping your wife stay comfortable with back rubs and positioning and emotional support. You will be needed to ensure that your birth plan and medical wishes regarding anesthetics are followed. And, finally, you will have the great privilege of being present at the moment your child comes into the world."

Another expectant father joined in: "Have any of the fathers ever fainted during their wife's labour?"

The nurse sighed before replying, "That is why we show you the video of birthing, so you can get that out of your system." (See www.medicalvideos.us/videos/1294/ for an example of a birthing video.)

When you are in your teens and twenties, you focus on contraception, but many couples in their late twenties and early thirties switch to a focus on getting pregnant rather than preventing pregnancy. They switch from not wanting a child to wanting one. Although the path for later fertility has many obstacles, such as higher rates of miscarriage and even more difficulty conceiving, one of the most interesting phenomena is the transition to wanting a child and the process of becoming a family.

TRANSITIONS

The birth of a child to either a couple or a single person represents one of the major life course transitions for many of us. This transition is significant because we add the **parental role**. We add this role—the very complex and age-graded role of parent—to our existing family roles such as son or daughter, sibling, and husband or wife. This in itself is interesting because most of the social roles we assume are age-graded for us. For example, when we are 16, we can drive; when we are 65, we can retire. The parent role is dictated by the age of one's child and the experiences that child brings to the parent, such as daycare, primary school, secondary school, dating, and soccer practices. This transition to the parent role is also significant because the child, whether adopted or genetically related, is treated as a consanguine (with blood) relative, and these relationships are "durable" in both cultural and legal ways. While one may separate or divorce a spouse, to leave one's child is considered abandonment and negligence by both society and the courts.

Besides the transition to the parent role, the birth of a child signifies dramatic changes in the relationship of many couples. It is estimated that about 75 percent of couples experience a decline in their feelings of love and less motivation to work on the couple relationship with the birth of the first child (Belsky & Rovine, 1990). This finding has been corroborated in several other studies (e.g., Cowan & Cowan, 1999; Feeney, Hohaus, Noller, & Alexander, 2001). This leads many researchers to ask: What is there about the birth of the first child that brings such declines in couple relationships? Just as interesting is the fact the some couple relationships actually improve with the birth of the first child. We may ask: What leads some couple relationships to decline and others to improve with the birth of the first child?

The actual day and time of birth is obviously the **transition point**, but the transition to the parent role is a process that involves deciding to have a baby, conception, gestation, birth, and adaptation to having the child at home. These are all complex experiences and this chapter addresses them in chronological order. In addition, these changes are clearly developmental. There are complex age- and duration-graded **timing norms** about relationships. For example, it may be an expectation of "good" parenting to breastfeed a child when he or she is an infant but not when the child is an adolescent. The norms about parenting are very much tied to the maturation of the child and the family relationships. Therefore, it is most appropriate that we examine this transition chronologically.

WHY DO COUPLES WANT A CHILD?

Over the years, many texts have enumerated some of the reasons why couples want children. It must be stressed, however, that if we really knew why couples wanted children, we could then predict and control fertility. The history of world fertility is full of surprises (e.g., the baby boom) and has proven difficult to predict. Furthermore, it is very likely that the "reasons" for fertility are *not* constant across time, culture, and place. Indeed, the study of fertility leads us to have more humility than hubris about our knowledge in this area.

Most explanations of fertility can be grouped as ones that rely on macro-structural causes such as the environment, social norms, and economic constraints. We commonly expect fertility to decline in tough economic times or during periods of social upheaval. On the other hand, some explanations of fertility focus on the micro-individual level, with cause most often being related to "choices" that individuals and couples make (Mitchell & Gray, 2007). These individual choices are often based on experiences that relate to macro-level phenomena, such as having a stable job or owning a home, and may lead couples to think that it is a good time to have child. Having a stable job and owning a home also may be related to other macro-level phenomena, such as a buoyant economy. We examine some of the macro-structural explanations of fertility later in this chapter, but for now we focus on the choices that individuals and couples make.

Typical Reasons

In this section, we address some of the most common reasons cited by couples for wanting at least one child.

Conformity is perhaps the most frequently cited reason why people have children. In other words, having children is simply what adults are supposed to do. This should not necessarily be viewed as a simple form of conforming to a pattern of behaviour. Scholars such as Aldous (1999) have argued that many people believe that one is not truly recognized as an adult until the parent role is in place. In other words, the social status of being a "mature adult" is tied to the social role of parent. Thus, one is motivated to have a child to achieve adult status in the eyes of one's parents, relatives, and even the larger society.

A second often-cited reason for having children is that people do not want to miss out on such a major *life experience*. The idea that giving birth and being a parent are experiences that are important to the richness of life is deeply ingrained. People argue that not to have a child is to miss out on life. This reasoning is found even among some feminist scholars, such as Betty Friedan (1981), who argues in her book *The Second Stage* that women should not have to sacrifice the experience of having children and a family in exchange for an occupational career.

A third reason cited for having children, closely linked to the two above, is that a couple's desire for children is really a desire for social capital (Schoen, Astone, Kim, Nathanson, & Fields, 1999; Schoen, Kim, Nathanson, Fields, & Astone, 1997). **Social capital** is defined as the network of relationships to which the individual has access. The basic idea is that social capital is necessary to the flow of social support and information from others. Schoen and his colleagues argue that in the developed world, many social organizations and networks are reserved for those who have children. For example, coaching soccer is tied to being a mom or dad. Most school and community organizations view having a child as the price of entry into those networks. Certainly, those who have no children would be looked at with suspicion if they wanted to coach children's soccer or attend student presentations at a school. Furthermore, relatives reawaken long-dormant relationships upon the birth of a first child. Certainly, there are social networks for single adults but consider the density and complexity of social organizations dealing with children and families, from ballet to baseball. Having a child is a way to enter these complex and rich networks.

Another very common reason often cited for wanting to have a child is *old age security*. In developing nations where there are no old-age security systems, having a child is viewed by many as assuring that someone will take care of you in your old age. In many of these countries, having multiple children has served the same purpose as an old age security system. The fact is that as countries invest in forms of old age security, their birth rates drop. Whether this is a cause-and-effect relationship or part of a larger process of development remains a question. Overall, we can say that having children for old age security is not as viable a reason for having a child in most of the developed world (Sleebos, 2003).

Other reasons are cited for having children, such as *entertainment*, but most of these can be grouped into one of the reasons discussed above. There are also vague proposals

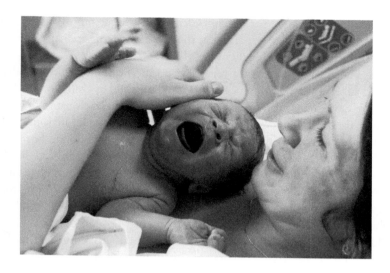

about biological imperatives to have children. Such biological reasons fail to explain differential fertility across time since we would not expect biological imperatives to fluctuate but certainly fertility has fluctuated, as has desired fertility. Thus, biological imperative explanations for fertility do not stand up to serious scrutiny and face the problem of trying to explain variability with a biological constant.

Actual and Desired Fertility

One of the first points we need to make about "wanting a child" is the distinction between **desired or intended fertility** and **actual fertility**. Desired or intended fertility is usually measured by asking men and women: How many children would you like to have? or How many children do you intend to have? Since these questions are usually asked before a couple or individual has any children, the answers may range from no children to five or more. It is interesting that indicators of desired or intended fertility are not good predictors of actual fertility. For example, in the Organisation for Economic Co-operation and Development (OECD) report on fertility, the authors found in their sample of developed nations that intended fertility tends to be higher for women than is their actual fertility (d'Addio & d'Ercole, 2005). In 2001, the average response among Canadian women was 2.47 desired children; however, the actual fertility at that time was approximately 1.5 children (Proudfoot, 2010). Because of this poor correlation between actual and desired fertility, it is best to consider these as two independent dimensions of fertility.

When examining fertility intentions in Canada over the last few decades, we find that most women, if they are going to have a child, prefer two children (2.4 in Canada and 2.5 in the United States, according to a 1997 Gallup poll; www.gallup.com/poll/9871/1997-Global-Study-Family-Values.aspx). Although this is the average response to desired or intended fertility, it clearly does not predict actual Canadian fertility, which has been consistently below two children per woman. Clearly, desired fertility is higher than actual fertility. In fact, an OECD study reports that the gap between desired and actual fertility is greatest in countries with low fertility rates (OECD, 2007).

To figure out what is happening regarding wanting children and actually having them, we need to separate the two processes. Wanting a child or children and deciding to have a child are quite different processes. Wanting a child is clearly attitudinal and more malleable than the actual process of having a child. For example, in young adulthood people are slightly more likely to say that they don't want any children, but as they age, they often change their minds. This means that the attitudinal measure of desired number of children is not stable. Furthermore, this brings up the awkward problem of whether those wanting no children are in same category as those wanting one or more. Indeed, in the 1960s there were several social movements to support voluntary childlessness. In addition, there is a significant grey area between those who do not want a child (**voluntary childlessness**) and those who cannot have a child (**involuntary childlessness**). Many people find that after trying to conceive for 12 months or more, they change their desired fertility to "no children." As a result, it is very difficult to know the real reason for wanting no children.

There is reason to believe that the "no children" group should be studied separately from those who desire a child or children. People who do not want children often cite overpopulation, lowering of our ecological footprint, and having time for the conjugal relationship. Indeed, the reasons traditionally cited by scholars for desiring a child simply do not make a lot of sense when applied to those not having children.

On the other hand, it is difficult to assume that *desired family size* represents much of a predictor of actual fertility. On the surface, it may seem that desired family size is the same as what people would do with their fertility if they were unconstrained by economic and social facts (McClelland, 1983). We can chart social and economic shifts, but they fail to act as mediators between desired family size and actual fertility. In other words, desired family size is a relatively poor predictor of actual family size.

When we review the various reasons that people cite for having children, it is not immediately clear why we have a disparity between the number of children people want (higher) and the number of children they actually have (lower). Mitchell and Gray (2007, p. 30) address this question in their research and conclude the following:

> In terms of labour market issues, we find that, of the measures of employment or material security, having a secure job and having a job with opportunities for advancement are far more important to those who expect to have a child in the future. Almost 95 percent of those who expect to have a child in the future say that having a secure job is important or very important, compared with less than 85 percent of those who do not expect to have a child in the future.

Although Mitchell and Gray consider this 10 percent difference to be meaningful, one could argue that the great majority of people (85 to 95 percent) want a secure job regardless of their fertility plans!

If we follow the logic of Mitchell and Gray's argument, the prevalence of contract positions rather than secure jobs with benefits for young people may result in curtailed desired fertility. A closer look at this requires that we examine actual fertility in Canada.

RECENT HISTORY OF FERTILITY IN CANADA

When we turn to an examination of actual fertility, we first need to clarify how fertility is measured. First, fertility is always measured only among women, not couples. At a simple level, we could count the number of live births to women in a year. This method is called the **crude birth rate (CBR)** and it has several drawbacks. The major drawback is that the CBR does not take into account whether the greatest bulk of women are in the early years of their fertility or are in the later years and have largely completed their fertility. For example, if Maggie is 22 years old, wants three children, and so far has one, she may well achieve a convergence between her desired and actual fertility. However, if Maggie is 45 years old, it is much more likely that she will not achieve her desired fertility simply because fewer years remain before menopause.

A better picture of a country's fertility is afforded by a measure called the **total fertility rate (TFR).** The total fertility rate is an estimate of fertility per woman based on the assumptions that (1) she will maintain the cohort rate of fertility for the past year, and (2) she will live to the end of her fertility (usually 45 to 50 years of age). Note that the TFR is an average and is usually reported as the number of children per woman that we expect in Canada. TFR is calculated yearly and is often used for comparisons with other countries. Another useful measure of fertility is age-specific fertility. **Age-specific fertility rates** are simply the number of children born to women in a given year for each age group. We often see ages grouped in five-year increments, such as 20 to 24 and 25 to 29.

We really would like to understand why people decide to remain childless, or have trouble conceiving, or wait so long to decide to have a child. To explain what is happening today, we often need to get a broader historical perspective. Figure 6.1 shows the TFR in Canada for more than 100 years.

Figure 6.1 shows that the TFR in Canada began to decline in 1961 after the postwar baby boom. It should be pointed out that if the baby boom (1941 to 1961) were eliminated, the decline in fertility would be consistent over the entire graph. Indeed, this downward trend is usually seen as part of the **demographic transition** from an agrarian economy favouring large families to an urban-industrial economy favouring small families. Goode (1963) argued that as the world industrializes and urbanizes, children become an economic liability, and therefore the number of children will decrease. As the number of children decreases, couples will spend increasing amounts of time in marital roles rather than parental roles. This change to an emphasis on conjugal roles is further buttressed by ideas of romantic love and individual mate selection. Goode called this new family form the **conjugal family.**

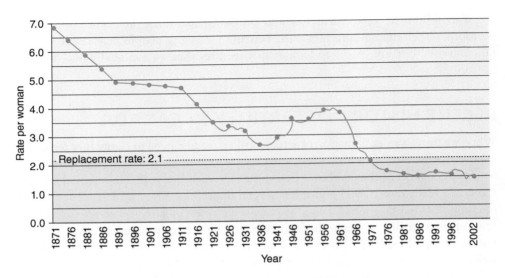

Figure 6.1 Total Fertility Rate, Canada, 1871 to 1996

Source: Health Canada. (2005). Changing fertility patterns: Trends and implications. *Health Policy Research, 10* (May). Reproduced with the permission of the Minister of Health, 2011.

Figure 6.1 also shows that around 1970, the TFR in Canada slipped below replacement level. **Replacement level fertility** is simply the fertility needed to replace each parent with a reproduction-age offspring. Clearly, there are two parents, so the assumption is that we need two children as replacements. The problem is that not all babies will survive to reproduction age. As a result, the TFR we need in Canada is slightly higher than two children (2.13). Each country computes its own replacement level based on child mortality statistics. Dropping below replacement level means that each parent is not replaced. Even though that may be the case, bulges in the population such as the baby boom will ensure that the population does not go into decline. **Population decline** is the point at which more people in a country die than are born (assuming that emigration and immigration are equal). Population decline has some obvious economic consequences since the labour force will shrink and the number of consumers will also shrink. As Career Box 6.1 illustrates, such demographic changes have consequences for your future career choices.

Fertility Timing

Fertility timing influences our measures of intended fertility and actual fertility. As you might guess, it is sometimes very difficult to assess the fertility of an age group (e.g., 20- to 45-year-old cohort) while its members are still in their fertile years. If women in a particular age group decide to delay fertility until 35 years of age, even our estimates of their fertility based on current behaviour would be inaccurate.

Demography and Your Decisions

As you think about declaring a major in university or your career direction, it may be useful to consult the demographic projections for your region, province, and country. Clearly, if fewer children are being born each year and this shortage is not being addressed by immigration, you might want to carefully consider the demand for teachers and child-care workers. Of course, this always must be balanced with other social trends such as mothers' timing for returning to work affecting demand for child care. Demographic trends also tell us about growth sectors. For example, the service sector serving the elderly will grow as the baby boomers enter their retirement years. This provides opportunities for new businesses and services to develop for this particular population bulge. You can access much of this demographic information through publicly available Canadian census data (Statistics Canada).

Furthermore, if women delay their fertility, they may not have sufficient time left in which to conceive in the manner they anticipated or expected. For example, if young women are taking more time to finish their education and then want to get a solid job with benefits before thinking of marriage and having a child, these institutional timing considerations could delay both marriage and fertility (Ranson, 1998). The fact that they wait so long may leave few years for child-bearing. These few years may be further eroded by increasing difficulties with conception among women over age 30 and increasing infertility of male partners due to low sperm counts. This, in turn, could explain some of the difference between the high number for desired fertility and the low number for actual fertility. Obviously, the way we time events such as education and work in our life course has important effects on the timing and even the ability to have children.

We need to take a closer look at the fertility rate in each age group (commonly referred to as age-specific fertility). Figure 6.2 shows that the traditionally most fertile age group (20- to 24-year olds) now has lower fertility than even the 30- to 34-year-old age group. This rather drastic change in fertility patterns since World War II is mainly due to both delay of fertility and increase in childlessness. The "good news" from these data is that teen births are declining, but this is part of an overall trend in fertility decline. Only the older age groups (30- to 34-year-olds and 35- to 39-year-olds) are showing some increase in fertility, but that has to be understood in the context that in most previous historical periods a couple would have completed their fertility by these ages.

Figure 6.3 graphically represents the delay of fertility in Canada. This figure compares fertility by age of the mothers for two years: 1976 and 1996. It is obvious that mothers in 1996 were having children at significantly older ages. What is perhaps less

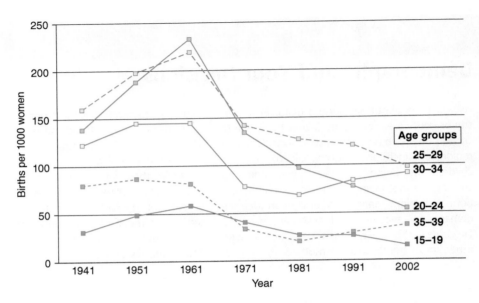

Figure 6.2 Age-Specific Fertility Rates, Selected Age Groups, Canada, 1941 to 2002

Source: Health Canada. (2005). Changing fertility patterns: Trends and implications. *Health Policy Research, 10* (May). Reproduced with the permission of the Minister of Health, 2011.

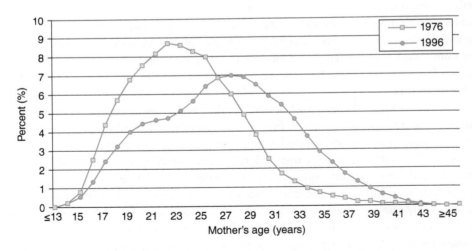

Figure 6.3 Distribution of First Births, by Age of Mother, Canada, 1976 and 1996

Source: Health Canada. (2005). Changing fertility patterns: Trends and implications. *Health Policy Research, 10* (May). Reproduced with the permission of the Minister of Health, 2011.

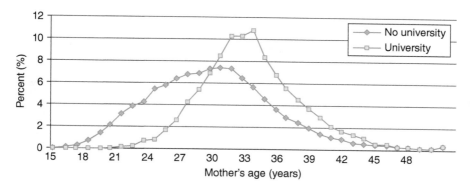

Figure 6.4 Distribution of First-Time Mothers, by Age and Education, Canada, 1996

Source: Health Canada. (2005). Changing fertility patterns: Trends and implications. *Health Policy Research, 10* (May). Reproduced with the permission of the Minister of Health, 2011.

obvious but just as important is the "spread" of the 1996 distribution. The 1996 curve is more spread out (platykurtic) than the more peaked distribution for 1976. Although these data are only limited to two time periods, such changes in distribution might suggest an overall weakening of social norms favouring having children. In general, when we have strong life course norms about the appropriate time to have children, we expect a very peaked distribution (leptokurtic). As timing norms weaken, the curve becomes more spread out (platykurtic). As the classical theorist Emile Durkheim pointed out in his work on suicide, anomie or "normlessness" can indicate social disorganization within an institutional sector of life.

Any attempt to explain why women are delaying fertility would certainly focus on the changing timing norms. Women's participation in the labour force doubled from 1970 to 2000. Previous age cohorts of women often did not enter the labour force until their children were teenagers or older. In 1970, the big switch was that women started to get more education and started their first major jobs after completing their education. Because of these timing changes, marriage and fertility were delayed. Figure 6.4 shows that mothers with post-secondary education are delaying their fertility longer than mothers with no university education. Clearly, extended periods of education are implicated in timing changes.

Education alone does not account for the changes in fertility. Another major factor is economic well-being. Interestingly, Mitchell and Gray (2007, p. 38) report that their sample of Australian couples reveals the following:

> . . . those who expect to have children, attach more emphasis to job security, career advancement and home ownership. Hence, those who want children express greater desire to set up an environment that is suitable to have children.

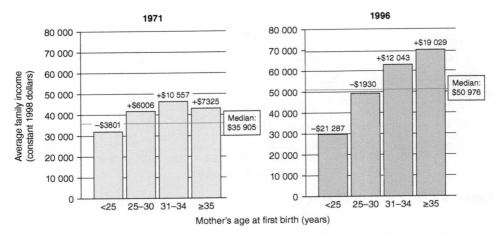

Figure 6.5 Difference between Average and Median Two-Parent Family Incomes, by Mother's Age at First Birth, Canada, 1971 and 1996*

*Data are based on two-parent families with the oldest child being 0–5 years of age. Average and median two-family incomes are measured in constant 1998 dollars.

Source: Health Canada. (2005). Changing fertility patterns: Trends and implications. *Health Policy Research*, 10 (May). Reproduced with the permission of the Minister of Health, 2011.

It is relatively easy to compare the median family incomes for two-parent families by age group of the mothers when they had their first child. Figure 6.5 clearly indicates that couples in 1996 did not achieve the median family income for Canada until the women were age 30 or older and then had their first birth. In contrast, couples in 1971 achieved this level of well-being when the women were about 25 years of age. This suggests that the findings in Mitchell and Gray's Australian sample may have a bearing on Canadian fertility patterns. It seems to suggest that couples who want children might delay fertility in part so that they can achieve a level of economic well-being previously achieved by much younger couples. The fact that achieving this economic well-being now requires two salaries rather than one would seem to be even more of a deterrent to fertility.

It may seem that the timing of fertility is largely irrelevant to Canada's TFR. After all, if a couple plans to have two children, what difference does it make whether the mother intends her fertility to occur between ages 25 and 30 or ages 30 and 35? This does make a difference, however. Certainly, male infertility and, more particularly, female infertility increase with age (Fox, 2000). In addition to infertility problems, problems of conception and miscarriage are associated with the mother's age. Figure 6.6 shows that the rate of miscarriage (spontaneous abortion) is 50 per 1000 married women in their early twenties but increases exponentially to more than 450 per 1000 after age 45. A woman in her late thirties has almost triple the risk of miscarriage as a 20-year-old woman. In 2007, Canada's

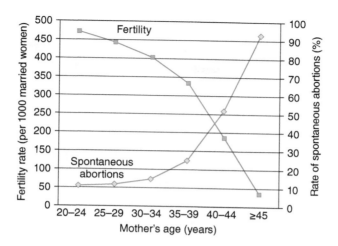

Figure 6.6 Fertility and Miscarriage Rates as a Function of the Mother's Age

Source: Health Canada. (2005). Changing fertility patterns: Trends and implications. *Health Policy Research, 10* (May). Reproduced with the permission of the Minister of Health, 2011.

average age of first-time mothers was 29.3 years, meaning that roughly half were above that age. As a result, some of Canada's lowered TFR is due to biological problems of infertility and miscarriage associated with delays in child-bearing.

CURRENT FERTILITY IN CANADA

The analysis of Canada's recent history of fertility is useful for developing a context in which we can understand current changes in Canadian fertility. The most recent data suggest that fertility in Canada is increasing somewhat. Table 6.1 seems to indicate that Canada is enjoying somewhat of an upward trend in births, although this is not an incipient baby boom. This seeming mini-boom levelled off in 2008 to 377 886 births (see Table 6.1). If we compare this 2008 number with Canada's highest number of births in the 1950s, Canada is producing only about two thirds of that earlier number even though the country's population was only 17 million in 1959 and was 33.5 million in 2008. In other words, Canada is producing many fewer children despite a much larger population

Table 6.1 Number of Births, Canada, 2003–2008

2003	2004	2005	2005	2007	2008
335 202	337 072	342 176	354 617	367 864	377 886

Source: Statistics Canada, Births, 84F0210XWE, September 2009; http://www.statcan.gc.ca/bsolc/olc-cel/olc-cel?lang=eng&catno=84F0210X

Data Box 6.1

Aboriginal People Surpass One-Million Mark

New data from the 2006 Census show that the number of people who identified themselves as an Aboriginal person has surpassed the one-million mark.

A total of 1,172,790 people reported Aboriginal identity, that is, North American Indian (hereafter referred to as First Nations people), Métis or Inuit. The census enumerated 976,305 Aboriginal people in 2001 and 799,010 in 1996.

In 2006, Aboriginal people accounted for 3.8% of the total population of Canada, an increase from 3.3% in 2001 and 2.8% in 1996.

The Aboriginal population has grown faster than the non-Aboriginal population. Between 1996 and 2006, it increased 45%, nearly six times faster than the 8% rate of growth for the non-Aboriginal population over the same period.

Of the three Aboriginal groups, the fastest gain in population between 1996 and 2006 occurred among those who identified themselves as Métis. Their numbers almost doubled (+91%) to an estimated 389,785. This growth rate was nearly three times as fast as the 29% increase in First Nations people, whose numbers reached 698,025. The number of people who identified themselves as Inuit increased 26% to 50,485.

Source: Statistics Canada (2008).

base. Indeed, we have seen only a modest increase in the TFR, to about 1.7 children per woman. The replacement level is about 2.13, so Canada is still very far from even maintaining its population through reproduction (or natural increase).

The type of relationship into which children are born has also changed dramatically over the last few decades. Increasingly, Canadian children are born to couples in cohabiting relationships or to single, never-married females rather than to married couples. It is interesting to note that, in Canada, 26.2 percent of births are to single, never-married females versus 61.6 percent of births to legally married couples. The most surprising fact about this is the rather incredible variation across different provinces. While only 11.6 percent of births in Ontario are to single, never-married women, British Columbia has a rate of 18 percent, Quebec has a rate of 59.9 percent, and Nunavut has a rate of more than 75 percent. Part of this variation results from the popularity of cohabitation in certain regions and the fact that cohabiting females are classified as single, never married. Regardless of classification, it is clear that births to single, never-married, and cohabiting women are increasing (Statistics Canada, 2006b).

In a monograph titled *Families Count*, the Vanier Institute of the Family (2010) concludes that given the current rate of decline in fertility, with the exception of the Aboriginal population (see Data Box 6.1), Canada cannot expect to maintain its population relative to death past 2030. At that point, the country would slip into population decline. Furthermore, they state that "International immigration is now the primary population growth engine, accounting for two-thirds of growth in 2006" (Vanier Institute of the Family, 2010, p. 4). They continue with the implication that after Canada reaches zero population growth in 2030, any population growth after that must be tied to immigration.

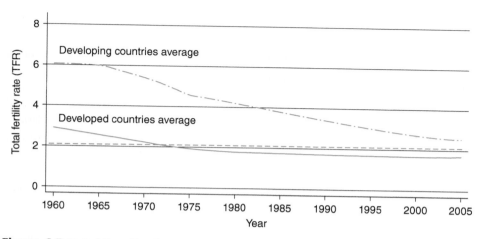

Figure 6.7 Total Fertility Rate over Time in High- and Low-Development Countries, Weighted by Population Size

Note: The population weights are based on 2000 population estimates. The dashed line represents replacement fertility (TFR = 2.1).

The implications of zero population growth can be seen as salutary from an ecological perspective and devastating from an economic perspective. From an ecological perspective, declining population could mean a smaller ecological footprint. Economically, however, we can sell our goods and services to our national population and see economic growth only if either the population is growing or we can convince consumers to buy increasing amounts of goods. Both of these scenarios are unlikely in a declining population with fewer children, teachers, schools, and houses needed. On the other hand, we can sell our goods and services to other countries if they represent consumer markets for us. This leads us to take a quick look at what is happening in other countries.

Worldwide, fertility is clearly declining. There is considerable variation as to the explanation for the decline, including human development indices that track education and health and women's labour force participation. Perhaps the clearest statement in this regard has been made by one of the leading demographers studying fertility, S. Philip Morgan. Morgan and Rackin (2010) present data showing that the average and country-specific TFRs have declined (see Figure 6.7). You can examine this for yourself by using the following tool: http://homepage3.nifty.com/sociology/motion.html. Clearly, developed countries have been below replacement level since the early 1970s but developing countries are approaching the replacement level as well.

Like many other developed nations, Canada is approaching a point of population decline where there are more deaths than births. Population for any year is defined by the following formula.

$$\text{Population (January 2010)} = \text{Population (January 2009)} + (\text{Births} + \text{Immigration}) - (\text{Deaths} + \text{Emigration})$$

Canada will be competing with many other countries for immigrants to maintain its population. The country is currently on track to begin population decline in 2030, so actions must be taken to redress this outcome, either by increasing the natural birth rate or by increasing immigration.

The assumption that immigration could solve both short-term labour shortages and longer-term fertility problems may be too optimistic. Indeed, Caron Malenfant and Belanger (2006) have demonstrated that visible minority women's fertility in Canada mainly falls below replacement level. Only in South Asian, Arab, and West African groups was fertility above replacement level, and that was probably due to these being more recent immigrant groups. Indeed, further analysis of data from the Ethnic Diversity Survey (Statistics Canada, 2003a) found that being in the first immigrant generation explains much of the variation in fertility among visible minority groups.

Many countries, such as France, have tried pro-natalist policies and some countries, such as Germany (via Chancellor Angela Merkel), have gone on record as saying that the policy of multiculturalism, which is tied to large-scale immigration, does not work. The perceived failure of multiculturalism in Europe has not yet surfaced in Canada. What is in doubt is whether immigration can address the shortfall in fertility. Indeed, Canada would have to increase its immigration rate considerably to keep from falling into population decline. It is perhaps even more important to maintain a labour force that can support the aging population. Therefore, even though immigration may not address fertility, it does address labour shortages. The only real alternative for countries eschewing immigration and multiculturalism is to pursue some form of pro-natalist policy to address fertility. Much of Europe has already made this investment, with varying degrees of success. Some of these policies include universal daycare, extensive paid parental leave, and payments or tax credits for births. In North America (with the exception of Quebec), we have not yet squarely addressed fertility as a problem. We can expect to see continuing debates throughout the world as countries try to address both labour and fertility shortages.

THE TRANSITION TO PARENTHOOD

Although the actual fertility rates in developed nations are below the replacement level of about 2.13, it is useful to recall that people continue to desire more children. As we have seen, some of the difference between desired and actual fertility results from delaying marriage and fertility to acquire post-secondary education and cement one's workforce participation and experience. We also noted that couples delay first birth until they feel financially stable and are living in an environment conducive to having a child. Now we turn our attention to the transition to parenthood.

The transition to parenthood is of great interest to family scholars for two reasons. First, this transition represents the assumption of the most responsible roles in a family, those of mother and father. These roles are well defined by both informal and formal social norms. While the roles are informally defined by expectations that parents will nurture their children, they are also formally and legally defined by laws governing parental abandonment, child neglect, and abuse. Even such areas as child discipline are surrounded by both formal and informal norms, which at times may be contradictory. The next chapter on parenting will develop some of these topics more fully.

The other major reason that the study of the transition to parenthood is important to family scholars is more practical. For several decades, we have known that the transition to parenthood is usually accompanied by significant declines in most areas of the marriage. Even though marriages with a child are more stable than marriages without a child at the same duration of time, these marriages may contain greater conflict and less love than was the case before the child joined the family. From a practical standpoint, we study this transition to solve the mystery about the decline in marriage.

Getting Pregnant and Pregnancy

Although most of us assume that the transition to parenthood begins with pregnancy, there is some evidence to suggest that the course of the marriage and indeed some child outcomes are tied to the "style" the couple adopts toward pregnancy. Cowan and Cowan (1999) argue that those who plan to initiate sex with the idea of having a child are in many ways better prepared throughout other phases of the transition to parenthood. On the other hand, some couples just stop using birth control and adopt a "whatever happens" attitude. Like the "sliders" discussed in the cohabitation studies, these couples are generally less prepared throughout the transition to parenthood.

We have already discussed involuntary infertility, but it should be clear that problems in conceiving a child are more noticeable to those who carefully plan intercourse during ovulation. We do not know all of the causes of involuntary fertility, but several have been speculated on in the popular press. One of these is the significant lower live sperm counts among males. The reasons for these lower live sperm counts are not clear but speculation has pointed to a host of environmental causes such as tight-fitting briefs

and plastic bottles containing synthetic estrogens. Female infertility is most commonly attributed to ovulation disorders, fallopian tube blockages, or pelvic inflammatory disease. Although estimates in Canada are difficult to come by, one preliminary estimate is that 7 percent were unsuccessful when measured over two years of attempting to get pregnant while 8.5 percent were unsuccessful when measured over one year (Norris, 2001).

Pregnancy is usually divided into three phases or trimesters. Although gestation to term is usually slightly longer than nine months, each trimester is roughly three months in duration. Although many discussions of pregnancy focus on the development of the fetus, our interest is in the developing couple. Each trimester has certain events that define it as unique for the couple and make it a developmental stage for them as well as for the baby.

In the first trimester, the couple discovers that they are going to have a child. Usually, suspicions of pregnancy are confirmed by a visit to a doctor. At that time, a series of appointments are scheduled to check on the development of the fetus. For planners, there is usually little ambiguity about the positive nature of the news, whereas for "sliders" the news may contain some ambiguity about the timing and whether a child is really wanted. For **primiparous** (first-time) mothers, the first trimester also is a source of anxiety since this is the most probable time for a miscarriage. Of course, if there is ambivalence about having the child and then there is a miscarriage, this usually results in feelings of guilt despite the fact that there is no evidence that ambivalence is related to miscarriages. The first trimester is also usually identified by "morning sickness" or nausea, although this may extend into other trimesters.

The second trimester is often reported by women as the most enjoyable trimester. Weight and balance are usually not yet a problem and many adjustments to being pregnant have already been made. In the second trimester, several diagnostic interventions such as amniocentesis may be suggested. Perhaps the least intrusive of these is ultrasound. Although these were routine at an earlier time in many areas, most provinces no longer fund this for all pregnancies. Many of these diagnostic interventions are routine for women over age 35 or with pre-existing risk factors.

The third trimester is important because the child will be born at the end of it. As a result, it usually involves preparations such as booking a hospital room, readying the child's room, and, perhaps most important, attending prenatal classes. Prenatal classes are essential for both partners to attend because as the couple draws up a birthing plan, the partner will know under what conditions the woman may want an epidural or other pain remediation. The experience of meeting other expectant parents who are at the same stage of pregnancy can be reassuring. Some prenatal classes also discuss post-birth issues such as diapers and bathing. After the prenatal classes, the couple usually packs a bag that will be ready to go to the hospital with them.

The First Birth and the Decline of Marriage

For the great majority of couples, the birth of a first child is a major life course transition. For some, this will be a home birth but for most, the birth will occur in a hospital. There is no doubt that hospitals socialize the new parents about many facets of early child care. Most hospitals offer assistance with and endorsement of breastfeeding the baby because of the protective maternal antibodies contained in breast milk and the overall nutritional value of breast milk. Another area addressed is how to hold and bathe the baby. Usually, the new parents take their child home within a few days of the birth. Some have equipped themselves with a list of things to check when the baby cries, such as wet diaper, last feeding, and so on. Unlike in some previous generations, first-time parents today are unlikely to have had infant brothers or sisters under their care or to have had much experience with infants.

Feeney et al. (2001) asked first-time parents what they disliked most about being first-time parents. As you may have guessed, most parents said that lack of sleep was unpleasant (48 percent), followed by not knowing what to do (35 percent). Certainly, these two factors could be related, though no examination of that was conducted by Feeney et al. At the beginning of the previous century, larger families afforded siblings experience in dealing with younger children as part of anticipatory socialization for parenthood. In addition, adult siblings may have experienced some anticipatory socialization when caring for a new nephew or niece. With increasingly smaller family size, these opportunities to learn are less available. Indeed, while preparation for birth is supported by prenatal classes, preparation for parenthood has yet to receive much support or attention. We will return to this issue later in this section. For now, note that it is not surprising that new parents report not knowing what to do as a problem.

Feeney et al. (2001) also report the "best" things that new parents list. The baby smiling (45 percent) and simply having the baby (31 percent) are mentioned at a relatively high rate compared to "being closer to my spouse" (10 percent). Many of the joys of having a first child are tied to either the increasing developmental and interactional ability of the infant or the notion of being a family. The early growth and development of the child as witnessed by increasingly complex parent and child interactions is an early source of joy. As well, by adding a child and becoming a family with the fully adult roles of mother and father, the couple attains a socially and legally recognized status.

Regardless of the joys, or even the hardships, of having a first child, most scholars have noted that this transition event is tied to changes in the course of the marriage. This was first noted by Blood and Wolfe (1960) in their landmark study of married couples in Detroit. They observed that the majority of wives were very satisfied with their marriages in the first few years of marriage, but that after 20 years only 6 percent were very satisfied. This research supplied impetus for scholars to examine marital satisfaction and marital quality throughout the life course of the family. The findings in this area have been very consistent. Starting with the life satisfaction research of Campbell, Converse, and Rogers (1976) and followed by that of Rollins and Feldman (1980), there has been a consistent finding that marital satisfaction follows a U-shaped curve (see Chapter 5, Figure 5.6) across stages of the family life course. This finding has been replicated by many other researchers in the United States (Anderson, Russell, & Schumm, 1983) and Canada (Lupri & Frideres, 1981; Rhyne, 1981). Only the U.S. study by Valiant and Valiant (1993) has failed to show strong support for this curvilinear relationship.

In the present context, we are only interested in the first two stages of this curve: the decline of marital satisfaction from the wedding day to the birth of the first child. Of course, it could be argued that this decline is simply the result of newly married couples moving from the romantic idealization of their partners to a more realistic viewpoint. This perspective would focus on a continuous decline as newly married couples find out increasingly accurate information about each other. Although some of this general decline may be due to removing the "rose-coloured glasses" of romantic love, researchers have discovered a much more abrupt process in the decline of marital satisfaction.

The decline in marital variables was first noted by Rossi (1968), although she focused mainly on the role of mother. She believed that the difficulties experienced in the transition to parenthood for mothers were due to four factors: the lack of support for a lifestyle other than motherhood, the shift in emphasis from the marital role to the mother role, the abruptness of this transition, and the lack of guidelines and support for parenthood. While all four of these factors may still make some sense today, we have come a very long way from the "lock-step" conformity of the 1960s about the automatic assumption of the mother role and the lack of lifestyle alternatives to motherhood. Rossi's (1968) study sparked decades of scholarly research on the transition to parenthood. Her work was followed by that of many scholars, including Russell (1974), LaRossa and LaRossa (1981), and Belsky, Spanier, and Rovine (1983).

Belsky et al. (1983) made a particularly instructive contribution to the study of the transition to parenthood because they followed a panel of married couples across three time points in the transition: pregnancy, three months postpartum, and six months postpartum. They concluded that statistically significant declines in many of their measures of marriage were evident for both husbands and wives with the first birth. This was followed by further analysis by Belsky, Lang, and Rovine (1985).

The most definitive statement about the changes in marriage associated with the first birth results from the three-year longitudinal study by Belsky and Rovine (1990). In this study, Belsky and Rovine followed married couples from pregnancy to three years postpartum. Their findings are unequivocal. Both husbands and wives showed significant declines on measures of marriage. The authors found that wives declined on all four measures, reporting decreased love, increased amount of perceived conflict, less effort on relationship maintenance, and more ambivalence about the marriage. Husbands reported declines in all areas except perceived conflict (see Table 6.2). Belsky and Rovine also tested for whether this was a linear or curvilinear (getting worse and then better) decline. They found that all trends were linear, with no support for measures improving after three years postpartum. Perhaps the only good news in their study was that while 75 percent of new parents declined, 25 percent of couples in their sample either stayed the same or improved on measures. This leads to an obvious question: Why and how do couples improve their relationships in the transition to parenthood?

Although we do not have a complete understanding of all factors that contribute to the decline of marriage during the transition to parenthood, Canadian researchers Cowan and Cowan (1999) shed considerable light on some of the major factors. They studied married couples over a 10-year period. During this time, many couples had a child and some opted to remain childless. The couples that had a pregnancy were followed throughout the

Table 6.2 Mean Husband and Wife Marriage Scores

Scale	Time of Measurement					Trend	
	Prenatal	3 Months	9 Months	36 Months	F	Linear	Quadratic
Wife							
(n = 128)							
df					3,381	1,127	1,127
Love	80.63	77.78	75.30	74.00	22.80***	51.02***	ns
Conflict	20.52	21.10	22.22	22.65	8.39***	18.35***	ns
Ambivalence	10.11	10.59	12.39	13.04	14.34***	28.46***	ns
Maintenance	31.77	29.80	28.64	28.27	20.91***	49.74***	5.46*
Husband							
(n = 117)							
df					3,348	1,116	1,116
Love	75.54	74.33	73.54	71.02	10.36***	23.51***	ns
Conflict	20.11	20.07	20.82	20.40	ns	ns	ns
Ambivalence	13.31	13.98	14.41	14.84	2.88*	5.43*	ns
Maintenance	29.92	28.89	28.53	27.09	12.25***	28.54***	ns

*$p < .05$. ***$p < .001$.

Source: Belsky and Rovine (1990).

duration of the study. Cowan and Cowan used both quantitative measures and interviews in this study. Because of the richness of the data, they were able to address the question of why and how couples prosper or flounder in the transition to parenthood. The answers are complex, of course, but overall a picture emerged about the expectations couples have regarding this new stage of the life course (being a family) and how these expectations could end up being disappointed.

For many couples, the most egalitarian roles in intimate relationships are found in cohabitation. Certainly, with the addition of the marital roles of husband and wife, the relationship becomes slightly less egalitarian. For the most part, however, marital roles before children are also egalitarian. Each partner negotiates and takes on part of the household labour and each is likely to maintain full-time employment in the workforce. When the woman becomes pregnant, the couple usually decides who will take parental leave, based on who is earning the higher salary, the need for rest after the labour of childbirth, and breastfeeding. Considering all this, it often appears to be "rational" that the woman should stay at home. Women tend to earn on average 80 to 90 percent of what men at the same level earn, and women of course give birth and breastfeed. Even though breast milk can be expressed and stored, this practice requires an understanding employer and on-site refrigeration. So, for many couples, the decision that the woman rather than the man will take parental leave seems "rational." This seemingly "rational" decision, however, begins to change the egalitarian marital roles and division of labour to much more gendered and non-egalitarian traditional roles.

With the birth of the baby, the mother is suddenly placed in a role in which she is expected to know more about the infant's care than the father. Cowan and Cowan document that this expectation is not only held by the couple but is also invoked and reinforced by the father's parents. Not only does the woman's role as mother intensify in ways she may not have anticipated, but the man also takes on his primary socially defined role as "breadwinner," often investing more hours and energy in work because of his new family responsibilities. As this role intensifies for the new father, work is seen from a family perspective as making legitimate "demands" on his time and energy, pulling him even farther from any egalitarian distribution of household labour. The father may come home in the evening tired from work only to find that the mother wants time away from the constant demands of the infant. The father may further expect that since his wife is home all day, she should naturally take care of the cleaning, cooking, and domestic chores. What transpires is that the couple that envisaged "being in this together" and "sharing the workload" of the baby suddenly finds themselves in the traditional roles they witnessed in their parents' and grandparents' relationships. The disappointment of these violated expectations of egalitarianism and the reality of the unexpected traditional roles create conflict between the couple regarding household labour, the value of each person's work, and the denial of help when both partners are exhausted from lack of sleep.

Certainly, the role of mother is increasingly intensified in our society. One example of this intensification is breastfeeding the baby. Most new mothers return to work somewhere between six months and one year postpartum (Statistics Canada, 2006f). Based on 2003 estimates, about 28.6 percent of infants aged six months to one year are in alternative care and 56.1 percent are in alternative care after one year of age (Statistics Canada, 2006e). The worldwide campaign by UNICEF and the World Health Organization (see Box 6.1) to have all mothers breastfeed their babies has placed some pressure on new mothers to make significant adaptations to achieve the breastfeeding goals. Many new mothers may wish to place their child in the care of a relative or in infant daycare when they return to work. However, if they are to continue feeding their infant breast milk once they return to work, they must express the milk using a breast pump and have refrigeration available. Of course, many offices are not equipped for these activities. The preferred situation would be work site infant care facilities, but such facilities are few. It is difficult for relatives and fathers to participate in infant feeding without the woman expressing and bottling her milk. Thus, the general expectation that mothers will breastfeed intensifies the gender specialization and reinforces traditional roles that move many couples further from an egalitarian division of labour.

The intensification of the gendered division of labour, the move away from egalitarianism, and the assumption of more traditional roles may all provide difficulties to marital relationships. However, recall that a few couples actually improve their relationships with the birth of the first child. This information led Cowan and Cowan (1999) to investigate ways to improve marital relationships for new parents. During the course of their 10-year study, Cowan and Cowan identified an intervention strategy. The strategy

Box 6.1

Baby-Friendly Hospital Initiative (BFHI)

In Canada the BFHI is overseen by the Breast-feeding Committee for Canada.

The BFHI is a global program initiated in 1991 by the World Health Organization (WHO) and the United Nations Children's Fund (UNICEF) in response to the Innocenti Declaration (1990). This program encourages and recognizes hospitals and maternity facilities that offer an optimal level of care for mothers and infants. A Baby-Friendly™ hospital/maternity facility focuses on the needs of the newborns and empowers mothers and families to give their infant the best possible start in life. In practical terms, a Baby-Friendly™ hospital/maternity facility encourages and helps women to successfully initiate and continue to breastfeed their babies, and will receive special recognition for having done so. Since the inception of the program, over 15,000 hospitals worldwide have received the Baby-Friendly designation.

The BFHI protects, promotes and supports breastfeeding through the Ten Steps to Successful Breast-feeding developed by UNICEF and the World Health Organization. In order to achieve Baby-Friendly™ designation, every hospital and maternity facility must:

1. Have a written breastfeeding policy that is routinely communicated to all health care staff.
2. Train all health care staff in skills necessary to implement this policy.
3. Inform all pregnant women about the benefits and management of breastfeeding.
4. Help mothers to initiate breastfeeding within a half-hour of birth.
5. Show mothers how to breastfeed and how to maintain lactation even if they should be separated from their infants.
6. Give newborn infants no food or drink other than breast milk, unless medically indicated.
7. Practice rooming-in, allow mothers and infants to remain together—24 hours a day.
8. Encourage breastfeeding on demand.
9. Give no artificial teats or pacifiers (also called dummies or soothers) to breastfeeding infants.
10. Foster the establishment of breastfeeding support groups and refer mothers to them on discharge from the hospital or clinic.

A Baby-Friendly™ hospital/maternity facility also adheres to the International Code of Marketing of Breast-milk Substitutes (1981). The Code seeks to protect breastfeeding by ensuring the ethical marketing of breastmilk substitutes by industry. The Code includes these ten important provisions:

1. No advertising of products under the scope of the Code to the public.
2. No free samples to mothers.
3. No promotion of products in health care facilities, including the distribution of free or low-cost supplies.
4. No company representatives to advise mothers.
5. No gifts or personal samples to health workers.
6. No words or pictures idealizing artificial feeding, including pictures of infants on products.
7. Information to health workers should be scientific and factual.
8. All information on artificial feeding, including the labels should explain the benefits of breastfeeding and all costs and hazards associated with artificial feeding.
9. Unsuitable products such as sweetened condensed milk should not be promoted for babies.
10. Products should be of a high quality and take account of the climatic and storage conditions of the country where they are used.

For more information about the Baby-Friendly Hospital Initiative, and the new Baby-Friendly Initiative in Community Health Services, please visit the Breastfeeding Committee for Canada.

Source: http://www.bcbabyfriendly.ca/BFHI.html

was simply to assist the couple during the pregnancy stage to talk realistically about the expectation each had for the postpartum division of labour as well as the social values and expectations of family and friends surrounding them. Although this could not be called an experimental test of the intervention strategy, the resulting difference in divorce rates certainly provides grounds for optimism. Cowan and Cowan (1999) report that six years after the beginning of their study, 20 percent of the new parents divorced compared with 50 percent of the childless couples, but only 4 percent of the couples in the intervention group divorced. Even though we may not have complete understanding of the factors contributing to marital declines during the transition to parenthood, there is certainly every reason to encourage prenatal discussions of accurate and realistic expectations for husbands and wives after the birth. Though not an argument in favour of traditionalism, it is likely that couples who adjust best to some of the postpartum realities are those who were most traditional even before pregnancy.

CONCLUSION

This chapter has traversed diverse areas of academic and scholarly research. The macroscopic discussion of worldwide declines in fertility is in bold relief to the microscopic declines of marital happiness with the birth of the first child. Yet both of these pictures of child-bearing are consistent with one another. At the macroscopic level, fertility is declining in most of the world and many developed nations will soon be entering population decline with all of its attendant economic and social implications. At the microscopic level, the first birth provides more challenges to egalitarian couples than it did to their parents or grandparents who had more traditional role expectations. These perspectives may seem overwhelming except that Cowan and Cowan (1999) point out that couples can talk about and renegotiate roles. Certainly, when we move to Chapter 7 on parenting, some of these themes will surface once again.

What are the ramifications for you of below replacement level fertility in Canada? Are you more likely to start a business selling walkers for the elderly than toys for children? During your lifetime, will schools and playgrounds become increasingly deserted? Will all countries in the developed world seek major increases in immigration to deal with workforce shortages? Undoubtedly there will be serious repercussions, but these will be spread over decades rather than a few years.

The transition to parenthood is changing dramatically. In the middle of the last century, almost all couples that had a child were married. Even those who had premarital pregnancies were soon married. Today, children are increasingly born to single, never-married, and cohabiting women. We know that the cohabiting relationship is the most egalitarian of family stages, so the dramatic changes in division of labour that accompany being parents may be even more uncomfortable for cohabiting couples. This discomfort with the demands of the parental role could spark a revolution in parenting, with fathers taking on more responsibilities for child care. However, it is also possible that these changes could simply further dampen fertility in Canada.

SUMMARY OF KEY POINTS

- The major reasons people often state for wanting a child are cited by social scientists as the following:
  - Conformity to others
  - Having the life experience
  - Increasing social integration (social capital)
  - Old age security
  - Entertainment
- Desired fertility is higher than actual fertility in most developed nations.
- While reports of voluntary childlessness may be confused with involuntary childlessness, it is clear that involuntary childlessness is increasing in North America.
- Mitchell and Gray (2007) argue that fertility timing is specifically linked to having a secure job.
- Canada's total fertility rate (TFR) has been below replacement level since 1971.
- Demographic transition theory argues that urbanization and industrialization (modernization) are related to lower fertility.
- The only age groups of women with slight increases in fertility are those 30 to 34 and 35 to 39 years of age.
- Post-secondary education is associated with women being older at the birth of their first child.
- Economic security measured by median family income is reached on average five years later today than in the 1970s.
- As women age past 21 years, fertility declines and the risk of miscarriage increases.
- Fertility is declining in both developed and developing nations of the world (see Figure 6.7).
- Many measures of marital happiness decline between the first birth and three years postpartum.
- Many aspects of the division of labour with infants are gendered, such as who takes parental leave and breastfeeding.
- Egalitarian expectations for the marriage after the birth of the first child may be unrealistic and should be discussed before the birth.

Critical Thinking Questions

1. Would you prefer to see Canada's population become larger, smaller, or stay the same? What are the economic and social costs attached to your preference?

2. If Canadians do not want to have children and the country cannot get sufficient levels of immigration to renew its labour force and tax base, should the government embark on

producing children in laboratory settings and training them in institutional daycare? Is this much different from today's two working parents sending their children to full-time infant daycare?

3. How do you think that early child care and nurturance can be made less gendered? How do breastfeeding initiatives and parental leave policies fit into your perspective?

Glossary

actual fertility Recorded live births collected as vital statistics.

age-specific fertility rates The number of children born to women in a given year for each age group. Often ages are grouped in five-year increments, such as 20 to 24 and 25 to 29.

conjugal family Goode's (1963) name for the small nuclear family form that emphasizes the conjugal or marital roles over the parental roles, in part because small family size means that less of one's lifetime will be spent in the parental role and more will be spent in the marital role with children having left home.

crude birth rate (CBR) The number of live births in a country in a given year.

demographic transition The change in fertility associated with changing from an agrarian economy that favours large families to an urban-industrial economy that favours small families.

desired (intended) fertility The number of children women say they would like to have by the time they complete their fertility.

involuntary childlessness The inability to conceive and birth a child after 12 months of unprotected sex.

parental role This role is composed of both formal norms (laws) and informal norms about the level of care, economic and social support, nurturance, discipline, and protection adults are responsible for regarding their children.

population decline The point at which more people die than are born (assuming that emigration and immigration are equal).

primiparous First-time mothers or couples.

replacement level fertility The fertility needed to replace each parent with a reproduction-age offspring.

social capital The network of relationships to which an individual has access.

timing norms Refer to age- and duration-graded relationships.

total fertility rate (TFR) An estimate of fertility per woman based on the assumption that (1) she will maintain the cohort rate of fertility for the past year, and (2) she will live to the end of her fertility (usually 45 to 50 years of age).

transition point An instantaneous point in time at which we demarcate one stage from another (e.g., the past stage from the new, current stage). For example, no matter how much preparation and anticipatory socialization a couple experiences, they do not become parents until the moment of their child's birth.

voluntary childlessness The decision and practice of birth control techniques to avoid having children.

Connections

www.bbc.co.uk/news/uk-england-cambridgeshire-13335037
www.medicalvideos.us/videos/1294/
http://homepage3.nifty.com/sociology/motion.html
www.youtube.com/watch?v=LJxshHjUvPc
www.gallup.com/poll/9871/1997-Global-Study-Family-Values.aspx
www.cprn.org/documents/46993_en.pdf
www.med.uottawa.ca/sim/data/Birth_Rates_e.htm
www5.statcan.gc.ca/cansim/pick-hoisir?lang=eng&searchTypeByValue=1&id=1024506
www.statcan.gc.ca/daily-quotidien/070619/dq070619d-eng.htm
www.statcan.gc.ca/pub/89-599-m/89-599-m2006003-eng.pdf

Remember to log on to the Companion Website at **www.pearsoncanada.ca/white** to find self-graded quizzes and useful resource tools for further study. You can log on to the Companion Website using the Student Access Code that comes packaged with your copy of *Families Across the Life Course*.

Chapter 7
Parent–Child Relationships

Learning Objectives

After reading this chapter, you should be able to:

1. Think about the goals of parenting in our society.

2. Critically explore preformational and experiential views about how children acquire knowledge and skills.

3. Understand the major sociogenic theories of child development.

4. Understand the "spanking debate" within the larger context of parental disciplinary techniques and child outcomes.

5. Explore the nature and transmission of social class from parents to children.

"What kind of parents are they? Their children are running all over the grocery store and they are going to knock something or somebody over," Ivana said indignantly.

Ivana's husband, Thomas, watched as the two children pulled cans off the shelf. "Ivana, I think they may be reading the labels! Perhaps they are just a little careless in their enthusiasm."

Just then, Maggie, the children's mom, strolled up with a shopping cart and said to her children, "Okay, which brand of tomato soup has the lowest calories and the highest protein?" The children correctly identified the brand and the relevant information while Maggie returned the cans to the shelf.

Ivana was still indignant. "Those unruly brats not only created a mess but, true to their upbringing, she couldn't even get them to clean up after themselves. She should have spanked them and made them pick up those cans after pulling them off the shelf! Of course, given where those kids are heading, they will get to do a lot of grocery shelf stocking in their future professions."

Ivana has many very firm ideas about how children should be raised. For example, she seems to favour obedient and well-behaved children over children who are exploring and more independent from their parents. Ivana assumes that such lack of discipline will result in these children not having high-status occupations. Furthermore, Ivana seems to think that children should be physically punished when they are not behaving well. Many may share her opinions, or some aspects of her position. This raises some very basic questions about parents and children. For example, we could ask: To what degree are parents the "cause" of their children's behaviour? We could also ask: Should parents primarily emphasize control of children, or are values about learning more important than being well behaved? Finally, we could ask if Ivana is correct: Will well-behaved and parentally disciplined children be successful as adults, and will the wayward children in the grocery store example have a more modest destiny?

Certainly, different parents will emphasize different techniques of parenting, such as intellectual challenges and discipline. Furthermore, the relationship that each parent builds with each child will be different as well. Of course, the nature of the work world and the economy do not always afford parents the choices they may prefer. Despite economic factors or even the personalities of each parent, almost all parents want the best outcomes for their children and would like their children to become independent adults. In a very important sense, the major goal of parenting (at least in North America) is the child's achievement of self-sufficiency and independence from the parents. That is, the goal is that children become independent "grown-ups."

Although this may seem like an obvious goal for parents in North America, it has not been the historical goal for many families. Indeed, most agrarian societies have viewed children as an economic resource to supply agricultural labour or home production of goods such as clothing. The Industrial Revolution changed this gradually.

At first, children could be employed in industry to the benefit of the parents. So, until the mid 1800s, parents could view children as an economic asset.

The major turning point when children shifted from an economic asset to an economic liability occurred because of two events. The first was the passage of child protection legislation in most industrialized countries to curb the exploitation of children. The second event was a bit more complicated. Since industrialism demands skills such as counting and record keeping, formal education became valued for all, not just for an elite few. With the advent of mass education came legislation that required children to attend school. As a result, children could not be in the labour force because they were in school. Mandatory schooling also made children more expensive. During agrarianism, children paid for their food, shelter, and clothing through their labour. With mandatory education, not only was the child's labour lost to the parents, but children now had to be provided with transportation, school supplies, and eventually expensive brand-name clothing and cellphones (see Goode, 1963; Parsons, 1954).

Although things are changing rapidly, parents in many developing countries still expect their children to stay with the family and eventually take care of them when they are elderly. Although the expectation of taking care of elderly parents vanishes as soon as countries develop old age security systems (Zhao, 2009), many in these semi-agrarian countries do not view children's independence from the parents as the goal of parenting. They view the goal of parenting somewhat more from the perspective that the adult child should repay the family with economic and service contributions.

Most North Americans and Europeans have embraced the goal of parenting as the successful rearing of the children to adulthood. The defining element is the interpretation of *success*. For North Americans, success means that the adult child is economically independent from the parents. Economic independence is usually viewed as the child's achievement of social integration and academic achievement. So, for many parents, the two major components of child rearing are to imbue the child with social skills and to help him or her achieve academically.

It would seem that today's parents simply want their children to grow up to be independent, and that entails developing the children's social and academic skills. This seems simple, but there is a great division among parents and even scholars as to how we can best achieve these outcomes. This chapter is about parent–child relationships. There are, however, many approaches to conceptualizing what this means and there are several theories about parental socialization of children. This is a large and complicated area of discourse and we will be able to touch on only some of the most salient topics, such as socialization, parental discipline and its effects on the child, and the transmission of social class.

MODELS OF PARENT–CHILD EFFECTS

Even Socrates (in Plato's *Meno, circa* 500 bc) was concerned with the socialization and learning of children. Indeed, in the early Socratic dialogues, two positions were argued. One position was that all learning depends on experience (**empiricism**); this would later become tied to the idea that children are a blank slate (John Locke's *tabula rasa*) upon which experience and socialization write. On the other hand, Socrates also argues in favour of the perspective that every human carries pre-existing forms of knowledge, especially analytic forms (**rationalism**). In this perspective, our experience is seen as requiring these pre-existing mental forms of analysis to process the information from experience.

When we "fast forward" to today, we still find these two distinct schools of thought about experience and forms of knowledge. Academically, we can find expressions of the pre-existing forms perspective in developmental theories of language (Chomsky) and cognition (Piaget). Even though these have been dominant theories, we also find the experiential theories to be powerful. We will have more to say about this when we review some of these theories later in the chapter.

These theories of learning and socialization have had an enormous influence on our concepts of parent–child relationships. As indicated, the experiential or empiricist view is associated with the idea that the child is a blank slate upon which experience writes. Because of this perspective, parenting involves writing upon the slate and monitoring access to others writing upon this blank slate. This perspective is one in which all effects on the child flow unidirectionally from the parents to the child (Peterson & Hann, 1999). This is often referred to as the **parent-to-child unidirectional model**.

As early as Hippocrates (500 bc), scholars discussed theories of "humours," which today are referred to as personality traits or temperament. Early personality theorists (e.g., Thomas, Chess, & Birch, 1968) pioneered the idea that children had innate differences in temperament from birth and that these differences must be considered in assessing child development. It became clear within this perspective that children were not simply blank slates at birth and that the success of parenting techniques could be dependent on the child's temperament. Certainly, the idea that a "difficult child" or a child with colic would have effects on the parents was not new. The perspective that the child's temperament affects the parents can be considered a **child-to-parent unidirectional model** (Peterson & Hann, 1999). Although the parent-to-child unidirectional flow was much more dominant in the scholarly literature, the idea that the child could have unidirectional effects quickly gave rise to the **bidirectional parent–child model**.

The bidirectional model evolved not only because of the work on child temperament but also because of advances in sociological theory, especially exchange theory. Richer (1968) amply illustrated the effect of exchange theory when he applied its propositions to the parent–child dyad. It was important, Richer noted, that the child could reward the parent with smiles for the parent's good behaviour and cries for the parent's bad behaviour as an interpretation of an interchange; such interchanges had previously been assumed by scholars to have all socializing power and effects flowing from parent to child. Bidirectionality is now assumed in most child developmental theories (e.g., Bronfenbrenner, 1979) and parent–child research (e.g., Peterson & Hann, 1999).

Today's bidirectional effects model assumes that, even in infancy, the child influences and conditions the interactions with parents and the parents influence the child.

It is just as important to recognize that parent–child interaction is dynamic over time, so that what would be perceived as nurturing socialization at one point in time, such as breastfeeding an infant, is simply inappropriate in a mother–teen interaction. Even in less noticeable units of time, there are sudden changes in interaction, such as when the infant acquires the ability to roll over. This new ability necessitates changes in parental caregiving, such as attending to where the infant is placed. Indeed, the dynamic developmental nature of the parent–child relationship is life long and continues as both the child and the parents age. This is one reason we might examine the parent–child dyad throughout the life course.

A Note on Parent–Child Levels of Analysis

Similar to the marital relationship, the parent–child relationship can be analyzed at several levels. Naturally, we can examine the *individual parent* or *individual child* regarding attitudes, beliefs, and actions. We can also examine the *dyad* (mother–son, mother–daughter, father–son, and father–daughter) in terms of relationship properties such as same-gender or cross-gender, conflict, agreement, consensus, and closeness. Finally, the parents and children can be analyzed as a *family group*. At the family group level of analysis, all of the lower-level measures such as individual attitudes and dyadic disagreements may be used, but we also now have group-level processes such as coalition formation and factions based on "two against one." Testament to the complexity of each of these levels is that they are all subject to development. For example, the infant has little power over decision making compared to the adolescent's verbal articulation and physical presence. We will have opportunity to discuss all of these **levels of analysis** (see Table 7.1) as we study parent–child relationships.

It should be clear from Table 7.1 that although we commonly refer to maturation and development as individual phenomena, they are much more complex. The cases of isolated children Anna and Isabelle, documented by Davis (1947), clearly demonstrate that without the dyad, family, or society, individual development does not take place. The more recent case of Genie (Rymer, 1993) demonstrates a similar point, except that physical abuse also may have been implicated in her early years. Such cases of early social isolation seem to document that without socialization and nurturance, there is very little in us that can be recognized as human. In other words, these cases are often used to assert

Table 7.1 Levels of Analysis for the Study of Parent–Child Relationships	
Level	**Appropriate Concepts and Measures**
Individual	Attitudes, beliefs, actions
Dyad	Cohesion, agreement and disagreement, negotiations
Group	Coalitions, factions, democracy

the *tabula rasa* position. Such cases, in part, led Bronfenbrenner (1979) to assert that the smallest unit of analysis at which we can study child development is the dyad and not the individual. If the biological human (nature) contains no inherent behaviour (feeding, standing, walking) that emerges independently from socialization, then individuals are dependent on socialization (nurturance) for the very essence of being human. Although Bronfenbrenner's assertion of the dyad as the minimum unit of analysis may have somewhat overstated the case for the "blank slate," as do some of those writing about the three cited cases of socially isolated children, these cases of isolated children supply the only direct observational evidence we have in this regard.

THE NATURE–NURTURE DEBATE

If we argue that a child is a blank slate and nothing without socialization, we run the risk of minimizing genetic contributions to child outcomes. As mentioned, children are born with personality traits that must be considered. At the same time, the cases of isolated children tend to argue effectively for the nurture side of the nature–nurture debate (see Box 7.1).

Today, much of the nature–nurture debate survives only when protagonists have either a naive perspective on biological inheritance or a view of humans as determined by their experience. In human development, it is usually the case that both genetic components (DNA and RNA) are dependent on the environment for protein. For example, no matter what genetic material a person may have to determine high intelligence, if there is insufficient protein during early life, that "potential" will not be realized (e.g., a child could develop kwashiorkor, a protein-energy malnutrition). Furthermore, we know that children with low intelligence have much better social functioning when they are raised in a supportive family with ample resources to develop the child's social and analytic skills. Box 7.2 shows two formulas depicting the independent effects of nature and nurture. Much of the nature–nurture debate focuses on the "either-or" construct found in the first formula. Increasingly, we see many more outcomes explained by the interaction of these factors, as shown in the second formula.

Box 7.1

The Nature–Nurture Debate

The nature–nurture debate refers to the continuing argument about whether most of a human being's outcomes, such as criminality and intelligence, are due to genetic or biologically determined causes or due to social experience and learning acquired from various socializing agents, such as parents, the media, and peers. The "blank slate" idea clearly falls on the *nurture* side of the argument. The idea of biological determinants of criminality or intelligence clearly falls on the *nature* side of the argument.

Box 7.2

Formulas for the Nature–Nurture Debate

Formula 1

Child outcome = Nature + Nurture
For example: Intelligence = Genes + Family background

Formula 2

Child outcome = Nature + Nurture + (Interaction of nature and nurture)
For example: Intelligence = Genes + Family background + (Genes × Family background)

It may help if we examine a relatively simple developmental case. Imagine that you are a parent and you are tired of changing diapers on your toddler. You want to know how to get your child to "go potty." This simple question has indeed baffled many scholars of child development. Some, such as Dr. Spock (1985/1946), thought that training was very important, whereas others emphasized the passage of time. In reality, it turns out that both are important. The child gains some voluntary control of the external anal sphincter valve at about 18 months of age. This appears to be a species characteristic. However, if the child is not exposed to appropriate socialization—that is, "potty training"—then the desired outcome may not be attained. When socialization (potty training) occurs at the same time as control of the sphincter, parents will have the success they anticipate. This is an interaction effect (nature × nurture) between biologically determined maturation and socialization. This effect is so widely acknowledged that most developmental milestones list 18 months of age as when a child is ready for toilet training. This interaction effect between biological development and socialization is presented in Table 7.2.

Table 7.2 Factorial Design of Toilet Training (Socialization) and Physical Maturation

Toilet Training	Independent Factor: Physical Maturation	Dependent Outcome: Potty Success
Present	18 months or more	Yes
	17 months or less	No
Absent	18 months or more	No
	17 months or less	No

THEORIES OF SOCIALIZATION AND DEVELOPMENT

Most of the theories about child development can be understood as putting differential weight on the factors within the interaction between nature and nurture. Some theorists place great weight on the maturational, age-graded physical developments that the child experiences. Such theorists believe strongly that the timetable for socialization is set by the physical maturations of humans. This perspective is called **ontogenetic development** and refers to the view that although socialization and learning are important, the guiding factor is the species-specific ontogenetic development. Since such development is true for the human species, we would explain variations in timing by different socialization experiences. This ontogenetic perspective is also responsible for the common infant and toddler developmental milestones used by many physicians and health service agencies.

On the other hand, some developmental scholars believe that the availability and experience of particular socializing agents create developmental outcomes. This perspective, illustrated in Box 7.3, is sometimes called **sociogenic development**. These scholars point out that since ontogenesis is a process shared by all humans, the age-grading processes would be constant and the explanation for differential outcomes such as criminality would be found in the experiences and socialization rather than the ontogenetic processes.

Box 7.3

Why Not Piano? Experience Trumps Physical Maturation?

When I was 6 years old, growing up in the 1950s, I desperately wanted to learn to play piano. Indeed, I was so passionate about music in grade 1 that I was expelled from school because I would not quit singing. When my parents looked into getting me music lessons, they were told that children lack the physical ability and manual dexterity to play a piano in grade 1 and they would have to wait until I was 8 years old. During this time it also was commonly thought that children were not developmentally ready to play violin until they were 10 years of age. My parents capitulated to the "experts" in Western child development at the very same time that the Suzuki method for teaching violin and piano was beginning in Japan. Suzuki argued that with nurturing experience, very young children could be taught both instruments. In other words,

Western experts were more heavily influenced by the nature side of the nature–nurture equation and Suzuki (and much of Asia) was more influenced by the experiential view of leaning.

By 8 years of age I had received much age-specific socialization in baseball and the piano lessons were scheduled at the same time as baseball practice. If I had started piano when I was passionate about music and unexposed to baseball, I wonder whether I would have avoided the fate of being a less than adequate right fielder. A more compelling question is whether there is a benefit to physical and biological determinism in child development and to withholding experiences for children on the basis that they are not ready. Do you think that the relative emphasis on biological determinism versus experience is an important cultural difference between the East and the West?

For example, George Herbert Mead focused on the learning of social roles and games rather than ontogenesis. Furthermore, some scholars argue (Rogoff, 2003) that many child developmental experiences are culturally organized by the **values** of the culture rather than by age grading. As we examine some of the theories, we will point out these different emphases (ontogenetic and sociogenic).

Besides seeing most development as biologically driven (ontogenetic) or a result of socialization, two other dimensions are important in distinguishing theories of development. One of these is the *time frame* the theory addresses. Though all theories of development view time as critical to the process, some theories (e.g., those of Freud and Piaget) view developmental processes as occurring mainly in childhood. Indeed, if we take childhood as our major concern, then everyone becomes smarter, stronger, and more socially adept as we age. There has been an important shift of focus for some developmental theories, however, so that they include later life, with its physical declines, social isolation, and economic dependence. While child development examines increasing strength and intellectual powers and optimistically stops at early adulthood, lifespan theories argue that stasis followed by decline and death is also part of human development.

Another dimension by which theories may be distinguished involves how a theory approaches stages of development. Many theories of development have conceptualized stages as occurring in an invariant sequence so that each stage must be completed successfully before moving to the next stage. This concept of *invariant ordering* and lockstep progression through stages is especially obvious in earlier theories. For many students and scholars, this deterministic progression is the very essence of what they identify as the process of development. As discussed in Chapter 2, there is a much more flexible view of development founded on the perspective that development is a branching process and that one can return to previous states as well as experience new states in the process.

Psychoanalytic Theories

Psychoanalytic theories are often founded on cases seen by a therapist during psychoanalysis. The basic unit of analysis is the individual patient. Certainly, some theories implicate other family members (e.g., the Oedipus complex), but the individual's psyche is the principal focus. Freud is, without doubt, the most well known psychoanalytic theorist.

Although scholars such as William James (1983/1890) had discussed the process of child development as a sequence of stages before Freud, there is little doubt that Freud's (2000/1905) psychosexual theory of development popularized the idea of invariant developmental stages. Accompanying the idea of invariant developmental stages is the idea that each stage is marked by certain developmental adjustments that, if not completed successfully, will detrimentally affect all future development. For Freud, psychosexual development was driven by the libido or sexual urges. These urges may focus on different objects as a child matures toward the final stage of focus on opposite-sex partners. Freud's stages are the oral stage, anal stage, phallic stage, latency stage, and genital stage. Because Freud's psychoanalytic focus was on the causation of neuroses, much of his discussion of the stages related to the production of mania or hysteria. Freud accepted case observation as evidence and most parts of the theory have failed to be empirically verified. Today, Freud's theory of development is seldom used in designing curriculum or driving research.

Erikson (1950; Erikson & Erikson, 1997/1982) was a neo-Freudian trained in psychoanalysis by Freud's daughter Anna. His major contribution to developmental theory was to extend Freud's view to adulthood and old age and to see developmental stages as representing deep conflicts that needed to be resolved before moving to the next stage. Erikson's stages are not expressed as psychosexual stages but are organized according to the conflicts inherent in the stages. His work did not reject the Freudian work so much as extend it. The major conflicts in the sequential order that Erikson identified are trust versus mistrust, autonomy versus doubt, initiative versus guilt, industry versus inferiority, identity versus role confusion, intimacy versus isolation, generativity versus stagnation, and integrity versus despair. The resolution of each of these conflicts is necessary to move on through the process. Thus Erikson, like Freud, believed that development was a progression through a set of invariant stages where completion and success at each stage is contingent on the successful resolution of previous stages. Erikson's extension of developmental stages to the entire life course, including old age and dying (integrity versus despair), indicated a major move away from Freud whose focus was on development as experienced only in childhood.

Psychological Theories

Psychological theories are different from psychoanalytic theories. Psychology is an academic discipline that studies the mental processes of individuals whereas psychoanalysis is within medicine and is clearly oriented toward pathology and treatment. Psychological theories are mainly "curiosity-driven" theories rather than "treatment-driven" theories. The basic unit of analysis in psychological theories is the individual's mental processes. Ontogenetic interpretations (nature) have been the hallmark of many psychological theories of development. Indeed, psychological theories of development have often sought to anchor theories in what may be perceived as the firm grounding of species-specific and biologically determined development. As we shall see, such motivation often pays scant attention to cultural variation and social determinants.

Without doubt, Piaget (1952/1936) constructed one of the most influential theories of child development. His theory of a child's cognitive and perceptual development relied on invariant stages that had to be experienced and learned before the next stage could be experienced. Piaget stages are detailed in Table 7.3.

Piaget influenced numerous scholars to follow his example and view development as invariant sequential stages. For example, Kohlberg (1971) envisioned moral development as having six sequential stages. However, Kohlberg differed from Piaget in one very important respect. Whereas Piaget had focused on child development, Kohlberg viewed moral development as a lifelong progression. As the study of aging has expanded

Table 7.3 Piaget's Stages of Development

Age Range	Stage	Properties of Stage
0 to 2 years	Sensorimotor	Differentiation of object from background and object permanence
2 to 7 years	Preoperational	Vocal and written language and nominal grouping
7 to 11 years	Concrete operational	Conservation of matter and ordinal series
11 years and greater	Formal operational	Formal symbolic logic: manipulation of symbols

Source: Adapted from Inhelder and Piaget (1958); also see Atherton (2010).

(see Chapter 10), increasingly the study of development has become less focused on childhood and more focused on a lifespan perspective.

Although Piaget's perspective was very influential and continues to be so in certain areas, its inaccuracies are readily apparent today. Piaget did not envision a flexible sequence but only a lockstep sequence. In other words, he did not envision Mozart writing music at the age of 3 nor chess masters at the age of 8, as both music and chess involve formal operations. Likewise, some elements of one stage may be experienced early while other elements may be delayed. Many of us can recall someone who had early acquisition of some skills but not others. Finally, the strict determinism of Piaget's model was questioned from the outset, with scholars reporting cultural variation (e.g., Levi-Strauss, 1949). After many decades of supremacy, Piaget's theory has at least "softened" into a probabilistic rather than deterministic theory, while some critics may even reject Piaget in favour of more social and experiential theories (e.g., Vygotsky, 1978). Certainly, the early learning of music and mathematics popularized by social and experiential views of learning such as the Suzuki violin method and early math programs have raised questions about Piaget's theory.

Sociological Theories

In contrast to the psychological focus on the ontogenetically developing individual, sociological theories of development have traditionally focused on the parent–child dyad, the family, or larger social units as the unit of analysis. Furthermore, the determinants of development are usually viewed as more social (nurture) rather than ontogenetically determined (nature). Most of the sociological approaches to child development refer to the process as *socialization*, a term that reflects the social nature of development. Although there are a great number of theories of socialization, we will discuss just three: G.H. Mead's theory, Bronfenbrenner's ecological approach, and attachment theory.

G.H. Mead's (1934) posthumously published book *Mind, Self and Society* gave a foundation to much of the child's development as a *social being*. G.H. Mead was not alone, since at this point in history numerous other scholars were vitally concerned with questions about socialization. Among these was the work of American anthropologist Margaret Mead, who authored several books on socialization, such as *Coming of Age in Samoa* (1928) and *Growing up in New Guinea* (1930). G.H. Mead focused on the social mechanisms that created an understanding of society so that the child could increasingly integrate as a participating member. He identified two crucial sequential stages in development. Unlike the psychiatric or psychological theories of development, Mead's theory conceptualized the outcome of development as the ability to take on and perform social roles in society.

According to Mead, for the child to be competent at performing social roles in a society, he or she must navigate two successive stages of development. The first stage is the **play stage**, which is marked by the child learning how to take on and *play* a social role. For example, a young boy may put on his father's shoes and coat to play "daddy." A young girl may play "mommy" to her doll. Mead argued that in these early play efforts, the child gradually learns that there is a range of expected and approved behaviours and unacceptable and unsanctioned behaviours. For example, when the young girl bashes her doll in the head, an adult may tell her that this is not acceptable behaviour for a mother and if the behaviour continues, the doll might be taken away until the girl could treat "baby" correctly. This initial stage is critical for developing the child's ability to take on a role and to understand that a role is determined by social rules (norms and expectations) and that unacceptable behaviour will be punished.

Mead, however, recognized that while role taking is an important process to learn and social roles are a basic building block of social systems, much more has to be learned. He argued that the second stage of socialization, the **game stage**, is required to teach the child that roles are always an organic and dynamic part of a larger social organization. In the game stage, the child learns that several roles can be performed as long as the actor knows the rules of the game. For example, in baseball a child may learn that assuming the role of a batter is contingent on his or her team being up to bat, and that after three outs the child will once again assume the role of a first baseman. In other words, social roles are dynamically linked to the rules of the game and to the time-oriented development of the game (e.g., the ninth inning). Likewise, a young child may play with a Barbie doll using a different set of roles and norms than used with a baby doll that wets itself and cries. By taking on multiple roles within and between games and time periods, children learn that roles are constructed within a larger system of norms and expectations and that these rules of the games may change over time. Furthermore, the child learns that he or she may take on multiple roles and thus have complex identities.

Bronfenbrenner (1979) developed a social and **ecological theoretical model of development** that has had a lasting effect in staging research on children. He argued that the smallest unit with which we could analyze development is the dyad. In other words, he asserted that the child did not develop alone but always in interaction with another human.

We have already seen that this is so with the reported cases of isolated children. Bronfenbrenner did not stop with the dyad, but further reasoned that development is an outward movement of the child's interaction and increasing competence with levels of interaction. First, the child might interact with only one or two significant adults, but soon the child is in daycare, kindergarten, elementary school, secondary school, the workplace, and community environments. Each level brings new forms of interaction and new relationships. Bronfenbrenner further argued that the age grading of these various interactions (what in 1989 he called the *chronosphere*) means that the child is gradually and systematically exposed to an expanding and increasingly complex set of interactions. Bronfenbrenner's theory has proven very useful in sensitizing developmental researchers to the many age-graded, life course interactions.

There is no doubt that the single most influential developmental theory today is **attachment theory**. In many ways, attachment theory stands between the determinism of ontogenetics (nature) and the models of socialization (nurture). As its name indicates, attachment theory is very much concerned with social relationships and how they are basic to human development and well-being. Bowlby (1953) initiated attachment theory. Observations of subhuman species suggested that animals may "imprint" on a caregiver from birth. Although Bowlby's observations did not suggest an immediate imprinting, he argued that humans develop a strong and important affectional bond with one consistently present significant caregiver, usually the mother. Bowlby's work received additional weight from the empirical and measurement expertise of the developmental scholar Marie Ainsworth (1967). In the 1980s, attachment theory was extended to adult attachment by Hazan and Shaver (1987). Today, forms of attachment and pathological consequences are recognized in the American Psychiatric Association's *Diagnostic and Statistical Manual of Mental Disorders*, 4th edition (DSM-IV, 1994).

Attachment theory argues that human infants need to form secure, affective attachments to one significant and consistent caregiver. The infant or child will explore and learn about his or her environment once assured that there is a stable and secure base from which to explore. This affective attachment is usually observable and measurable by 6 months of age. For example, the familiar phenomenon of 9-month-old children "making strange" by crying when held by strangers can be interpreted as an indicator of attachment. Ainsworth, Blehar, Waters, and Wall (1978) conducted famous "strange situation" laboratory observations of children aged 12 to 18 months. They observed mother and child pairs as the mother stayed in the laboratory room with the child, a stranger entered the room, the mother left the room, and then the mother re-entered the room. Based on these observations, Ainsworth and colleagues developed three attachment styles. Later, Main and Solomon (1986) added a fourth attachment style. These attachment styles are outlined in Table 7.4.

Originating in the work of Hazan and Shaver (1987), the extension of attachment theory into adult relationships has developed "attachment styles" for adult romantic relationships based on the schema an adult uses to interpret relationships. For example, adults may want a close relationship but be afraid of being emotionally hurt. Such adult

Table 7.4 Child Attachment Styles

Observed Style	Properties from "Strange Situation" Observation
Secure	Firmly attached to caregiver, explores with checking back for caregiver
Anxious-resistant	Disturbed when caregiver absent, angry with caregiver on return
Anxious-avoidant	Treats stranger and caregiver similarly but avoids caregiver on return
Disorganized	Lacks coherent pattern of response to caregiver leaving and to stranger

Source: Ainsworth et al. (1978); Main and Solomon (1986).

attachment styles are then correlated with retrospective accounts of child attachment or simply treated as an adult phenomenon.

MATERNAL DEPRIVATION AND DAYCARE

Attachment theory has been important to one of the most debated areas in the last 50 years: alternatives to maternal care. Starting about 1970, women's labour force participation began to grow throughout the world. As a result, women experiencing childbirth after 1970 were increasingly more likely to return to work than stay at home with their children. The debate has focused on the possibility of harm to children placed in alternative care situations, and attachment theory has been central to this debate.

Much of the early literature on institutionalized daycare as an alternative to maternal care was conducted in high-quality daycares that were often part of laboratory settings at major universities. The first tests used were typically based on Ainsworth et al.'s (1978) "strange situation" observations. The overall conclusion in most of these early studies was captured in a review by Belsky and Steinberg (1978). Given the constraints of these early data, they concluded that there was no evidence that daycare was harmful or that maternal care was superior for infants. They also noted that there was no evidence that daycare was harmful to the mother–child bond. Furthermore, they noted that daycare does increase the frequency of peer interaction.

A decade later, the research had changed. Belsky (1988) again summarized the research literature, but this time concluded that infants in the first year of life with more than 20 hours per week in daycare were at higher risk for developmental difficulties at a later age. Belsky and Eggebeen (1991), based on their longitudinal study, determined that children under 3 years of age with more than 20 hours per week in daycare were significantly more likely to have compliance problems in elementary school.

The change in Belsky's conclusions prompted a host of criticism from advocates of daycare. Although much of this criticism was aimed at the data or at the relatively small but nonetheless statistically significant effects for child non-compliance, some of the criticism was aimed at attachment theory. Most notable is the criticism by Hays (1998), who argued that the "strange situation" protocol for attachment theory may be methodologically flawed in that children in daycare who experience independence earlier may simply be coded as less attached. Certainly, there have been other criticisms of attachment theory, such as that it fails to control for child temperament; to account for family background factors such as income, social class, and ethnicity; and to account for community and school variables.

The research in this area continues to expand and, as appropriate for the role of a scholar, Belsky (2003–2005) has modified his position according to new research findings. In his most recent summary of the research, Belsky concluded that children are at greater risk for developing insecure attachment if they are in daycare for more than 10 hours per week during the first year and the mother is insensitive to the relationship with the child. This not only softens earlier admonitions but also adds that there is an interaction effect between the mother's insensitivity and daycare. Belsky still maintains that children in daycare through the first four and a half years show more difficulties with their behaviour through grade 1. Children who spend more time in daycare (regardless of the quality of the daycare) show more problem behaviour through grade 3. Belsky also reports that high-quality daycare is associated with higher levels of language and cognitive functioning in children. For Belsky, the implications are clear: Countries should pursue family policies favouring parental leave and should avoid alternative care as a decision into which parents are pushed for economic reasons.

It is important to view care arrangements in the broader context of parent–child relationships. Although parents and parenting techniques have an effect on children, increasingly children are affected by daycare arrangements, pre-kindergarten, kindergarten, and elementary and secondary school. The mass media, which include television, internet, movies, and cellphone "apps," all have early and prolonged access to the developing child. We cannot easily separate the effects of parental techniques on the child from those of peers and mass media. Because of this complexity, any statistically significant effect on child outcomes may be moderated by these many other variables.

PARENTING TECHNIQUES

To a child, it must seem that the parents have supreme power over him or her. For the parents, however, the perception may be entirely different. In previous centuries, parenting techniques were largely the choice of the parent. Certainly, in the Roman *pater familias* (*circa* ad 100), the patriarch had complete control of even the life and death of children as well as the ability to sell them into slavery. This absolute authority of the father and head of the family was eventually narrowed by law. The steady increase in individual rights has resulted in today's parents being much more tightly controlled than at previous times in history. Today, parental behaviours toward their children are constrained by laws about neglect, exposure to danger (failure to supervise), mandatory schooling, child abuse, abandonment, and use of physical force. Child assistance phone numbers help to ensure that children can report infractions. The mother who leaves a child unattended in the car while she uses an automated bank machine could be charged with neglect or abandonment (see Box 7.4). The father who fails to supervise a child using playground equipment, resulting in an injury to the child, could be charged with failure to supervise. If the government agency responsible for child welfare deems that parents are not adequately caring for and protecting their child, the child may be seized and placed in foster care.

Today's parent–child relationship is not only more defined by legislation than ever before, but also more controlled by informal social norms as to what is "correct" parenting. Public inspection of parental behaviour is at an all-time high, in part because of the moral and legal beliefs about spanking. Certainly, a mother or father who uses physical punishment in public may well be reported to authorities. In addition, there are very strong feelings about abandonment. Some of the cases of moral outrage toward parents are humorous, such as the March 2009 case in which a car thief found an infant in the back seat, returned to find the child's parents, and scolded them for leaving their child alone in the vehicle.

The parent–child relationship is life long and the academic study of parent–child relationships spans a long duration from early childhood until the death of either the parent or the child. However, most developmental sociologists study parenting as it pertains to the young child from infancy through the elementary school years since, during this period, parents are charged with the greatest responsibility for the child, the child has the least amount of power, and the parental socialization of the child is most effective. Indeed, if you review brainwashing techniques, you will find that brainwashing involves first stripping a person of prior socialization; developing a warm and close relationship between

Box 7.5

Explaining Things to Billy

"Billy, get back here!" shouted the boy's alarmed father. Billy's dad was mowing the lawn and two-and-a-half-year-old Billy had been playing on the driveway. His dad had yelled because Billy was headed for the street in front of the house and there was a fair amount of automobile traffic.

Billy's dad kneeled down to have a talk with the boy. "Billy, if you go into the road, a car might smush you, and then you would be hurt or dead. It's like a really big 'ouchy' and you don't want that, do you?"

Billy obediently said, "No, Daddy." Then he paused thoughtfully and asked, "If I were dead, would I still get to go to the birthday party tomorrow?"

Billy's dad quickly incorporated the idea that Billy could not conceptualize death or even being "smushed." He replied, "If you go into the street, you will end up in your room, and you will *not* go to the birthday party." Billy's dad was not confident that even this deterrent could be understood by Billy.

the captive and one significant captor; totally controlling the environment in terms of rewards, punishments, and all other influences; and finally rebuilding the socialization. Parents do not have to strip previous socialization and identity since the infant is unencumbered by these. They largely control the environment, the rewards, and the punishments of the infant. They can limit playmates and select alternative care and preschools according to their religious, cultural, and moral values. Of course, as the child grows, the parents increasingly lose control over rewards and punishments and the environment expands to include influences of peers and mass media. This early socialization, however, forms the child's world view, morals, and identity and is perhaps the single most powerful influence throughout one's lifetime.

In the academic study of the early parent–child relationship, emphasis is usually placed on two broad areas for child outcomes: child compliance and child achievement. **Child compliance** involves the child's response to the directions from responsible adults such as parents, teachers, caregivers, and authorities. Compliance is essential in early childhood (ages 0 to 4), before the child can reason and conceptualize consequences (see Box 7.5). As the child begins to be able to understand consequences and reason, compliance becomes less important than autonomy and creativity. However, when the child is young, it is essential that compliance is emphasized for the child's own safety.

Child achievement is usually divided into two areas: social achievement and academic achievement. Most parents want their children to have friends and to develop social skills. At the same time, parents also want their children to be respectful of teachers and adults, and these, too, are social skills. However, in addition, parents want their children to do well in school and to receive good grades and praise from their teachers. The balance between these two areas of achievement may be difficult at times. For example, how much time does a child spend playing with other children (social) rather than taking special math courses or violin lessons (academic)? On the other hand, some activities, such as group violin lessons or chorus groups, may involve achieving both social and academic skills.

Parents have available to them several techniques and strategies to help their children reach these outcomes. Parental warmth and support are used to encourage and bolster desired behaviours. However, many parental techniques are aimed at control and discipline, to achieve either immediate compliance to commands such as "don't go in the street" or compliance to longer-term goals such as "practise your violin." To achieve compliance, parental techniques include coercion, ridicule, withdrawal of love, threats, punishments such as physical isolation ("time out") or physical discipline, and reasoning.

Some psychologists have approached parenting as a static and relatively stable phenomenon. For example, the noted psychologist Diana Baumrind (1967) argued that parents fall into just three styles of parenting: authoritative, authoritarian, and permissive (a fourth style, uninvolved, was added by Maccoby and Martin [1983]). Today, rather than placing parents in one parenting category, we know that many variables determine which techniques and strategies parents adopt in relation to a child's behaviour. In fact, this process is complex and parental techniques change with such variables as the age of the child, the gender of the child, the type of behaviour being monitored, and the place or situation (school or home). For example, most parents reduce spanking frequency starting at about 3 years of age, and by 10 years of age it is virtually nonexistent in most families (Day, Peterson, & McCracken, 1998). Boys receive different treatment than girls, and the frequency and duration of spanking also depends on the gender of the parent. In other words, parental techniques are clearly developmental in that they depend on the age of the child, the immediate environment, and the duration and development of the relationship. Parental techniques change with the development of the child, so to slot parents into a particular parenting style seems to lack an understanding that the parent–child relationship is dynamic rather than static. Indeed, Belsky (1984) produced a more dynamic view of parenting in his process model of parenting shown in Figure 7.1.

In Belsky's process model, the child's developmental history includes both previous stages and experience and these are integrated with personality and temperament. Parenting effects on child development are the product of the parents' marriage and the parents' work as they interact with the child's temperament. Finally, the effect of parenting is always joined with the characteristics of the individual child. Clearly, Belsky's model incorporates the bidirectional effects of child to parent and parent to child. Perhaps the largest oversight in Belsky's model is that it does not actively and deliberately incorporate influences from the media, peers, the school, and the community. To do so would of course make the model more complete, but also make it so complex as to lose some of its clarity. Some of these additional variables will be incorporated into the following discussion of parental disciplinary techniques. What the Belsky model does achieve when compared to static categorizations of parenting styles such as "authoritarian" and "permissive" is that it recognizes the bidirectionality of the parent–child influences and allows for dynamic changes over time as the parents and child grow and develop together.

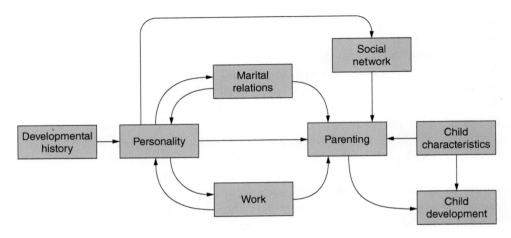

Figure 7.1 Belsky's Process Model of Parenting

Source: Reprinted with permission from Figure 1, page 84, Belsky, J. (1984). The determinants of parenting: A process model. *Child Development*, 55, 83–96.

Parental Disciplinary Techniques

Among all topics surrounding parenting, the disciplinary techniques used by parents are probably most frequently discussed. There is hardly a social group or organization without some opinion on this topic, including religious leaders, the media, political lobbying groups, schools, and legislators. Even such august bodies as the United Nations Study on Violence against Children set a target date (now passed) of 2009 for the worldwide prohibition of spanking. At least 13 countries, including Norway, have adopted zero tolerance laws regarding the spanking of children. At the same time, there are warnings from religious fundamentalists that if we spare the rod, we will spoil our children (see, for example, www.tldm.org/news6/child.discipline.htm). This area is so fraught with emotion and conflict that few academics or scholars want to venture into these complex issues.

The major finding on the harmful effects of spanking concerns heightened aggression in children who have been spanked. The problem with much of the literature on spanking and aggression is that we cannot perform research that uses an **experimental design**, because this obviously would be not only cruel but also unethical. As a result, most of our knowledge is based on research that uses a **correlational design**. Correlational design does not allow us to analyze separately whether aggressive children are simply more likely to produce behaviours that result in spanking or whether spanking actually produces aggressiveness in children. In other words, we need to control for the traits and attributes of the child before examining the effects of spanking. Seldom do researchers establish baseline data of child temperament. Correlational designs for spanking outcomes are complicated further by estimates that 94 percent of all U.S. parents spank 3- and 4-year-old children and 52 percent of Canadian parents do the same (Larzelere & Kuhn, 2005). The prevalence of spanking means that the "no exposure" group is numerically difficult to include in research samples.

There are many other significant problems with research in this area, some of which were noted early on by Steinmetz (1979). One major problem concerns the dependent variable "aggressiveness." This variable confuses **prosocial aggression** with **anti-social aggression**. Most societies consider prosocial aggression as valuable since it leads people to intervene when another is being hurt or attacked. Another problem with the research is that the direction of the effects of corporal punishment (whether they are positive effects, such as reducing anti-social aggression, or negative effects, such as increasing anti-social aggression) tends to change with conditions such as the gender of the disciplining parent, whether the act being disciplined is aggressive or non-aggressive, whether corporal discipline is conjoined with reasoning, whether the discipline occurs in school or at home, and the age and gender of the child being disciplined. In addition, the degree of physical discipline (low, moderate, or high intensity) often has curvilinear effects on child outcomes. All of this is very confusing in terms of interpreting findings, but it does tell us that any good research would have to account for all of these variables to be able to make any claims about the effects of spanking.

Although there has been a host of ideologically and politically biased "research" on spanking, there has also been some outstanding research on its effects. Straus (1996) argued that spanking creates a violent society. Later, Straus and Paschall (1999) found that spanking has a negative influence on the child's intellectual development. Slade and Wissow (2004) found that spanking before age 2 is associated with behaviour problems four years later. In addition, Straus and Paschall's (2009) global data found that children from geographic areas that use less spanking have higher intelligence quotients (IQs) than those in areas that use more spanking. They also reported some notable exceptions in Asian countries where spanking and other forms of physical punishment are practised. They attributed this region's higher IQs and academic performance to strong parental academic values. Naturally, this explanation brings up the possibility that IQs in all countries may be determined more by parental values than by spanking, and that spanking may be spuriously related to IQ.

All of these researchers used longitudinal data so that the causal influences could be better identified. Nonetheless, it is virtually impossible to control for or account for the many variables associated with parents' use of spanking, such as race, class, income, and social development. All of these associated variables have effects on the child's IQ and cognitive development, as do more subtle variables such as the school system and community supports.

There is also a sizable literature arguing that spanking leads to positive outcomes for children. This research makes a distinction between spanking and other forms of corporal punishment such as slapping, hitting with a belt or other object, and kicking. Spanking is often defined as the hitting of the child's clothed buttocks with the palm of an open hand. Some researchers go further and suggest that the number of hits be limited to three and that the hitting not produce welts, bruises, or scars. Some use of spanking is contingent on the desired outcome. For example, when immediate compliance is required, spanking may be the most effective way to achieve such compliance (obedience). For example, if a 2-year-old wants to run into the road (see Box 7.5), a threat of spanking or an actual spanking may gain immediate compliance. However, if the outcome of interest is long-term intellectual development, spanking may be inappropriate. This conditional position on spanking (e.g., Baumrind, Larzelere, & Cowan, 2002) is further complemented and complicated by the fact that when most parents use spanking, they conjoin it with at least one or more other forms of discipline. For example, Larzelere, Sather, Schneider, Larson, and Pike (1998) found that spanking of toddlers used in conjunction with reasoning was more effective in delaying the target behaviours. Indeed, this has led to a new category of spanking where parents use spanking if and only if the child does not obey some other method of discipline. For example, if a child is put in his or her room for a "time out," refuses to stay there, and the parents state that the child will get a spanking if he or she comes out of the room again, that is termed *conditional spanking* (Benjet & Kazdin, 2003).

More recently, a question originally raised by Steinmetz (1979) has become central to the spanking debate: Are the outcomes for other disciplinary techniques any less harmful than the outcomes for spanking? The early assessment of this question by Steinmetz indicated that most forms of discipline, such as "time out," withdrawal of love, scolding, isolation, and use of reasoning, were often associated with increased aggression similar to that seen with spanking. It seems that children do not like to be disciplined! A recent review (Larzelere & Kuhn, 2005) of 26 outcome studies regarding different disciplinary tactics concluded that conditional spanking is better associated with positive child outcomes (prosocial behaviour, self-esteem, etc.) than are alternative disciplinary strategies. Surprisingly, spanking achieved long-term outcomes equal to or better than those associated with alternative forms of discipline. The authors of this study were careful to exclude forms of physical abuse and overt assault as disciplinary tactics.

Among academics, the spanking debate certainly has not been resolved. Clearly, we need large longitudinal samples and detailed diary reports of discipline to address many of the remaining questions about causation. Furthermore, we need much more information about the target child's personality and behaviour before disciplinary tactics are ever used by the parents to ensure that spanking is not the result of problematic traits or temperament in the child. Nevertheless, a more complete picture is emerging about the many complicating control variables (age of child, temperament, gender, type of behaviour being punished, place, gender of disciplinarian) as well as the types of discipline being used (spanking, conditional spanking, other forms of physical punishment, "time out," withdrawal of love, ridicule) and the associated outcomes (long-term and short-term compliance, self-esteem, anti-social aggression, prosocial aggression). This complex debate is far from resolved but we have gained considerable sophistication in the questions we now ask. Even if we had all of the scientific answers, those factual answers would not address the moral question about the use of spanking and corporal punishment.

Intergenerational Transmission of Social Class

One of the most interesting areas of research about parenting techniques is on the association between parenting techniques and the intergenerational transmission of social class. This is an important area for sociological study since it involves the transmission of inequality. For example, a recent Organisation for Economic Co-operation and Development (OECD) report by Cristina d'Addio (2007, p. 4) shows that intergenerational income mobility is higher in Nordic countries, Canada, and Australia than in the United States, Italy, and the United Kingdom. Rates of intergenerational income mobility show the degree to which inequality is tied to the status into which you are born (**ascribed status**, such as a caste system) or the degree to which status can be changed through hard work or affirmative action programs (**achieved status**). Cristina d'Addio argues that education, especially early childhood education in families, is responsible for much of the inequality and mobility.

According to Cristina d'Addio (2007), early economic work on the transmission of social class and inequality (Becker & Tomes, 1979, 1986) argued that mobility was composed of parentally transmitted "endowments" to children, financial transfers to children, and the constraints on mobility in the social system (equality of opportunity). Later, the idea of "endowments" was broken down into the components of physically transmitted endowments (e.g., genetic IQ, athleticism), the human capital the child receives (knowledge, skills), and the cultural capital the child receives (cultural practices appropriate to a class). Clearly, the second and third of these, human capital and cultural capital, are more subject to social policy and inquiry.

For many years, sociologists thought that the most important part of social class was human capital. Even indicators such as socio-economic status were composed of years of education, occupational prestige, and income. Indeed, education was thought to give a person the skills and training needed to get a good job with high income. Much of the research on intergenerational transmission focused on formal education as a key to mobility. For example, Cristina d'Addio (2007) argues that wealthy families can afford an enriched environment for early learning and language and good schools that aid the child's later success in education and acquiring human capital. Human capital was

then seen as instrumental to high income, and income was a significant dimension of class. Early social class characterizations such as Warner, Meeker, and Eells's (1949) six classes relied heavily on income, as have many more recent class characterizations (see Beeghley, 2004).

In today's post-industrial economy, this supposition has run into some trouble. The correlation between education and income has weakened as labour unions successfully negotiate lucrative contracts for lower-skilled workers and social programs address income inequalities. In addition to the weakening correlation between education and income, there has been a change in the economy. Previously, industrial economies were limited by their labour supply and production constraints. In highly automated post-industrial societies, the limits on the economy are often set by the market. How many cars you can sell is tied to convincing each Canadian consumer that he or she needs two or three cars rather than one car. In addition, there is a need to compete for global export markets and consumers.

These changes have been tied to the increasing popularity of a view of social class as a system of values and practices linked to the idea of *cultural capital* (Bourdieu, 1984). As income has become less of a predictor of social class, the other measures constructing socio-economic status (SES) have been more closely scrutinized by researchers (see Cristina d'Addio, 2007; Bourdieu, 1984). Bourdieu argues that in a world where patterns of consumption rather than production are more important in distinguishing social class, a detailed examination of the mechanisms tied to different patterns of consumption is required. He analyzes descriptive data from a national survey of French tastes and consumption using a statistical technique (correspondence analysis) that reveals clusters of associated behaviours. An example of the patterns Bourdieu found is that those persons who like soft-ripened cheeses such as Camembert also like opera and new age classical music and read books. Those people who like beer and steak also like to watch sports on TV and tend not to read books but only magazines. Naturally, there was some correlation with income, but cultural patterns could be shared by lower-income groups such as artists and intellectuals as well as wealthy industrialists.

These associations prompted Bourdieu to theorize that "tastes" are important not only in announcing one's social class but also in attaining and maintaining social class. He argued that children acquire basic habits early in life that become so ingrained that they will later seem "natural" or almost "inborn." These early patterns and the situation in which they are acquired are called the **habitus**. The habitus equips the child with immediate reflexive behaviours such as saying "please" and "thank you" or using a tissue rather than a sleeve to blow one's nose, and that these behaviours announce social class to teachers and peers. Later, the child is thrown in with peers and the child from an upper social class will understand the *rules of the game* for talking about art or music but perhaps be less able to relate to common knowledge. The upper-class child may be more comfortable with Chopin's music yet readily believe that a "hockey pool" is what happens when an ice rink melts in the summer. Furthermore, the habitus is associated with early values about creativity and learning.

Other scholars across the developed world have given some credence to the perspective on social class argued by Bourdieu (1984). For example, Bernstein (1971) argues that speech patterns carry social class so that it can be distinguished by those who use restricted codes (such as demonstrative pronouns *this* or *that* rather than the elaborated codes used by higher classes that name the object). The difference between saying "could you close that?" and "would you please close the door?" announces one's background or what Bourdieu would call one's habitus. Similarly, Lareau's (2003) study of 88 families and parenting practices documents how parenting practices are clearly structured and patterned by social class. Her work must be seen as an extension of the extensive theoretical and empirical work on this topic by the sociologist Melvin Kohn (1969). Kohn developed a detailed theoretical model of intergenerational social class transmission (see Figure 7.2).

Tracing through the steps in the model from left to right, we find that the model begins with the **social class** influence in the family of orientation. This influence includes what Bourdieu calls habitus along with the early socialization of the "rules of the game" and value orientation. The social class that the child exhibits is translated into the form and type of education. For example, those in the upper class are more likely to believe that education involves inquisitiveness and curiosity rather than being an onerous task required to get a job. Education combined with social class background lead to an occupational status such as those tied to professions or trades.

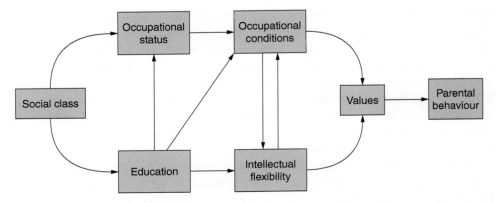

Figure 7.2 Kohn's Model of the Intergenerational Transmission of Social Class

Source: Reprinted with permission from Gecas, V. (1979). The influence of social class on socialization. In Burr et al. (1979). *Contemporary theories about the family, Vol. 1* (Figure 15.1, p. 382). New York: The Free Press.

The type of occupational status is related to the **occupational conditions**. Occupations in which people work to project production rather than to punch a time clock and that require problem solving at a high intellectual level will tend to emphasize independent thought, creativity, and intellectual flexibility. Some "jobs" will require obedience to union rules, punching a time clock, and doing what one is told and these are associated with low intellectual flexibility. Both the intellectual flexibility and the occupational conditions determine the **values** of the parent. If the parent perceives the rewards at work as being tied to a high value on obedience and following directions, that parent will likely choose techniques of discipline and parenting that emphasize those values. On the other hand, if the parent perceives that creativity and independence get one ahead in this world, those values would lead to adopting certain other parenting techniques. Kohn recognizes that over time the values articulated by the professional work world and social class may change, and his model is sufficiently dynamic to address this. Career Box 7.1 illustrates how Bourdieu's and Kohn's arguments about the intergenerational transmission of social class values and cultural consumption could affect one's job interview skills.

Overall, Kohn's model proposes an explanation for the long-term association between physical discipline of children, with its emphasis on obedience and compliance, and homes with lower socio-economic status. Kohn's theory states that the replication of social class is complex and involves aspects of Bourdieu's habitus, but that occupational conditions and the tacit values on intellectual flexibility are more proximally related to parenting techniques. There is certainly an impressive array of research on this theory spanning more than 40 years (e.g., Luster, Rhoades, & Hass, 1989; Ritchie, 1997). Kohn's model identifies the links between how we are raised, school, work, and the values that parents transmit to their children.

The Real Interview and Cultural Capital

The board of directors had spent the afternoon interviewing Ray for the job. Now it was time to relax. The directors took Ray to a very fancy restaurant, and he was a little uncomfortable with the array of eating implements that confronted him once he was seated. As the company's directors chatted about the new surrealism exhibit, Ray noticed that his hosts had all placed their napkins on their laps. However, before Ray could follow their lead, the waiter elegantly whisked the napkin from the table and placed it on Ray's lap. Ray cringed slightly at the attention this garnered from his hosts.

One of the directors asked if Ray had decided on any menu items and recommended the clams on the half shell. Ray said that he didn't like "live food" and continued to look over the menu.

Later, Ray laughingly said to one of the directors that his menu must have been misprinted because the restaurant had left the prices off.

Will had been looking forward to chatting with members of the board after a long job interview.

The "arsenal" of forks and utensils at the restaurant did not intimidate him since he had been raised with such place settings at home. He was completely comfortable.

Will was happy when the topic of conversation turned to the surrealism exhibit and talked knowledgably about the impact of Max Ernst's work in establishing surrealism as a viable school of art. As it turned out, many of the directors had an interest in art and several were involved in painting and collecting.

One of the directors suggested the clams on the half shell but Will pointed out that they were littleneck clams and said he would rather have the Nova Scotia Digby scallops as an appetizer. Later, Will ordered the osso buco and noted how difficult it is to find on menus due to the length of cooking time required.

Days later, Will was offered the job and told that the board was especially pleased with his social skills and intellectual flexibility. The directors felt that Will could serve as an outstanding representative of the company in almost any context.

CONCLUSION

Although the previous discussion assists us in understanding the social mechanisms for the transmission of social class, it should be obvious that the availability of occupations, the financial security tied to these forms of employment, and the climate of independence and creativity in such professions are all linked to economic and social structures outside of the control of individuals and families. Regardless of the fact that the 2007 OECD report places Canada near the top of the list of countries with high rates of social mobility, other data are more troubling regarding our country's future. In a recent report by the Vanier Institute of the Family (2010, p. 112), a disturbing trend for families is noted:

> The 20% of families with the lowest adjusted after-tax income saw an increase of 14.2% from $14,100 in 1989 to $16,100 in 2007, while families in the second quintile experienced a gain of 14.1% from $23,400 to $26,700. Families in the third and

fourth quintiles saw their after tax incomes increase by 17.5% and 20.5%, respectively, between 1989 and 2007. Stated in another way, the incomes of families in the top 20% were increasing twice as fast as those in the bottom two quintiles (at 31%).

It should be obvious that the individual family and the school system may fully prepare people for intellectually flexible careers, but it is critical that economic and social structures continue to maintain equality of opportunity and well-being. The data cited in the Vanier Institute of the Family (2010) report suggest that Canada may be becoming increasingly like the more rigid class-structured societies and have less social class mobility than we have formerly enjoyed.

We have seen that parent–child relationships are very complex. The infant comes equipped with his or her own personality and characteristics as well as with a species calendar for ontogenetic development. Each parent also has these characteristics as well as his or her own family history, values, and integration into the adult world of work. The ideas and values of the parent will be expressed in numerous ways, such as choices favouring experience over readiness of the child and forms of discipline to achieve the child's compliance, social success, and academic success. The child's success will depend on subtle characteristics of family background and values but also on the social and economic structures that the adult child confronts.

The parent–child relationship is so complex that only one major conclusion can be reached. Although social scientists may offer tentative generalizations about parent–child effects, there is simply no one way of disciplining that is correct for all children, no one way of motivating a child that is correct, and no one way of igniting a child's creativity that is correct. Each child and each parent has his or her own personality. Each disciplinary technique interacts with a complex array of variables, such as age, gender, place, and type of act being disciplined, which make any answers about child discipline exceedingly complex. As we have seen, even success as measured by social mobility contains historical variables, parental variables, and variables outside of the control of parents and families.

SUMMARY OF KEY POINTS

- Parsons (1954) and Goode (1963) argue that children in agrarian societies supplied labour and were economic assets, whereas in industrial societies children are economic liabilities because of compulsory schooling and the lack of need for their unskilled labour.

- The goal for most North American parents is to raise children to be socially and economically independent.

- Empirical or experiential perspectives on learning believe that parents and society transfer their knowledge and skills to the "blank slate" of the child.

- Rational theories of learning believe that pre-existing structures or forms of analysis allow experience to occur.

- There are three dominant models of "effects" or causation between parents and children.
  - Unidirectional: Parent → Child
  - Unidirectional: Child → Parent
  - Bidirectional: Parent ⟷ Child

- Development or maturation could be discussed in terms of the maturation of the social group (family), a dyad (husband–wife, father–daughter, mother–son), or the individual.

- Theories of development are conceptualized by how they deal with the following:
  - Ontogenesis versus sociogenesis
  - Sequential invariance versus variable sequential flexibility
  - Stages of development

- Psychoanalytic and psychological theories focus on ontogenesis and invariant stages of development rooted in the individual.

- Sociological theories of development focus on sociogenesis, sequential variation of stages rooted in the social system (norms, family, school).

- Among the sociogenic theories of development are G.H. Mead's play and game stages, Bronfenbrenner's ecological theory, and Bowlby's attachment theory.

- Belsky and attachment theorists argue that full-time institutionalized daycare before 3 years of age has detrimental effects on the children's level of compliance in school and at home later in life.

- Child abandonment (see Box. 7.4) is a criminal offence in Canada.

- Most scholars studying parent–child relationships emphasize the child outcomes of compliance and achievement. Achievement is further divided into social achievement and academic achievement.

- Parent–child relationships are dynamic and numerous variables affect child outcomes (see Figure 7.1).

- Social scientists usually cannot use experimental designs to study effects of different forms of discipline on children but they can use correlational designs to study child outcomes.

- Discipline results in higher levels of child aggression, though it may be either prosocial aggression or anti-social aggression.

- The "spanking debate" is empirically unresolved by social scientists, who disagree on the role of child traits, complex interactions between factors (e.g., gender and type of discipline), definitions of spanking, and definitions of outcomes. The moral debate cannot be resolved by social science.

- Physical punishment is tied to the transmission of social class in that it does not reinforce values of creativity or intellectual flexibility in the child (see Kohn, 1969; Figure 7.2).

- Bourdieu's concept of habitus suggests that external conditions of social class (cultural capital) are socialized into the child so that, as an adult, his or her values and culture reconfigure a similar social structure in the next generation.

Discussion Questions

1. To what extent do you think your parents have passed on their social class background to you?
2. How much prosocial aggression does our society need? Do we reward anti-social aggression, such as fighting in hockey games?
3. Do you think that children should be exposed to only developmentally appropriate challenges? Who decides what is appropriate and how do they know this?

Glossary

achieved status A level or strata in society attained by the individual's effort and training.

anti-social aggression Aggression (behaviour intended to injure or harm a person or property) that is antithetical to or fails to support the norms of society (e.g., butting in line, hitting).

ascribed status A level or strata in society attained by the individual based on characteristics outside the individual's control, such as race, gender, family status, and caste.

attachment theory Bowlby's theory that infants must securely attach to one principal caregiver for optimal psychosocial development.

bidirectional parent–child model A theoretical approach that recognizes that parents both affect and are simultaneously affected by their children. The same holds true for children (that is, they affect and are simultaneously affected by their parents).

child achievement Children are expected to achieve higher levels of competency in academics and socializing. Social achievement is often measured by the child's ability to work and play in groups as well as to maintain friendships. Academic achievement is often measured by school grades, test scores, and teacher reports.

child compliance The ability of the child to comply with the instructions of authorities such as parents, teachers, and other adults.

child-to-parent unidirectional model The child conditions (rewards and punishes) the parent to produce the behaviour he or she desires. The more modest version states that parenting responds to the temperament and desires of the child.

correlational design A field research design that measures two variables only and can show if they are related but cannot show if they are causally related.

ecological theoretical model of development Bonfenbrenner's (1979) theory argued that a child's ontogenetic development always occurs in a social context. Humans begin their development in the context of the mother–child dyad and throughout the life course they enlarge their context to family members, school, community, and eventually major social institutions. In this perspective, ontogenesis is simply a part of a complex picture of interactions between the individual and the social and physical environments.

empiricism Theories of learning that emphasize sensory data as the source of ideas and experience.

experimental design A research design aimed at controlling all relevant variables except the hypothesized cause to demonstrate its causal effect on an outcome variable. It commonly uses the state or level of the outcome variable *before* the introduction of the causal variable and then measures the change in the outcome *after* the introduction of the causal variable.

factorial design A design based on a statistical model known as the general linear model (see Table 7.2). More specifically, the general linear model identifies independent causal or associative factors (independent variables) related to some dependent variable (in Table 7.2, the child's success with toilet training). The design is a way of thinking about research and cause and effect. The joint level of two factors (such as the combined effect of toilet training and being 18 months or older) is called an interaction effect. The direct or main effects are simply the independent effect of toilet training regardless of age and the independent effect of age regardless of toilet training. For further information and explanation, see www.socialresearchmethods.net/kb/expfact.php.

habitus Bourdieu's term forthe early habits an individual acquires that are part of and express the values of the social class structure. For example, saying "please" and "thank you" or using a handkerchief rather than a sleeve to blow one's nose.

game stage G.H. Mead's game stage is the time when the child learns that various social roles (such as batter or catcher in baseball) are meaningfully structured by social rules (norms) to construct a game. By playing a game, the child learns to take on various social roles and execute them based on the rules of the game. The child also learns that he or she may take on different roles, such as first being "it" or the "seeker" in a game of hide and go seek and later being one of the "hiders." This is critical to learning the way in which roles and norms function in human societies.

levels of analysis Maturation and development occur at all levels of analysis. Societies develop, social groups develop, dyads and marriages develop, and individuals develop, though the processes for each level of analysis may be quite distinct and different.

occupational conditions Kohn argued that the work conditions of an occupation relate to the values that parents try to instill in their children. Work conditions that are inflexible and have routinized time demands (punching a time clock) tend to emphasize a high value on obedience. Work conditions that are oriented to project completion and require creativity (software producer, lawyer) emphasize time flexibility, internal motivation, and intellectual flexibility.

ontogenetic development Development in which the progression is set by species-specific genes. All humans (in a normal range) progress through the same stages of development at about the same ages.

parent-to-child unidirectional model The parent transfers knowledge and skills to the child.

play stage G.H. Mead's stage of child development in which the child learns that social roles are constructed by norms and sanctions by playing "mommy" or playing "doctor."If a child beats his or her doll, an adult might say, "That is no way to treat your baby!"

prosocial aggression Aggression (behaviour intended to injure or harm a person or property) that enforces or supports the norms of society (e.g., defending the helpless, standing up to bullies, reporting a crime).

rationalism The view that there are pre-existing structures in the mind (ideas) that allow us to channel and form sensory data into "experience."

social class The idea of social class is based on the view that all societies are hierarchically stratified into groups (classes) and that these groups are distinguished by differentials in opportunity, background, culture, and material wealth.

sociogenic development The view that maturation and development are affected mainly by cultural learning and socialization within social groups as opposed to being inherent to the species in the form of a necessary timetable.

values The worth or valuation of an act, thing, or person relative to other elements being evaluated. Parental values have to do with the importance (value) that parents place on elements such as obedience, moral behaviour, and creativity.

Connections

www.andosciasociology.net/resources/
　　Davis$2C+Kingsley+-+A+Final+Note+on+a+Case+of+Extreme+Isolation.pdf
www.youtube.com/watch?v=dEnkY2iaKis
www.ncbi.nlm.nih.gov/pubmed/3119812
www.ncbi.nlm.nih.gov/pmc/articles/PMC1419949/pdf/gut00400-0056.pdf
www.med.umich.edu/yourchild/topics/devmile.htm
www.health.qld.gov.au/cchs/growth_approp.asp
www.socialresearchmethods.net/kb/expfact.php
http://people.ucsc.edu/~brogoff/William%20James%20Award.pdf
www.child-encyclopedia.com/documents/BelskyANGxp_rev-Child_care.pdf
www.tldm.org/news6/child.discipline.htm
www.oecd.org/dataoecd/27/28/38335410.pdf

Remember to log on to the Companion Website at **www.pearsoncanada.ca/white** to find self-graded quizzes and useful resource tools for further study. You can log on to the Companion Website using the Student Access Code that comes packaged with your copy of *Families Across the Life Course*.

Chapter 8
Institutions

Learning Objectives

After reading this chapter, you should be able to:

1. Understand that the family is one of several social institutions that shape the way individuals live their lives.

2. Think through the symbiotic nature in which the family is influenced by other institutions and the family also influences these institutions.

3. Identify the ways in which work, education, religion, and government institutions influence the day-to-day activities of families.

4. Understand the way in which institutions affect families differently at different stages of the life course.

5. Learn about the direct and indirect ways in which institutions affect and are affected by the family.

It is Monday morning and Cam and Wanda Phillips are gearing up for a new week. The week ahead is pretty much set for them, with school trips and work deadlines as well as the events their religious community has planned. It looks particularly busy and they wonder if there is any way to slow it all down. They have thought about home-schooling their two older children, but that would mean that Cam or Wanda would have to put his or her career as a lawyer on hold; after spending all that money and time in law school, it doesn't seem as if that is going to happen. If only they lived closer to Cam or Wanda's family and hadn't moved across the country for new jobs, they wouldn't have to deal with the daycare issue of their youngest each morning. Wanda was legally entitled to an extended maternity leave package at her firm, but she returned to work just two months after the baby was born. She hopes to make partner one day and the thought of being put on the "mommy track" scared her. She wanted her company to know that she could work just as hard as the men there. With BlackBerry in hand, school planners signed, and breakfast in a glass, Cam heads off to take the older children to school while Wanda buckles in the baby to take him to daycare. It will be another day of wondering whether this craziness will ever end.

The Phillips may have a little more money in their retirement account, drive nicer cars, and have a bigger house than most couples, but their day-to-day life is not that different from most North Americans as they try to juggle multiple demands on their time. This chapter looks at the impact that other common social institutions have on the family, and how that impact changes over the life course. See Box 8.1 for more detail on what we mean by social institutions. The family is one of several social institutions that influence one another. In the Phillips family, we see the influence of the educational system throughout the day in the form of rides to school and tightly packed schedules, but it also affects people across the life course according to the type and location of the school selected as well as the length of time spent in formal education. The education one chooses earlier in life is usually tied to career choices made later in life, which may in turn require the need to relocate to obtain work. The labour institution has influenced where the Phillips have chosen to live. Religion will also affect the family's schedule in terms of when and where they gather with their faith community. Although government as an institution isn't mentioned directly, it has also affected the family by establishing laws regarding universal child education, parental leave policies, retirement payouts, and the way in which child care is provided and funded. At the end of the day, the Phillips family must navigate the difficult terrain set in front of them by these often competing institutions.

Institutional influence does not remain constant across the life course of individuals or the family. As people move through the educational system, they are steered toward career choices as well as toward potential mates who reflect their own values. These early

Box 8.1

Social Institutions

The term "social institution" is somewhat unclear both in ordinary language and in the philosophical literature (see below). However, contemporary sociology is somewhat more consistent in its use of the term. Typically, contemporary sociologists use the term to refer to complex social forms that reproduce themselves such as governments, the family, human languages, universities, hospitals, business corporations, and legal systems. A typical definition is that proffered by Jonathan Turner (Turner 1997: 6): "a complex of positions, roles, norms and values lodged in particular types of social structures and organising relatively stable patterns of human activity with respect to fundamental problems in producing life-sustaining resources, in reproducing individuals, and in sustaining viable societal structures within a given environment." Again, Anthony Giddens says (Giddens 1984: 24): "Institutions by definition are the more enduring features of social life." He (Giddens 1984: 31) goes on to list as institutional orders, modes of discourse, political institutions, economic institutions and legal institutions.

Source: Miller (2011).

life choices have a lasting impact across the rest of the life course. How much education we receive, what careers we choose, and the people with whom we develop early, committed, intimate relationships will give the rest of our lives structure that becomes more difficult to change later in life. Newly married couples are not concerned about daycare issues or school day activities, nor are couples later in life after their children have left home. While younger couples may be more concerned about child-care policies, older couples may focus on the government's approach to Old Age Security payments and health care funding priorities. As we move through the life course, the institutions around us continue to affect us in ever-changing ways.

We begin this chapter with a brief discussion of the theoretical perspectives applied to examining the institution of the family, to give us a framework in which to discuss the dominant social institutions that influence and are influenced by the family. We will look at the impact of labour, education, religion, and government on the family over the life course.

The ancient Greek philosophers Plato and Aristotle had strong but conflicting views of the family and its place among institutions such as the government. Plato had little regard for the family while Aristotle saw it as a key component to a healthy, stable society. More recently, sociological theorists Karl Marx, Emile Durkheim, and Max Weber addressed this issue of family among other institutions. Marx and Weber shared similar ideas regarding the economic importance of the family. Weber felt that close family ties hindered the growth of capitalism. Consistent with his work on the **Protestant Reformation**, Weber concluded that the transfer of affinity from kin to one's religious community freed individuals to produce goods and services more rapidly, which helped to fuel the expansion of capitalism. Durkheim wrote more extensively on institutions and saw the institutions of family and religion as the foundation of societal development. His traditional views on gender interdependence and divorce would not make him popular today yet his emphasis on the structural importance of working together rather than pure patriarchal leanings motivated his logic. Durkheim viewed the developmental progression of mechanical solidarity into organic solidarity as support for the theory that family size will continue to shrink as development increases, passing through the stages of extended family to a focus on **conjugal families** and ultimately to single-parent families. Mid-twentieth-century scholars continued to study these ideas and express their concern for the family amid the competing influence of other institutions.

American sociologists Carle Zimmerman (1947) and William Ogburn (1937) both documented the family's interaction with other social institutions. Ogburn and Zimmerman would have agreed on the trend that saw the family's steady loss of functions to increasingly powerful corporations and government, although they would have disagreed on the importance of this trend. Ogburn viewed the American home as becoming "merely parking places" for parents and children, who spend most of their time elsewhere, and argued that the state should assist people with this inevitable path. It could do this by ensuring full-time employment for mothers and universal daycare for children. The goal would be the individualization of society. In stark contrast, Zimmerman did not view the course of society as linear but as cyclical. With a focus on the amount of power a family has over its members, he observed three types of families over history: (1) the **trustee family**, which has the locus of power in kinship connections; (2) the **atomistic family**, characterized by strong individualism and weak influence of family on its members; and (3) the **domestic family**, in which a balance of power exists between the family and other social institutions. The trustee family is followed by the domestic family and then the atomistic family, which is similar to Ogburn's description except that Zimmerman viewed this progression as eventually leading to societal collapse, only to see the cycle repeat itself. Zimmerman documents two previous historical cycles, with the Roman Empire being the last to collapse, and suggests that the North American family is close to becoming the third.

Current scholars continue to examine the family and its interaction with surrounding institutions. The latter half of the twentieth century has seen a significant contribution to the study of the family in its institutional context by feminist scholars such as Lynne Casper, Suzanne Bianchi, Phyllis Moen, Marty Blair-Loy, Anne-Marie Ambert, and Stephanie Coontz. These women and many others like them have provided a more complete picture of the challenges and obstacles that men and women must navigate within both the family and competing social structures.

The family, as an institution, is bigger than the individual members within it and is subject to the influences of other social institutions, such as religion and education, on the behaviours of its individual members. Durkheim (1888) argued that the family had an important effect on reducing the prevalence of suicide. The family provided social cohesion, thus reducing the potential levels of anomie. As a social institution, the family has a direct impact on many life course outcomes that affect individuals. Uhlenberg and Mueller (2004) list four outcomes of well-being that family context influences: survival and physical health, mental health, socio-economic status, and relational success.

Before moving on to discuss specific institutions, it is important to note that social influence is never unidirectional. Not only is the family influenced by other institutions, but the family as an institution also influences these other institutions. The family is just one of many institutions at work shaping the lives of individuals and other institutions. Riley (1998, p. 45) illustrates this point when she discusses the reciprocal nature of women's career aspirations and the social norms regarding women in the paid workforce over the last century:

> We uncovered historical data on the work lives of successive cohorts of U.S. women spanning an entire century that reveal a consistent and striking transformation: In each more recent cohort, larger and larger proportions of women have spent their adult lives in the labor force. From generation to generation, this wave has mounted until, with the changes in lives, structures began to change. As women in those early cohorts demonstrated what they could do, more and more work roles opened up for them at every age up to retirement. Gradually, the norms changed as well. First it became acceptable for women to work. Now it is expected, even required, that women (at all income levels), even young mothers, should work. Clearly, changes in the individual lives of millions of women in successive cohorts (and their employers) have revolutionized both work and family structures.

WORK AND FAMILY ACROSS THE LIFE COURSE

Research in the area of work and family has been stimulated by social, economic, and demographic transformations affecting both institutions. These changes have affected the way in which Canadians experience family life (Duxbury, Higgins, & Coghill, 2003) and the way in which they see the family interacting with work. The dual-earner family is now the norm as women participate in the workforce at almost the same level as men and more and more families become dependent on two paycheques to maintain their standard of living (Jacobs & Gerson, 2004; McQuillan & Ravanera, 2006). As women now outnumber men in institutions of higher learning, the trend of women in the paid workforce can be expected to continue at historically high levels. Recent Statistics Canada data show that women have increased their labour force participation from 42 percent in 1976 to 63 percent in 2008 (Girard, 2010). Women are not only entering the workforce in greater numbers, but also remaining there even after having children. Married women who had children had a rate of departure from the workforce of 26.7 percent in the 1970s; that number decreased to 10.4 percent only 20 years later (Even & Macpherson, 2001). With people living longer and the population aging, the care of dependant parents is also becoming a significant family concern for working Canadians.

As the profile of the Canadian worker shifts to reflect more of a gender balance, the work environment is changing. Although it appears that the average length of the workweek has remained relatively stable for most North American workers, some people are working fewer hours than they would like and others are working more hours than they would like, creating a cancelling-out effect (Jacobs & Gerson, 2004). Accompanying a divergence in non-preferred work hours is the trend for Canadian workers to have non-standard work schedules (Beaujot & Andersen, 2008). This trend toward **non-standard employment** continues, with no change in that pattern in sight (Vosko, Zukewich, & Cranford, 2003). With many workplace cultures still operating under assumptions representative of only a minority of Canadians, such as those of the male breadwinner and the female homemaker, conflict is inevitable. Confusion and lack of institutional clarity confront workers and family members alike. While the lack of clarity may be universal, the way in which it is experienced is divergent. Social norms regarding ideal workers benefit men more than they do women (Williams, 2000).

Early research on work–family interaction focused on the dysfunctional aspects of the interaction. Coser (1974) referred to work–family interaction as the tension between two "greedy institutions." Hogan (1978) looked at the importance of the temporal order of significant life events. He demonstrated that negative consequences were associated with non-normative patterns of life events. For example, marital instability was higher in those cases that did not follow the normative pattern of completing one's education followed by gaining employment and then beginning a family. More recent work has framed the interaction as being more normative and having the potential for positive outcomes and enhancing one's life (Carlson, Kacmar, Wayne, & Grzywacz, 2006). The dynamic nature of work–family interaction has been addressed through longitudinal research. These studies have looked at the transition from school to work (Schoon, McCulloch, Joshi, Wiggins, & Bynner, 2001); career pathways (Blair-Loy, 1999; Huang, El-Khouri, Johansson, Lindroth, & Sverke, 2007); job stability and interruptions (Fuller, 2008); employment, housing, and marital status (Pollock, 2007); and the importance of time in the work–family interaction in general (Han & Moen, 1999). Voydanoff (1987) and White (1999), in their research on the staging of work and family careers, recognized the importance of studying work–family interaction from a systemic perspective. Finally, when work–family research acknowledges that the interaction influences not just individuals but also work environments and families, the institutional dimension is incorporated into the research design. Grzywacz, Almeida, and McDonald (2002) look at the bidirectional effect of positive and negative spillover in both families and the workplace. Drobnic, Blossfeld, and Rohwer (1999) examine the cross-cultural differences in women's employment patterns across the family life course.

Work–family interaction, with its ebb and flow of conflict and resolution, has always existed in various forms (Voydanoff, 2007). Family and work are universal institutions, existing across time and in all societies. Economic theory reminds us that markets are always changing as well, adapting to forces of supply and demand, economic cycles, and innovation and bureaucracy. Early sociologists of the family saw the family as "an organization that is in the constant process of adaptation to changing conditions" (Angell, 1965/1936, p. 14). The latter part of the twentieth century saw rapid change in work environments as the technical information age replaced the labour-intensive industrial age. In addition to changes in work environment, families have been forced to adapt rapidly to a changing world with different family forms and evolving social norms. However, neither of these large social changes are new phenomena.

Historical Context

As family composition changes over time and workplace cultures continue to be transformed, the intersection of these two institutions will affect each other in ways that will challenge both. Benoit (2000) describes the pre-modern historical epochs of work and family in the context of the gender inequity at different times through history. She begins with a brief description of hunting and gathering societies and continues through to large-scale farming societies. Her premise is that in more simple societies, women experienced status on par with men. With few possessions and no surplus wealth, there was little to differentiate women from men economically. As societies moved to small-scale farming, equality remained relatively intact, although gender roles began to diverge. As societies entered large-scale farming, inequity was at its greatest. Men controlled the rudimentary means of production and the income and wealth that accompanied it. In terms of work–family interaction, pre-industrial societies are best described as involving equally hard work for both men and women, with men being the greater benefactors of that hard work.

From the onset of the Industrial Revolution, work and family continued to transform and intersect. Benoit develops another continuum of change for women, outlining the gender inequity from early mercantilism to the current post-industrial society. She concludes that mercantilism picked up where large-scale farming left off—that is, with women at the lowest level of social status. As societies move through the manufacturing stages, first small-scale and then large-scale, women begin to gain in social status as the distribution of wealth extends to females though economic opportunity and less patrilineal inheritance customs. In the post-industrial society, Benoit sees women making large gains in social status because of men's income stagnating while women's income grows. The dominance of the service sector and alternative, non-standard working arrangements provides opportunities to women not previously available. Despite these large gains in social status, Benoit notes that inequity continues between men and women, with women overrepresented in the more precarious working environments.

From a functionalist perspective, Rothman (1978) paints a historical work–family picture similar to Benoit's. She describes the previous 100 years of work–family interaction and notes that in the nineteenth century men were vacating the home as a place of work to go to the cities and work in factories. There seemed to be little concern about this at the time, and men being removed from the household is generally taken for granted today. Initially, wives and sometimes children worked alongside the men, but eventually middle-class values were projected on a larger portion of society and women were relegated back to the home, where they often looked after boarders or did laundry to earn extra income.

With the technological advancements of the Industrial Revolution, time-saving devices began to reduce the energy required to look after the home and children. During the middle of the twentieth century, following World War II, the functionalist work of Parsons and Bales (1955) applied Durkheim's (1933) concept of the division of labour to describe how the family could be organized as efficiently as industry; with men as the breadwinners, fulfilling the **instrumental role**, and women as the homemakers, fulfilling the **expressive role**, the family was seen to be functioning optimally. When organized labour's power peaked in the mid twentieth century and with the postwar economy expanding rapidly, large numbers of men were able to earn a family wage, eliminating the economic need for women to earn an income as well.

Coontz's (1992) denunciation of this ideal functionalist image of the middle-class nuclear family helps to convey just how prevalent this ideal type was as the standard in North American culture. Coontz argues that the family was never like the Cleaver family depicted in the 1950s television show *Leave It to Beaver*. Despite Coontz's attempt to clarify the heterogeneity of family forms, this almost monolithic functionalist image continues to influence many people's definition of how the family used to be and ought to be today.

Early feminist scholars focused on the simplistic nature of seeing all men and all women as homogenous groups with identical environments and roles. Damaske and Gerson (2008, p. 235), citing several authors, state: "More recent theoretical approaches, along with a host of empirical studies, have extended this early work by focusing on variations among women (and men) as well as by examining the institutional and cultural paradoxes and contradictions that leave modern mothers facing deep conflicts and dilemmas." They highlight the importance of understanding the differences that emerge among women when ethnicity, race, and socio-economic stratification are considered.

They cite Collins (1991) to make two important points. First, as Coontz noted, the traditional breadwinner family was an anomaly among white middle-class women and could never accurately be applied to black women. For black women, motherhood has always taken a different form. This inaccurate ideal also does not apply to working-class and working-poor families that have always depended on women's workforce participation.

Work and Family Today

As the first decade of the twenty-first century ended, demographic and geopolitical changes continued to alter the landscape of both workers and families and challenge the institutions of the family and work. The competing institutional demands of work and family are reinforced in a national report by Duxbury et al. (2003), which shows that Canadians are experiencing higher levels of **role overload** as a direct result of spending more time both at work and with their family. The tension caused by the limited resources of time and energy trying to meet the expanding demands of work and family means that something will need to change, just as it always has.

Rapid changes to both the family and the workplace over the past century highlight the need to view work–family interaction in its changing context. The institution of the family has seen a rise in the prevalence of cohabitation and divorce, as well as a move toward increased education, delayed child-bearing, and smaller families. These trends both affect and are affected by the institution of work. The transition from an industrial-based economy to an information-based economy has necessitated more education for the average worker. Greater female representation in the paid workforce, especially of young mothers, has led to a reduction in the size of families. Workplace changes in the form of flextime, non-standard work, the baby boom bubble, and an increase in precarious employment have also influenced and been influenced by the family. Dual-income families may seek non-standard work schedules that do not overlap to alleviate child-care needs and costs. As the baby boom generation begins to enter traditional retirement years, there will be an increased demand for workers in sectors of the economy such as financial services, health care, and technology.

Work–family interaction must be understood as a dynamic process requiring concepts and theories that understand it as such. More than 10 years ago, Han and Moen (1999, p. 100) stated: "Scholars are only beginning to consider the work–family interface as it unfolds over time and across multiple domains." Since then, the dynamic nature of the work–family interface has garnered more attention in journals and books. Kalliath (Kalliath & Brough, 2008), in an interview regarding the state of work–family balance theory, said, "I believe work–family conflict is an intermediate state in a continuous process of creating harmony between work, family and personal life." Books such as It's About Time (Moen, 2003), The Time Divide (Jacobs & Gerson, 2004), and Changing Rhythms of American Family Life (Bianchi, Robinson, & Milkie, 2006) look at the interaction of work and family as a dynamic process that changes across the lifespan. Each book uses the family as the unit of analysis but also outlines the gendered nature in which these dynamics unfold. All three volumes present a variety of studies that involve the measurement of time spent at work and with family, each specifically separating the findings for each gender to provide a more detailed summary of work–family interaction.

As constantly intersecting, constantly changing institutions, work and family are also subject to age, historical period, and cohort effects. In looking at work–family interaction, age effects are going to be the result of an individual's maturation over time. An individual who is young and just out of school may possess little human and social capital in comparison to their situation later in life. Different chronological ages can be more highly correlated to life events such as the birth of a child or the last child leaving the home. These events affect a person's family and work dynamics. Different periods in history are influenced by different socio-historical and political events such as war, economic crisis, or important legislative changes. These periods need to be understood as having different influences on work–family interaction. For example, during World War II, millions of families were left for years without a father physically present when men went to war. At the same time, historically high numbers of women were in full-time employment as part of the war effort. Within a few years after the war, the social context of both work and family environments were quite different. Women left the workforce to make room for returning male soldiers, fertility rates began to climb, and a growing number of women entered institutions of higher learning. These sudden changes also help to explain cohort effects. Women born prior to these changes and women born after them experienced the labour market in different ways. Blair-Loy (1999) looks at the role that cohort and period effects have on female financial executives' success in their field. After outlining the social and legislative changes of the 1960s that helped to integrate women into male-dominated fields, Blair-Loy demonstrates that earlier cohorts' efforts and sacrifices paved the way for later cohorts' success. Earlier cohorts had to deal with a male-dominated field and the challenges that presented, such as lack of female role models, job mobility inequity, discriminatory practices, and sex typing of jobs in the field. Blair-Loy finds that subsequent generations of female financial executives were relatively unaware of the path paved for them by their female predecessors.

As the twenty-first century entered its second decade, the institutions of work and family continued to morph and change as they interact with one another (see Career Box 8.1). This reciprocal impact is well noted in the areas of child and family care, non-paid domestic work, and division of labour. The study of work and family continues to look at these areas as families adjust to new roles and social expectations. Some of the most recent research has highlighted the importance of social support to the well-being of mothers returning to the labour force (Seiger & Wiese, 2011), as well as for new mothers and marital satisfaction levels (Dew & Wilcox, 2011). At the other end of the life course, Kahn, McGill, and Bianchi (2011) found that as men retire from the workforce, they become more involved in the care of grandchildren, to the point where there is no gender difference between grandparents in providing care by the time they are in their sixties.

Intersecting Institutional Influences

As Mindy sat in the orientation meeting, she could not believe that she was finally able to fulfill her lifelong goal of completing a seminary degree. Her father was a pastor, his father's father was a pastor, and now she was going to be the first female pastor in her family. After years of theological debate, her denomination concluded that the ordination of female clergy would now be recognized.

Mindy knew that challenges lay ahead of her. Her decision to have four children and develop a home-based business had been a direct result of her not thinking this day would ever come. She had consigned herself to the role of mother, homemaker, and entrepreneur early in her marriage. Now that the doors had opened to her lifelong calling, her family was going to have to make some significant adjustments. Her business was very profitable yet provided no extended health coverage. Would her husband quit his lower-paying job to take over her business and help with the children? Mindy had home-schooled all of them and now they would have to be integrated into the public school system. When Mindy graduated and received her first parish assignment, where would it be and would her family be willing to relocate?

All of these issues will be a challenge, but her biggest concern is whether she will be able to get back into an academic environment alongside all of the younger students. After all, she was becoming a student all over again with others half her age. Mindy is optimistic, but a little scared as well.

One major concern often brought up in regard to the increased labour force participation of women, especially young mothers, has been the issue of child outcomes. The logic is that as women work more hours, their children receive less care and suffer as a result. It is therefore interesting to note that women spend more time with their children today than they did just decades ago (Bianchi et al., 2006). Bianchi et al. (2006) show that employed mothers have found a way to balance home and work by reducing time spent on housework, even though they have an average combined workload of five hours more per week than working fathers. When aggregating the workloads of all fathers and mothers, the results indicate gender equality. This time equality is something that the authors indicate reflects the continuing pattern from the mid 1960s. They conclude, based on detailed data gathered from time diaries, that families have adapted to the changing institutional norms.

EDUCATION AND FAMILY ACROSS THE LIFE COURSE

Education repeatedly has been connected to a variety of advantages in life. It is by far the single most important factor in determining future economic well-being. It has been shown to be associated with improved health and longer life. It also affects a variety of life course transitions associated with the family, such as marriage, fertility, and divorce.

Box 8.2

Residential Schools

Education was seen as a primary tool in effecting the transformation. In a vein similar to the government's notion of "getting them while they are young," the Oblates saw tremendous possibilities in the establishment of residential schools. Here the students could be isolated from the cultural influences of their parents and a daily, systematic inculcation of Christian theory and practice became possible. Attempts to control became close to absolute in that students were expected to attend from August to June and visits from home were strictly limited.

Source: Haig-Brown (1988, pp. 35–36).

What makes education so important to the study of the life course is that it is something one normally does early in life rather than later. This is important because life course theory has at its foundation the concept that earlier life events have implications for later life events (Mayer, 2004, 2009). Life course trajectories and pathways always contain some form of education early in life, whether it occurs in a formal school environment or is a result of parents and elders who invest time and energy in preparing young members of society for adulthood. It should be noted that this early influence has also been used to subjugate disadvantaged populations, as the case of residential schools in Canada has shown. Residential schools were established to educate and re-socialize young Aboriginal children into the dominant Western culture of the new nation of Canada. Box 8.2 contains a paragraph from Celia Haig-Brown's 1988 work titled *Resistance and Renewal: Surviving the Indian Residential School*. This book is an ethnographic account of those who attended the residential school in Kamloops, British Columbia.

Recent tradition has made completing one's education a key event in the transition from childhood to adulthood (Arnett, 2001). This life event marking the transition to adulthood becomes even more culturally relevant when we consider the fact that young adults are extending their time spent in formal education for periods unlike those seen in the past. This extension of formal education has created ripple effects in the life course, such as delayed union formation and delayed and reduced fertility. The rest of this section summarizes the impact of education on events across the life course also associated with the family.

Early Childhood Care and Education

The importance of early childhood education has been well documented (Mustard, 2006). Families benefit from education and from the implementation of early child care and child education. Canada, like many other **OECD countries**, has been working toward an integrated program of early childhood education and child care. However, like its OECD counterparts, Canada has some demographic challenges. These include a high and increasing rate of young mothers in the paid labour force, an ethnically diverse population, a fertility rate below replacement level, and a relatively high rate of child poverty (Friendly, 2008).

Economic Well-Being

Education is an investment of time and money early in life that has an expected increased economic return later in life. Education usually leads to greater economic returns across the life course in the form of higher and more stable income. The time spent in formal education is often time lost to earning income, so education is usually viewed from a long-term or lifelong perspective. From a relational perspective, time in formal education usually is associated with delays in entering committed relationships and having children.

Family Transitions

Cohabitation and Marriage Higher education is consistent with improved communication and problem-solving skills, both of which equip individuals for entering and maintaining relationships. Higher educational levels may benefit one gender more than the other in the preparation for family formation. Men become more attractive marriage partners due to increased education and the earning power that comes along with it. Women, on the other hand, do not experience the same benefits. Better educated women have prepared for careers that are usually less flexible and more demanding, which makes these careers less compatible with finding a partner and having children (see Figure 8.1). In addition, women who have more rewarding careers may not feel the same desire for a family in order to feel fulfilled in life.

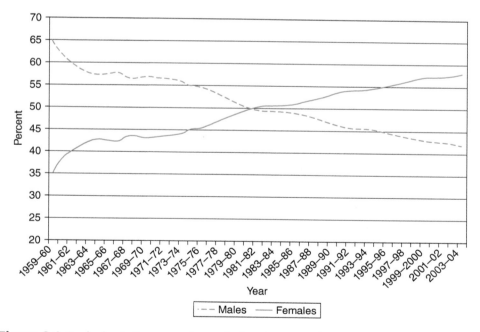

Figure 8.1 Bachelor's Degrees Awarded to Men and Women in the United States, 1959 to 2004

Source: Buchmann and DiPrete (2006, p. 516).

The type of relationship that people enter into is also affected by education attainment. Individuals with higher levels of education are more likely to marry rather than to cohabit. Higher levels of educational attainment are associated with delayed entry into committed unions. Much of this delay can be accounted for by the extended period spent in formal education, but outside of this effect, the acquisition of education is positively related to union formation and, in particular, marriage rather than cohabitation. This relationship has been explained as being consistent with an economic dual-earner model of union formation (Oppenheimer, 1994).

Divorce and Separation Research overwhelmingly supports the relationship of increased education and decreased levels of divorce and separation, although this relationship may not be so direct or linear. Recent research indicates that those with some college education may be more likely to divorce than those with little education or those with a college degree, conveying a curvilinear relationship. Social economic theorist Gary Becker (1981) suggests that this is a result of increased education among women decreasing the economic benefits of marriage for them. It has also been shown that more highly educated women are better equipped financially and psychologically to deal with divorce (Blossfeld, De Rose, Hoem, & Rohwer, 1995). Härkönen and Dronkers (2006) summarize the existing theories connecting education with divorce outcomes and state that the common element in each prevailing explanation is that as long as the benefits of the union outweigh the costs of divorce for the partners, the relationship will remain intact. They suggest that the main difference between prevailing theories involves the mechanism, like those suggested above, as being responsible for tipping the balance toward divorce.

RELIGION AND FAMILY ACROSS THE LIFE COURSE

Many scholars believe that the family is the most influential socializing agent in children's development of religiosity. Although exceptions (e.g., Hoge, Johnson, & Luidens, 1994) and inconsistencies can be found, numerous studies have demonstrated a link between parental and offspring religiosity (see, for example, Clark, Worthington, & Danser, 1986). Religion and family come together in the socialization process as family members pass on their beliefs and behaviours from one generation to the next. The major world religions exist today because of this very process. Hundreds and even thousands of years separate the founding of each major faith and its current adherents. A powerful dimension of religious socialization is the **rite of passage** ceremonies practised by most faiths in unique ways.

Rites of Passage and Religious Ceremonies

Religion and family not only have developed hand in hand over time, but also interact with one another across the life course. Religion and family come together in diverse ways across religious traditions. Some Christian families have their newborn infants

baptized or christened, while others wait for their children to be confirmed in later childhood as a sign of acceptance into the religious community. Jewish families have their male children circumcised on the eighth day of life as part of an ancient covenant God made with their ancestor Abraham. The bar mitzvah occurs when a Jewish male turns 13 years old. This ceremony marks the age of accountability and responsibility for his actions. Rites of passage ceremonies are common in many other religious and cultural traditions as well. Young Buddhist males are carried around on the shoulders of older men during the three-day ceremony of Poy Sang Long before being ordained as novice monks. The corporate nature of Poy Sang Long contrasts with the Australian Aboriginal walkabout, which sees preadolescent boys sent out into the wilderness for six months on their own to mark their transition to adulthood. In many Latin American countries, families celebrate a girl's fifteenth birthday with the Fiesta de Quinceañera, which marks her transition to womanhood. In addition to these religious ceremonies, there are the universal traditions of marriage and burial that link religion and family across the life course.

Religious and Family Socialization

Religious convictions and customs are strongly held beliefs carried forward by groups through religious socialization. This process is facilitated by two primary institutions: the formal religious authorities and the families that embrace the religious teaching. The first of these takes a literal cradle-to-grave life course perspective of the individual, as can be seen in ceremonies involving infants and those remembering the deceased. The family takes an active role in religious socialization by exposing children to religious custom, reinforcing the teaching of the religious institution, and modelling behaviour consistent with the religious community, as shown in Box 8.3. The sacred texts of the three **Abrahamic-based religions**—Christianity, Islam, and Judaism—speak to this point:

> [6] These commandments that I give you today are to be on your hearts. [7] Impress them on your children. Talk about them when you sit at home and when you walk along the road, when you lie down and when you get up. [8] Tie them as symbols on your hands and bind them on your foreheads. [9] Write them on the doorframes of your houses and on your gates. (Deuteronomy 6:6–9)

Box 8.3

A Study of Religious Socialization

Overview

In this study we look at the influence parents, peers and faith communities have on adolescent faith transfer. We examine the transmission of religiosity among Protestant youth using "faith maturity" as operationalized by Benson, Donahue, and Erickson (1993) and Roehlkepartain and Benson (1993). Both of these authors define faith maturity as: ". . . the degree to which a person embodies the priorities, commitments, and perspectives characteristic of vibrant and life transforming faith, as these have been understood in 'mainline' Protestant traditions" (p. 3).

Contradictions in the Literature

Research on religious socialization shows that there are inconsistent results when studying the influence of parental religiosity on the religiosity of their offspring. First, there is the question of whether there is any significant influence. Although most researchers (Clark, Worthington, & Danser, 1986) believe parental religiosity to be central in determining adolescent religiosity, Hoge, Johnson, and Luidens (1994) concluded that parents' involvement in a local church had no determining influence on the patterns of their children. Their study showed a negative relationship between the religiosity of the mother and the church involvement of the youth.

Another example of the inconsistencies is the significance of family types and styles of parenting. Nelsen (1980) found that warmth between the parent and adolescent was not a factor in religious transmission. On the other hand, Myers (1996) reported that family type and style of parenting were significant in aiding or hindering parental influence in religious socialization. Myers found families that were described as warm and caring were more fertile to parental intergenerational transmission of religiosity. Myers also noted that traditional single-income family structures aid in the process of religious inheritance. In contradiction, yet another report indicated that parental education, income, and class had no significant effects on the religiosity of offspring (Francis & Brown, 1991). Results became even more confusing when Wilson and Sherkat (1994) noted that parents of higher income may produce offspring that are less likely to resemble themselves.

Clark et al. (1986) provide a final example of contradictory findings in their review of twelve different studies analyzing the influences of gender of parent on the child's socialization. In seven of the studies, the mother was more influential in determining the offspring's religiosity, two found the fathers more influential, and three found no difference. Some researchers have suggested that the pattern of religious participation has little to do with family transmission at all, but is more the result of macro influences that shape the life course. Stolzenberg, Blair-Loy, and Waite (1995) showed that by separating the effects of marriage and childbearing from the effects of age alone, the data demonstrated that current age and family formation change religious participation. Firebaugh and Harley (1991) supported this perspective and concluded that church attendance is simply a result of aging.

Findings

The importance of this study is that it helps to clarify the importance of all three socializing institutions. It demonstrates that congregational influences are significant in adolescent development of faith maturity. It provides strong evidence for the strength of the peer influence in the process and finally it shows the lasting impact that parents have in influencing the faith maturity of their offspring. Furthermore, there is

support for peers as a mediating variable in the channeling model.

Many studies examining religious socialization have focused on religious socialization as measured by the similarity between the parents and the offspring. However, religious socialization is not necessarily the replication of a list of belief or behavioral items. These intergenerational comparisons do not convey what is sought by religious socialization. In a study of a similar grouping of denominations as used in this study, Hoge et al. (1982) found that parents rated the goal of moral maturity as number one for their children. Since cohorts and period have changed, the meaning and behaviors indicating such maturity may also change. Indeed, parent–child similarities may indicate a lack of moral maturity. What this study has shown is that parents play an important role in the development of their offspring's faith maturity.

Source: Martin, White, and Perlman (2001).

Religion and Family Influence on Couple Formation, Fertility, and Marital Control

Frans Van Poppel and Renzo Derosas (2006), in their book *Religion and the Decline of Fertility in the Western World*, examine some interesting questions. In the late nineteenth century, early researchers were confronted with the almost simultaneous decline in fertility across Europe. This led to resources being directed toward the study of fertility. Greater attention to demographic records confirmed the trends in fertility. Because of the increase in data collection, more opportunities for studying fertility differentials occurred at various levels. Provinces, states, countries, towns, and regions could now be compared.

Countries with religious diversity showed religious differentials almost immediately. This was very apparent in Protestant–Catholic comparisons (Knodel, 1974). Although other religious groups such as Jewish populations were studied, the early debates and discussions revolved around explaining why the fertility rate was higher among Catholics than among Protestants. Each group developed rationales supportive of their cause and political parties were established around each religious group. Van Poppel and Derosas (2006) state that the early twentieth century research of religion and fertility was primarily motivated by fear of losing political power to those producing more offspring. They cite Julius Wolf, a German economist in the late nineteenth and early twentieth centuries, who showed that the regions with the highest percentage of Socialists votes had the largest decline in fertility, while the areas that voted for the Confessional Party had the smallest decline. Based on this kind of information, projections were made by demographers about which regions would grow fast enough to secure power or which groups would decline to the point of losing power.

As the level of sophistication of information gathering and data analysis increased, so did the objectivity of the study of religion and fertility. Researchers emphasized that they focused on scientific study and were not motivated by religious, political, or any other motives. Van Poppel and Derosas (2006) cite an Indianapolis study carried out in 1941 as a seminal work in religious differentials regarding fertility. The study looked at the details of social networks and personal factors that may influence the decision to limit family size. Freedman and Whelpton (1950) continued a series of articles testing various hypotheses regarding the influence of religion on fertility. They tested the hypothesis that the more importance religion had to a person, the less likely he or she would take steps to limit fertility, an assumption based on the pro-natalist nature of religion. They concluded their study by saying that their data did not support this hypothesis, even though earlier studies had showed support for it.

During the second demographic transition of the 1960s and beyond, the rapid decline in European fertility led to very low reproduction levels (Lesthaeghe, 1995). During this time, most Western countries lost interest in the role that religion played in fertility (Van Poppel & Derosas, 2006). With very low fertility levels and decreased religious influence in society, only small differentials were found between groups based on religion.

Presently, as a result of the theoretical contributions of authors such as Goldscheider (1971), Kertzer (1995, 1997), and Greenhalgh (1995), new theories are being explored concerning how fertility and religion correlate. McQuillan (2004) and Chatters and Taylor (2005) have begun to look not just at religion but also at the aspects of religion that may be working to influence fertility. McQuillan (2004) looked at qualities of religion that must be present for it to influence fertility. First, the religion in question must have statements of belief concerning behaviour that specifically relates to fertility outcomes. Norms concerning abortion and contraceptive use have some connection to most religious groups, although those norms may change over time. Second, the religious group must have the means not only to communicate these teachings, but also to enforce compliance to these norms. This enforcement need not occur at the institutional level but often comes through informal social pressure from the community itself. Goldscheider (2006) makes the same argument in response to those who have studied families exposed to the stricter Islamic schools. Goldscheider believes that the coercive nature of the communities these families come from reinforces the strict gender role segregation that encourages higher fertility. The same coercive nature at work in these strict Islamic sects would also explain higher levels of fertility in strict religious sects of Judaism and Protestantism. Finally, McQuillan (2004) argues that religious groups influence the fertility of their members only when those members feel a strong sense of attachment to the group.

Chatters and Taylor (2005, p. 518) list the following general links between religion and family behaviour:

- Religion condemns certain forms of behavior and promotes specific beliefs and practices that are conducive to family solidarity and assistance;
- It provides a framework for beliefs, norms and practices that reinforce the fulfillment of certain family roles;
- It gives guidelines for the handling of life difficulties and conflicts between family roles;
- It fosters positive feelings that promote certain family characteristics;
- Religious settings provide benefits and support for families.

Both McQuillan (2004) and Chatters and Taylor (2005) encourage further study of the religion–fertility link in context to gain a better understanding of what religion means. The connection between religion and fertility has regained some stature in the eyes of researchers. With fertility data and religious scholars from non-Western countries contributing to the literature (King & Beattie, 2004), broader approaches and a greater understanding of the process at work will emerge.

Religion and Gender Roles

Ursula King and Tina Beattie (2004) produced an entire volume on the topic of gender and religion from a cross-cultural perspective. They gathered a diverse group of scholars from various religious traditions to write on the topic of gender and religion. This builds on earlier work by King (1995) on gender and religion. These works highlight the increased interest in the interaction of gender and religion, especially from a feminist perspective.

Many social scientists have attempted to understand and explain the high participation rate of women in religious communities (Finke & Stark, 1992; Stark & Bainbridge, 1985). Women of all ages have higher scores on measures of religiosity. Female membership continues to outnumber men even in newer faith movements (Howell, 1998). This pattern of higher female participation seems to continue across the life course and across religious organizations (Ozorak, 1996). It is not limited to North America, as the same phenomenon occurs in Europe and among Latin American women (Martin, 1990). Because of the high female participation rates and gender differences in religious adherence, some feminists have criticized women's participation as having a "false consciousness" (Furseth & Repstad, 2006). Feminist scholars continue to contribute to the understanding of the gender issue in the context of religion. The Abrahamic-based religions of Christianity, Islam, and Judaism are presented as a dichotomized version of gender equality. Each supports spiritual equality but each also sustains a version of social inequality. This dualistic approach filters into gender role attributes. King (1993) suggests that many world religions are based on the idea that women are associated with the body, nature, and earth, whereas men are associated with the mind, spirit, and heaven. Each of these traditions is also marked by complementary marriage scripts, although there have been significant moves toward a more egalitarian model in some religious communities representing each of these faiths.

Sexuality is an area in which religion has a voice. Once again, across the faith traditions, women have been seen through the lens of their reproductive function. Ancient religions focused on fertility gods. Contemporary religions have vacillated between the evils of sexuality, tolerated procreative value, and a separation of procreation and the sex act. Foucault (1976) considered religion a central part of culture. In his work on sexuality, "Foucault argues that religion actually is always about sexuality and the body because discourses about religious practice and belief center around the body and are always concerned about what people do with their bodies" (Furseth & Repstad, 2006, p. 65).

The Christian texts and traditions speak extensively about the role of sexuality, often in a contradictory manner. Most traditionally seen as sanctioned in the context of marriage, sex is mentioned in both a procreative and a non-procreative way. Paul, an early disciple of Jesus and a missionary of the Christian faith, tells husbands and wives that

> The husband should fulfill his wife's sexual needs, and the wife should fulfill her husband's needs. The wife gives authority over her body to her husband, and the husband gives authority over his body to his wife. Do not deprive each other of sexual relations, unless you both agree to refrain from sexual intimacy for a limited time . . . (1 Corinthians 7:3–5).

This passage makes no reference to procreation and gives no sense of gender inequality. This seems consistent with the teachings of Jesus himself when he was asked about the role of marriage in the future kingdom to come. Jesus stated frankly that after the resurrection of the dead, people will not marry but be like the angels (Luke 20:24–36), a reference, presumably, to their sexless nature. The early church fathers moved away from this mutual view of sexuality and began to see it as a necessary evil. Soble (2002) discusses Augustine's theology of sexuality in which sexual activity between married spouses, if done for pleasure only and not for procreation, is a sin but forgivable. Thomas Aquinas continues this sinful view of sexuality by referring to women as inferior and mandating a need to separate sexual pleasure from procreation (Furseth & Repstad, 2006). Over the next 500 years, sexual abstinence was viewed as a superior form of earthly living. After the Reformation, Protestant sects slowly began to adopt a move love-centred view of sexuality and marriage. Today, the Catholic Church maintains strict teachings on marriage, divorce, contraception, and abortion. However, a brief study of the very low fertility levels in predominantly Catholic countries would reveal a form of cognitive dissonance in this area.

With the resurgence of religion (Christianity and Islam) in the late twentieth century, scholars began to look more closely at the role religion has in family life. Recent immigrants to Canada come from a variety of religious traditions and ethnic backgrounds. Caron Malenfant and Belanger (2006) note that 80 percent of new immigrants adhere to the Christian faith. That rate is slightly higher than in the general population, in which 72 percent identified with Christianity. Morgan (1987) argues that religion has increased impact on family and gender-related issues. Using Scanzoni's (1975) research, Morgan focuses on the symbiotic relationship between religious devotion and sex role traditionalism. She highlights the role that religion has played in the creation and maintenance of traditional family roles, which also contributed to assigning privileged patriarchal rights in the realm of politics, business, and the judicial systems (Burlage, 1974).

In the Islamic sacred text, the Quran, women are spoken of as having equal spiritual status as men, but that equality is not extended socially. Swenson (2008) builds a case for Islamic patriarchy by citing several passages from the Quran. Women and men were both created by Allah (Sûrah 4:1 and 49:13) and they both have the opportunity to enter paradise in the afterlife if their deeds are considered righteous (Sûrah 4:124 and 33:35). Physically, both women and men are considered protectors of one another (Sûrah 9:71) and they should treat each other with kindness. Despite these spiritual and physical statements of equality, men have been placed in charge of women because Allah made one to excel compared to the other and because men economically support women (Sûrah 4:34).

Islamic traditions do not see sexuality and spirituality as being at odds. Sexuality is described as a sign of God's mercy (Furseth & Repstad, 2006). The control of women's sexuality using the hijab or the veil has its roots in pre-Islamic notions of honour and shame. Hassan (1995) describes the role of men's honour and shame being connected to women's chastity. As a result, it is extremely important for men to control women's bodies and their sexuality. Furseth and Repstad (2006) cite Natayanan (1990) in describing the Hindu scriptural sources as being primarily male centred. This focus has significant implications in Indian culture. Women suffer from labels of being unclean and impure during menstruation and childbirth, but fertility is celebrated and mother images are worshipped.

Morgan (1987) references several authors (Burlage, 1974; Daly, 1974; Richmond-Abbott, 1983) to support the statement that traditional religious belief systems have also viewed women's primary function as that of bearing and raising children. Historically, Hindu marriages were for having children, with a greater appreciation for sons who would be able to carry on the family line in the patriarchal society (Jain, 2003). Morgan's (1987) study revealed that as religious devoutness increases, gender role attitudes become more traditional. In support of this finding, Pearce (2002) concluded that the greater a woman's involvement in and valuation of religion, the larger the size of family she desired. Pearce (2002, p. 337) states: "These findings suggest that gender-oriented studies of family issues such as child-bearing dispositions cannot ignore the influence of religion."

Religion and gender roles—whether through direct instruction, sexuality, or cultural mandates—are intricately connected. Religion's influence in establishing gender roles and maintaining those gender roles connects well to McQuillan's (2004) tripartite requirements for religion influencing fertility. After establishing the link between religion and its history of influencing gender roles, particularly gender roles consistent with fertility decision and outcomes, the link between gender roles and fertility can be examined.

Gender Roles and Fertility Goldscheider (2006) suggests that as the roles of women become less family based, fertility levels are likely to decline. He sees this as a central research emphasis. Illustrated by the complex social structure of Muslim Israelis, Goldscheider illustrates that large family size is consistent with traditional family roles. These Muslim women represent powerlessness on two fronts: their gender and their religious orientation. Because of their powerlessness, they are unable to move out of a gender role that values and reinforces large families. Consequently, large family size ties women to households and families in a way that reinforces and maintains their gender segregated roles. This illustration provides a good summary of the literature on the effects of gender roles on fertility outcomes.

GOVERNMENT AND FAMILY ACROSS THE LIFE COURSE

Governments are keenly interested in the citizens of their country. They are concerned that their constituents are relatively satisfied and have their basic needs met. Different types of governments have different approaches to how this may look. For example, the welfare capitalist state may encourage an environment of maximum productivity, whereas a socialist state may be more concerned about the equal distribution of resources among the population. The point is that each type of government will be active to some extent in influencing the life course of individuals and families through policies and laws. For example, the state legally defines marriage (see Box 8.4); decides who is financially responsible for children; and determines whether procedures affecting fertility, such as abortion, are considered legal. The state may also define who is family (see Box 8.5).

Aldous Huxley's brave new world (see Box 8.6) really isn't all that new after all, just an old idea told in a new way. As discussed, Greek philosophers debated the role of the state in the family. Plato, in *The Republic*, abolishes the family and replaces it with guardians instead. This was his solution to nepotism and the amassing of private wealth

---

Box 8.4

Bill C-38: The Civil Marriage Act

Bill C-38, An Act respecting certain aspects of legal capacity for marriage for civil purposes, or the Civil Marriage Act, received first reading in the House of Commons on 1 February 2005. The bill codifies a definition of marriage for the first time in Canadian law, expanding on the traditional common-law understanding of civil marriage as an exclusively heterosexual institution. Bill C-38 defines civil marriage as "the lawful union of two persons to the exclusion of all others," thus extending civil marriage to conjugal couples of the same sex.

Source: http://www.parl.gc.ca/About/Parliament/ LegislativeSummaries/bills_ls.asp?ls=c38&Parl=38&Ses=1

Box 8.5

Bill C-31: Defining Who Is Family and Who Is Not

In June 1985, the Canadian government amended the Indian Act through Bill C-31. The impact on Aboriginal women and their children was particularly important. Prior to this legislative change, an Aboriginal woman who married outside her band automatically became a member of her husband's band. A transfer between bands is still possible but occurs only through the woman's choice and the receiving band's consent. In addition, prior to the legislation, Indian women who married non-Indian men lost both their status and their band membership. These patterns robbed thousands of women of their traditional kinship and lineage and removed their children from those same family ties.

During the first five-year period (1985 to 1990) following the amendment to the legislation, the population of Status Indians rose by 19 percent, with women representing the majority of that number (Indian and Northern Affairs Canada, 1990).

Box 8.6

Brave New World

In the year of our Ford 632, children are created, sex is purely recreational, and the world's economic goals are being achieved with the help of carefully crafted castes of humans who could boast of up to 95 identical siblings thanks to the Bokanovsky process. Aldous Huxley's futuristic depiction of society was written in 1932 but is set in the Gregorian equivalent of AD 2450. Huxley's utopian world is at peace and its 2 billion inhabitants have everything they could possibly want. The world economy is running smoothly and is populated by the five controlled castes. Fertility is no longer an option or a concern. The state-run hatcheries allow the fetuses of the highest (or Alpha) caste to develop naturally in "decanting bottles," while fetuses predestined to become members of the lower castes (Beta, Gamma, Delta, and Epsilon) are exposed to chemical treatments that retard their physical and intellectual abilities and make them uniquely suited to obedience and functionality. When one young boy is foolish enough to inquire about the value of this Taylorized incubation process, the Director of the Hatcheries and Conditioning Centres promptly replies,

"My good boy! Can't you see? Can't you see? Bokanovsky's Process is one of the major instruments of social stability. Stability," said the Controller, "stability. No civilization without social stability. No social stability without individual stability. Stability," insisted the Controller, "stability. The primal and the ultimate need. Stability. Hence all this."

The mass production of human beings with predetermined IQs allows for the easy division of society members into castes with minimal questioning or potential social unrest. With limited cognitive and physical abilities, these beings represent ideal citizens in the Brave New World. All of the children are socialized with subconscious messages appropriate to their caste. This approach ensures conformity to designated social roles as well as the adoption of morals, behaviours, and a class consciousness consistent with the needs of society.

Any connection between sexuality and procreation was long forgotten. Sexuality was for recreational purposes only. Parental identification had become so removed from society's consciousness that the use of a familial term such as *father* was considered pornographic. Women relied on a "Malthusian belt" and a regular supply of contraceptive cartridges to avoid pregnancy.

(*Republic*, book 5, 416–417, and 462–464). "Wives and children are to be held in common by all, and no parent is to know neither his own child nor any child his parents—provided it can be done" (*Republic*, book 5, 457). In his other works, Plato took a less drastic position on the family but still felt that the state should control the number of children to avoid having too many for the state to care for or too few to meet the needs of the state (*Laws*, book 5, 740). Plato's student Aristotle did not embrace his mentor's opinion about the state and the family. He felt that when things are held in common, they receive less care than when individuals are responsible. "For besides other considerations, everybody is more inclined to neglect something which he expects another to fulfill; as in families many attendants are often less useful than a few. Each citizen will have a thousand sons who will not be his sons individually, but anybody will be equally the son of anybody, and will therefore be neglected by all alike" (*The Politics of Aristotle*, 1261 b34–1262 a2).

With the increased prevalence of towns and cities coming together during the sixteenth and seventeenth centuries to form nations, the state began to gain more importance and became more concerned about their populations. These more clearly defined nation-states focused on their increased need to protect their borders and their trading markets. The increased interest in the individuals making up the nation led to a strategic division of the life course. The state divided those who were dependent on care (children and the elderly) from those who were productive workers able to provide that care. Leisering (2004) describes this period as the time when the tripartite division of childhood and youth, working age, and old age gradually evolved. The welfare state's concern for the care of its population developed and, as a result, legislation was implemented to ensure that these groups worked together and their needs were met. The primary function of the government in a **welfare state** is to ensure that the basic needs and expectations of the individuals in the nation are achieved. The more the state is involved, the more the state feels it can do a better job of making the choices associated with the redistribution of the nation's resources.

Leisering and Walker (1998) provide a succinct overview of the welfare state's interaction with the family over the life course in their model shown in Figure 8.2. They present the state's role in minimizing certain economic and security risks associated with various stages of the life course. Leisering (2003) points out that social scientists have examined the key examples of the state's influence in the areas of education, old age pensions, and risk management. The concern is that these contributions have been looked at in isolation and instead need to be studied holistically.

Childhood

State policies that directly relate to the first stage of the life course, childhood, need to start with birth and fertility. State policies affecting fertility may be as direct as the Chinese government's strict one-child policy or cash incentives for having more than two children, as was tried in Quebec during the 1990s. More indirect policies—such as

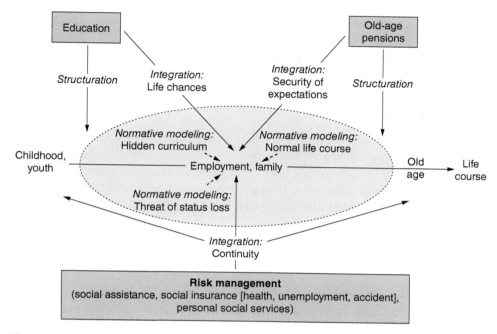

Figure 8.2 Life Course Policies in the Welfare State: Programs and Modes of Operation

Source: Leisering and Walker (1998, p. 10).

parental leave allowances and universal child-care programs—often encourage women to approach their desired fertility level without fear of it negatively affecting their career goals.

Child-care policies and universal education legislation play an important role in the structure and functioning of the family across the life course. With children in the care of alternative caregivers, women are able to engage in the paid workforce at a similar level to men who are the fathers of young children. One of the most significant trends in the twentieth century was the rise of woman in the paid workforce. Nowhere has that effect been more pronounced than among woman with preschool-aged children.

Labour Force Participation

Government policies benefit some segments of society more than others (e.g., two-parent families versus single-parent families, wealthier families versus poorer families). Gornick and Meyers (2003) point out that policies in the United States favour intact families and that poorer families spend a disproportionate amount of their income on child care compared to wealthier families. In Canada, economic fluctuations and state intervention strategies are not experienced in the same way by poorer or non-traditional families. Legal immigrants do not experience the same benefits as the native population (Papademtriou & Terrazas, 2009). Although many companies have increased their focus on family-friendly policies, workplace norms still segregate serious employees from those on the **"mommy or daddy track"** who consider family care an integral part of their identity (Cummins, 2005; Duxbury et al., 2003) and something they are not willing to sacrifice to get ahead in the workplace.

Another form of indirect state intervention that affects families in the working stage is the way in which governments choose to tax earnings of single individuals compared to family units. A country may tax individuals who are part of a family differently than individuals who are unattached from a family, or it may present family-based tax credits that benefit only one individual within the family (e.g., a child tax credit paid to the mother).

Marriage and Divorce

Marriage and divorce are important family life-course markers. They also are regulated by the state. Who can legally marry is at the discretion of the government and may change. Multiple-partner marriage, or polygamy, was made illegal in North America in the late nineteenth century. Most recently, Canada changed the definition of who could marry from one man and one woman to include same-sex marriages (see Box 8.5). The state is interested in marriage because it legally establishes the mutual responsibility of each partner as well as the physical and emotional care of any children who come from the union. No-fault divorce or divorce without cause (irreconcilable differences) is a relatively new phenomenon that involves the division of assets between the parties without attributing blame to either partner. This is in contrast to the experience of previous generations, when the state would often mandate spousal support payments, usually paid by the husband to the wife. The state continues to decide the amount of child support that must be paid when joint custody of working spouses is not awarded in a divorce.

Retirement

The third stage of the tripartite division of the life course by the state is retirement. Mandatory retirement of older workers was first instituted in Germany in the 1880s. People are now living longer and healthier lives, so it is not a surprise to see countries such as Canada repeal mandatory retirement laws. A person born in 1960 can expect to live 20 years longer than someone born in 1900. Yet even though an individual is not required to retire at age 65, government pension rules help to create a typical retirement age around this period. The state also influences housing and health care decisions in old age. Government housing is common in welfare and socialist states as a means of providing housing for low-income and elderly citizens. These housing units are built where the state chooses, which leaves those who need this type of housing with few options

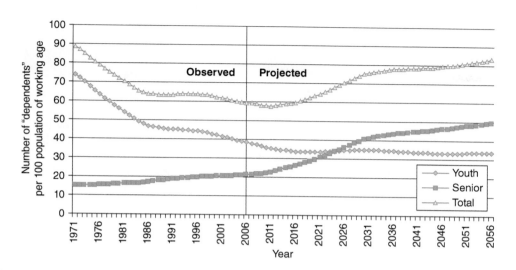

Figure 8.3 Observed and Projected Youth, Senior, and Total Demographic Dependency Ratios, Canada, 1971 to 2056

Source: Statistics Canada, CANSIM Tables 051-001 (1971 to 2008) and 052-0004 (2009 to 2056).

regarding where they will live. Other housing concerns affect those seniors no longer able to live on their own. Institutionalized care homes are in increasing demand as the populations of Western countries age.

Income during retirement is usually made up of a variety of sources, the primary ones being personal savings, work-related pensions, and government pensions. Each of these sources is affected by the state. Government pensions are distributed to elderly citizens in amounts that vary by marital status and, to a certain degree, financial need. These funds are dispersed from tax dollars and from contributions made by the retired individuals earlier in the life course. The government's ability to continue to pay these amounts to an aging population has caused some concern, particularly among younger Canadians. The **dependency ratio** in Canada is projected to increase (see Figure 8.3). The total demographic dependency ratio is the ratio of the combined youth population (0 to 19 years) and senior population (65 years or older) to the working-age population (20 to 64 years). It is expressed as the number of "dependants" for every 100 "workers." In other words, it is the number of youth (ages 0 to 19) plus the number of seniors (ages 65 and older) per 100 workers (ages 20 to 64).

The state affects not only the amount that elderly people can expect to receive from the government, but also the way in which work pensions and individual savings are collected and distributed. Through legislation, the government can create tax incentives for companies to pay pensions as well as laws that benefit individual savers. Registered retirement savings plans and tax-free savings accounts are examples of the ways in which the state can influence savings and ultimately retirement income.

Box 8.7

Get in Line . . . and Wait

Date: Jun. 3, 2009

MRI wait lists in British Columbia are approaching one year—and expensive private clinics may be the only alternative.

Victoria resident Vicki Clark is reeling from an old sports injury. Doctors say she needs an MRI scan to diagnose the problem, but Clark was shocked when she learned how long she would have to wait.

"I have an appointment for 7 a.m. in Victoria, March 20, 2010," Clark said.

Mike Conroy, of the Vancouver Island Health Authority, had a similar reaction.

"I was a little surprised by that," Conroy said.

In 2008, the province gave the health authorities $120 million in one-time funding to clear up MRI wait lists—and it worked. But now the money is drained up, and wait lists have shot up dramatically.

Clark also called a private clinic. She was told she could receive the same scan within a week—but for a cost of more than $1,200.

"I'm not adverse to private treatment, but at the same time I think our health system should be revamped," Clark said.

Source: http://www.ctvbc.ctv.ca/servlet/an/local/CTVNews/20090603/bc_mri_waits_090603

An aging population is concerned with health care availability and affordability. State health care policies govern who receives treatment and when that treatment can take place. Even in countries with universal health care, barriers exist that restrict the availability of care. Universal health care is not synonymous with unlimited resources. For example, limited magnetic resonance imaging (MRI) machines means that queuing is used to limit the number of people who have access to this type of imaging (see Box 8.7).

The state also influences the cost and availability of drugs through pharmaceutical regulations and drug approval processes. The elderly as a group are most affected by this because of their greater use of medication and medical processes.

In summary, the influence of the government on families across the life course is much more prevalent than the casual observer might expect. It is present when we consider formalizing our relationships, influences how many children we choose to have, and decides at what age our children go to school. It gives us incentives to save for the future and controls the medical process on which we ultimately become dependent. The government, like religion, can be described as affecting our lives from cradle to grave.

CONCLUSION

The family represents one of the foundational social institutions of any society. Researchers and scholars may not agree on the future or value of the family, but they do agree that the family continues to have important social implications. Alongside other important social institutions such as religion, government, education, and labour, the family continues to shape and influence the behaviours of individuals across the life course.

SUMMARY OF KEY POINTS

- The family is one of several social institutions that influence one another. Some other important social institutions are:
  - Work
  - Education
  - Religion
  - Government

- The family is influenced by other social institutions and also influences those social institutions.

- Classic and modern scholars have debated and continue to debate the importance of the family as a social institution.

- The dual-earner family has now become the norm in Canada.

- Early research on work–family interaction focused on the dysfunctional aspects of the interaction, but current work continues to examine the benefits of multiple roles.

- The idyllic depiction of the North American family in *Leave It to Beaver* in the 1950s continues to influence people's definition of how the family was and ought to be today, despite it being an anomaly in recent family history.

- Despite the increasing rate of young working mothers, women spend more time with their children today than they did just decades ago (Bianchi et al., 2006).

- Concerning family care and paid work, the differences between men and women are decreasing, but men continue to do more paid work and less family care than women.

- Education is an excellent example of an early life course event that has an impact on later life course events. Individuals and families benefit from early education.

- Completing one's education is recognized as a marker in the transition to adulthood.

- Economic theory suggests that as income goes up, divorce rates go down because of the costs associated with divorce. Highly educated and highly paid women are less likely to be financially dependent on a male provider and therefore are more likely to divorce.

- Religious influences on family socialization revolve around important life course events such as marriage, birth, death, and coming of age ceremonies.

- Religion influences family life in both direct and indirect ways. Direct influences include doctrinal propositions regarding marriage and divorce scripts as well as the socially acceptable use of sexuality. Indirect influences include reinforcing patriarchal approaches to family life that affect decisions on the roles of family members and fertility.

- The government is or has been involved in virtually every aspect of the family:
  - Who can legally marry and divorce (see Bill C-38)
  - Who is related to whom (see Bill C-31)
  - Accepted forms of sexual expression
  - When you can start working and when you must stop
  - Issues of child custody and obligations among former partners

Critical Thinking Questions

1. Do you feel that changes occurring in the workplace are shaping the way in which families function, or are the ways in which families are changing leading to changes in the workplace? Why?

2. To what extent do macro forces such as global economic changes and geopolitical instability affect our local institutions? In other words, how does the fall of Libya or the default of a foreign nation such as Greece affect our families, our work environment, and educational system?

3. Institutional conflict occurs when the roles we fulfill in life demand that we be in two places at the same time, such as at a board meeting and at a child's baseball game. Discuss other ways in which the institutions that influence us put us in situations that are impossible to harmonize.

Glossary

Abrahamic-based religions The religions of Judaism, Islam, and Christianity, which all trace their historical roots to the patriarch Abraham.

atomistic family A family that has the individual as its focus. This is the third stage in Zimmerman's cyclical theory of family development and is depicted as the state having a dominant role in the life of the family.

conjugal family A family that has the partner dyad as its focus. Goode predicted that this family type would be a natural result of modernization.

dependency ratio The ratio of the population considered to be below and above working age to the population in the labour force.

domestic family The second stage of Zimmerman's cyclical theory of family development in which the state has increasing influence in the life of the family.

expressive role A gendered term that refers to family roles that are most often associated with females, such as caring and nurturing.

instrumental role A gendered term that refers to family roles that are most often associated with males, such as economic provision and physical protection.

mommy and daddy track A symbolic pathway that parents who value family more than career are often placed on by company supervisors.

non-standard employment Employment that falls outside of the more traditional working hours of 8 a.m. to 5 p.m., Monday through Friday.

OECD countries The Organisation for Economic Co-operation and Development represents a group of countries committed to democracy and the market economy. Founded in 1961, the original group of 20 states has now expanded to 34 countries.

Protestant Reformation A general religious movement of the European Christian faith in which dissenters separated from the Roman Catholic Church in protest of perceived religious abuses.

rite of passage A significant life course event in which individuals pass from one life stage to another. This typically involves a ceremony that marks the transition to adulthood.

role overload A concept that was developed by family researchers from a functionalist perspective who felt that additional roles in a person's life would reduce the effectiveness of the existing roles. This concept was applied to the roles of women as they began to enter the paid labour force in large numbers.

trustee family The first stage in Zimmerman's cyclical theory of family development. He considered this stage as a time in which families relied on each other for survival and the state was either undeveloped or not yet interfering with family functions.

welfare state A term used to designate government systems that seek to enhance the economic and social well-being of their citizenry. Welfare states exist in most current nation-states and lie on a continuum of involvement and intervention.

Connections

http://en.wikipedia.org/wiki/Parental_leave
www.parl.gc.ca/About/Parliament/LegislativeSummaries/bills_ls.asp?ls=c38&Parl=38&Ses=1
www.statcan.gc.ca/pub/82-229-x/2009001/demo/dep-eng.htm#hg
www.ctvbc.ctv.ca/servlet/an/local/CTVNews/20090603/bc_mri_waits_090603
www.cbc.ca/news/canada/calgary/story/2009/11/03/calgary-flames-h1n1-swine-flu-shot.html

Remember to log on to the Companion Website at **www.pearsoncanada.ca/white** to find self-graded quizzes and useful resource tools for further study. You can log on to the Companion Website using the Student Access Code that comes packaged with your copy of *Families Across the Life Course*.

Chapter 9
Divorce and Repartnering

Learning Objectives

After reading this chapter, you should be able to:

1. Understand the historical background of divorce and how it compares to current data and trends.

2. Describe the divorce fluidity and variation model used to understand the ecology of divorce as well as see it as a process and not just an event.

3. Identify the correlates and predictive variables understood to explain divorce and identify the ways in which divorce rates are calculated as well as the strengths and weaknesses of each method.

4. Describe the research on the outcomes of divorce, particularly its effect on children as seen across the life course.

5. Identify the various pathways that people take after divorce.

Ms. Baker couldn't help noticing that Haley had been looking out the window for most of the class. She knew that Haley's parents were going through a divorce and, based on Haley's declining school performance, she thought things were probably not going well. Jordan, on the other hand, seemed to be much happier now that his parents had sorted through their divorce issues. He was glad he wasn't going to have to move and that his mom was going to live close to their old house so she and Jordan could still spend a lot of time together. Emma also seemed to be doing well with her new family. After a tough year, she was much more focused on her studies and seemed to be getting along better with the other kids in the class. When Emma's mother got remarried to her childhood girlfriend, it was quite a transition for everyone, but they seemed to be adjusting well with the support of extended family.

With all of these children making progress, Ms. Baker examined her own feelings about her mother getting divorced again. Given her mother's age, Ms. Baker was worried about things like home care, grocery shopping, and doctors' visits. It looked as if her mother's needs would once again become her own.

In 2010, a Canadian news article began with the following statement: "The traditional definition of family is changing in Canada, with four in 10 first marriages ending in divorce, according to a new study" (www.cbc.ca/news/canada/story/2010/10/04/vanier-study004.html). In 1997, Barbara Dafoe Whitehead wrote *The Divorce Culture*. Fifteen years later, it is now possible to examine the influence of marital breakdown on a generation of people who grew up with divorce as a normative family life-course event. In this work, Whitehead argues that divorce is now part of everyday North American life. It is embedded in our legal system, part of our pop culture, and so common that it is now considered normative. One need only ask the average adolescent or adult what he or she knows about divorce and the response typically will be that half of all marriages will experience it. Is this true? Do we live in a divorce culture? Are current times drastically different from other periods in history? If so, what implications does divorce have for adults, children, and society as a whole?

This chapter looks at the divorce process in three parts. We begin by providing the historical context of divorce. Then we look at the diversity of divorce, considering the many different experiences people have while going through it. Finally, we look at the implications of divorce for adults and children across the life course as a means of giving us a better appreciation for the topic. The final section of the chapter discusses the new experiences and challenges that face families confronted with divorce: single-parent families, re-entry to the dating scene, and more complex family types with the introduction of remarriage and stepfamilies.

DIVORCE IN CONTEXT
Historical Overview of Divorce

For the purposes of understanding divorce across the life course, the history of divorce has two primary stages: an ancient historical phase and a modern historical phase. Divorce is not a new social entity. It was developed as a stage in the life course shortly after marriage was created! The ancients discussed divorce in historical records and sacred texts. Divorce and its place in society are discussed at length in the Jewish Pentateuch, which is dated to well over 3000 years ago. According to Dionysius, Roman law regulated divorce from the time of Romulus onward. Roman law allowed divorce under certain conditions and could be initiated only by males (Woolsey, 1882).

In this ancient historical period, divorce was characterized as an event that took place infrequently. When it did occur, it was highly regulated and permitted only to men of influence. Not much changed through history in Western nations. The strong influence of the church through much of the previous two millennia subdued any attempts for divorce to grow. The Roman Catholic Church currently does not recognize divorce, consistent with their doctrinal history. Apart from the church granting an annulment (deciding that a marriage is not officially recognized because of some undisclosed pre-existing condition or fraudulent representation at the time of marriage), a couple must remained married until one of the partners dies. This strong church position changed for some Christians because of the influence of reformers such as Martin Luther and John Calvin, who taught that divorce was permitted for specific reasons such as adultery. King Henry VIII is often thought to have established the Church of England because of the issue of divorce, but that was not the case. He wanted to marry Anne Boleyn after his first wife, Catherine of Aragon, was unable to produce a male heir, and sought an annulment from the Pope in Rome. When it wasn't granted, King Henry VIII formed the Church of England and was issued an annulment by the archbishop. Divorce continued be rare in England and was made available to the average citizen only in 1857. In 1901, there were 512 divorces in England and Wales, compared to 141 135 in 2001 (Wilson and Smallwood, 2008).

Divorce continued to remain unattainable for several hundred years after the Protestant Reformation in areas of Europe where Catholicism dominated. The ecclesiastical influence of the church on divorce continued to be felt in Western nations until the end of the twentieth century, with Ireland not making divorce legal until 1995. The situation in North America was different. Apart from Quebec, North America was originally settled mostly by Protestants and divorce, although difficult to obtain, was not uncommon.

The history of divorce in North America is described in detail by Cherlin (2009) in his book *The Marriage-Go-Round* (see also Phillips, 1991). He emphasizes the U.S. government's desire to have Christian marriage viewed as a fundamental aspect of American society. Legislation and judicial decisions were used to ensure that aberrant unions such as polygamy and Aboriginal marriage customs were unable to continue.

Divorce laws and practices varied from state to state and divorce rates began to rise in the mid 1800s. Cherlin states that, by the 1890s, divorce had become a national issue. He cites President Theodore Roosevelt's comments to Congress in response to a 1905 study on the topic: "There is widespread conviction that the divorce laws are dangerously lax and indifferently administered in some states, resulting in the diminished regard for the sanctity of the marriage relation" (O'Neill, 1965). The rate of divorce in the United States doubled between 1865 and 1890 (Cherlin, 2009).

In Canada, the divorce rate was held down by the Catholic influence in Quebec and by the fact that divorce in Canada required a parliamentary act. According to Statistics Canada, only five divorce acts were passed prior to Confederation in 1867. From 1867 until the first major legislative change regarding divorce, a person had to petition the government for an Act of Divorce, placing the request publicly in the *Canada Gazette* as well in two local newspapers. This petition remained in the paper for a six-month period. The rare nature of divorce in Canada continued into the twentieth century, with only 11 divorces registered in 1900. Until 1968, the only common grounds for divorce were adultery or seven years of desertion.

The increased participation of women in the paid workforce allowed them to reduce their economic dependency on a breadwinning partner. Women were no longer required to remain in unfulfilling marriages for financial security. This employment trend also provided women with a greater diversity of roles and identities beyond those of wife, mother, and homemaker. Changes in legislation regarding divorce and the increasing numbers of women in the labour market contributed to a change in divorce patterns.

The **Divorce Act** of 1968 was the first significant piece of Canadian legislation to affect divorce rates. It granted divorce for couples who had experienced marital breakdown and been separated for three years. Grounds-based divorce continued to exist as well. The number of divorces almost doubled between 1968 and 1970. Less than 20 years later, an amendment to the Divorce Act in 1985 reduced the waiting period from three years to one. Once again, the divorce rate spiked, with the number of divorces reaching 90 900 in the following year (Oderkirk, 1994).

During the twentieth century, the divorce rate continued to rise in the United States. The one exception to this trend occurred during the 1950s, when the divorce rate remained stable (Cherlin, 2009). Cherlin estimates that approximately one in three marriages ended in divorce at that time, compared to one in two today. The divorce culture discussed by Whitehead (1997) coincides with Cherlin's summary of the last 40 years. For this period, he refers to marriage as individualized and uses Whitehead's term *expressive divorce*. Concern over fraudulent attempts by couples to feign adultery as a means of expediting divorce hastened the social and legislative changes that made divorce easier. Cherlin connects California's no-fault automobile insurance legislation to this new and easier type of divorce. The idea that divorce is not either partner's fault was not intended by legislators, but the name stuck and other states began to adopt **no-fault divorce**. This change led to an increase in divorce rates after the brief levelling out period of the 1950s. The rate of divorce climbed during the 1960s and 1970s and remains high today. In fact,

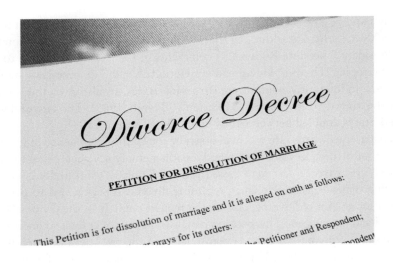

it is much higher in the United States than anywhere else in the world, a distinction that country has had throughout the entire twentieth century (Goode, 1970). This is partly because the United States has a continued high rate of marriage compared to other developed countries, which have seen a more rapid trend toward cohabitation replacing marriage. These cohabiting unions are not counted as marriages, so they are also not counted as divorces if they dissolve.

Determinants of Divorce

The rapid rise and sustained high levels of divorce in North America lead to a question about cause. What is causing this important and enduring social trend? A review of divorce research in the 1980s reveals three clusters of study: macro-structural influences, the life course and demographics, and family process (White, 1990).

Concerning macro-structural influences, the focus was on several institution-level factors. Legislative changes had large impacts in Canada and Australia, where no-fault divorce laws caused a spike in the number of divorces (Balakrishnan, Rao, Lapierre-Adamcyk, & Krotki, 1987). The institutional importance of the family was found to be waning with the advent of other competing institutions. The conclusion made by several researchers was that family is not as important as it has been in the past (Becker, 1981; Popenoe, 1988). White (1990) quoted Schoen, Urton, Woodrow, and Baj (1985, p. 113): "Recent economic changes have undermined the social and economic forces that maintained the institution of marriage." The increased labour force participation of women was correlated to an increase in divorce, as was a lack of social integration. These macro-level factors have all been consistent, with the general rise of individualism identified by family scholars as contributing to a rise in divorce (Popenoe, 1988).

The second cluster identified by White (1990) includes life course and demographic factors. More complex family forms and secondary marriages were found to be at a greater risk of dissolving (Martin & Bumpass, 1989; White & Booth, 1985). The intergenerational impact of divorce was identified as an important factor in divorce (McLanahan & Bumpass, 1988). Cohabitation along with premarital pregnancy and childbirth led to higher levels of divorce (Teachman, 1983; White, 1987) as well as to marriages at earlier ages. Martin and Bumpass (1989) found age at marriage to be the strongest predictor of divorce in the first five years of marriage, while additional researchers found this age effect carried well into the marriage (Heaton, Albrecht, & Martin, 1985). Fertility was also a factor in divorce. The birth of a child reduced the likelihood of divorce in the year immediately following the birth, and additional births had an additive effect in preventing divorce. Couples who were childless were more likely to divorce and the process, when it happened, occurred more rapidly (Booth, Johnson, White, & Edwards, 1986; Wineberg, 1988). White (1990) highlights what she feels was the most important finding of the decade. Morgan, Lye, and Condran's (1988) study found that parents of sons are less likely to divorce than parents of daughters. The interpretation of these findings is that fathers spend more time and have greater involvement with sons than daughters, and that this greater father involvement has been shown to reduce divorce (Seccombe & Lee, 1987). South and Spitze (1986) concluded from the use of longitudinal data that, irrespective of the stage of the life course, the detriments of divorce remain consistent.

The final cluster of White's (1990) decade in review focused on the process of divorce. Reflecting on a review of the research from a decade earlier, White concluded that although much is known about the relationship of demographic variables and divorce, we still know little about the mechanisms at work in the couples or individuals who choose to divorce. Most of the findings supported a rational choice or exchange theory approach. Couples with high cost for divorce because of the presence of children or with relatively low alternatives to divorce because of age or employment status (particularly women) were much less likely to entertain the divorce option. General predictors of divorce such as socio-economic status and women's labour force participation also received attention. More family income = less divorce and more female employment = more divorce were the general findings. Conflicting reports of women's labour status and family stability gave some hope that things were changing for the better, but White (1990) pointed out that the bulk of the research from the 1980s still pointed to the conflict that home care and paid employment for women creates in terms of family stability. Individual anecdotal data collected from a handful of studies focused on issues of alcoholism, drug abuse, physical and emotional abuse, gender role disagreements, infidelity, sexual incompatibility, and financial disagreements as some of the key factors precipitating divorce. White summarized her final cluster by saying that due to small samples and selectivity issues (all participants were divorced), these studies were difficult to generalize from but did provide fertile areas for future research.

Reducing the Risk of Divorce

If your annual income is more than $50,000, the risk of you getting divorced reduces by 30%.

If you marry after you reach 25 years of age, your divorce risk reduces by 24%.

If your parents are happy in their marriages, your divorce risk reduces by 14%.

Your risk of divorce goes down by 14% if you have strong religious beliefs.

If you're college educated, divorce risk reduces by 13%.

Source: Whitehead and Popenoe (2006).

Current Trends

More recently, Teachman (2002) came to a conclusion similar to that of South and Spitze (1986). He found that the research-identified covariates of divorce have remained relatively stable across more recent cohorts. Using data from the National Survey of Family Growth, Teachman was able to study marriages that spanned a 35-year period (1950 to 1984). Apart from race, the other major variables of age at marriage, education, premarital births and conception, religion, and parental divorce continued to be predictors of divorce (see Data Box 9.1). Teachman concluded by stating that in a period of widely varying divorce rates, there is a consistency in risk factors across cohorts.

The twenty-first century has also seen its fair share of divorce and divorce research. Paul Amato (2010), like White (1990) 20 years earlier, reviewed a decade of research in the area. The major risks of divorce are listed as marrying before age 20, low socioeconomic status, periods of unemployment, cohabitation with the partner one marries or with another partner, premarital birth, stepchildren, interracial marriage, growing up in a home without two continuously married parents, and second and **higher-order marriages** (that is, marriages after a first marriage) (Amato & DeBoer, 2001; Bramlett & Mosher, 2002; Bratter & King, 2008; Sweeney & Phillips, 2004; Teachman, 2002). Amato (2010) cautions that although these variables are correlated to divorce, we cannot assume that they are the causes of divorce. Each of these variables needs further and more detailed study to understand how it may affect the life course in different ways.

Amato (2010) uses cohabitation as an illustration of the changing divorce landscape and the need to look more closely at the correlate's role in the process. Even with the majority of premarital cohabitation findings concluding a negative effect, some research has found the opposite. This illustrates the complicated and complex nature of studying the interconnectedness of social phenomenon across the lives of diverse populations in different periods. A further example provided by Amato (2010) is that of female paid employment. Earlier researchers hypothesized that increased roles in a woman's life would have a detrimental impact on her other roles. For example, if a woman fills the roles of wife and mother, it would be expected that those roles would suffer if she added the role of worker. More recent research does not support this conclusion (Schoen, Rogers, & Amato, 2006). Although increased roles may create the potential for increased tension between spouses, other factors such as inequitable distribution of tasks and responsibilities were more often cited as reasons for marital stress. Married mothers with children report a greater sense of satisfaction with their other roles when they are employed outside the home (Korabik, Lero, & Whitehead, 2008).

THE DIVORCE PROCESS

Using a life course perspective to study the family reveals the diverse nature that virtually every life stage takes as it unfolds across a population, with divorce being no different. Divorce tends to be thought of in a monolithic way, as if everyone who gets a divorce goes through the same process. Although the act of a divorce may produce the same result of dissolving the marriage contract, the pathway into and out of divorce is anything but similar. The divorce of a couple without children is quite different from that of a couple with children. **Blended families** going through a divorce have more complex challenges than a family facing a first divorce. The following sections look at the diverse ways in which divorce plays out in the lives of those affected, the diverse ways in which divorce is explained and theorized, and the diverse ways in which divorce rates are calculated.

The Diverse Nature of Divorce

Examining divorce as an event in time is like looking at marriage or the birth of a child as a single momentary event. The marriage planning process is quite elaborate for some, as are the preparations for childbirth. Understanding the process helps us to understand the event in context. Divorce is a process, not something people decide to do on a whim and never think about afterwards. The experiences of people who have gone through divorce are varied and, as a result, the outcomes on those involved (child well-being, financial or social costs) will also vary. David Demo and Mark Fine (2009, p. 49) describe divorce as "a complex and multidimensional process that unfolds over many years." In their divorce variation and fluidity model, or **DVFM** (Figure 9.1), they describe an ecology of divorce in which socio-historical context, gender, race, cultural values, legal context, and economic conditions are part of the ecosystem with which couples and families must contend as they go through the process of divorce. The impact on both child and adult well-being is considered both leading up to the divorce event and following it. Risk factors and protective factors are recognized as influencing the adjustment of both the children and the adults affected. Risk factors include pre- and post-divorce family conflict, financial consequences, and the reality of reduced parent–child interaction. Protective factors include human and social capital qualities such as coping skills and support communities. Demo and Fine also suggest that new partnering for the adult members may be a positive support for the family.

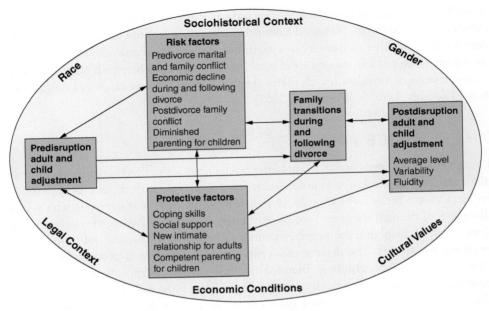

Figure 9.1 Divorce Variation and Fluidity Model

Source: Demo and Fine (2009, p. 49).

The DVFM model highlights the diversity of potential pathways into and out of divorce. Some of the factors affecting that diversity are the family form or composition as the divorce process unfolds. A young couple without any children may move through the divorce process with less discomfort than a larger family. The family structure may change in the middle of the process with the birth of a child or the acknowledgment of a third person involved. Children may leave home or extended family may move in. The economic circumstances surrounding the loss of a job or the acquisition of a new job by one of the spouses may also affect the divorce pathway. If only one spouse is involved in the wage economy, the other spouse may be at a financial disadvantage in seeking legal counsel or securing other housing arrangements. Divorce is a dyadic event that affects individuals differently. There is also a gendered aspect to divorce. Kalmijn and Poortman (2006), in their sample of the Dutch population, found that women tend to initiate divorce more often than men. They also found that women's decisions to divorce were tied more to economic implications than were men's and that men's decisions were more strongly constrained by the presence of children than were women's.

The age of the spouses and the duration of the union at the onset of the divorce process is another differentiating factor. With age at marriage rising and women delaying childbirth, the standard life course timetable is adhered to less. Divorce at an early age may provide greater opportunity for remarriage, while divorce at an older age may take place when children are no longer at home, resulting in different experiences. Shorter marriages may involve less personal investment and be easier to end. Cultural norms also affect the divorce experience, as illustrated by changing social sanctions regarding divorce. During the first half of the twentieth century, divorce was frowned upon and few chose it as a result. The rise of expressive divorce in the latter third of the twentieth century ushered in a new approach. Divorce had become an avenue for self-expression and individual actualization (Whitehead, 1997). Society no longer viewed divorce as failure but as an option for the freedom to start over. The divorce experience today is generally not met with scorn or social stigma but considered a natural part of the life course for many people.

Legislative changes can alter the experience of divorce with the stroke of pen. In Canada, the Divorce Act of 1968 and revisions in 1985 changed the way people in this country go through divorce. The time a couple was required to be separated before a divorce could be granted changed from seven years to three years and now is one year. In the United States, each state has its own waiting period, which may vary from as soon as a couple can agree on terms to up to 18 months. People going through a divorce across these different waiting periods would have diverse experiences in areas of housing, economic and social conditions, and alternative relationships.

No-fault divorce, whether in its unilateral form (able to be initiated by one spouse) or non-unilateral form, requires no cause for the divorce. The introduction of no-fault divorce in the United States is said to have increased the divorce rate by an average of 6 percent in states that adopted it. After a large jump in divorce rates after the introduction of no-fault divorce, there has been a general convergence of divorce rates among states. Research has pointed to the effects of no-fault divorce laws dying out (Wolfers, 2006) and indicates that some no-fault regions actually have fewer divorces (Weiss & Willis, 1997). This has been explained as a selection effect. Locations in which divorce laws make getting a divorce easier lead to women marrying later in life, which is attributed to a more careful mate selection strategy. The presence of no-fault divorce laws has been found to be correlated with greater equality in the distribution of work within marriages, which enhances a woman's negotiating strength (Yodanis, 2005).

Research in Europe has also demonstrated the diverse pathways into and out of divorce because of divergent divorce legislation. González & Viitanen's (2009) comparative study of 18 European countries spanning from 1950 to 2003 found that countries that allow unilateral divorce saw an increase of 0.3 to 0.4 divorces per 1000 people for several years after the legislative change. The authors state that these findings are consistent with findings in the United States (Wolfers, 2006). More recent research on the impact of unilateral divorce law on divorce rates confirmed the lasting effect of increased divorce rates (Kneip & Bauer, 2009). Figure 9.2 presents an overview of the diverse nature of divorce patterns among countries in the Organisation for Economic Co-operation and Development (OECD).

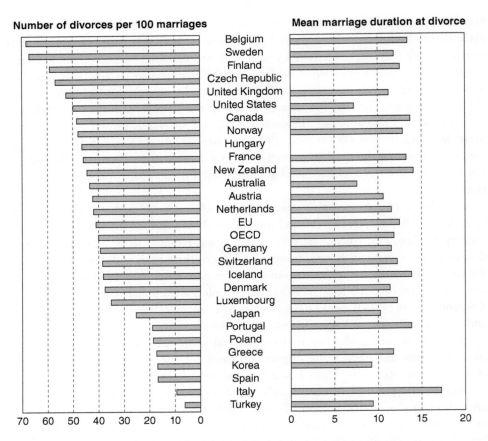

Figure 9.2 Number of Divorces per 100 Marriages and Mean Marriage Duration at Divorce, 1995

Source: Organisation for Economic Co-operation and Development (2001).

Diverse Explanations of Divorce

Apart from the Holy Grail or a cure for cancer, nothing is more elusive than the causes of divorce. Here, we discuss *potential* causes of divorce since we are discussing factors correlated with divorce. We already presented an overview of the determinants of divorce, so this section focuses on the diverse explanations for why divorce happens. The complex life courses for those affected by divorce are attested to here by the diverse ecologies. An ecological approach is not the only theoretical approach to studying divorce but it does provide a comprehensive template to locate factors associated with divorce on a micro to macro continuum. Miller, Perlman, and Brehm (2007) present a detailed look at **ecological correlates of divorce** from the individual ecosystems (Table 9.1) while Fine and Harvey (2006) state that the study of causes of divorce relies on numerous theories and

Table 9.1 Ecological Correlates of Divorce

Micro-sociological causes	Individual issues	■ Alcoholism and drug abuse ■ Infidelity ■ Incompatibility ■ Physical and emotional abuse ■ Disagreements over finances, especially among older people
	Dynamics of the relationship	■ Poor communication ■ Poor conflict resolution skills ■ Lack of commitment ■ Perceived inequality
Meso-sociological causes	Age at marriage	Strongest predictor in first five years of marriage. Young spouses: ■ Lack emotional maturity needed for marriage ■ Have ill-founded expectations ■ Become disappointed or disillusioned with marriage
	Cohabitation	Adverse selectivity explanation: ■ "Kinds of people who cohabit have lower commitment to marriage and disregard stigma of divorce" As it becomes normative, cohabitation will no longer be a predictor variable.
	Second marriage	Adverse selectivity explanation: ■ "Kinds of people who get divorced once will do so again" ■ May be "divorce prone" ■ Competing theory: stress of remarriage ■ Integration of stepchildren ■ Interaction with ex-spouses
	Parental divorce	■ Less likely to believe that marriage can last ■ "Learned how to divorce" from parents
	Child-bearing	Get married for wrong reasons: ■ To legitimize birth, not because committed to one another

(continued)

Table 9.1 Ecological Correlates of Divorce *(continued)*

		Family size:
		■ Women with small or medium-sized families have lower rates of divorce
		■ Women with no children or large families have high rates of divorce
		Sex of child:
		■ Sons reduce the risk by 9 percent
		■ Fathers are more involved when raising sons
	Stage of marriage	■ Longer duration means lower rate of divorce
		■ Having invested more time and energy in marriage means higher cost of starting over
		■ Couples are more aware of being badly matched early on (first three years)
	Place of residence	Urban greater rates than rural
		Adverse selectivity explanation:
		■ Rural people migrate to urban areas before, during, and after divorce
		■ Migrants have weaker social ties, therefore fewer barriers to disruption
		Alternate explanation:
		■ People who move are risk-takers willing to make changes
	Religion	■ More religious have fewer divorces
		■ Divorce rate increases when spouses have different religions
		■ No particular religion has the highest divorce rate
	Socio-economic status	Increased rates among poor:
		■ Higher financial insecurity equals stress
		■ Poor have less to lose in divorce and less to gain in staying married
Macro-sociological causes	War	■ War separates couples, who grow apart

		▣ Lonely people get together under conditions that encourage involvement
		▣ Strain of postwar reunion
	Economic cycles	▣ Less likely to divorce during recession
		▣ Divorce is costly: establishing two households, dividing assets
	Sex ratios	Ratio of available alternatives affects divorce rate.
	Gender expectations	▣ When social structures allow women economic independence, divorce rate increases
		▣ Divorce rate most stable when gender roles are egalitarian or when both spouses are high on "feminine" characteristics (nurturance, sensitivity, gentleness)
	Social integration	▣ Higher social integration equals lower divorce rate
		▣ Highly integrated communities support "pro-family" ideals
	Legislation	No-fault and unilateral divorce laws increase the divorce rate.

Source: Adapted from Miller, Perlman, and Brehm (2007).

models. The diverse list of theories range in scope from social-psychological to macro-sociological, as can be seen in the following list:

- Stress and coping
- Risk and resilience
- Social exchange and resource
- Investment
- Behavioural theory
- Deinstitutionalization of marriage
- Gender
- Ecological theory
- Symbolic interactionism and identity

- Disaffection
- Crisis
- Vulnerability, stress, and adaptation
- Cognitive theory
- Cognitive-behavioural theory
- Cognitive-developmental theory
- Account-making
- Coping with loss
- Family systems

- Feminist theory
- Social penetration
- Disillusionment model of dissolution
- Perpetual models of dissolution
- Stage models

- Relational depenetration
- Cognitive emotional adaptation
- Social network
- Stress-related growth
- Relational deterioration model

The use of so many theories to explain one social phenomenon emphasizes the diversity and complexity involved. Fine and Harvey (2006, p. 4) summarize the positives and negatives aspects of this absence of focus:

> It is strength in that there is a wealth of different perspectives on divorce and relationship dissolution—in the midst of the diversity of perspectives is, one would hope, a complementarity and synergy that is beneficial for the development of our knowledge base. Creative and innovative solutions to new research questions are more likely when an array of varying theoretical perspective is available to address them; however, the multiplicity of theories is a deficit in that the lack of a singular, unifying perspective makes it more difficult to integrate findings across studies.

Diverse Calculations of Divorce Rates

Calculating divorce rates serves as a good lesson in the importance of knowing how reported statistics have been determined. We are presented with percentages and ratios on a continual basis as social scientists—see, for example, Figure 9.3—but where do those numbers come from and how were they calculated? The most common statistic people are aware of when it comes to divorce is the 50 percent number. You may be surprised to learn that not everyone agrees that 50 percent accurately represents the divorce rate in our society (see Data Box 9.2).

Before looking at the most popular methods of calculating divorce rates, it is valuable to review some important aspects of the data that are used to calculate divorce. Rates tell us the relationship between two items. For example, our rate of speed while driving compares the distance we travel in a standard metric of time, hence kilometers (distance) per hour (time). Divorce rates compare the number of divorces and the number of marriages. To begin with, a person is at risk of divorce only if he or she can actually divorce. In other words, he or she must be married (single, widowed, and divorced people cannot get a divorce). To be married, you must be of legal age (typically 18), of sound mind, and (in North America) not already married. It is also important to recognize that divorce is a dyadic-level event. It affects two people yet it is a single divorce, so care must be taken to not double-count divorces. The most common approaches to calculating divorce rates follow, along with the advantages and disadvantages of each.

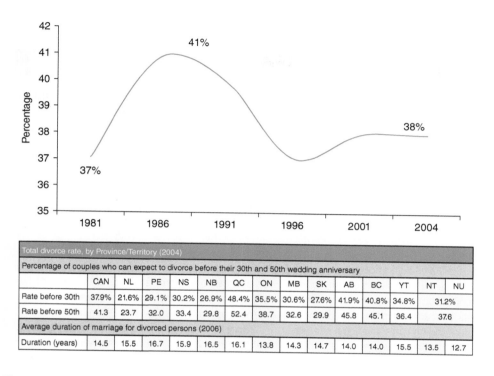

Figure 9.3 Total Divorce Rate—Percentage of Couples Who Can Expect to Divorce Before Their Thirtieth Wedding Anniversary, 1981 to 2004

Source: Vanier Institute of the Family (2010, p. 47).

Divorces per Marriage

$$\frac{\text{Number of divorces in year XXXX}}{\text{Number of marriages in year XXXX}}$$

This calculation divides the number of divorces in a given year by the number of marriages in the same year. This method is quite popular because of its ease of calculation and isolation to one specific year. The problem with this method is that it overestimates the actual divorce rate because the denominator (number of marriages in the year) is a smaller set of people than are actually at risk of divorce. Everyone married prior to the year of calculation is not included in the set of people who are at risk of divorce.

Crude Divorce Rate

$$\frac{\text{Number of divorces in year XXXX}}{\text{Mid-year population in year XXXX}}$$

Total divorce rate, by Province/Territory (2004)													
Percentage of couples who can expect to divorce before their 30th and 50th wedding anniversary													
	CAN	NL	PE	NS	NB	QC	ON	MB	SK	AB	BC	YT	NT	NU
Rate before 30th	37.9%	21.6%	29.1%	30.2%	26.9%	48.4%	35.5%	30.6%	27.6%	41.9%	40.8%	34.8%	31.2%	
Rate before 50th	41.3	23.7	32.0	33.4	29.8	52.4	38.7	32.6	29.9	45.8	45.1	36.4	37.6	
Average duration of marriage for divorced persons (2006)													
Duration (years)	14.5	15.5	16.7	15.9	16.5	16.1	13.8	14.3	14.7	14.0	14.0	15.5	13.5	12.7

Data Box 9.2

Four in Ten First Marriages End in Divorce

The traditional definition of family is changing in Canada, with four in 10 first marriages ending in divorce, according to a new study.

For the first time in Canadian history, there are more unmarried people than legally married people age 15 and over in this country, says the study from the Vanier Institute of the Family released Monday in Ottawa.

It was based on data from the 2006 census, and some of the information has been reported in the years since.

"Marriage is still a vitally important part of the experience of families in the fabric of our country and most young people do aspire to marriage," said Clarence Lochhead, executive director of the Vanier Institute, adding that even people who have divorced or separated will end up partnering up again.

"We just have to come to grips with the diversity that actually is within our experience. Then we need to find ways to address and take on the challenges that face families, but do it in an inclusive way that makes sense for the reality and not some ideal notion of what a family is or ought to be."

According to Statistics Canada, about 38 percent of all marriages taking place in 2004 will have ended in divorce by 2035. The total divorce rate was down slightly from its peak of about 41 percent in the mid 1980s, but slightly higher than the rate of about 37 percent recorded in the mid 1990s.

Newfoundland and Labrador had the lowest rate of divorce at 21.6 percent—while Quebec had the highest at 48.4 percent.

The highest proportion of married people was in Newfoundland and Labrador where 54.3 percent were married, while Quebec had the lowest proportion of married couples with only 37.5 percent of adults falling in this category.

For the first time in Canada, there were more couples without children than with children, and this was true throughout the country, with families with children representing a minority of families in all provinces and territories.

For married families with children, 18.6 percent of children live with only one parent. Common-law families are growing faster than any other type of family with one in 10 Canadians living in such relationships and 14.6 percent of children living with common-law parents.

The 2006 census was the first to report on same-sex marriages and 16.5 percent of same-sex couples now marry.

The recent economic downturn has proven to be a stressor for families. The higher cost of living means most families now require two income earners to achieve an average standard of living.

More families are also struggling with debt and poverty. Men are also working longer hours and spending less time with their families.

Top 8 Reasons People Marry

1. Feeling that marriage signifies commitment
2. Moral values
3. Belief that children should have married parents
4. It is the natural thing to do
5. Financial security
6. Religious beliefs
7. Pressure from family
8. Pressure from friends

Top 5 Reasons Couples Separate or Divorce

1. Different values and interests
2. Abuse—physical and emotional
3. Alcohol and drugs
4. Infidelity
5. Career-related conflict

Source: CBC News (2010).

The **crude divorce rate** is calculated by dividing the number of divorces in a given year by the mid-year population. This rate is also quite simple to measure but it is inherently conservative since the denominator (mid-year population) includes many people who are not at risk of a divorce, such as babies, children, and single and widowed individuals.

Cohort Ever-Married Divorce Rate

$$\frac{\text{Number of first divorces among those born in year XXXX}}{\text{Number of ever-married persons born in year XXXX}}$$

The **cohort ever-married divorce rate** is a more fine-tuned approach that accurately gives a historical account of a group of individuals who are all born in a similar period. The limitations of this approach are that the data are less generalizable to the rest of the population and that the rate will change depending on the year in which it is calculated. The longer the time, the greater the likelihood that divorce may occur.

Refined Divorce Rate

$$\frac{\text{Number of divorces in year XXXX}}{\text{Number of currently married in the population in year XXXX}}$$

The **refined divorce rate** is a very accurate measure but it is difficult to calculate since, apart from census years, the data are hard to gather.

AFTER THE DIVORCE
Effects of Divorce

The dissolution of marriage has been a popular topic of research in the study of the family across the life course. Its importance is found not in the actual divorce decree itself but in the family interaction leading up to and following it. As a transitional family event, it does not end the family but leads to a reconstruction of it. More complex versions of the family may be created from the divorce as the result of remarriage or cohabitation. Step-parents and stepsiblings create new opportunities for adjustment that may be handled successfully or not. Research on divorce continues to try to understand its effects on both children and adults. Although more refined research methods are helping to expose the heterogeneity of pathways into and out of divorce and the divergent outcomes on the participants, the general picture is not good. A recent review of divorce research from the previous decade showed that both children and adults who go through divorce are negatively affected (Amato, 2010). Children of divorced parents, when compared to children of continuously married parents, scored lower on social, emotional, health, and academic outcome measures (Frisco, Muller,

& Frank, 2007). The negative effect of divorce on children remains into adulthood. Adult children of divorced parents are more likely to attain less education, to have lower psychological well-being, to report having troubles in their own marriages, and to see these marriages end in divorce (Amato & Sobolewski, 2001; Barrett & Turner, 2005; Teachman, 2002; Wolfinger, Kowaleski-Jones, & Smith, 2003). Amato (2010) concluded by stating that these more recent findings replicate earlier research and help to establish the relative consistency of the links between the negative impact of divorce on adults and children.

> Research during the last decade has reinforced previous work by showing that divorced individuals, compared with married individuals, exhibit more symptoms of depression and anxiety, more health problems, more substance use, and a greater risk of overall mortality (Bierman, Fazio, & Milkie, 2006; Hughes & Waite, 2009; Lorenz, Wickrama, Conger, & Elder, 2006; Waite, Luo, & Lewin, 2009; Williams & Umberson, 2004; Zhang & Hayward, 2006). The strength of associations between divorce and measures of mental health appear to be comparable for women and men. (Amato, 2010, p. 658)

Research continues to reinforce the information already known about the detrimental effects of divorce on those involved. New cohorts of young adults will form ideas and experience intimate relationships in a divorce culture (Whitehead, 1997). New and important areas of study in the negative implications of divorce will focus on the diversity of experiences people have with divorce. Past research focusing on group average effects will be replaced by studies that reveal the extensive differences that families experience as they go through the divorce process (Demo & Fine, 2009). More emphasis will also be placed on the process itself, recognizing that the consequences of divorce on both children and adults are rooted in the quality of the family relationship prior to the marriage ending.

Protective and Mitigating Factors

An examination of the effects of divorce on children across the life course reveals a consistent negative impact. It is important to understand that the event of divorce itself is not the direct cause of these negative outcomes. Causes are more accurately understood to be found in the stressful events leading up to and following the divorce. Many of the correlates to negative outcomes, such as diminishing family income, poor parental interaction, separation from non-resident parent, and continuing conflict between co-parents, point to the potential protective factors that can mitigate the harmful effects of divorce. Recent research has reinforced the belief that children show little negative affect and may even show improvement if divorce ends a high-conflict marriage (Booth & Amato, 2001; Strohschein, 2005). Stability for children, regardless of their parents' marital status, has been shown to mitigate negative child outcomes as well. Divorce is not a single event or a single transition. It often involves a series of changes and transitions as the family members must adjust and adapt to new residential, custody, economic, and relational environments. Cavanagh and Huston (2006) have shown that the number of family structure transitions is linked to child behaviour problems throughout the life course.

Children

The impact of divorce on children and adolescents has been well documented. The topic, like divorce itself, is complicated and even controversial at times. In *Handbook of Stressful Transitions Across the Lifespan*, edited by Thomas Miller (2010), Barczak, Miller, Veltkamp, Barczak, Hall, & Kraus (2010) provide a summary of the most current research and clinical data. They conclude that the quality of the pre- and post-divorce parental relationship is the most important factor in mediating the long-term effects of divorce on children and adolescents.

> While some may argue or assume that children and adolescents are sufficiently resilient to simply "get over" the negative effects of divorce throughout their lives, the most recent clinical research findings refute this claim. (Barczak et al., 2010, p. 210)

Barczak et al. (2010) felt that maternal parenting style is the major factor in mediating the experience of divorce concerning younger children's perceived attachment style. This finding is important in terms of understanding the implications of secure attachment versus anxious-ambivalent or avoidant attachment. The researchers believe that current parent–child visitation approaches and guidelines are outdated. The best interests of the child are not being addressed because of the unnecessarily rigid and restrictive approach. Early parental divorce or separation is found to be more negatively related to children's external and internal behavioural expression when compared to parents who divorced later. However, academic grades are seen to suffer more with later divorces. Family breakup is significantly associated with poor adjustment among adolescents, manifested in self-harm behaviours such as drug use and alcohol consumption. Parental divorce is associated with increased adolescent anxiety and depression as well as negative effects on subjective well-being and self-esteem. The divorce experience was found to affect adolescent males, but not females, in the form of school problems.

An independent effect of divorce and parental distress was also identified. Adolescents of divorced parents report double the levels of distress when compared to adolescents of intact and non-distressed parents. Females seem to demonstrate anxiety and depressive symptoms more openly over the long term than do males. Females of divorced families report more psychological problems and indicate greater interpersonal relationship challenges than their unexposed peers. These findings do not seem to apply to males in similar circumstances. Barczak et al. (2010, p. 213) highlight five summary clinical findings about children and adolescents of divorce.

> (1) Depressive symptoms appear to change in a curvilinear pattern throughout the adolescent years (especially among the females) (depressive symptoms appeared to increase during early- to mid-adolescence and then subsequently declined as subjects approached late adolescence and young adulthood); (2) Females experience an ongoing greater number of depressive symptoms in adolescence and early adulthood when compared to their male counterparts; (3) Adolescents who experienced parental divorce by age 15 tend to display a sharper increase in the number of expressive symptoms experienced when compared to their peers from non-divorced families; (4) Stressful life events experienced shortly after parental marital disruption and divorce appear to mediate the actual effects of parental divorce on the adolescents' depressive symptoms; and finally, (5) Time-variable stressful events throughout the adolescents' lives (especially those related to either personal losses or relationship losses) are significantly associated with the trajectories of depressive symptoms in the typical adolescent member of a divorced family.

The conclusion of this report is that there is a price to be paid for marital conflict between parents: the disruption of their children's overall physical and mental health.

Adult Children

Ahrons (2007) assessed the findings of three longitudinal studies of the impact of divorce on family members' well-being. The Binuclear Family Study followed the lives of divorced families for 20 years. Ninety-eight pairs of former spouses were interviewed in 1979. All had at least one minor child and were randomly selected from the public divorce records in Dane County, Wisconsin. Interviews with both parents were conducted at one, three, and five years after the legal divorce. In the follow-up interviews, family transitions such as remarriage and cohabitation were identified and recorded. Five typologies were created after examining the life courses and responses of the participants. These five types formed a continuum, with very friendly ex-spouses (perfect pals) at one extreme and couples who had nothing to do with each other (dissolved duos) at the other extreme. The three other groups (co-operative colleagues, angry associates, fiery foes) formed the middle of the continuum. Ahrons (2007, p. 58) states: "No single factor contributed more to children's self-reports of well-being after divorce than the continuing relationship between their parents. Children whose parents were cooperative reported better relationships with their parents, grandparents, stepparents, and siblings." Ahrons (2007) concludes by saying that most divorcing parents have a short-term, narrow view of the implications of their continuing relationship. Box 9.1 highlights the fact that adult children also face challenges because of their parents divorcing later in their life course.

Box 9.1

Adults Dealing with Their Parents' Divorce

Sonja and Carson met for a coffee to talk about the announcement that their parents were going to divorce. They grew up in a household that was not always peaceful, but their parents seemed to make it through the challenges and difficulties that life presented. Now grown, with families of their own, it seemed difficult for Sonja and Carson to grasp that their parents were getting a divorce. They had been married almost 40 years and neither parent seemed to have any other romantic interests on the side. What was going on?

Sonja was concerned about her mother's relationship network. Her parents had decided to sell the family home and divide the assets. The intergenerational costs of older adult divorces have been researched and the picture for some adult children and their parents is not pretty (Hans, Ganong, & Coleman, 2009). Mom was not going to be able to afford a home in the neighbourhood where all her friends were. What about their parents' shared acquaintances? How would they deal with that?

Carson was concerned about what to tell his own children. How would they deal with Christmas, birthdays, and other family celebrations? It was all very disconcerting.

Remarriage and Repartnering

In Canada, nearly 40 percent of marriages will end in divorce; in the United States, that number is closer to 50 percent. Because a significant portion of the population divorces, the number of people who repartner and remarry is also large (Figure 9.4). It is only the growing segment of post-marriage cohabitors that has kept the number of higher-order marriages in a narrow band of 35 000 to 37 000 per year over the past generation. In Canada, about 10 percent of those who have ever married do so again, with less than 1 percent marrying more than twice. The Vanier Institute of the Family (2010) states that the majority of Canadians will repartner after a divorce or separation. As time passes, a greater percentage of the divorced population re-enters some form of intimate partnership. After three years, approximately one quarter (26 percent) of the women and more than one third (37 percent) of the men re-enter conjugal unions. After five years, those numbers climb to 36 percent and 51 percent, respectively. Twenty years later, 69 percent of women and 82 percent of men have entered into committed relationships at least a second time (Table 9.2).

Andrew Cherlin has followed the marriage and divorce trends in the United States for more than 30 years. To describe the American culture, he used the phrase *marriage, divorce, remarriage* in 1981. Cherlin (2009) points out that, throughout its history, the United States has had simultaneously higher marriage rates and higher divorce rates than much of the rest of the world: "They partner, unpartner, and repartner faster than do people in any other Western nation . . . " (pp. 14–15). In other words, having several partnerships is more common in the United States not only because people *exit* intimate partnerships faster but also because they *enter* them faster and after a breakup *re-enter*

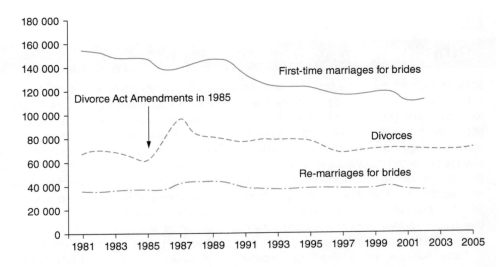

Figure 9.4 Number of Marriages and Divorces, Canada, 1981 to 2005

Source: Vanier Institute of the Family (2010, p. 47).

them faster. Data from the previous decade in the United States show that 69 percent of women and 78 percent of men remarry after divorce. With age comes a decrease in remarriage rates, presumably because of the elderly seeing more risks than benefits to remarriage (King & Scott, 2005).

The frequency of divorce and remarriage has led to research about the quality of and dynamics within remarried relationships. Sweeney (2010) provides a summary of recent remarriage literature. It shows that remarried couples are less likely to communicate in both a positive and a negative fashion than first-married couples. Remarried couples

Table 9.2 Cumulative Percentage of Repartnering after Marital Disruption

	Women			Men		
Year	Remarried	Cohabited	Total	Remarried	Cohabited	Total
1	0.7%	9.5%	10.2%	0.6%	14.9%	15.5%
2	2.7	17.3	20.0	2.7	23.5	26.3
3	4.2	22.1	26.3	6.3	31.0	37.3
4	5.6	25.9	31.4	10.1	35.8	45.9
5	7.2	28.8	36.0	11.8	38.6	50.5
10	13.5	39.1	52.5	20.4	49.2	69.6
15	16.4	45.4	61.8	23.4	54.3	77.7
20	19.2	49.4	68.6	26.6	55.5	82.1

Source: Vanier Institute of the Family (2010, p. 47).

are also more likely to withdraw in conflict (Halford, Nicholson, & Sanders, 2007). They also tend to be more egalitarian and more autonomous in decision making about finances and child rearing (Allen, Baucom, Burnett, Epstein, & Rankin-Esquer, 2001).

Second and higher-order marriages tend to be less stable. Bumpass and Raley (2007) report that 40 percent of second marriages will end in divorce or separation by the end of the marriage's first decade, compared to 32 percent for first marriages. Sweeney (2010) reports that, consistent with the increased complexity of remarriages and reconstituted family structures, second marriages report greater marital instability yet no noticeable difference in marriage quality. One explanation put forth is selection effect. The least stable relationships will dissolve quickly and, as a result, not factor into cross-sectional results (Amato, Booth, Johnson, & Rogers, 2007).

Stepfamilies and Blended Families

The stepfamily has been termed the *incomplete institution* (Cherlin, 1978). It struggles with unscripted norms and pathways throughout the life course. How affectionate can a stepfather be with his stepdaughter before he is viewed as crossing a line? How much authority does a stepmother have over her stepson's messy room before an abusive verbal exchange takes place? What are the rules for grandparents of stepchildren when it comes to birthdays and other important holidays? These scenarios represent a few of the emotionally charged areas in addition to everyday mundane issues that stepfamilies must try to resolve.

In Canada, 46 percent of all **stepfamilies** are blended families. Blended families are distinct from stepfamilies in that they may include children from both previously married parents or a child from one of the parents plus the addition of a biological or adopted child to the union. It is well documented that higher-order marriages are more likely to break than first marriages, and each subsequent remarriage has an even bleaker outlook for success. Stepfamilies into which a child is born have better odds of remaining together, as do stepmother families, the latter being indistinguishable from intact families (Vanier Institute of the Family, 2010).

Stepfamilies are more likely to be found in the United States than in any other industrialized country (Sweeney, 2010). Data from the 2004 Survey of Income and Program Participation show that 5.7 million children lived with one biological parent and either a stepparent or an adoptive parent (Kreider, 2008). This represents 10.5 percent of all children living with two parents and is statistically unchanged from 11 percent in 2001 and 10 percent in 1996 (Figure 9.5).

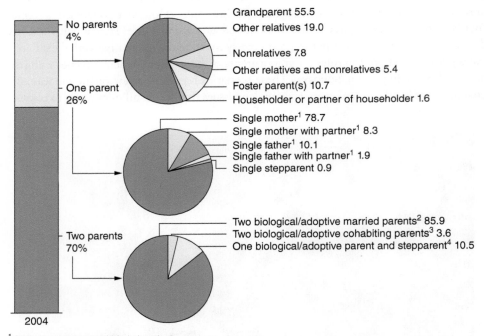

[1] Child points to one parent, biological or adoptive.
[2] Child points to two parents, who are married to each other—either two biological, two adoptive, or one biological and one adoptive.
[3] Child points to two parents, who are not married to each other—either two biological, two adoptive, or one biological and one adoptive.
[4] Child points to two parents, either married or cohabiting—one is biological or adoptive parent; one is a stepparent; or both are stepparents.

Figure 9.5 Percentage of Children Aged 0 to 17 Living in Various Family Arrangements, 2004

Source: Kreider (2008).

The effects on children residing in blended families or stepfamilies are consistent with expectations. Children raised in stepfamilies do not fare as well as those living with two biological parents in numerous areas of social development. Sweeney (2010) cautions that although recent scholarship supports lower outcomes in the child's educational, cognitive, emotional, and behavioural measures (Artis, 2007; Barrett & Turner, 2005; Brown, 2004, 2006; Deleire & Kalil, 2002; Hofferth, 2006; Manning & Lamb, 2003), the differences tend to be modest. It is also important to note that children raised in stepfamilies have gone through other significant family transitions. Some have lost a parent to death, but the majority has gone through the divorce process along with their biological parents. This alone exposes them to the detrimental effects already attributed to divorce. More sophisticated studies are needed to distinguish the effects of the divorce process from the effects of the stepfamily living environment.

According to Sweeney (2010), topics in need of further research in the area of stepfamilies are cohabiting family arrangements, the roles and influences of step-grandparents and step-grandchildren, and same-sex parents. Children being raised in a stepfamily environment in which the adults are not married is an increasing phenomenon. How this may affect marital quality and stability and resultant child outcomes compared to stepfamilies in which the adults are married will be a fruitful area of research. The increase in reconstituted families also means that there are more step-grandparents. The roles they play and how they may mitigate negative effects through the family transitions are areas that need further attention (Ruiz & Silverstein, 2007). Lastly, there is the area of same-sex parents. Patterson (2006) asks the question: "Does parental sexual orientation have an important impact on child or adolescent development?" She concludes that, based on recent research, more important than the sexual orientation of the parents is the quality of the family relationships.

CONCLUSION

Divorce and remarriage are aspects of family life that many people experience. This chapter focused on these topics as processes and not simply as point-in-time events. As we continue to study the family across the life course, we are reminded that pathways are diverse and more frequently less linear. Divorce signals the end of a marriage, a stage that some believe should last a lifetime, but it also signals a new beginning that may involve remaining single, cohabiting, remarrying, and possibly even getting divorced again. Divorce and remarriage highlight the family transitions that influence and affect all of those involved. Divorce may or may not involve children, but when it does, the outcomes require our attention. The lasting negative impact of the average divorce has been well established. Whether anyone ever experiences an *average divorce* is quite another issue.

SUMMARY OF KEY POINTS

- Social customs regarding divorce have been well documented in Western culture for more than 3000 years.

- Both secular and religious influences have worked to define the place and role of divorce in society.

- According to Statistics Canada, only five official divorces took place prior to Confederation in 1867.

- A variety of social changes over the past 100 years has seen divorce move from a rare to a normative event.

  - Secularization and modernization

  - Increased female paid employment, causing a decrease in financial dependency

  - Legislative changes, particularly the Divorce Acts of 1968 and 1985 in Canada

  - Greater individualization

  - Lower fertility rates

- Divorce is not just an event but also a diverse and varied process. Demo and Fine (2009) describe divorce as "a complex and multidimensional process that unfolds over many years."

- In the search for causes of divorce, multiple ecological-level variables have been identified as contributors.

  - Individual and relationship dynamic issues at the micro level

  - Age at marriage, the number of marriages, a history of cohabitation, parental divorce, and religious and socio-economic factors at the meso level

  - Sex ratios, geopolitical events, and legislation at the macro level

- Divorce rates are calculated in a variety of ways that produce different reported levels.

  - Divorces per marriage

$$\frac{\text{Number of divorces in year XXXX}}{\text{Number of marriages in year XXXX}}$$

  - Crude divorce rate

$$\frac{\text{Number of divorces in year XXXX}}{\text{Mid-year population in year XXXX}}$$

  - Cohort ever-married divorce rate

$$\frac{\text{Number of first divorces among those born in year XXXX}}{\text{Number of ever-married persons born in year XXXX}}$$

- Refined divorce rate

$$\frac{\text{Number of divorces in year XXXX}}{\text{Number of currently married in the population in year XXXX}}$$

- A recent review of divorce research from the previous decade showed that both children and adults who go through divorce are negatively affected (Amato, 2010).

- A key mitigating factor in reducing the potential negative effects of divorce for children is to reduce the number of transitions experienced and maintain a level of stability. Other mitigating factors include maternal parenting style and parental conflict.

- With high divorce rates, remarriage has also been on the rise. The Vanier Institute of the Family (2010) states that a majority of divorced Canadians will go on to remarry.

- Blended families are the result of bringing children into a new family from a previously constituted one. These diverse family forms provide additional stress and a need for healthy adjustment if the new unions are to survive.

Critical Thinking Questions

1. In just 100 years, divorce has gone from being a socially stigmatized event to one that most people will experience across their life course. What mechanisms have been at work to bring about such a change?

2. The process of divorce is complex and diverse. Given the variables and explanations listed in the chapter, do you think we are any closer to understanding the "cause" of divorce?

3. What do you think of the term *expressive divorce* and how it reinforces the idea of marriage becoming more individualized? Is this a good thing?

Glossary

blended families A term used to describe families in which children from one or both of the partners are brought into the union.

cohort ever-married divorce rate The rate calculated by dividing the number of first divorces among those born in a given year by the number of ever-married persons born in that same year. This is a more accurate rate but lacks generalizability to the general population and fluctuates depending on the date on which the rate is calculated.

crude divorce rate The rate calculated by dividing the number of divorces in a given year by the mid-year population. Although easier to measure than some of the other rates, it is inherently conservative since the denominator (mid-year population in a given year) includes many people who are not at risk of a divorce, such as babies, children, single individuals, and widowed individuals.

Divorce Act The Divorce Acts of 1968 and 1985 changed the conditions under which a divorce would be permitted. Permanent marriage breakdown as grounds for divorce was maintained and could be claimed because of adultery, cruelty, or desertion. The main change was a move away from fault-based grounds for divorce to include no-fault grounds. The waiting period for no-fault divorce was reduced to one year in the Divorce Act of 1985.

DVFM The divorce variation and fluidity model was developed by David Demo and Mark Fine (2009). The model highlights the potential diversity of pathways into and out of divorce.

ecological correlates of divorce

Micro level: individual and relationship dynamic issues

Meso level: age at marriage, the number of marriages, a history of cohabitation, parental divorce, and religious and socio-economic factors

Macro level: sex ratios, geopolitical events, and legislation

higher-order marriages Subsequent marriages beyond an individual's first marriage.

no-fault divorce A divorce in which one party's actions are not solely responsible for the divorce. Irreconcilable differences are often the reason stated for a no-fault divorce.

refined divorce rate The rate calculated by dividing the number of divorces in a given year by the number of people currently married in the population in that same year. This is a very accurate measure of the divorce rate but is difficult to calculate since, other than in census years, the data are hard to gather.

stepfamilies See *blended families*.

Connections

http://dsp-psd.pwgsc.gc.ca/Collection-R/LoPBdP/CIR/963-e.htm
www.collectionscanada.gc.ca/databases/divorce/001070-130-e.html
www.oecd-ilibrary.org/social-issues-migration-health/society-at-a-glance-2001_soc_glance-2001-en
www.vifamily.ca/node/371
www.nytimes.com/2005/04/19/health/19divo.html
www.census.gov/prod/2008pubs/p70-114.pdf

Remember to log on to the Companion Website at **www.pearsoncanada.ca/white** to find self-graded quizzes and useful resource tools for further study. You can log on to the Companion Website using the Student Access Code that comes packaged with your copy of *Families Across the Life Course*.

Chapter 10
Aging Families

Learning Objectives

After reading this chapter, you should be able to:

1. Examine your own views of "aging" and "being old."

2. Describe Canada's aging population today (statistical trends).

3. Identify the gains and losses that occur during later life.

4. Compare and contrast life course experiences in later life with respect to gender and culture.

5. Decide what decisions can be made earlier in life to increase the probability of "successful aging."

Bill and Sue were married and best friends for more than 35 years. Since they had no children, they spent most of their time in retirement doing things together—whether going on vacation or simply going for a walk in the park. Bill passed away from cancer, leaving Sue alone in their large home. Most of Bill's relatives had been unaware of his condition because he was a private man. At the funeral, several family members noticed that Sue was asking the same questions over and over again.

In the following weeks, Sue seemed to get worse. She started to do strange things such as not remember how to make toast and answer the door half-dressed. Her nieces and nephews, all of whom had their own spouses, children, and grandchildren, did not know how to best care for Sue. It seemed she had dementia, a diagnosis that was confirmed by a psychologist. How could Bill not have told anyone about Sue's condition, knowing he was sick and not going to outlive her? Why didn't he ensure that Sue had care arranged for her when he was gone? Or, being with her every day, had he not noticed Sue's symptoms of forgetting? What were her nieces and nephews supposed to do? Sue needed 24-hour care so that she would not wander onto the street or burn down her house, but they all had responsibilities to their own families and lived a good distance away.

Luckily, Bill and Sue had managed to save a good amount of money for their retirement, so it was possible for Sue's extended family to arrange for formal care. However, they didn't know what the best option would be. Sue didn't want to leave her home but she was becoming progressively more forgetful and her personality was changing to the point where she often verbally abused the live-in caregiver. She also called her nieces and nephews every day, asking them to come over because she was feeling lonely. Then she would forget that she had called already and would fill up their voicemails with multiple messages. Would a nursing home that specialized in people with dementia be a better option? How would the family get Sue to agree to move there? Would it be wrong to suggest to her that it was her idea, knowing she wouldn't remember if she had made that decision or not? If Sue and Bill had had their own children, would this have made a difference now that she needed care? What would have happened if Bill and Sue hadn't saved for retirement and there were no funds to pay for formal care?

As you can see from the opening vignette, later life can bring a unique set of experiences to both the elderly person and their family members. For the elderly person, later life can be a time of new or renewed opportunity. One has the free time to travel and pursue hobbies and interests that had to be put on hold to fulfill work and family demands earlier in life. Later life can also bring its own set of challenges. The elderly person must adjust to physical and social changes, declines in health, and the death of loved ones. Family members of the elderly person also must make adjustments, most specifically in terms of planning care for the elderly family member within the context of their own busy lives. This chapter discusses some of the opportunities and challenges that later life brings to families.

WHAT IS AGING?

Research on aging looks at the effects of "getting older" in two ways. We can examine population aging and individual aging. Before we examine the effects of aging on the individual and his or her family, we need to examine briefly why the study of population aging is becoming increasingly important and the implications of population aging for family life.

Population Aging

Demographers examine **population aging**, or the distribution of a population's age structure. We say that a population is "old" when it contains a large proportion of elderly people (those individuals 65 years of age and older). In 2006, 13.7 percent of Canada's population were elderly individuals aged 65 years and older (Statistics Canada, 2007c). In comparison, in 1981 the elderly made up only 9.6 percent of Canada's population. It is expected that by 2026, the elderly will make up approximately 21.2 percent of our population (Statistics Canada, 2006c).

There are three major components that affect the aging of a population: mortality or death rates in a population, fertility or birth rates in a population, and migration or movement of people internally (within country) and externally (between countries). The combination of these three components causes changes in size and composition of a population. When at least 10 percent of a population is over 65 years of age, the population is considered "old." We can also look at the median age of a population (if we put all the people living in Canada in order from youngest to oldest, the middle person in this distribution would have the median age). In 2006, the median age in Canada was 39.5 years (Statistics Canada, 2007c).

Demographers, or people who study changes in populations, are interested in the age of a population because this will affect the need for specific types of social supports and resources (e.g., health care) and can help to inform policy-makers on where to allocate resources based on need. Since the population is expected to get older, we can expect that a greater number of elderly individuals will need assistance with such things as health care and assisted living housing. Areas of need in a population are measured by examining dependency ratios. There are three common ways to measure dependency in a population. The **aged dependency ratio** is measured as the number of persons 65 years and older divided by the number of persons between 20 and 64 years old. Note that the 20- to 64-year-old group is considered the group in society that will be working and thus be able to support the "dependent" segments of the population. The **youth dependency ratio** is measured as the number of individuals aged 0 to 19 years divided by the number of individuals aged 20 to 64 years. The **total dependency ratio** in a given population is measured as the number of individuals aged 0 to 19 years plus the number

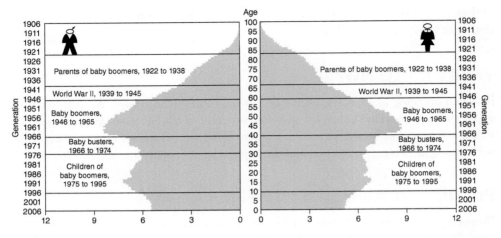

Figure 10.1 Canada's Population Pyramid, 2006

Source: Statistics Canada, Annual Portrait of the Canadian Population in 2006, by Age and Sex, 2006 Census, 97-551-XWE;
http://www12.statcan.gc.ca/census-recensement/2006/as-sa/97-551/index-eng.cfm

of individuals aged 65 years and older divided by the number of individuals aged 20 to 64. These dependency measures can tell us roughly the proportion of dependency in a population as well as where the majority of that dependency is located (young or old). This can affect family life directly as government resources are moved from one area (e.g., funding for youth) to another (e.g., funding for seniors). See Boxes 10.1 and 10.2 for a consideration of structural changes related to immigrant and Aboriginal elder groups that may require changes in policy and resource allocation in the near future.

Population pyramids are graphs that show the distribution of individuals in a population by age. Often these pyramids are also divided by gender. Figure 10.1 is an example of a population pyramid. This pyramid represents Canada's population structure in 2006. Notice that there are more elderly women than men at the top of the pyramid. Also notice the bulge in the population pyramid that represents the baby boom generation (those born between 1943 and 1960). These baby boomers are just starting to reach old age (65 years and older). If we think about this in terms of dependency ratios, there is some concern as to how the working cohort (those 20 to 64 years old) will be able to support such a large elderly population in the coming years. Another concern is the lack of children being born to "replace" the older group as they die. Notice the much smaller proportion of children than adults at the bottom of the pyramid.

Canada is not the only country in the world with an aging population. In fact, population aging is a worldwide phenomenon. Many populations have slow growth or no growth, meaning that the rate at which children are being born into a population is not replacing or is barely keeping up with the rate of people leaving a population (through mortality or migration). This phenomenon is split according to development. More developed countries, such as Canada and the United States, have an aging population.

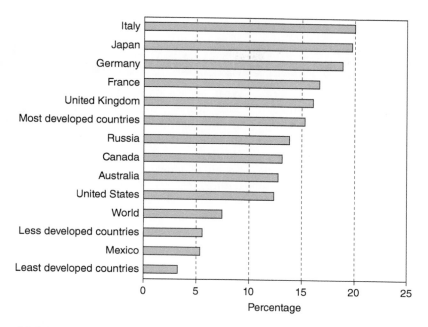

Figure 10.2 Percentage of the Population Who Are Seniors, Selected Countries, 2005

Source: Statistics Canada, A Portrait of Seniors in Canada, 89-519-XIE200600, February 2007; http://www.statcan.gc.ca/bsolc/olc-cel/olc-cel?catno=89-519-XIE&lang=eng#formatdisp

Less developed regions, such as Africa and Latin America, have "younger" populations since they have higher fertility rates as well as a shorter life expectancy. However, the birth rates in less developed regions are expected to decline (Kalache, Barreto, & Keller, 2005) and life expectancy is expected to increase (Hayward & Zhang, 2001), leading to aging populations in developing regions in the near future. Figure 10.2 is a graph of the percentage of the population who are seniors in select countries in 2005. Notice that Italy has the highest percentage of seniors while Mexico has the lowest (keep in mind that this graph represents only select countries).

Individual Aging

Individual aging consists of the biological, physiological, psychological, and social changes that occur over the life cycle. For example, individual aging includes the greying of one's hair and the development of dementia. These changes have an impact on the elderly individual as well as on his or her family members, in both positive and negative ways. In this chapter, we examine common changes that occur as we move to the later stages of the life cycle.

Box 10.1

Structural Changes in Ethnic Diversity: Immigrants

As mentioned, the structure of a population can change due to births, deaths, and immigration and emigration. Figure 10.3 shows that a large segment of the working cohort (aged 20 to 64 years) in Canada is made up of immigrants, those individuals who were not born in Canada or who did not have Canadian citizenship at birth (the figure compares the rates in 1981 and 2001). These immigrants will soon move into old age and will thus become "dependants."

What implications might this have on social policy geared toward the elderly and specifically toward elderly immigrants? What additional supports need to be put in place to serve this elderly group? Figure 10.4 shows the distribution of immigrant seniors by province and territory in 2001. Note that Ontario and British Columbia have the highest proportions of immigrant seniors compared to the other provinces and territories in Canada.

Who Is Old?

When we talk about the elderly, we must keep in mind that there is intragenerational diversity within this group. As a result, subcategories for the elderly group have been developed. The **young-old** comprise those aged 65 to 74 years, the **old-old** are aged 75 to 84 years, while the **oldest-old** are aged 85 and older. We can measure "old" by **chronological age** (one's age in years) or by **functional age** (one's age measured by competence or performance). A person can have a functional age that is younger or

Box 10.2

Structural Changes in Ethnic Diversity: Aboriginals

First Nations and other Aboriginal groups make up about 4 percent of the Canadian elderly population (Statistics Canada, 2005c). According to Statistics Canada, it is expected that the number of Aboriginal elderly will double by 2017. Although in terms of the whole population the proportion will still be relatively small (about 7 percent), this is a significant change for Aboriginal communities. Many Aboriginal elderly live in poverty. For example, according to the National Advisory Council on Aging (2004), half of the elders in Nunavut and the Northwest Territories receive the Guaranteed Income Supplement, and many more are eligible but have not applied to receive it. Levels

of post-secondary education are at one third the rate of the rest of Canadians. More than one third work in unskilled labour (compared to 20 percent for non-Aboriginals). All of these factors affect the quality of Aboriginal people's old age. Due to modernization and information exchange through mass media, the elderly are not sought out for their knowledge as much as they once were. However, elderly Aboriginals provide a significant link to Aboriginal culture, especially in terms of maintaining language. What kinds of social policy should be put in place to help retain Aboriginal culture and to better serve elderly Aboriginals today and in the future?

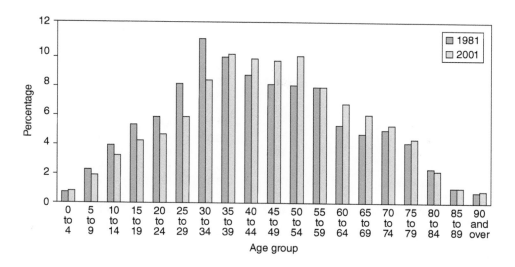

Figure 10.3 Distribution of the Total Immigrant Population, by Age Group, 1981 and 2001

Source: Statistics Canada, A Portrait of Seniors in Canada, 89-519-XIE200600, February 2007; http://www.statcan.gc.ca/bsolc/olc-cel/olc-cel?catno=89-519-XIE&lang=eng#formatdisp

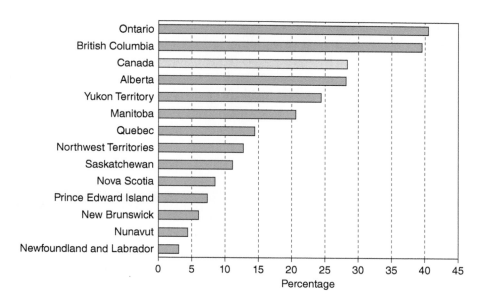

Figure 10.4 Percentage of Immigrants among Seniors, by Province and Territory, 2001

Source: Statistics Canada, A Portrait of Seniors in Canada, 89-519-XIE200600, February 2007; http://www.statcan.gc.ca/bsolc/olc-cel/olc-cel?catno=89-519-XIE&lang=eng#formatdisp

	Both sexes	Men	Women	Male/Female difference
Canada	79.7	77.2	82.1	4.9
Newfoundland and Labrador	78.3	75.7	80.9	5.2
Prince Edward Island	78.8	76.2	81.3	5.1
Nova Scotia	79.0	76.4	81.5	5.1
New Brunswick	79.3	76.5	82.0	5.5
Quebec	79.4	76.6	82.0	5.4
Ontario	80.1	77.7	82.2	4.5
Manitoba	78.7	76.2	81.1	4.9
Saskatchewan	79.1	76.3	82.0	5.7
Alberta	79.7	77.4	81.9	4.5
British Columbia	80.6	78.2	82.9	4.7
Yukon	76.7	73.9	80.3	6.4
Northwest Territories	75.8	73.2	79.6	6.4
Nunavut	68.5	67.2	69.6	2.4

Figure 10.5 Life Expectancy at Birth, by Sex and Province or Territory, Canada, 2002

Source: Statistics Canada (2002, p. 45).

older than his or her chronological age. We can also think about "old" in terms of **life expectancy**, or the number of years an individual born in a particular year (cohort) can expect to live (that is, how many years of life he or she can expect to have left). Figure 10.5 shows the life expectancy at birth of Canadians by sex and province or territory, estimated in 2002. Box 10.3 highlights individuals who have lived past their expected lifespan.

Box 10.3

What Are the Limits of the Human Lifespan?

According to the *Guinness World Records*, the oldest person alive (at the time of writing) is Besse Cooper, who was born in Sullivan County, Tennessee, on August 26, 1896. *Guinness World Records* states that based on authenticated records, Jeanne Louise Calment (from France) is the person who lived the longest. She lived to 122 years and 164 days; she was born on February 21, 1875, and died on August 4, 1997. Keep in mind that this is based on documented evidence. Record keeping in the past was not as good as it is today and these claims have been contested. A simple Google search will show many different individuals listed as the oldest man or woman alive.

AGING: A CHALLENGE OR AN OPPORTUNITY?

Individual aging can be perceived as a challenge or an opportunity, or both. Several theorists have marked mid to later life as a time that involves a shift from a focus on self to a focus on other. Erikson (1950), for example, describes mid-life as being a challenge between generativity and self-absorption and stagnation. **Generativity** is the ability to move beyond your own interests and toward helping the generation to come. Stagnation, in contrast, is the inability to find value in guiding and aiding the next generation. Erikson describes this as feeling bored with life tasks and feeling that life is adequate but unsatisfying. Late life, according to Erikson, has its own challenge between finding integrity and living in despair. **Integrity** is the ability to accept one's life as something that had to be rather than regretting what it was not. Despair is the feeling that life has been in vain and is felt by a person who is still not satisfied with how his or her life turned out. Later life, then, can be a time for reflection on the life that was lived with integrity or in despair.

Kotre (1984) also talks about generativity as a major life task for the older adult. He expands generativity to four primary areas in life. There is **biological generativity**, in which people contribute to society by having children. **Parental generativity** involves nurturing and socializing children (who may or may not be one's biological children). **Technical generativity** involves contributing by teaching skills to the next generation, while **cultural generativity** involves passing on cultural values and traditions to the next generation. A person can be generative in one or all of these areas, suggesting that an individual can contribute to society in a number of important ways and, in the process, give their life purpose.

Baltes (1987) suggests a proportional shift in the ratio of gains to losses one experiences over the life course (see Figure 10.6). As we age, we may experience more losses

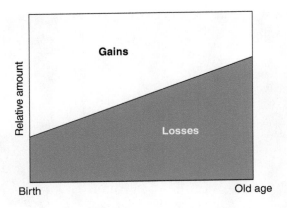

Figure 10.6 Gain–Loss Ratio Shift Across the Life Course

One theoretical expectation concerning the average course of gain–loss ratios is a proportional shift across the lifespan.

Source: Baltes, P. B. (1987). Theoretical propositions of life-span developmental psychology: On the dynamics between growth and decline. *Developmental Psychology, 23,* 611–626. Copyright 1987 by the American Psychological Association.

than gains, but it is important to remember that there are still gains to be made in later life! The following sections discuss some of the major changes that occur in later life, both in terms of loss and gain.

Ageism

One challenge that the elderly face is **ageism,** or the stereotyping of older persons (see Box 10.4 for myths about aging). This is usually negative but may be positive. Ageism is thought to be the result of our fear of and vulnerability to our own aging and eventual death (Martens, Goldenberg, & Greenberg, 2005) and of the fact that, in Canada, the young and old cohorts are largely separated in society (Hagestad & Uhlenberg, 2005). For example, leisure activities are often age-based, which keeps younger and older individuals from interacting with one another. This separation does vary depending on ethnic or cultural background, with many First Nations cultures, for example, integrating the young and the old in traditions and rituals (which may result in less ageism among these groups).

One important point to consider when studying the elderly is that our research must be designed in a way that age, cohort, and period effects are not confused. **Age effects** are outcomes that occur due to one's age or developmental stage. **Cohort effects** are outcomes that occur because one is born in a particular cohort. People born in a particular period share certain socio-historical experiences. For example, individuals who were working adults during the Great Depression often have a "save for the future" mentality and are reluctant to spend money frivolously. **Period effects** are outcomes that occur due to what is happening at the time of measurement. For example, there may be period effects in studies

Box 10.4

Myths of Aging

1. Senility is a normal part of the aging process.

   ■ Becoming a little forgetful is a normal part of aging. Forgetfulness so severe that it disrupts one's daily life is not normal. Dementia is a severe form of memory loss and is not a normal part of aging.

2. Most older people are lonely.

   ■ Actually, the number of close friends a person has remains relatively stable over the adult life course. The number of casual friends may decrease. Family is also an important part of life and older people see their adult children and grandchildren often.

3. Most older people are sick.

   ■ Physical changes do occur as we age but most older adults state that their health is "good" or "excellent."

4. Most older people are victims of crime.

   ■ Older individuals are more fearful of crime but they are less likely to be robbed, assaulted, or raped. They are more likely, however, to be victims of crime committed by their own family members.

5. The elderly become more religious as they age.

   ■ The **lifetime stability theory** states that people remain the same throughout their lives. Thus people do not become more religious but rather have been religious throughout their lives. This myth is a result of cohort differences in religiosity.

6. Most older people are non-productive.

   ■ Older individuals may not be as active in the workforce due to retirement. However, they are "productive" in that they are active grandparents, involved in volunteer activities, and sometimes employed part-time.

7. People who retire experience a decline in health and die quickly after retirement.

   ■ This used to be true when the typical lifespan was 46 years. Today, with people living well into their eighties and nineties, this is simply not true.

8. Older people have no interest in and lack the ability for sex.

   ■ Once again, the lifetime stability hypothesis applies here. People who were active sexually in early adulthood will continue to be so in later life. The way in which people express sexuality may change (e.g., more cuddling) to accommodate physical changes, but sexuality is still a large part of life.

9. Most older people end up in nursing homes.

   ■ The majority of elderly people live in their own homes or with family and friends. Community support makes it possible to live independently. Only about 5 percent live in nursing homes long term. Often these residences are used for rehabilitation purposes and the older individual returns home afterwards.

Source: Adapted from Wilken (2002).

conducted during the bursting of the dot-com bubble or during the introduction of a particular technology (e.g., televisions, computers, ultra-broadband). Failing to separate age, period, and cohort effects leads to the **developmental fallacy** in which cross-sectional age differences are interpreted as developmental change. For example, in early studies of intelligence quotient (IQ), it was believed that IQ drops with age (e.g., see Wechsler, 1939).

This is because the effects of age (natural aging) and cohort were not taken into account (separated). Giving the same IQ test to an elderly individual and a young adult may show a drop in IQ. However, we need to consider different educational standards and opportunities (young adults today largely finish high school and attend university, while a very small proportion of the elderly had the opportunity to go to university in the past) (Novak & Campbell, 2010). The way in which tests are constructed may also be a factor (again, young adults today have much more practice with multiple-choice exams, whereas the elderly may not have had as much exposure to these types of tests). Longitudinal studies of intelligence (in which the same individuals are followed and retested over time) show much less decline in intelligence (Schaie, 1990).

Types of Aging

Aging can be examined in several ways. **Chronological aging** is measured as the passage of time. Some events that occur during the life course are based on our chronological age. For example, Canada has a legal drinking age (which varies by province or territory), a legal driving age (assuming that you pass the driving exam), and a legal voting age. **Biological aging** deals with the physiological changes that occur over time. For example, bone mass loss (Bee, 1998) and a reduction of growth hormones occur as we age (Murray, Zentner, Pangman, & Pangman, 2006). **Psychological aging** deals with changes in personality, cognition, emotional arousal, memory, learning, and motivation. **Social aging** includes the changes in our social roles and social status over time (e.g., retirement is a status change from "working" to "non-working"). We will focus on biological and psychological aging in the following subsections. A discussion of social aging follows that.

Biological Aging Biological aging is a process of physical deterioration that occurs over time. Biological aging can occur due to internal (intrinsic) factors. For example, as we age, we lose lung capacity and brain cells and our arteries harden (McPherson & Wister, 2008). Biological aging can also occur due to external or (extrinsic) factors. For example, exposure to the sun and loud noise and our personal health habits (diet and exercise) can all have effects on the aging process (Health Canada, 2003).

There are three main areas of physiological effects with regard to aging: effects on the musculoskeletal system, effects on the endocrine system, and sensory changes. Musculoskeletal effects include losses in muscle mass and bone density as we age (Bee, 1998). This process begins between the ages of 20 and 30 years! Exercise can help to reduce muscle loss and the rate of bone decline. Weight-bearing exercise, in particular, builds muscle, increases bone density, improves balance, maintains weight, and lubricates joints (Blumenthal et al., 1991).

In the endocrine system, during later ages, a water imbalance in the kidneys may occur due to a malfunctioning hypothalamus (Gormly, 1997). Adrenal glands also decrease the production of sex hormones (Murray et al., 2006). Menopause begins between the ages of 45 and 55 years in women. Men, too, experience decreases in testosterone levels beginning in their twenties.

Box 10.5

The Drug Dilemma: The Need for "Elder-Friendly" Medications

Katherine asked her elderly father if he would mind taking care of her dog while she was away on a business trip. The dog, also in its elderly years, and her father were very fond of each other and had spent many afternoons going on long walks together while Katherine was at work. Katherine's father immediately agreed.

The dog needed to take several different medications twice a day, as it had developed a heart condition. To make things easier for her father, Katherine arranged the dog's pills in a pillbox that had compartments for each day of the week (Monday to Sunday) and also had AM and PM compartments per day. All her father had to do was open the correct compartment (e.g., Monday AM or Monday PM) and add the pills to the dog's food.

As Katherine was settling into her hotel room, her father called in a panic: "I opened the pill box and all the pills fell onto the floor—all of the pills for the *whole* week! I picked them up but now I don't know what pills to give the dog! They all look the same!"

"Don't worry, Dad," Katherine said, "I will tell you which pills you need over the phone.

Just write this down. She needs one large white pill, one small white pill, one-and-a-half green pills, and one blue pill."

Her father started to get agitated. "Okay, I have the large white pill and the small white pill, but I only see green pills. There aren't any blue pills . . . there aren't any blue pills!"

Suddenly Katherine realized that this wasn't going to work. Because her father was elderly and had some yellowing of the lenses in his eyes, he could no longer distinguish between the colours light green and light blue. Giving the wrong pills in the wrong doses could cause her dog to have heart failure.

"Don't worry, Dad," she said, "I'll call Frank. He'll be able to sort this out." Frank was Katherine's brother.

"Katherine," her dad said, "what if these were my pills and you or your brother weren't around to help? How would I know what pills to take?"

"If that time comes, Dad, I'll be sure to get the pharmacist to cut the pills into shapes for you," she said.

Sensory changes also occur. A decrease in our ability to smell can cause a loss of interest in food and an inability to smell rotten food (Stevens, Cruz, Marks, & Lakatos, 1998). A loss in temperature and vibration sensations (touch) can lead to slower reaction time to pain and the potential for burns (Gescheider, 1997). Several changes in vision can occur (see reviews by Fozard & Gordon-Salant, 2001; Kline & Schaie, 1996). A reduction in our ability to make tears can lead to "dry eye" syndrome. Yellowing of the lenses can make distinguishing between colours such as green and blue or yellow and white difficult (Murray et al., 2006). This can be problematic when taking several medications that are all the same shape but "colour coded" for the normal eye (see Box 10.5). Weakened eye muscles can lead to limitations in eye rotation (and thus have effects on peripheral vision). A loss of sensitivity to light can make it difficult to drive or to read a menu in a dimly lit restaurant. Hearing loss can lead to social isolation and depression since the individual is not able to participate fully in discussions (Murray et al., 2006). Older adults also report sleep difficulties (Dowling, 1995). They may compensate by taking naps, but one aspect of sleep called "slow wave" sleep declines as we age (Weiten & McCann, 2007). Loss of this type of sleep does not allow an individual to wake up feeling refreshed from a good night's sleep. Other sleep disorders that occur with age include respiratory problems, sleep apnea, and restless leg syndrome (American Nurses Association, 1995). Elderly individuals and their families must learn to cope with these changes. Although these changes sound negative, keep in mind that these sensory changes occur gradually and individuals generally learn to adapt and adjust as they occur.

On the positive side, the **compression of morbidity hypothesis** states that more people today than in the past postpone the onset of chronic disability; therefore, the period between being seriously ill and death has been compressed (shortened). The three most prevalent illnesses causing death and functional disability in later life are heart disease, cancer, and stroke (Statistics Canada, 2007b).

Acute (short-term) conditions are more debilitating and require more care. Chronic conditions are considered long term (more than three months), and often these are permanent conditions that require long-term management. Assessing an older person's capacity to be able to perform basic self-care is measured by the activities of daily living (ADL) and instrumental activities of daily living (IADL) scales. The ADL scale assesses whether individuals can bathe themselves, dress themselves, go to the bathroom on their own, get out of a bed or chair on their own, walk on their own, get outside, and feed themselves. The IADL scale measures more complex activities, such as one's ability to prepare meals, go shopping, manage money, use the phone, do light housework, and do heavy housework. Difficulties in these areas have been found to be related to age and sex. Increasing age is associated with more difficulties with these tasks, as is being female. There are three proposed reasons why women report more difficulty with items on the ADL and IADL scales. Culturally, it is more acceptable for women to be ill (the stereotype that women are fragile), and therefore women are more comfortable reporting such difficulties. Women also use medical services more than men, so difficulties with ADL and IADL tasks are more likely to be detected. Finally, women's roles may in fact be more stressful (e.g., the double shift), and therefore there may be more real illness among women (McPherson & Wister, 2008).

Psychological Aging As mentioned in Box 10.4, there are some losses associated with memory as we age. Large losses occur in **episodic memory**, or memory for personal events and experiences (Bäckman, Small, Wahlin, & Larsson, 2000), and in **working memory**, or our ability to hold a small amount of information in an available state (Hoyer & Verhaeghen, 2006). Smaller losses are found in **implicit memory,** a type of memory where you do not need to think to perform a task—a sort of automatic pilot based on previous experiences and skill development. For example, once you learn how to play the piano, as long as you continue to practise you will not have huge deficits in your ability to play. You certainly will remember where to place your fingers on the keyboard. There are also smaller losses associated with **semantic memory**, or memory for factual information (Hoyer & Verhaeghen, 2006).

The main factor that affects our ability to process information is attention (Weiten & McCann, 2007). **Selective attention** is the ability to focus on relevant information while ignoring what is irrelevant. **Sustained attention** is the ability to stay focused on a particular thing over time. **Attentional control** is the ability to multi-task with our attention, so to speak—to allocate our attention over several different things at the same time. These abilities are learned! Therefore, losses in these areas as we age are a result of our lack of practice.

One of the "gains" in terms of physiological change in later life is the development of wisdom. **Wisdom** is the ability to apply knowledge of life events and conditions to make optimal decisions when trying to solve life problems. What this means is that older people may be better at foreshadowing problems (problem finding) and problem solving due to their vast life experiences (Dixon, 2000). First Nations cultures hold their elderly in high regard because they are believed to hold wisdom. In this sense, later life is a stage one aspires to reach, as one becomes the holder of valuable life knowledge.

The most common psychological disorders in later life are depression, anxiety, dementia (including Alzheimer's disease), and alcoholism (McPherson & Wister, 2008). However, for most elderly individuals, global or subjective well-being does not decline with age (McPherson & Wister, 2008). Compared to younger adults, older adults tend to have less negative emotion, comparable positive emotion, more emotional control, and more emotional stability. Thus for most individuals in later life, negative emotions are not a problem; instead, the elderly tend to be as happy as those in mid-life (Ebersole & Hess, 2004).

What causes some elderly individuals to be depressed while others feel happy? Ryff (1995) proposed seven key dimensions of well-being. These include (1) positive self-evaluation and self-acceptance, (2) positive relationships with other people, (3) having autonomy and self-determination, (4) having mastery over one's environment, (5) effectively managing one's life, (6) having a sense of purpose, and (7) having a feeling of growth and development as a person. Among older individuals, environmental mastery and autonomy are higher but purpose in life and personal growth are lower than for younger adults (Ryff, 1995).

Problems occur when psychological stress develops. Negative cognitive and emotional states result when the demands of life exceed one's ability to cope. As stress increases, negative emotions increase. For the elderly, stress leads to related impairments in cognitive ability (such as the ability to perform a task), attention, concentration, memory, and judgment. One important side effect of stress is that stress causes the body to release a chemical that stops the activity of the thymus gland (Karren, Hafen, Smith, & Frandsen, 2006), which is the master gland involved in the immune system. When an individual is highly stressed or stressed for long periods, the thymus gland stops producing T cells, which are needed to fight viruses and bacteria. This makes the individual more vulnerable to infectious agents.

There are three basic types of coping associated with positive emotions during chronic stress. **Positive reappraisal** occurs when an individual tries to focus on the good aspects rather than the bad. **Problem-focused coping** occurs when an individual focuses his or her thoughts and behaviours on things he or she can do to manage or resolve the underlying cause of the stress. The third method of coping is to create positive events for oneself. For example, a person can take pleasure in a beautiful day or have a good laugh.

Coping is also dependent on one's locus of control. If a person has an **internal locus of control**, he or she believes that control over life events resides within himself or herself. Thus, the individual is more likely to confront a problem directly because he or she expects that his or her behaviour will make a difference in the outcome. The individual is more likely to accept responsibility for what is happening in his or her life. If a person has an **external locus of control**, he or she believes that life outcomes are due to fate, chance, God, or other people. The individual tends to respond defensively to a problem or deny that it exists. He or she lacks action to deal with the problem. Research has shown that individuals in later life with an internal locus of control tend to have higher well-being and a more positive view of themselves (Karren et al., 2006). Therefore, it seems that having an internal locus of control is the better way to go. However, when the cause of stress is something that cannot be controlled (e.g., a life-threatening disease such as cancer), individuals with an internal locus of control have lower well-being than those with an external locus of control because they cannot actually control the outcome!

Thus far we have discussed changes within the individual with which the elderly person and his or her family members must learn to cope. This stage of life also has several social changes that affect interactions between family members.

Changes in Relationship Status

As in other life stages, changes in relationship status occur during later life. Although most young-old continue to remain married, one new stage that occurs for the majority of elderly individuals is widowhood. According to Statistics Canada (2006d), approximately 30 percent of individuals aged 65 years and older are widowed. Widowhood occurs more frequently for women than for men. About half of women aged 75 to 79 years are widowed, while only 16 percent of men of this age are widowed. This occurs in part because women marry older men (about two years older on average) and are less likely to remarry (Beaujot, 2000).

Only about 5 to 6 percent of the elderly are divorced and 10 to 13 percent of those aged 65 years and older have experienced a divorce in their lifetime (see Figure 10.7). We expect these rates to increase as younger cohorts move into later life, since there is more acceptance of divorce today than in the past. An interesting point to consider when talking about rates of divorce and remarriage across the life course is that for many older individuals, there are few benefits to divorcing. Often older adults will simply separate and live the rest of their lives as separated individuals. Without the need or desire to remarry, the costs of a formal divorce may outweigh the benefits. Divorce in general is more difficult economically for women than for men (Galarneau & Sturrock, 1997), because traditionally men are the breadwinners and women are the homemakers depending on their husbands for financial support and because women are less likely to form a post-divorce union.

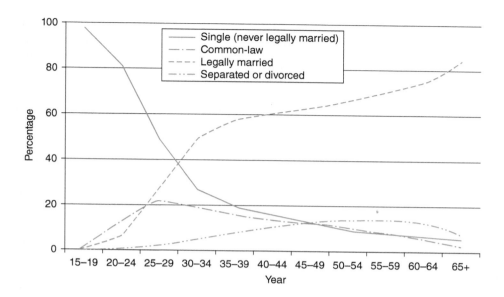

Figure 10.7 Conjugal Status of Population by Age Group, Canada, 2006

Source: Statistics Canada (2006c).

However, older men also lose financially after divorce because they cannot regain their lost income since they are no longer working (at least not full time) (Keith, 1985). Divorce also erodes one's support network (Martin-Matthews, 1991). Friends do not want to have to pick sides in terms of to whom they will be loyal. The loss is said to be greater for men than for women, as men typically have a smaller support network (friends who they can emotionally talk to and rely on) (Lin, 2008). Women are often **kinkeepers**, or the individual in the family who keeps family members connected, so men tend to lose family connections as well. Divorce can also affect grandparent–grandchild relations as it changes the balance of resources (Downs, Coleman, & Ganong, 2000). Whereas the older person could once buy things for the grandchild, he or she may no longer be able to do so as easily. Divorce also disrupts family links, making it difficult for adult children and grandchildren to spend time with both parents, especially on holidays.

Following divorce is the potential for remarriage. Remarriage rates are higher for men than for women (Calasanti & Kiecolt, 2007). Often this is due to a marriage squeeze (discussed in Chapter 5). An imbalance in the **sex ratio** (the number of marriageable men to the number of marriageable women) can make it difficult for older women to find new partners. Since women live longer than men (there are fewer men in the oldest-old group) (Statistics Canada, 2002) and men tend to marry women younger than themselves, older women often are squeezed out of marriage (Chappell, McDonald, & Stones, 2008). Generally, those in poor health, those with poor finances, and the very old do not remarry. There also are fewer incentives to remarry at this stage in life. There is no need to conform to life cycle timing for marriage (which occurs in the late twenties and early thirties), the elderly are not going to have children together (another main reason why people decide to get married when they are young), and often older individuals feel the need to protect their estate (and sometimes there is strong pressure from the family to do so!) (Talbott, 1998). Positive reasons to remarry include enlarging your kin network, being generally happy with the relationship, having increased financial and emotional stability, and enhancing relationships with your children (if the children are supportive) since you will become less of a burden to them.

One group of elderly we don't want to forget about is those who never married. Educated women make up the largest proportion of this group (Seccombe & Ishii-Kuntz, 1994). With no economic need for a spouse, decreasing stigma associated with remaining single, and the marriage squeeze as described above, getting an education before getting involved in a serious relationship often leads women to be squeezed out of marriage. The assumption about never-married individuals is that they are lifelong social isolates (Gubrium, 1975). Although they do spend less time with their relatives (Seccombe & Ishii-Kuntz, 1994), never-marrieds have a high rate of co-residency (Stull & Scarisbrick-Hauser, 1989), strong friendship groups (McDill, Hall, & Turell, 2006), and close ties with their siblings (Rubinstein, Alexander, Goodman, & Luborsky, 1991). Never-married individuals usually have no children, although this isn't always the case. Some say that they regret never marrying (Rubinstein, 1987) and some report being lonely, but they generally have high well-being and are spared spousal bereavement and desertion (Pudrovska et al., 2006).

Empty Nest

A new stage for most elderly individuals (those who have children) is called the **empty nest**. This occurs when their children leave the family home to start their own lives and establish their own residences. For most, this is a time of increased satisfaction (Guttman, 1994). The job of parenting is more or less done and one has time to pursue new or old hobbies and interests that may have been put on hold while busy with parenting (see Box 10.6 for an example). Children leaving the home is called **launching**. Delayed launching, however,

Box 10.6

The Red Hat Society

The Red Hat Society is an international society for women in mid-life and later life. It was founded by Sue Ellen Cooper in 1998 and currently has more than 20 000 chapters across the United States and in 25 foreign countries. Women over age 50 are called "red hatters" and women under age 50 are called "pink hatters."

The purpose of the group is to encourage women to pursue their lifelong dreams, fun, freedom, friendship, and fitness. The group is dedicated to "reshaping the way women are viewed in society" by raising the visibility of aging women. Members wear red and purple at their events (or pink and lavender if under 50).

can decrease satisfaction. Parents think that they have failed in some way because their children are not moving on to become responsible, productive members of society. As more and more young adults pursue higher education, taking longer to settle into careers and as a result partnering at older ages, launching often does not occur until the children reach their late twenties (Statistics Canada, 2001). This varies by culture and ethnicity, with many individuals of South Asian, Asian, and European descent staying in the parental home well into their late thirties (Gee, Mitchell, & Wister, 2001).

Another issue is the return of adult children to the parental nest. This may occur due to the children's separation or divorce, job loss, or simply an inability to "make it" on their own. When children refill the nest, they are called **boomerang children**. Sometimes, children never leave but rather establish their new families as co-residents in the family home. Once again, this varies by cultural background; it is a common residential pattern for those of Asian descent, for example. In these cultures, the adult child is expected to reside with his or her parents and take care of them. This is called a **cluttered nest** and occurs when the family home has more than one family of procreation living in it. According to the Vanier Institute of the Family (2010), 60.3 percent of adult children aged 20 to 24 years and 26 percent of adult children aged 25 to 29 years lived in the parental home in 2006. Approximately 34.7 percent of boomerang children return home to attend school, 24 percent return for financial reasons, and 10.5 percent return due to a relationship ending.

Finally, there is a growing trend for the elderly to take on the responsibility of raising their grandchildren as primary caretakers (see Figure 10.8). This, however, is not

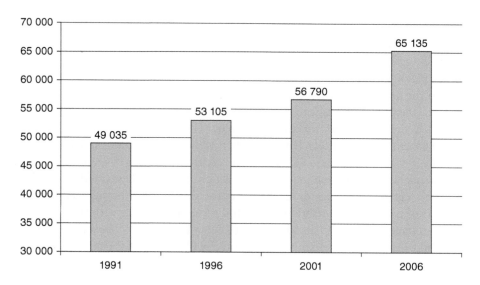

Figure 10.8 Children (All Ages) Living with One or More Grandparents with No Parent Present, Canada, 1991 to 2006

Source: Statistics Canada (2006d).

normative (Stepan, 2003) and may occur for a number of reasons. The biological parents may be in trouble with the law, have addictions, be dead or ill, or be teen parents who are unable to cope with the demands of parenting.

Grandparenthood

Grandparenthood usually occurs in middle age. By the time a person reaches later life, they usually have teen grandchildren. However, since the age at marriage and the age at first birth have been increasing, this may not remain the case among future generations of the elderly. There has been a steady increase in the number of grandparents who become custodial caregivers of grandchildren (see Figure 10.8), although this is not the dominant role of grandparent. Generally, the role of grandparent is more flexible than that of parent. Grandparents are usually told what not to do by their adult children. The role of grandparent is also not chosen; you become a grandparent if your own children choose to become parents. As well, parents often mediate the relationship between the grandparent and the grandchild. For example, they do not get to visit each other unless the parent approves.

There are three main types of grandparents. The **companionate grandparent** is the most common type. These grandparents are close to their grandchildren but do not have a parental role. **Remote grandparents** are the next most common type. Here the grandparent is less involved in the grandchild's life, usually because they live far away from one another. **Involved grandparents** are the least common type, but they have parent-like duties. They are less warm than companionate and remote grandparents (because they must discipline their grandchildren). Grandmothers generally tend to emphasize closeness and fun. Grandfathers like to assume the role of adviser (Russell, 1986). Gender differences are exaggerated depending on lineage. Paternal grandfathers are more masculine (e.g., they play-fight more often) than maternal grandfathers (who are more nurturing).

When the grandchild becomes a teenager, the relationship may become more withdrawn as the teen tries to become more independent (Cherlin & Furstenberg, 1986). Often teen grandchildren do errands for the grandparent. The age of the grandchild affects the amount of control the parents can have in mediating the grandparent–grandchild relationship (Troll, 1985). Young grandchildren have no control over visits by grandparents. Teen or adult grandchildren can form independent relationships with their grandparents. Thus, contact with a grandchild depends on the age of the grandchild. Another factor affecting the amount of contact is the relationship with the parent. Conflict with their own adult children can limit contact with grandchildren (King & Elder, 1997). Separation or divorce of adult children can also have an impact. Contact will increase if the grandparent's own child has primary custody of the grandchildren (Hilton & Macari, 1997). Conflict with ex-spouses reduces contact. Since child custody used to go to mothers more often than not, maternal grandparents tended to have more contact with grandchildren than paternal grandparents (Uhlenberg, 2004). With child custody arrangements changing, the impact on grandparent–grandchild relationships is also changing. In addition, as middle-aged

children repartner or remarry, the elderly also may become step-grandparents. This is a new role with few established expectations and thus one that may require some negotiation.

Retirement

In the past, retirement was viewed as a negative event. The purpose of one's life (especially for men) was diminished since they were no longer in the workforce. This is no longer true. Early retirement is now seen as a worthwhile goal (only those that "have made it" can afford to do so in style). Greater retirement income makes it possible for some workers to quit earlier than the established standard retirement age of 65 years. Typically, people choose to retire earlier rather than later (Statistics Canada, 2003b). An equal number of individuals say that they retired "just because" as say that they did so for health reasons.

As the provider role for men is diminished in retirement, they must search for substitute activities. For an elderly couple, this can be a challenging time if the couple failed to establish shared interests before retirement. More time available to spend together can lead to irritation or to greater intimacy (Chappell et al., 2008). Men seek increased companionship from their wives. Many homemakers, however, report less freedom as they increase couple activities at the expense of individual ones. Married women tend to retire earlier than unmarried women. This is due to economics (having adequate income saved) as well as to the age of their spouse (women tend to retire around the same time as their husbands do, although this trend is in decline; see Figure 10.9). Older couples also make other adjustments, such as reducing their work hours. According to the Vanier Institute of the Family (2010), 11 percent of older men and 28 percent of older women worked part-time in 2006.

Among the current cohort of elderly, the pattern of work and retirement is rather uncomplicated. The general life course was to marry young (women marrying men slightly older than themselves) and soon after have children. Divorce was unlikely and there was a gendered division of labour (men as the breadwinners and women as the homemakers).

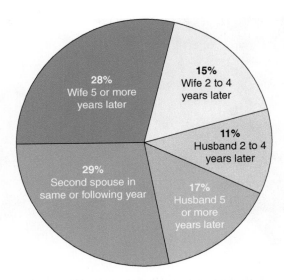

Figure 10.9 Spousal Retirement Transitions of Dual-Earner Couples, 2001

Source: Schellenberg and Ostrovsky (2008).

Men tended to go to work once they finished their schooling and worked until retirement. Women worked in the domestic sphere and if they did work outside the home, it was secondary to their domestic work (McDonald, 2002). Thus, "retirement" is less meaningful for the current cohort of elderly women, as domestic work continues regardless of one's age (that is, you don't get to retire from doing housework).

Income of unattached elderly (never married, separated, divorced, and widowed) has increased. According to the Vanier Institute of the Family (2010), these improvements reflect gains from "market" sources (private pensions, investment income, and earnings) as well as significant increases in transfer payments received through government programs (see Figure 10.10). The poverty rate among the elderly has declined from 29 percent in 1976 to 4.8 percent in 2007 (Vanier Institute of the Family, 2010). Levels of poverty are higher for unattached elderly individuals than for those in families, but have dropped to 13 percent and 14.3 percent for unattached elderly men and women, respectively (Vanier Institute of the Family, 2010). See Figure 10.11 for median net worth by age of the major income recipient in the family.

Caregiving

As the vignette at the beginning of this chapter illustrated, family members often face the need to provide care for their aging relatives. In 2006, about 21 percent of women and 16 percent of men provided care to an elderly individual. Individuals aged 45 to 54 years are most likely to provide care (Vanier Institute of the Family, 2010). Many of these individuals are also providing care to their children. Thus,

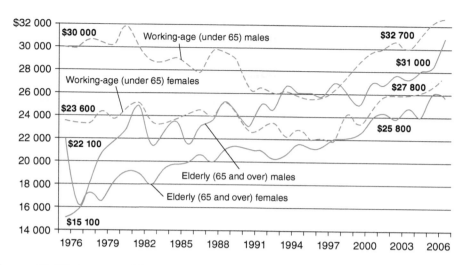

Figure 10.10 Average After-Tax Incomes of Unattached Individuals, in Constant 2007 Dollars, 1976 to 2007

Source: Statistics Canada (2009).

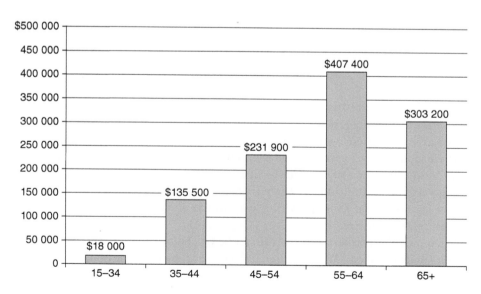

Figure 10.11 Median Net Worth by Age of Major Income Recipient, 2005

Source: Statistics Canada (2006g).

Table 10.1 Profile of Caregivers Providing Elder Care to Seniors with Long-Term Health Conditions, Population Aged 45 Years and Older, 2007

	Percentage Distribution	
	Caregivers	Non-Caregivers
Age		
45–54	43%	38%
55–64	32	28
65–74	16	18
75+	8	16
Gender		
Men	43	49
Women	57	51
Marital Status		
Single	7	6
Married or common-law	76	72
Widowed	7	11
Divorced	10	11
Work Status		
Employed	57	51
Retired	31	34
Other	12	15

Source: Cranswick and Dosman (2008).

they are often referred to as the **sandwich generation**. Most caregivers report coping "very well" (54 percent), many said they were "managing" (42 percent), and others reported giving up their own social activities (34.7 percent) and spending less time with their spouses (17.5 percent) and their children (15.1 percent) as a result of caregiving (Vanier Institute of the Family, 2010). As shown in Table 10.1, the majority of caregivers are in mid-life, partnered (married or common law), employed, and female, suggesting that those providing care to the elderly are juggling other family and work responsibilities.

When an older person needs care, it can be psychologically difficult for both them and their family members. Adult children feel a sense of irredeemable obligation; they can never do enough for their parents. The elderly parent, however, feels a loss of power. The primary reason why children report caring for their parent is because the parent looked after them when they were young (Dwyer, Lee, & Jankowske, 1994). If they were parented poorly, they feel less obligated to their aging parent. Although less able to provide forms of support that require physical functioning, an elderly person generally can still provide emotional, practical, and financial help to the adult children. This helps to maintain a sense of power. However, when an elderly person receives assistance due to his or her own failing health, an emotional strain is felt (Newsom & Schulz, 1996). Interestingly, the amount of help received from a child is not equal to the level of affection an elderly person feels for that child. The **generational stake hypothesis** states that "older parents have a greater stake than children do in the parent–child relationship because of their desire to see their value and lives continued through their children" (Connidis, 1989, p. 60). Thus, the elderly parent will report more affection between themselves and their children than the children do.

Abuse

Abuse occurs across the life course, and later life is no exception. **Elder abuse** is defined as any act occurring within a relationship where there is an implication of trust that results in harm to an older person. Abuse can be physical, psychological, sexual, financial, or neglect. **Physical abuse** includes any use of physical force against the elderly person. This can include an inappropriate use of drugs or restraints, or punishing the elderly person for misbehaving. **Psychological abuse** includes verbal threats, intimidation, enforced social isolation, and humiliation. **Sexual abuse** is any non-consensual sexual contact. This also includes having sexual contact with a person incapable of giving consent (e.g., a person with dementia). **Financial exploitation** is the illegal or improper use of an older person's funds, property, or assets. This can include cashing cheques without permission, forging a person's signature, misusing or stealing possessions, coercing or deceiving a person into signing documents he or she does not fully understand, and improper use of conservatorship, guardianship, or power of attorney. Elder neglect can include active neglect, passive neglect, and self-neglect (although in this last case, the elderly person is abusing himself or herself). **Active neglect** occurs when a caregiver refuses to provide the services that the elderly person needs. **Passive neglect** is the non-intentional failure of a caregiver to provide appropriate services to the elderly individual because he or she does not have adequate knowledge of what is available and what is necessary for proper care. **Self-neglect** occurs when the elderly person himself or herself fails to follow medical directives (intentionally or unintentionally) and does not take proper care of himself or herself.

Who is abusing the elderly? Research has shown that 71 percent of abusers are adult children and spouses. Elderly women are equally as likely to be abused by a child (37 percent) as by a spouse (36 percent) while elderly men are most likely to be abused by a child (43 percent) (National Advisory Council on Aging, 2003–2004). Risk factors for abuse include shared living situations, dementia, social isolation, caregiver mental illness or substance abuse, and the caregiver being dependent on the elderly person (Lachs & Pillemer, 2004)

There are many reasons why elder abuse is hard to detect and prevent. The older adult may not seek help because he or she may not recognize the situation as abuse (McPherson & Wister, 2008). Often abuse starts earlier in the life cycle and becomes "normal" in the eyes of the elderly individual. For example, a spouse could be psychologically abusive for many years before becoming half of an older couple. Older persons may not report abuse because they think they will not be believed, they think nothing will change, or they think their caregivers will get angry and the abuse will get worse (Beaulaurier, Seff, Newman, & Dunlop, 2007)! Often they are also ashamed and embarrassed. The abusing caregiver is usually a family member, and thus older adults are reluctant to let others know they have a "bad" son, daughter, or spouse. They may even blame themselves for the abuse, thinking that if they weren't such a problem or so much work, their caregiver would not get so angry. Some individuals cannot report abuse because they are socially isolated (by the caregiver or by their own disabilities) and physically unable to report the problem (McPherson & Wister, 2008). Cognitive diseases and communication deficits make reporting difficult. The elderly are also prone to bruising and falling, so outsiders may not be sure whether outward signs of abuse are actually the result of abuse.

End of Life

The response to impending death varies from person to person and can be influenced by cultural or religious beliefs about what occurs to the individual following death. Dying is more than just a biological act. There are social and emotional implications for the individual and his or her family and friends. Kübler-Ross (1969) proposed five stages that an individual will go through in the process of dying: (1) denial, (2) anger, (3) bargaining, (4) depression, and (5) acceptance. Not everyone will go through all of these stages or go through the stages one at a time, but this describes the general pattern of moving to acceptance for most individuals in North America. The grieving process for those left behind includes letting go of the dying individual as well as coming up with new ways to maintain connections with other family members and friends. Conflicts may occur as family members try to determine how the loved one should be cared for at the end of life (Matthews, 2002). The role of non-kin is often unclear. They may be cut off from the loved one and excluded from end-of-life planning. Institutions often will not allow non-kin to visit those who are critically ill and dying. This has been a concern among older gay and lesbian couples. They are concerned that their role in their partner`s health care plan will not be recognized by service providers (McFarland & Sanders, 2003).

"Death rituals are rites of passage that provide formal recognition of the transition from life to death" (Chappell et al., 2008, p. 432). These rituals help family and friends to accept the death of their loved one and provide support so they can continue in life without them. Common options in Canada include burial, cremation, and entombment. Cremation is becoming more and more popular, as it costs less than a traditional

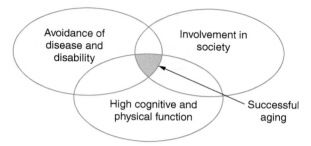

Figure 10.12 Model of Successful Aging

This model assumes that all three components must exist for successful aging to occur.

Source: Rowe and Kahn (1997).

burial. First Nations groups celebrate the "circle of life" and see death as another stage in that circle.

CONCLUSION

This chapter has examined what it means to "age," both from a demographic and individual point of view. Demographically speaking, we are concerned about the aging of a population since it may have implications for available resources and the allocation of these resources to various segments of the population. From an individual perspective, this stage in the life course can bring many changes—physical, psychological, and social—that the individual and his or her family members must adjust to and negotiate. These changes can be seen as new opportunities (e.g., retirement, grandparenthood) or as new challenges (e.g., physical slowing and decline, widowhood). Maintaining a positive attitude throughout these changes can help to ease the transition, but what else can one do to age successfully?

Successful aging is defined as a combination of physical health, psychological health, and an active involvement with society (Rowe & Kahn, 1997; see Figure 10.12). A few key tips to successful aging are eating a low-fat diet and getting adequate exercise (Health Canada, 2003). Having a body mass index (BMI) that is either too low or too high causes health burdens (Must et al., 1999). Thus, eating a proper diet can help to increase longevity. Both heart disease and cancer have been found to be reduced by exercise. Staying fit can prevent, delay, or even ease some chronic conditions (Ebersole & Hess, 2004). Exercise also has psychological benefits (Blumenthal et al., 1991). Having an exercise partner, education about appropriate exercises to perform, and recommendations from doctors can boost exercise regimens. Finally, having a strong social support network (family and friends) can help to buffer an individual from the effects of stress (Ross, Mirowsky, & Goldsteen, 1990). As well, these social supports can step in to help when needed.

SUMMARY OF KEY POINTS

■ Research on aging examines both population aging and individual aging. Population aging is the distribution of a population's age structure. A population is considered "old" when 10 percent or more of the population is made up of people aged 65 years or older. Three components that affect the aging of a population are fertility rates, mortality rates, and migration.

■ Population pyramids are graphs that show the distribution of individuals in a population by age; they are often also divided by gender. As the baby boomers move into old age, there is concern that the working cohort will not be able to support such a large number of elderly dependants.

■ Population aging is becoming a worldwide concern. Old populations are found in more developed regions (e.g., Canada and the United States) while developing regions (e.g., parts of Africa and Latin America) have younger populations. The developing regions are predicted to have aging populations in the near future.

■ We can measure chronological age (one's age in years) or functional age (one's age measured by competence or performance). We can also think about age in terms of life expectancy, or the number of years an individual born in a particular year (cohort) can expect to live.

■ One of the challenges the elderly face is ageism, or the stereotyping of older persons. This is usually negative but may be positive. There are several myths of aging that perpetuate ageism.

■ Aging research must be designed in a way that age, cohort, and period effects do not get confused. Non-separation of age, cohort, and period effects leads to the developmental fallacy in which cross-sectional age differences are interpreted as developmental change.

■ The compression of morbidity hypothesis states that more people today than in the past postpone the onset of chronic disability; therefore, the period between being seriously ill and death has been compressed.

■ Assessing an older person's capacity to be able to perform basic self-care is measured by the activities of daily living (ADL) and instrumental activities of daily living (IADL) scales.

■ There are some losses associated with memory as we age. Large losses occur in episodic memory and in working memory. Smaller losses are found in implicit memory and semantic memory, or memory for factual information. One of the "gains" in terms of physiological change in later life is the development of wisdom.

■ The most common psychological disorders in later life are depression, anxiety, Alzheimer's disease, and alcoholism. However, for most elderly individuals, global or subjective well-being does not decline with age.

- According to Statistics Canada, approximately 30 percent of individuals aged 65 years and older are widowed. Widowhood occurs more frequently for women than for men. About half of women aged 75 to 79 years are widowed, while only 16 percent of men in this age group are widowed.

- Only about 5 to 6 percent of the elderly are divorced and 10 to 13 percent of those aged 65 years and older have experienced a divorce in their lifetime.

- Remarriage rates are higher for men than for women. An imbalance in the sex ratio (number of marriageable men to number of marriageable women) can make it difficult for older women to find a new partner. Since women live longer than men (and there are fewer men in the oldest-old group) and men tend to marry women younger than themselves, older women often are squeezed out of marriage.

- The empty nest stage occurs when children leave the family home to start their own lives and establish their own residences. As more and more young adults pursue higher education, taking longer to settle into careers and partnering at older ages, launching often does not occur until the children reach their late twenties or early thirties. This varies by culture and ethnicity.

- There has been a steady increase in the number of grandparents who are becoming custodial caregivers of grandchildren. There are three main types of grandparents: companionate, remote, and involved.

- In the past, retirement was viewed as a negative event. Early retirement is now seen as a worthwhile goal. Married women tend to retire earlier than unmarried women.

- Income of the unattached elderly has increased in recent years. The poverty rate of the elderly has also declined from 18 percent in 1976 to 1.5 percent in 2007 (Vanier Institute of the Family, 2010). Levels of poverty are higher for unattached elderly individuals than for those in families.

- In 2006, about 21 percent of women and 16 percent of men provided care to an elderly individual. Individuals aged 45 to 54 years are the most likely to provide care (Vanier Institute of the Family, 2010). Many of these individuals are also providing care to their children and are referred to as the sandwich generation.

- Elder abuse is defined as any act occurring within a relationship where there is an implication of trust that results in harm to an older person. Abuse can be physical, psychological, sexual, financial, or neglect. Elder neglect can include active neglect, passive neglect, and self-neglect. Seventy-one percent of abusers of the elderly are adult children and spouses. Risk factors for abuse include shared living situations, dementia, social isolation, caregiver mental illness or substance abuse, and the caregiver being dependent on the elderly person (Lachs & Pillemer, 2004).

- Successful aging is defined as a combination of physical health, psychological health, and an active involvement with society (Rowe & Kahn, 1997).

Critical Thinking Questions

1. Since population aging is becoming a worldwide concern, should we create policy (e.g., laws or incentive programs) with the goal of shifting the population structure? If yes, what specifically should we implement?

2. Should an elderly individual with dementia be allowed to date and have sexual relations? Why or why not?

3. If you could reverse, stop, or control any one physical or mental component of aging, what would it be? Why?

4. If you were an elderly person abused by a family member, what could you do to stop it? What are some potential obstacles you would face in doing so?

Glossary

active neglect Neglect that occurs when a caregiver refuses to provide the services that an elderly person needs.

age effects Research outcomes that occur due to one's age or developmental stage (e.g., greying hair).

aged dependency ratio A measure of elderly dependency in a population measured as all persons 65 years and older divided by all persons aged between 20 and 64 years in a given population.

ageism The stereotyping of older persons.

attentional control The ability to multi-task with our attention—to allocate our attention over several different things at the same time.

biological aging Physiological changes in the body that occur over time.

biological generativity Contributing to society by having children.

boomerang children Adult children who return to their parents' home to live with them again after having moved out.

chronological age One's age in years.

chronological aging Measured as the passing of time.

cluttered nest This occurs when two or more generations of family members live in the same family home.

cohort effects Research outcomes that occur because one is born into a particular cohort.

companionate grandparent A type of grandparent defined by a close relationship with grandchildren, without the parental (disciplinary) role.

compression of morbidity hypothesis A hypothesis that states that more people today than in the past postpone the onset of chronic disability; therefore, the period between being seriously ill and death has been compressed.

cultural generativity Contributing to society by passing on cultural values and traditions to the next generation.

demographers People who study stability and change in populations.

developmental fallacy An error made when cross-sectional age differences are interpreted as developmental change.

elder abuse An act occurring within a relationship where there is an implication of trust that results in harm to an older person.

empty nest This occurs when children leave the family home and the parents are alone in the household.

episodic memory Memory for personal events and experiences.

external locus of control The belief that life outcomes are due to external factors (e.g., fate, chance, God, or other people).

financial exploitation The illegal or improper use of an (older) person's funds, property, or assets.

functional age One's age measured by competence or performance on tasks.

generational stake hypothesis Parents and grandparents (older individuals) have more of an interest in the parent–child or grandparent–grandchild relationship because they want to see their values and lives continued through their children or grandchildren. Thus the older individual will invest more in the relationship than the younger individual.

generativity The ability to go beyond one's own interests and help the generations to come.

implicit memory A type of memory in which you do not need to think to perform a task (e.g., acting on automatic pilot).

individual aging The biological, physiological, psychological, and social changes that occur over the life cycle.

integrity According to Erikson, the ability to accept one's life as something that had to be rather than having regret over what it was not.

internal locus of control The belief that control over life events resides within oneself.

involved grandparent A type of grandparent that has parent-like duties toward the grand-children (e.g., providing care and discipline).

kinkeeper The individual in the family who keeps family members connected with one another.

launching This occurs when children leave the family home and move out on their own.

life expectancy The number of years that an individual born in a particular year can expect to live.

lifetime stability theory People remain the same throughout their lives (e.g., if an individual is active when young, he or she will be active when old).

Old-old Individuals 75 to 84 years of age.

Oldest-old Individuals 85 years of age and older.

parental generativity Contributing to society by nurturing and socializing children.

passive neglect Neglect that is a non-intentional failure of a caregiver to provide appropriate services to an elderly individual because he or she does not have adequate knowledge of what services are available and what is necessary for proper care.

period effects Research outcomes that occur due to what is happening at the time of measurement (e.g., feelings of safety would show serious decline if safety was measured right after September 11, 2001).

physical abuse Any use of physical force against an (elderly) person.

population aging The distribution of a population's age structure in which there are increasing proportions of older people.

population pyramids Graphs that show the distribution of individuals in a population by age (and sometimes by sex).

positive reappraisal A form of coping in which an individual tries to focus on the good aspects of a situation rather than the bad aspects.

problem-focused coping A form of coping in which an individual focuses his or her thoughts and behaviours on things that can be done to manage or resolve the underlying cause of stress.

psychological abuse Verbal threats, intimidation, enforced social isolation, and humiliation of an (elderly) individual.

psychological aging Changes in personality, cognition, emotional arousal, memory, learning, and motivation over time.

remote grandparent A type of grandparent that is less involved with the grandchildren, usually due to physical distance between them.

sandwich generation Middle-aged adults who must look after their elderly relatives as well as take care of their own children.

selective attention The ability to focus on relevant information while ignoring what is irrelevant.

self-neglect Neglect that occurs when an elderly person fails to follow medical directives (intentionally or unintentionally) and does not properly take care of himself or herself.

semantic memory Memory for factual information.

sex ratio The number of marriageable men to the number of marriageable women in a given population.

sexual abuse Any non-consensual sexual contact.

social aging Changes in our social roles and social status over time.

sustained attention The ability to remain focused on a particular thing over time.

technical generativity Contributing to society by teaching skills to the next generation.

total dependency ratio A measure of dependency in a given population, calculated as the number of individuals aged 0 to 19 years and 65 years and older divided by the number of individuals aged 20 to 64 years.

wisdom Knowledge of what is true or right coupled with the ability to act appropriately in a given situation.

working memory The ability to hold a small amount of information in an available state (often called short-term memory).

young-old Individuals 65 to 74 years of age.

youth dependency ratio A measure of dependency in the young, calculated as the number of individuals aged 0 to 19 years divided by the number of individuals aged 20 to 64 years.

CONNECTIONS

www.go60.com/myths.htm
www.redhatsociety.com/aboutus/index.html
http://intraspec.ca/rc2006_e.pdf
www.ccsmh.ca/en/default.cfm
www.caregiver.org/caregiver/jsp/content_node.jsp?nodeid=569
www.cnpea.ca
www.qelccc.ca/Home

Remember to log on to the Companion Website at **www.pearsoncanada.ca/white** to find self-graded quizzes and useful resource tools for further study. You can log on to the Companion Website using the Student Access Code that comes packaged with your copy of *Families Across the Life Course*.

Chapter 11

Stress, Conflict, and Abuse Across the Life Course

Learning Objectives

After reading this chapter, you should be able to:

1. Understand the differing explanations for family stress and dysfunction.

2. Describe the ABC-X and Circumplex models of family functioning as well as their historical roots in the work of Reuben Hill.

3. Understand the ways in which family stress and conflict play out at different stages across the family life course.

4. Discuss less well-known expressions of family stress conflict and abuse such as sibling violence, adolescent–parent abuse, and elder neglect, as well as date rape, spousal abuse, and corporal punishment.

5. Outline the research supporting the intergenerational transfer of dysfunctional family behaviour.

Even through the walls, they could hear the screaming and the crying. Bob and Jan had their own financial challenges, but ever since their neighbour Kwan had lost his job, he and Juanita had been fighting more than usual. It probably didn't help that that the twins had been demanding most of Juanita energy and attention; with four children under 4 years of age, Kwan and Juanita must be pretty taxed. But this time seemed worse, and the crying was not from the kids but from Juanita. It sounded like cries of pain rather than of frustration.

Jan recognized the sound. She had been involved in an abusive relationship prior to Bob and the slow constriction of her freedom and the isolation from her family ultimately led to a situation ripe for her partner's violent outbursts, which she hates to admit were preferable to the degrading names he would call her.

As the sound of the sirens began to get louder, Bob and Jan figured that someone must have called the police. They guessed that it probably had been Mrs. Chan, who lived in the apartment on the other side of Kwan and Juanita. They knew she was home because she had just gotten back from hospital. Her arm was in a cast and her adult son who accompanied her had said she'd had a fall. Mrs. Chan hadn't seemed to hear him and must have been in a rush, because she hadn't even looked up or attempted to make eye contact.

The family is held up as the basic building block of society, a place where intimacy is encouraged and where children are nurtured. So why is it that the family is also a place where stress is prevalent, conflict seems to be the norm, and abuse in its most hideous forms can be found? The **universal taboo** is not neglecting your children, but sexually abusing them. In addition to incest, there are the controversial topics of abortion and infanticide, both of which have been practised by the family across cultures and throughout history. Homicide also often has family connections (Figure 11.1). Current research shows that the family members most likely to be killed are younger children, particularly those under 1 year of age (Cavanagh, Dobash, & Dobash, 2007). Gender is not a factor, as boys and girls are equally likely to be victims of fatal child abuse. The act is most likely to take place in the home and occurs more often when the child is in the solitary or temporary care of a parent, typically a father or stepfather. Direct blows and physical force often take the life of younger children, with shaking widely reported as a cause of infant deaths.

This chapter looks across the life course at the common family issues of stress and conflict as well as the less frequent but too often present issues of abuse and violence. After a brief overview of social science's explanation of extreme family dysfunction, we discuss a few relevant research models used to understand how some families deal more effectively than others with the challenges of family functioning. The last section in this

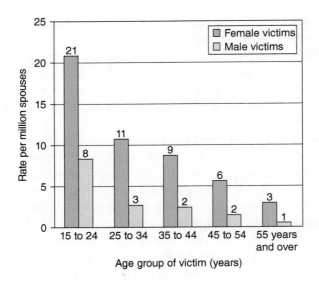

Figure 11.1 Spousal Homicide Rates Highest Among Young Female Spouses, 1998 to 2007

Notes: Rate per 1 000 000 legally married, common-law, separated and divorced spouses, 15 years of age and over, based on estimates provided by Demography Division, Statistics Canada. Spousal homicides reported by police include a small number of victims who were separated from a common-law relationship. As population estimates are unavailable for this sub-population, the overall rates of spousal homicide may be slightly overestimated. Same-sex partners were excluded from the analysis due to the unavailability of population estimates. Homicides of same-sex partners represented 1% of spousal homicides.

Source: Statistics Canada, Canadian Centre for Justice Statistics, Homicide Survey, http://www.statcan.gc.ca/pub/85-224-x/2009000/ct014-eng.htm

chapter presents a systematic approach to stress, conflict, and abuse across various stages of the life course, beginning with the formation of intimate relationships and concluding with the topic of elder abuse.

ORIGINS AND EXPLANATIONS OF HARMFUL DYSFUNCTION

The explanations for why something so good can become something so bad are numerous. We provide a brief overview of four of these explanations: sociobiology and evolutionary psychology, psychological explanations, sociological explanations at both the macro and the micro level, and family theory explanations.

Sociobiology and Evolutionary Psychology

Sociobiology is concerned with examining the combination of sociological and biological factors to explain human behaviour. At its core, this approach applies the Darwinian theory of evolution to explain the motivation behind social conduct. Genetic evolution-ists believe that certain human behaviours exist as the result of weeding out poor adaptive social patterns over the course of human history. At the heart of sociobiology and the closely related discipline of evolutionary psychology is the **nature verses nurture** debate. How much of what we do in our individual and social lives is the result of being socialized (nurture) to behave in a certain way, and how much of it is the result of genetic qualities that we have inherited from our parents (nature)? Evolutionary psychology attempts to minimize the controversy associated with sociobiology once the discipline moved from explaining animal survival behaviour to explaining human social behaviour.

Central to a discussion of the dysfunctional aspects of the family are sociobiology's explanations for the negative social behaviours closely related to intimate relationships and family life, such as lying, jealousy, rape, violent acts, infidelity, and murder. This theoretical approach would describe these acts as successful adaptive strategies for survival that improve reproduction opportunities. Murder becomes an adaptive strategy because it can be employed to eliminate threats from rivals, which may include non-genetic rela-tives such as stepchildren. Genetic fitness would be encouraged by murdering deformed infants, the infirm, or the chronically ill. Infanticide may be practised to ensure that male (rather than female) offspring survive to adulthood or because of contested resources such as available food sources, land, or inheritance rights. Rape may be practised by those who are less sexually desirable to improve their reproductive chances.

David Buss, an evolutionary psychologist, developed a theory regarding sexual mating strategies (Buss & Schmitt, 1993; see Figure 11.2) that views men and women as differing in terms of the quest for short-term mates and long-term mates. Both sexes are motivated by the desire to perpetuate themselves through offspring. Their strategies are socially devel-oped to increase the probability of raising as many healthy offspring to adulthood as pos-sible. Males are more concerned with short-term strategies than are women, but both must

Short-term reproductive challenges		Long-term reproductive challenges	
Men	**Women**	**Men**	**Women**
Partner number	Immediate resource extraction	Paternity confidence	Identify men willing to invest
Identify sexually accessible women	Judge as possible long-term mates	Assess woman's reproductive value	Physical protection
Minimize cost, risk, and commitment	Get high-quality genes	Identify women with positive parenting skills	Identify men who will commit
Identify fertile women	Cultivate backup mates	Get woman with high-quality genes	Identify men with positive parenting skills and positive genes

Figure 11.2 Short-Term and Long-Term Reproductive Challenges

Source: Adapted from Buss and Schmitt (1993, p. 207).

come to consensus in order to survive. These differing strategies create conflict between the sexes and foster other negative aspects of relationships in differing magnitude. Conflict occurs as men and women disagree on the timing of the onset of sex as well as on the frequency of sex and partner exclusivity regarding sex. These conflicts are accompanied by jealousy, infidelity, and a cadre of psychologically and physically abusive behaviours. Men are more likely to be jealous of their partners' sexual infidelity than their emotional infidelity, whereas women demonstrate the opposite pattern. According to sociobiologists, "The ultimate function of male jealousy is to increase the probability that one's wife will conceive one's own rather than someone else's child" (Symons, 1979, p. 242).

Psychological Explanations

Several authors have looked at psychological explanations for violent behaviour in intimate relationships. Dutton (2010) has identified borderline personality organization (BPO) as one explanation. He describes the person with BPO as having an unstable sense of self, uncomfortable being alone, suffering from abandonment anxiety, having intense anger, being demanding and impulsive, and usually connected to substance abuse and promiscuity. This combination leads to inevitable instability in interpersonal relationships and often undermines the success of any close relationships (Box 11.1). The abusive personality has been an area of study by social scientists only for the past 40 years. The *Journal of Marriage and Family*, the dominant journal in the study of family intimacy, contained no reference to violence between 1939 and 1969 (Dutton, 2007). Researchers must have deluded themselves into thinking that marriage may contain conflict but not violence. It is clearly understood now that this is not the case.

Box 11.1

University of British Columbia Rallies Behind Attacked Grad Student

A horrific attack on a University of British Columbia graduate student, home visiting her family in Bangladesh, has led to renewed discussion at the university of defending the right of women to an education. *The Globe and Mail* reported that the husband of Rumana Monzur, a graduate student in political science at [the University of] British Columbia and an assistant professor at Dhaka University, has been charged with gouging out her eyes, leaving her blind. While Monzur was planning to return to Vancouver to defend her thesis, her husband reportedly opposed the idea of her leaving the country.

Stephen J. Toope, president at [the University of] British Columbia, sent a letter to students and faculty members in which he said: "This tragic occasion is a poignant marker of the need to work to protect the fundamental human right of all women to pursue education. The allegations that her commitment to her studies was a factor in the attack are of grave concern."

Source: http://www.insidehighered.com/news/2011/06/24/qt

Other researchers have demonstrated that not all abusive personalities should be equated (Johnson, 2008; O'Leary, Malone, & Tyree, 1994). These authors view the motivations for lower-level partner violence as being distinct from those influencing men who commit severe abuse. O'Leary et al. (1994) point to mildly abusive men having greater tendencies toward impulsiveness, suspicion of others, and aggressive tendencies, but state that those who commit extremely violent acts usually are diagnosed with one of several psychological disorders such as schizophrenia or severe narcissism. Johnson's (2008) work looks at two distinct categories of interpersonal violence. **Situational couple violence** is distinct from the more severe category of **intimate terrorism** in that it tends to be less severe and more mutual. In one Canadian study using data from General Social Survey 2004, independent research found that those categorized as being in the situational violence group had an 8 percent frequency score for ongoing violence and that 9 percent of the victims feared for their lives. This contrasts with 57 percent and 60 percent, respectively, for those categorized as being in the more severe violence group (Ansara & Hindin, 2009).

Sociological Explanations

Macro Explanations Macro sociological explanations for harmful family behaviour focus on the institutional level of analysis. What are the prevailing ideologies regarding violence, how violent is the society in which we live, and what punishments or sanctions are connected with different forms of violence? This approach argues that societal factors explain why families and members of families behave poorly toward one another. The culture of violence theory sees a general social acceptance of violence, leading to greater prevalence of violence in the family and among individuals. Greater exposure to violence through violent video games, television programming (Kahlor & Eastin, 2011), and sporting events (Sabo, Gray, & Moore, 2000) lowers the general consciousness in terms of what is considered a violent act.

The dominant sociological theory used to explain the negative side of the family is the feminist-inspired theory of patriarchy. A patriarchal society is one dominated by males. This domination spreads across all dimensions of society, from kinship structure, to inheritance rights, to social and political power, to family structure and functioning. According to this perspective, a society structured around male domination facilitates the abuse of power between men and women and leads to detrimental family behaviour. The power imbalance makes women vulnerable to men who seek to gain and maintain control and power through coercion and abusive behaviour (Yodanis, 2004). Feminist scholars are critical of psychological and sociobiological explanations because they believe that these explanations provide excuses for abusive male behaviour and do not address the root cause of how abusive behaviour is learned, encouraged, and permitted at the societal level.

Micro Explanations Micro sociological explanations of family dysfunction concentrate on what is going on in the life of the individual or in the lives of the couple. Exchange theory explains hurtful and harmful behaviours as goal-achieving activities that outweigh the costs associated with those activities. If a husband receives no legal or social sanction for abusing his wife, he may continue the practice because it works in terms of him achieving dominance and control. If an elderly woman extends financial help to her adult son, conflict and potential abuse may be alleviated (Wallace & Roberson, 2010). Investment theory assumes that as an individual invests more in a relationship over a longer period, the harder it becomes to leave the relationship. This theory explains why happily married newlyweds may be less stable and at greater risk for divorce than older unhappy couples, who have a greater investment in the relationship (e.g., children, combined assets, social networks). With little investment in the relationship, the lack of barriers such as religious beliefs or children may make the newly married couple more susceptible to the pulls of alternative partners, who may appear to be a better option than the spouse. Becker (1991), a noted economic theorist who applied his research to family patterns, feels that individuals are constantly looking for new mates throughout the life course, even when they are married. As time goes on, the investment in a relationship increases and the alternatives for relationships decrease, leading to greater marital stability later in life.

Family Theory Explanations

In addition to the explanations already discussed, theories regarding family dysfunction treat the family as a level of analysis and not simply as an aggregate of the individuals in the family. We highlight two of these theories here: **family development theory** and **family stress theory**. They share a similar intellectual background.

Family development theory has as its focus the systematic and patterned changes that families experience over the life course. Family development theory dates back to the late eighteenth century (Mattessich & Hill, 1987). However, it was Hill and Rodgers (1964) who presented the theory's basic tenets, which are used by current family scholars. Family development theory's important contribution to our discussion of the negative side of families is based on propositional statements regarding the consequences of family transitions, such as marriage and childbirth, being out of sequence or off-time from social norms. For example, a couple with children will experience considerably more stress if one of the partners decides to go back to school full-time rather than if that person's education had been completed before the formation of the union and the arrival of children. White and Klein (2008) list the following propositions of family development theory:

1. Family development is a group process regulated by societal norms and sequencing norms.
2. If a family or individual is out of sequence with the normative ordering of family events, the probability of later life disruptions is increased.
3. Within the family group, family members create internal family norms.
4. Interactions within the family group are regulated by the social norms constructing family roles.

5. Transitions from one family stage to another are predicted by the current stage and by the duration of time spent in that stage.
6. Individuals and families systematically deviate from institutional family norms to adjust their behaviour to other institutional norms, such as work and education.

Items 2 and 6 emphasize that there may be costs and rewards to the family for functioning in a certain way in a given social context. The costs can accumulate and create challenges that the family must try to address. The way in which the family handles these challenges may be beneficial or detrimental to the overall health of the family. These two outcomes provide a link to family stress theory, which we use to structure the rest of the chapter.

STRESS, CONFLICT, AND ABUSE ACROSS THE LIFE COURSE

The negative side of family relationships takes many forms but whether the discussion is about the magnitude of the hurt or the severity of the pain, the negative behaviours begin when smaller, seemingly insignificant events are not dealt with in a constructive manner. Family stress theory builds around what Hill (1949) termed the **ABC-X model** and focuses on how families deal with stressors to the family system.

Hill's ABC-X Model

Reuben Hill's (1949) study of role theory at the individual level of analysis was expanded to examine the role of stress at the family level. His work emphasizes systems and the importance of family development across the life course instead of simply looking at individual development. His construction of the ABC-X model used to understand family stress flows specifically from research on families' adjustment to the absence of fathers during World War II and their eventual return. Hill was concerned with identifying the factors found to mediate stress in those families. Hill defined A as the provoking event or stressor, B as the family's resources or strengths at the time of the event, and C as the meaning attached to the event by the family. In the ABC-X model, the X represents the stressor and crisis. Hill viewed stressors not as either positive or negative but as normative. Yet even in its neutrality, stress has the potential to initiate change in the system it affects. Hill and others (McCubbin, Sussman, & Patterson, 1983) continued to develop the ABC-X model as well as its longitudinal version called the **double ABC-X model** (Figure 11.3). In the double ABC-X model, time is introduced to capture both the multiple concurrent stressors that may be present in the family system and the stressors that may be occurring sequentially across the life course. Multiple crises happening at one time could include the birth of a child during a major housing relocation for work, or a job change that coincides with a child's illness.

The ABC-X model is frequently used in the study of family stress, conflict, and abuse. It has been shown to be relevant cross-culturally and was used by Lee (2009) to

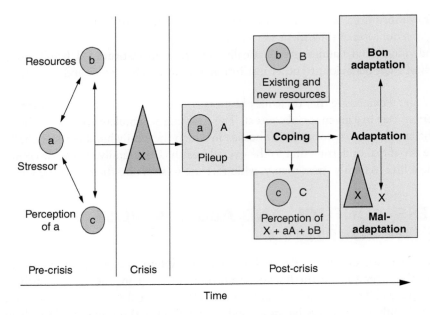

Figure 11.3 Long-Term and Short-Term Mating Strategies

study elder abuse among South Korean families. It also has been shown to be valuable in the study of racially diverse families with autistic children. Manning, Wainwright, and Bennett (2011) found that the model's focus on family adaptation helped to explain the variance in family functioning and parental distress. Reconstituted families (Greeff & Du Toit, 2009) and military families (Westhuis, Fafara, & Ouellette, 2006) have also been researched using this model. Family therapists are often guided by this theory in assisting families going through crisis (Mendenhall & Berge, 2010).

Circumplex Model

The existence of stress and conflict in family life does not mean that abuse must take place. The proper handling of stress and crisis can actually strengthen a family and help its intimacy to grow. Before moving on to examples of stress and abuse across the life course, we briefly look at one popular model for dealing with the challenges that family life sends our way.

The **circumplex model** was developed by David Olson and built on the interaction of three empirically identified important dimensions of family functioning: cohesion, flexibility, and communication (Olson, Sprenkle, & Russell, 1979). Cohesion refers to the amount of physical and, more importantly, emotional connectedness that a family experiences. Five categories range from *overly disconnected* to *overly connected*, with *balanced* in the centre. Flexibility is a measure of the family's level of comfort with role rigidity— for example, a male breadwinner and a female caregiver. The five categories for this dimension range from

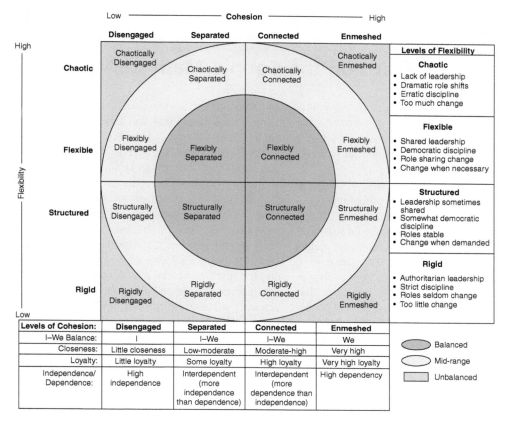

Figure 11.4 Circumplex Model: Couple and Family Map

Source: Olson, Sprenkle, and Russell (1979, p. 7).

overly flexible to *inflexible*. The communication dimension is overlaid on the intersection of the cohesion and flexibility dimensions and assesses the quality and health of family communication, especially in the areas of problem solving and conflict resolution.

The circumplex model has been used to examine a number of family function areas, such as marriage preparation and enhancement, and as a predictive tool for couples at heightened risk for divorce. It has been used in more than 500 research studies and has been validated cross-culturally and with a variety of different family forms (see www. prepare-enrich.com and www.facesiv.com/home.html for further information on these studies and data). Figure 11.4 provides an overview of the different dimensions and the combinations of family functioning that are created by the circumplex model. The model is dynamic in that it is useful in tracking couple and family units across time, whether through different stages of life or through the challenges of a particularly stressful event, such as the loss of a loved one or the birth of a child (see Career Box 11.1). The goal of the healthy, well-functioning family is not to aim for the middle of the diagram, but to

Finding Your Place on the Couple Map

When Carla met Troy on an online dating site, she was ecstatic. They seemed to be compatible in almost every aspect of life. When they finally met in person, Carla was convinced that Troy was the one for her.

As the relationship progressed, the couple found themselves in a marriage preparation class run by a local certified family life educator. During one class, Carla and Troy were asked a variety of questions that would help the counsellor determine the type of family they both came from and how they viewed their own relationship as a couple. Carla was surprised when she saw that her impression of the relationship on the couple map (circumplex model) was quite different from Troy's. She thought that they were quite balanced but he thought that they were overly connected and very inflexible. Troy documented that he came from a family that was chaotic and disengaged. Carla's family was enmeshed and rigid.

What concerned Carla most was that Troy was happy with the type of family he came from and used the class as an opportunity to tell Carla that he was concerned about her tendencies toward controlling him and not giving him his freedom. Troy liked to live week to week with his paycheques and Carla was a meticulous budgeter. Was truelove.com just another dead end in Carla's pursuit of a soul mate, or was the mapping exercise revealing something they could work to make their relationship stronger? As each of them reflected on the exercise, the question of whether this was the person the other wanted to build a life with came to the forefront.

understand that different stages of life and of an individual crisis will necessitate movement around the diagram. After a crisis, a flexibly connected family may become chaotically enmeshed as they initially deal with the event. As the family members work through the crisis together, they may move into the rigidly connected category before moving back into one of the balanced inner quadrants. A family's movement across the life course may see newlyweds being more enmeshed than a retired couple and parents being more flexible with teenage children than they were when their children were young.

THE FAMILY ACROSS THE LIFE COURSE

We now turn our attention to the family life course to discuss a sampling of the negative side of families across time. We begin with the relationship formation stage and then move through cohabitation, newly married couples, parenting, and the empty nest period. This is the traditional pathway through life, but family life courses today are quite diverse and the challenges they face may not be so neat and are likely change over time.

Relationship Formation

The transition to adulthood is defined differently in different cultures and across time, but one universal benchmark is the development of an intimate relationship leading to

family formation. According to Arnett (2000), partnering is one of three primary tasks for emerging adults. Other researchers reinforce this idea: "Learning how to form, maintain, and gracefully end romantic and sexual relationships with others is arguably one of the critical developmental tasks of adolescents and early adulthood" (Snyder, 2006, p. 161). It can be expected some individuals will negotiate this task with less grace than others. The implications of this lack of grace may range from embarrassment and discomfort to conflict and abuse. Along the road to mastery of navigating oneself into and out of romantic relationships, a few bumps will certainly be encountered.

Jealousy William Shakespeare called jealousy the green-eyed monster, research shows that it is a key factor in 80 percent of spousal homicides (Wilson & Daly, 1998), and others argue that jealousy has no boundaries and that it penetrates all social positions, intellectual levels, ages, races, and economic strata. Jealousy has been demonstrated to be a precursor to interpersonal violent acts (Babcock, Costa, Green, & Eckhardt, 2004). It is certainly a poignant illustration of the negative side of families, specifically concerning mate selection and relationship formation. Jealousy is an emotional reaction to a perceived threat to an existing relationship. Typically, it is invoked when a third person is attracted to one of the partners. Although jealousy may be a part of all stages of relationships and family life, it is most often a factor in developing relationships where commitment and security may be fragile.

White and Mullen (1989) define jealousy as coming in two flavours: **chronic jealousy** and **relationship jealousy**. The former is more of a character trait, while the latter is situational and predicated on the condition of the relationship.

> Romantic jealousy is a complex of thoughts, emotions, and actions that follows loss of or threat to self-esteem and/or the existence or quality of the romantic relationship.

The perceived loss or threat is generated by the perception of a real or potential romantic attraction between one's partner and a (perhaps imaginary) rival. (White & Mullen, 1989, p. 9)

Fatal Attraction Hollywood may have made the expression *fatal attraction* more popular through highly sexualized imagery, but it usually manifests itself in more pedestrian ways. Fatal attraction, in the sense of foreshadowing rather than being deadly, occurs when someone is attracted to a certain quality or characteristic in his or her partner that ends up being a major irritant. For example, a person may consider his partner's spontaneity an attractive quality, only to later describe that same characteristic as irresponsible and undisciplined. Women have a slightly higher proclivity to fatal attraction, and personality characteristics rather than physical characteristics tend to more prevalent (Felmlee, 1998). The idea that opposites attract (Winch, 1955) does not find support in the literature. Fatal attraction is much more likely to occur between people who do not share a certain characteristic. Felmlee (1998) concludes that although opposites may attract initially, that attraction sows the seeds of eventual repulsion and the dissolution of the relationship. The intriguing aspect of this dark element of relationship formation is that when the relationship dissolves, increased conflict and emotional strain occur over a quality that was evident at the beginning of the relationship rather than something that occurred during the relationship itself. With this knowledge, one questions how a pleasing attribute could become so detestable and why it is not recognized as such earlier in the relationship formation process.

Date Rape and Sexual Coercion The formation of intimate relationships, a precursor to a committed relationship, must negotiate the timeline and degree of physical and emotional intercourse. Canadian data show that more than 80 percent of those 20 to 24 years old have engaged in sexual intercourse at least once (Statistics Canada, 2005b). Other research in North America shows that among those aged 20 to 24 years, males have a higher average number of partners (3.8) than females (2.8). Men in this age group are also more likely (30 percent) than women (21 percent) to report having had seven or more sexual partners. Ten percent of young women aged 18 to 24 years who have had sexual intercourse before age 20 report that their first intercourse was involuntary. The younger they were at first intercourse, the higher the proportion reporting it as involuntary. A study of date rape victims in the Vancouver area (McGregor et al., 2004) showed an increasing trend in the percentage of victims who report the administration of an unsuspected drug during the assault (Table 11.1). Regardless of whether sexual coercion is physical or nonphysical, women who have been sexually coerced by an intimate partner experience negative physical and psychological consequences (e.g., Campbell & Alford, 1989; Campbell & Soeken, 1999).

Violence Research on the health effects of dating violence among college students (DuRant et al., 2007) summarizes the prevalence of dating violence and its resultant health implications. The students themselves describe it as significant health problem. Data cited

Table 11.1 Hospital-Reported and Drug-Facilitated Sexual Assault (DFSA) for Vancouver and Surrounding Communities, January 1993 to May 2002*

Year of Assault	Total Number of Sexual Assaults	Number of DFSAs	Proportion of DFSAs (%) among Total Sexual Assaults
1993	186	17	9.1
1994	147	12	8.2
1995	130	8	6.2
1996	164	14	8.5
1997	165	17	10.3
1998	162	16	9.9
1999	208	45	21.6
2000	156	40	25.6
2001	180	51	28.3
2002 (Jan–May)†	90	26	27.1

* Excludes individuals presenting to the SAS who resided outside the SAS catchment area (Vancouver, Richmond, North Shore, Howe Sound)

† Data only available to May 31, 2002

Source: McGregor et al. (2004, p. 442).

show that the percentage of those in grades 6 through 12 who have engaged in dating violence ranges from 7 percent to 51 percent for both victim and perpetrator. DuRant et al. (2007) explain the wide variance in percentages as being due to the diverse nature of the samples and the lack of clarity regarding the definition of dating violence. Studies defined dating violence as ranging from verbal threats and intimidation to physical fighting or other forms of violence; however, DuRant et al. feel that the consensus among researchers is that adolescents may underreport dating violence. They conclude from their representative sample of 3900 college students that "among men, date fight victimization was associated with early onset of alcohol consumption, current tobacco and amphetamine use, and recent threats of physical violence. Female victims of date fighting were more likely to have been the victim of other violence, to have had multiple sex partners, to have had a history of heavy alcohol consumption, and to have used illegal drugs" (DuRant et al., 2007, p. 295).

DuRant et al.'s findings are not consistent with previous research that suggested that women were more likely than men to suffer the negative effects of violence from an intimate partner. Foshee (1996), using a broader definition of dating violence that included threatening communication, verbal abuse, and sexual victimization, found that 39.4 percent of younger adolescent males and 36.5 percent of younger adolescent females had been a victim of dating violence at least once, and that 15.0 percent of men and 27.8 percent of women reported perpetrating dating violence.

Cohabitation

Recent union formation trends have identified cohabitation as a stage leading to marriage in which many young adults engage. As discussed in Chapter 4, there are diverse motivations for cohabitation, but a majority of cohabitors choose this form of union as a trial marriage or as a prelude to marriage. Because of this trend, more research has explored the experiences of cohabiting couples and has found that cohabitation does have a negative side. Refer back to Chapter 4 for the selection and experience explanations for some of the negative outcomes of cohabitation. Here, we provide a brief overview of the known negative correlates of cohabitation as it relates to union formation.

Cohabitation is not limited to any particular age group yet is more common among young adults. When viewed as either a trial marriage or a prelude to marriage, the implications for later relational outcomes become more important. A large body of research was cited in Chapter 4 to show that premarital cohabitation increases the odds of later marital dissolution. Although some evidence to the contrary has been put forward (Hewitt & DeVaus, 2009), the general body of evidence shows that cohabitation before marriage leads to higher rates of divorce. Cohabitation as a relationship status is also correlated to higher rates of partner violence (Brown & Bulanda, 2008; Brownridge, 2008). Even more severe dysfunction was found in a study by Cavanagh et al. (2007), which looked at fathers who fatally abuse their children. This study showed that the majority of men (62 percent) who committed this crime were not the biological father of the victim, and that the great majority were cohabiting with (81 percent) rather than married to (15 percent) the biological mother. It should be noted that, in this study, cohabitation involving non-biological fathers was the family type highlighted.

Some researchers suggest that one potential effect that cohabitation can have on later relationship stability is that it creates inertia, leading to marriage, that is much stronger than that experienced while just dating (Kline et al., 2004; Stanley, Markman, & Whitton, 2002; Stanley, Rhoades, & Markman, 2006). These researchers make it clear that they do not feel that the experience of cohabitation increases the risk of future marriage instability so much as that cohabitation makes it more likely that couples with more risks will stay together than they would if they were only dating.

Newly Married Couples

The fears and anxiety that a couple experiences as they prepare for marriage may be one of the major roadblocks to people marrying. Immersed in a divorce culture, fear of failure seems to affect most couples. The first few years of marriage have been shown to be important in later martial success (Huston, Caughlin, Houts, Smith, & George, 2001). "Most marital dysfunction either exists at the beginning of marriages or arises in the first few years" (Glenn, 1998, p. 437). Marriage as a life course stage does not materialize out of thin air. As a result, the early stages and challenges of marriage cannot be separated from the relationship formation process that preceded it.

Marital Adjustment Marriage is a time of adjustment, a time when two people must work through the difference that each brings to the committed, legally bound relationship. Poor marital adjustment may lead to dissatisfaction or even to divorce. Several studies have linked poor marital adjustment to increased risk for physical aggression by one's partner, which is preceded by marital distress (Schumacher & Leonard, 2005).

Expectations Most people enter marriage with expectations and a degree of idealism that are soon challenged by the realities of life. The sobering reality is that those who have the highest expectations for married life will be the least happy spouses later in the relationship (Miller, Todahl, & Platt, 2010). McNulty and Fisher (2008) found that of the almost 100 married couples that they followed for 4 years, those who had the most realistic expectations of married life were the happiest. Those who had unrealistic expectations were the most disappointed after the honeymoon ended. It seems safe to say that what brings you into a relationship is not enough to keep you in a relationship.

Conflict "The most important advice I can give to men who want their marriages to work is to try *not* to avoid conflict" (Gottman & Silver, 1994, p. 159). Conflict is a normal part of any relationship. People are not identical and their tastes and preferences are not always the same. Whether it is what movie to watch or what restaurant to go to, couples will sometimes experience conflict. As we have seen, how that conflict is handled is much more important than trying to eliminate the conflict. The ability to deal with conflict in a healthy manner early on may set the stage for conflict resolution patterns later in the marriage. Handling conflict in a constructive way can facilitate the growth of an intimate relationship (Helmick & Petersen, 2002).

Carrere and Gottman (1999) examined the marital conflict discussions of 124 newlywed couples, hypothesizing that the first few minutes of a discussion are a good predictor of divorce. Using a detailed coding system that divided approaches into the three categories of positive, negative, and positive-minus-negative affect, measures were taken across five three-minute intervals. The researchers found that it was possible to predict marital outcome over a six-year period using just the first three minutes of data from both the husband's and the wife's conversational patterns.

Parenting

Bill Cosby has said, "No matter how calmly you try to referee, parenting will eventually produce bizarre behaviour, and I'm not talking about the kids. Their behaviour is always normal." After marriage, the arrival of children may be the next most challenging stage of a family. Two people with the cognitive capacity to rationally solve disagreements and work through conflict are suddenly confronted by a child who is completely dependent on them for survival. Children are an incredible addition to a couple's life, but their arrival also may expose the weaknesses in the family.

Early research on the impact of children on the marital relationship showed both the good and the bad. Couples who had children were more likely to stay together (the good), but also reported a general decrease in marital satisfaction (the bad). More recent studies have demonstrated that not all pathways into parenthood are the same. The arrival of children has been described as "instigating a shift in the marriage whereby most couples are expected to experience a qualitative change in their relationship that is relatively abrupt, adverse in nature, relatively large in magnitude, and likely to persist" (Lawrence, Rothman, Cobb, Rothman, & Bradbury, 2008, p. 41). The good news is that the more discrete data confirm earlier qualitative research that showed that the arrival of a baby is unlikely to have any lasting negative impact on well-functioning marriages (Cowan & Cowan, 1999). The arrival of children does mark a new phase in family formation. The challenges facing a couple with this arrival involve not only their own satisfaction but also the raising and nurturing of the child. The negative side of parenting is illustrated by the topic of discipline.

Corporal Punishment It is generally agreed that children need guidance and direction as they move from complete dependence on caregivers to independence. How that discipline should look has less consensus. Academic literature over the past 40 years has been dominated by reports of the detrimental effects of physical discipline being used on children. These dark elements resulting from physical discipline include aggression, anti-social behaviour, psychological distress, and behavioural issues later in life such as increased delinquency, substance abuse, a greater proclivity to violence, and reduced socio-economic attainment (Gershoff, 2002; Straus, Sugarman, & Giles-Sims, 1997; Turner & Finkelhor, 1996). Nevertheless, at the end of the twentieth century, 94 percent of American parents of 3- and 4-year olds felt the need to use physical discipline.

The central issue with regard to the discrepancy between research and practice is whether all forms of **corporal punishment** lead to the same negative outcomes in children or whether some forms of physical discipline may have positive outcomes. Ellison and Bradshaw (2009) argue that the motive behind physical discipline may hold a clue to the direction of the outcomes. They point to a growing body of literature that "indicates that the effects of corporal punishment may differ across cultural and other subgroups within the population (Baumrind, 1997; Deater-Deckard & Dodge, 1997; Gunnoe & Mariner, 1997). Specifically, within cultural communities in which this practice is common, even normative, its effects are less harmful, or perhaps not harmful at all (Ellison & Bradshaw, 2009, pp. 336–337). Durrant, Trocmé, Fallon, Milne, and Black (2009) examine the Supreme Court of Canada's attempt in 2004 to distinguish between reasonable and abusive coercive force on children. Table 11.2 shows maltreatment investigations involving children aged 0 to 15 years in all provinces and territories except Quebec. Sixty-three of 400 child-welfare service areas across Canada were included in the survey.

Child Neglect and Abuse There is no ambiguity regarding child neglect and abuse. Although the definitions of neglect and abuse may be debated, the social

Table 11.2 Estimated Substantiated Child Maltreatment Investigations by Primary Category of Maltreatment, Canada (Excluding Quebec), 2003

| | Primary Category of Maltreatment | | | | | |
	Physical Abuse	Sexual Abuse	Neglect	Emotional Maltreatment	Exposure to Domestic Violence	Total
Estimate	25 257	2935	30 366	15 569	29 370	103 298*
Percent of total sample	24	3	34	14	26	100
Incidence per 1000 children	5.31	0.62	6.38	3.23	6.17	21.71

*Based on a sample of 5660 unweighted substantiated child maltreatment investigations.

Source: Trocmé et al. (2005, p. 3).

abhorrence of child neglect and abuse is unanimous. The social context that defines child neglect and abuse is illustrated in the discussion of corporal punishment. It is not uncommon to hear anecdotes from adults regarding being taken to the woodshed and being given a "licking" with a switch or a rod. This behaviour may have been normative in the not too distant past, but it would not be accepted even by proponents of corporal punishment today. One only needs to look at other cultures to realize that physical punishment remains a normal part of educational institutions' approach to discipline.

Child abuse may take the form of neglect rather than violent acts. The results can be equally devastating. Mills et al. (2011) found that abuse and neglect, independent of one another, are correlated with decreased levels of cognitive performance at age 14 years. Data collection occurred from children's mothers at 3 to 5 days after delivery, 6 months of age, and 5 years of age. Outcome measures were gathered from assessments of the children's abilities at 14 years of age. Even after controlling for potential confounding factors, Mills et al. (2011) noted that abuse and neglect have detrimental implications for child development.

Family dysfunction continues to have a negative impact on children as they age. Research on children aged 4 to 9 years shows that prolonged high levels of family dysfunction have distinct gender implications (Pagani, Japel, Vaillancourt, & Tremblay, 2010). Girls in particular demonstrate higher levels of indirect aggression, defined as more underhanded and relational means of causing harm to another, such as generating rumours, cattiness, social exclusion, or indiscriminate disclosure of confidential information (Lagerspetz, Bjorkqvist, & Peltonen, 1988).

Box 11.2

Mother Allegedly on Facebook while Baby Drowned

An American mother who told police her 13-month-old son drowned in the bathtub while she was playing a game on Facebook was charged on Friday with child abuse resulting in death.

Shannon Johnson, 34, of Colorado was advised of the charge against her via a video hookup from the jail where she is being held on a $100,000 bond, said Jennifer Finch, spokeswoman for the Weld County District Attorney's Office.

Johnson requested a public defender during the brief hearing and another hearing was set for later in the month, Finch said.

Under questioning by police after the boy died at a Denver-area hospital last September, Johnson admitted she placed the baby in the bathtub and went into another room to play the Facebook game "Cafe World."

She also checked in with friends and watched videos on the site while the boy bathed alone, according to an affidavit filed in the case.

When she didn't hear any sounds from the boy after 10 minutes, she found him slumped over face down in the bathwater making "gurgling" sounds, according to the affidavit. Johnson then called 911, and the boy was airlifted to the hospital where he was pronounced dead from drowning.

When police arrived at Johnson's home they found a laptop opened to Facebook.

Johnson told police that she frequently left the boy unattended in the bathtub because he was "independent," he liked to be left alone, and she didn't want him to be a "mama's boy," according to the affidavit.

Police also questioned the boy's grandmother, who said he suffered a seizure while she was baby-sitting him a month before he died. She told police she warned her daughter about leaving her grandson alone in the tub after the seizure.

When police asked Johnson about the wisdom of leaving a young child with a history of seizures alone in water, Johnson admitted that "it was so stupid."

She faces up to 48 years in prison if convicted.

Source: http://www.torontosun.com/news/world/2011/01/16/16907941.html

---

Box 11.2 contains a news article on a disturbing new phenomenon that involves child neglect because of internet addiction. Young (2009) reports that studies on internet addiction originated in the United States but that recent studies show that internet addiction is a growing problem in countries such as Italy, Pakistan, Czech Republic, Korea, China, and Taiwan. Child neglect is no longer the result of chemical addictions but of online addictions as well.

Incest Nothing epitomizes the negative side of the family like the universal taboo of incest. Anthropologists, historians, and sociologists discovered early in their work that sexual relations between two close kin was met with general social disapproval in virtually all societies and across all social strata and times. Research conducted more than 25 years ago found that an estimated 1 million Americans were victims of father–daughter incest (Finkelhor, 1984). This form of incest is the most widely reported form, followed by stepfather–stepdaughter and brother–sister. Lester (1972) found little incest between mother and son, a finding supported by other researchers.

Speculation as to why reports of male incest may be lower centre around socialization issues that may make males less likely to disclose incest. They may fear that it will signify weakness or homosexuality. This is consistent with data that indicate that 80 to 90 percent of reported victims are female and 90 percent of perpetrators are male (Russell, 1986). The disturbing nature of incest is that, according to Vanderbilt (1992), perpetrators can be uncles, aunts, nephews, nieces, grandparents, stepparents, stepbrothers, stepsisters, brothers, or sisters and that the abuse typically takes place within the family home. The pattern of incest usually begins in preadolescence (Phelan, 1986), when children are more vulnerable and more easily intimidated by adult perpetrators.

Parent–Adolescent Issues Increased stress and conflict during the adolescent years is almost taken for granted in Western culture. Adolescence is viewed as a time of growing independence, and that seeking of independence does not always correspond to the parents' comfort level. Conflict at this stage is not restricted to one or two particular areas of concern. Early adolescence in particular is a time of elevated conflict (Laursen, Coy, & Collins, 1998; Steinberg, 1990). In a study of middle school–aged children, Allison and Schultz (2004) found that the frequency of conflict was at its highest level in grade 7 and was significantly lower in grade 8 for males. This is consistent with the view that parent–adolescent conflict peaks during the transition to adolescence and then subsides (Laursen et al., 1998). Allison and Schultz (2004) also point to the gendered nature of parent–adolescent conflict. Research found that parental conflict with daughters was higher than with sons (Smetana & Asquith, 1994) and that mother–daughter conflict was more prevalent than conflict in other dyads (Holmbeck & Hill, 1991).

Autonomy and independence are sought by emerging adolescents, but parents are concerned about responsibility and the development of good life choices. Conflict is less likely to occur over the choice of friends, clothing, personal hygiene, and going out unsupervised than over character issues such as lying, swearing, and getting into trouble outside the home, with the highest frequency of conflict reported over substance abuse (smoking, drinking, drug use). Parents may feel that if these character issues are not a concern, then greater freedom can be given to the teen (Smetana & Asquith, 1994).

The issue of household responsibility has been identified as a common area of parent–adolescent conflict. As teens seek greater independence, they become less excited about being told what to do and contributing to family functioning. Allison and Schultz (2004) again highlight the gendered nature of family conflict. Their research showed that parent–daughter conflict was more frequent than parent–son conflict. Greater expectations for daughters to perform household duties, dress appropriately, and not be disruptive at home during the early years of adolescence seem to be the cause of this difference (White & Brinkerhoff, 1981). This gender difference was also manifest in parents being more restrictive of their daughters' freedom to go places alone, choose friends, make decisions about money, and decide how to spend their free time.

Sibling Violence

A form of family abuse seldom discussed in the popular media is one that occurs between siblings. Mackey, Fromuth, and Kelly (2010) cite several scholars who found that sibling violence is one of the leading forms of childhood victimization (Finkelhor, Ormrod, Turner, & Hamby, 2005) yet goes unrecognized (Cornell & Gelles, 1985). They point out that the way in which sibling abuse is classified often leads to wide variety in its reported prevalence. Some studies state that 35 percent (Duncan, 1999) to more than 60 percent (Goodwin & Roscoe, 1990; Hoffman, Kiecolt, & Edwards, 2005) of respondents reported committing physically violent acts against a sibling. Mackey et al. (2010) report that the highest levels of victimization were indicated by Simonelli, Mullis, Elliott, and Pierce's (2002) study of college undergraduates, in which 71 percent of men and 88 percent of women reported physical aggression by a sibling.

Abuse of Parents by Adolescents

Most of the discussion regarding abusive family dysfunction has been unidirectional, or parent to child. Unfortunately, the abusive pattern operates in both directions. Data confirm that some children are physically and psychologically abusive to their parents, most often the mother. Stewart, Burns, and Leonard (2007) cite several authors (Cottrell, 2001; Cottrell & Finlayson, 1996; Cottrell & Monk, 2004) who argued that parent abuse is a serious social problem that has received inadequate attention from researchers and service providers. Cottrell and Finlayson (1996) noted that restricting the definition of abuse to physical assaults can cloud the severity of the problem. Research shows that threats, emotional manipulation, and other non-physical abuse can cause equal distress. Stewart et al. (2007) state that in Cottrell's sample of Canadian parents, there were reports of physical, verbal, and psychological forms of abuse, including "emotional terrorism." The profiles of the victim and the abuser were similar. Mothers and stepmothers were the most likely victims. The perpetrator's abusive actions were often associated with substance abuse or with psychiatric problems. Estimates of the prevalence of child to parent violence are in area of 10 percent. Based on interviews with parents in intact families, Cornell and Gelles (1985) estimated that 9 percent of all 10- to 17-year-olds in the United States had assaulted one of their parents in the previous year. Another national sample estimated that between 6.5 and 10.8 percent of adolescent males in the sample had assaulted their parents (Peek, Fisher, & Kidwell, 1985).

Adult Children and Elder Abuse

Child to parent abuse is not confined to the adolescent years. Adult children have also been found to be physically, psychologically, and financially abusive to their parents, again primarily their mothers. In a large British study, Cooper, Selwood, and Livingston (2008) found that more than 6 percent of the older general population, a quarter of vulnerable adults, and a third of family caregivers reported being involved in significant abuse.

One explanation given for the onset of abusive behaviour toward the elderly is the stress that caregivers are under. Most informal care is provided by family members. In a comparison of caregivers serving relatives with dementia to those serving relatives without dementia, Ory, Hoffman, Yee, Tennstedt, and Schulz (1999) reported higher rates of stress and conflict among those caring for relatives with dementia. Identifying who is perpetrating the abuse is a challenge, with some studies indicating that adult offspring are most likely to commit abuse (Paveza et al., 1992) and other studies pointing to spousal caregivers as more likely to abuse (Pillemer & Suitor, 1992).

Intergenerational Issues

The final area to touch on regarding the negative side of the family is the unsettling knowledge that most of the topics discussed in this chapter are often found to repeat from one generation to another. Sassler, Cunningham, and Lichter (2009, p. 759) discuss the intergenerational patterns of relationship formation and conclude: "High rates of union dissolution and remarriage in the past have obvious implications for current marriage patterns. Demographic momentum is built into current family patterns through the intergenerational reproduction of divorce and family instability (Amato, 1996; Amato & Rogers, 1997; Teachman, 2002)." Abusive behaviour has also been linked to intergenerational influences. Primarily relying on social learning theory (Bandura, 1978), which states that exposure to violent acts provides a script for future behaviour, research has showed a link between exposure to physical, psychological, and sexual abuse and later likelihood of similar personal behaviours. Box 11.3 provides an up-to-date, comprehensive summary of the literature on intergenerational transmission of family dysfunction.

Box 11.3

Empirical Evidence of Intergenerational Transmission (IGT) of Family Dysfunction

Evidence supporting the IGT of violence theory has been accumulated for married couples as well as dating relationships for both adolescents and emerging adults (Ballif-Spanvill et al., 2007; Breslin, Riggs, O'Leary, & Arias, 1990; Carr & VanDeusen, 2002; Craig & Sprang, 2007; Dubow, Huesmann, & Boxer, 2003; Ehrensaft et al., 2003; Foshee et al., 1999; Kwong, Bartholomew, Henderson, & Trinke, 2003; Stith et al., 2000; Whitfield, Anda, Dube, & Felitti, 2003; Yexley, Borowsky, & Ireland, 2002). For example, large-scale studies have reported clear evidence of an IGT of marital aggression (Doumas, Margolin, & John, 1994; Pagelow, 1981; Straus & Gelles, 1986; Straus, Gelles, & Steinmetz, 1980). Considering adolescents, between 7% and 15% of youths have experienced serious physical victimization by an intimate partner (Avery-Leaf, Cascardi, O'Leary, & Cano, 1997; Bergman, 1992; Coker et al., 2000; Silverman, Raj, Mucci, & Hathaway, 2001), and social learning of violence has been supported in varying degrees for this cohort (O'Keeffe, Brockopp, & Chew, 1986; Schwartz, O'Leary, & Kendziora, 1997). For instance, Foshee et al.'s (1999) findings support this theory whereby 21% of female perpetration and 15% of male perpetration was accounted for by social learning theory—mediating variables such as aggressive conflict-response style, expecting positive outcomes, and accepting dating violence. However, several null findings have been reported between witnessing interparental violence and subsequent dating violence (Capaldi & Clark, 1998; Carlson, 1990; Hotaling & Sugarman, 1990; MacEwen & Barling, 1988;

Simons, Lin, & Gordon, 1998), leading to the conclusion that the majority of children experiencing violence in their homes do not grow up to be violent adults (Kaufman & Zigler, 1987). In addition, some studies have found an association only for males but not for females (e.g., O'Leary, Malone, & Tyree, 1994). This has led some researchers to suggest that main effects may vary within subgroups (Foshee, Ennett, Bauman, Benefield, & Suchindran, 2005) or that methodological and measurement inconsistencies exist in previous research.

The prevalence of college-age students witnessing serious interparental physical violence while growing up typically ranges from 10% to 30% (Edleson, 1999; Jankowski, Leitenberg, Henning, & Coffey, 1999). Similarly, college students report rates at 20% to 50% for experiencing physical abuse in their own current intimate relationships (Arias, Samios, & O'Leary, 1987; Avery-Leaf et al., 1997; Fiebert & Gonzalez, 1997; Jankowski et al., 1999; Neufeld, McNamara, & Ertl, 1999; Riggs & O'Leary, 1996). Although psychological violence has gained less empirical attention, one study (Lane & Gwartney-Gibbs, 1985) suggested that psychological aggression might occur in up to 80% of young adult dating relationships. These high rates were supported in a sample of undergraduate students, whereby Riggs & O'Leary (1996) found that at any time in their relationship only 7% of men and 3% of women reported that they had not engaged in any verbal/psychological aggression within any intimate relationship.

Source: Black, Sussman, and Unger (2010).

CONCLUSION

The universal social institution of the family has provided for the care, nurturance, and socialization of humanity through time. In the twenty-first century, the motivation for family formation has shifted from survival to one better described as self-fulfillment. As a result, it seems that there is even greater awareness of the negative side of the family. The conflict and abusive behaviours described in this chapter have always existed within the family, to one degree or another. Explanations of why they occur and why they continue to occur are varied. The important point is that they have occurred and will continue to occur. These negative behaviours and actions are more palatable if they occur in times of war or at the hands of a deranged character in a horror movie. Yet when they occur in the very institution that we consider a safe haven and protection from the negative elements of society, we are caught off guard. How could these things happen? How could something so good become so bad? The only somewhat plausible overarching explanation may simply be that if the potential for the family wasn't so good, the opportunity for it to become so bad would not exist.

SUMMARY OF KEY POINTS

- Despite all of its good qualities, the family also has a negative side that ranges from increased stress to intimate violence and abuse.

- The nature versus nurture debate is important in the context of interfamily dysfunction. Why do people who share the same genetic material or who commit themselves to one another sometimes harm each other?

- Two important family theories used to understand the negative side of family behaviour are the family development theory and the family stress theory.

- Reuben Hill developed the ABC-X model of family stress through research on families' adjustment to the absence of fathers during World War II and their eventual return. His concern was identifying the factors found to mediate the stress in these families.

- Hill defined A as the provoking event or stressor, B as the family's resources or strengths at the time of the event, and C as the meaning attached to the event by the family. In the ABC-X model, the X represents the stressor and crisis.

- The circumplex model identifies the three dimensions of flexibility, cohesion, and communication as foundational in examining how stress affects families.

- Families across the life course face challenges in dealing with stress and conflict. Each family stage provides unique challenges that must be negotiated. Stress, conflict, and abuse have the potential to occur.

- Drug-facilitated sexual assaults as a percentage of all sexual assaults have been on the rise in Canada.

- Dating violence has been reported to affect more than a third of both male and female college students (Foshee, 1996).

- John Gottman highlighted the normative nature of conflict in relationships when he stated, "The most important advice I can give to men who want their marriages to work is to try *not* to avoid conflict" (Gottman & Silver, 1994, p. 159).

- Corporal punishment continues to be a hotly debated social issue in the twenty-first century. Most researchers and government agencies would like to see it eliminated as a disciplinary technique.

- Child neglect as a form of abuse has been in the headlines more frequently as parents form internet addictions.

- Family conflict is not always hierarchical. Sibling conflict in the form of physical aggression was reported by 71 percent of men and 88 percent of women in study of college students (Simonelli et al., 2002).

- Children abusing their parents is another part of the negative side of the family. Studies have looked at both adolescents and adults who have been abusive toward their parents. Elder abuse often results from the stress that caregivers are under.

- Unfortunately, abusive family patterns are often transferred from one generation to another. Black, Sussman, and Unger (2010) provide a comprehensive overview of the current literature in this area.

Critical Thinking Questions

1. This chapter presents stress within a family context as normal. With this lens, consider stressful situations in your own family of origin and how you felt during those times.

2. Considering the different plausible explanations of the origin of family stress (sociobiological, psychological, and sociological), which do you feel stands on its own the best?

3. Many unhealthy examples of family stress are presented in this chapter. Which behaviours do you find most difficult to comprehend?

Glossary

ABC-X model A model originally developed by Reuben Hill to aid in understanding the way in which families adjusted to fathers being away during World War II. *A* is the provoking event or stressor, *B* is the family's resources or strengths at the time of the event, *C* is the meaning attached to the event by the family, and *X* represents the stressor and crisis.

chronic jealousy A more permanent quality of a person's character with little variation attributed to situational circumstances.

circumplex model A model of family functioning made popular by David Olson. It incorporates three distinct dimensions of family functioning identified by most contemporary family researchers as being important to family health. Cohesion is the degree to which a family balances the "we" and "me" identity within a family, flexibility is the degree to which a family balances the rigidity and adaptability of family roles, and communication is the dimension of family functioning that facilitates change and adjustment between the other two dimensions.

corporal punishment The term commonly used to describe child discipline that involves physical means such as spanking.

double ABC-X model An expanded version of the ABC-X model that incorporates the additional dimension of time and allows the model to be applied over the life course.

family development theory A theory focused on the systematic and patterned changes that families experience over the life course. It is unique in its attempt to use the family rather than the individuals in the family as the level of analysis.

family stress theory A theory that uses the ABC-X model as a means of understanding family functioning.

intimate terrorism The most destructive form of couple violence. It almost exclusively involves males causing extensive bodily harm to or the death of their female partners.

nature versus nurture The debate over how individual characteristics are developed. Nature assumes that the characteristics have biological origins while nurture attributes characteristics to social influences.

relationship jealousy In contrast to chronic jealousy, relationship jealousy is situationally based and predicated on the condition of the relationship.

situational couple violence A term used to describe the less extreme forms of violence that are quite prevalent in relationships and are less gendered in their use.

universal taboo The term applied to incest, or sexual relations between two close family members, since it has been found to be socially unacceptable in one form or another across societies and across time.

Connections

www.prepare-enrich.com
www.facesiv.com/home.html
http://agecon.uwyo.edu/eruralfamilies/ERFLibrary/Readings/CircumplexModelOfMaritalAndFamilySystems.pdf
www.informaworld.com/smpp/section?content=a907454261&fulltext=713240928
http://jacksonville.com/news/crime/2010-10-27/story/
    jacksonville-mom-shakes-baby-interrupting-farmville-pleads-guilty-murder

Remember to log on to the Companion Website at **www.pearsoncanada.ca/white** to find self-graded quizzes and useful resource tools for further study. You can log on to the Companion Website using the Student Access Code that comes packaged with your copy of *Families Across the Life Course*.

Chapter 12
Changing Pathways and Emerging Alternatives

Learning Objectives

After reading this chapter, you should be able to:

1. Incorporate the rapid changes in marriage and family structure during the last decade into your knowledge of families in Canada.
2. Acknowledge the socio-cultural changes such as labour force participation and immigration that are concomitant with family changes.
3. Analyze the changes in family within the dynamics of the family life course and the changing alternative models of family.
4. Appreciate the non-normative pathways to family forms that may become dominant during your lifetime.
5. Analyze current social changes and produce scenarios for the future of the family in Canada.
6. Identify the policy implications of different social goals regarding the family, parenting, and marriage in Canada.

Emory couldn't understand it. Even though he had just graduated from university, he still couldn't understand it. His mother and father had just told him that they were going to separate, but then had added "not *really* separate." Emory's dad worked as a senior accountant with an international pharmaceutical company and would be moving to Milan, Italy. Emory's mom had just accepted a new position in the United Kingdom and was excited about living in London. His parents tried to assure Emory that this physical separation was not an emotional one, and that their marriage would continue.

"How can you have a close relationship when you are not living together and are countries apart?" exclaimed Emory.

His dad replied, "Emory, in Europe they do this all the time. It's called a LAT, which means 'living apart together.' Just think of this as your good old parents getting more cosmopolitan and being less staid, conservative Canadians.

Emory said, "It may be European, but it certainly is *not* Canadian!"

Trost (2010) identified **LATs** (living apart together) as a newer form of couple relationship that he believes is on the rise in Europe among both cohabiting and married couples. Trost discussed LATs in the context that 50 years ago, most of the developed world could not have imagined that cohabitation would become normative in their societies and that marriage rates would fall precipitously (see Lee & Payne, 2010). Trost also argued that social scientists failed to predict these changes, and in some ways were even slow to realize the magnitude of these changes once they had occurred. So, do Emory's parents represent the vanguard of a new form of couple relationship or will LATs not survive the decade as a form of coupling?

This final chapter examines the changes in the family life course that we have documented throughout the book, places these changes in the context of the theory of life course development, and attempts to speculate about the future changes we might expect.

SUMMARY OF CHANGES TO CANADIAN FAMILIES

Family Structure

Family structure in Canada is changing dramatically. In 1986, the majority of couples with children (55 percent) were married, whereas in 2006, only 38.7 percent were married with children. The big change during this time was the increase in lone-parent families (up 4.6 percent) and the increase in common-law couples with children (up 5.0 percent) (Statistics Canada, 2006c). These changes are even more startling when examining Figure 12.1. In addition, 26.2 percent of births in Canada are to single, never-married women, although some of these births occur within common-law relationships

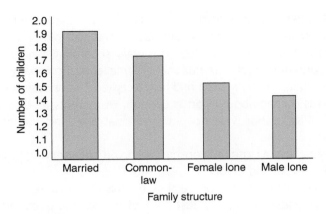

Figure 12.1 Average Number of Children by Family Structure, 2006

Source: Statistics Canada (2006c).

(Statistics Canada, 2006c). When we examine with whom children under 15 years of age reside, we find that 66.0 percent live in married couple families, 14.8 percent live in common-law couple families, and 18.7 percent live in lone-parent families (Statistics Canada, 2006c). The average number of children per family type (see Figure 12.1) has declined over the last 20 years for all family structures except common-law couples, where the number has remained relatively stable (Vanier Institute of the Family, 2010).

Dating

There is little doubt that dating is changing, but perhaps not in as predictable way as we might imagine. Certainly, Goode (1963) and others have speculated that global dating patterns will increasingly become romantic, voluntary, and autonomous. Although this is true in general, there is great diversity in patterns of dating, including internet dating, speed dating, and various types of dating combined with some family or parental control. Many cultural groups in Canada view "dating" with suspicion, since it seems to encroach on mate selection. Hence, we may find Canadians who begin dating as early as 10 years of age and others who are in their mid-twenties and have never dated.

Mate Selection and Cohabitation

Selecting a mate is difficult. Although we saw in Chapter 3 that several mechanisms are involved in the selection of a mate, there is no longer one simple path that people follow (e.g., dating → engagement → marriage). The single largest change in this area is the growth and prevalence of cohabitation.

In 2006, about 10 to 11 percent of the adult population in Canada was cohabiting (Vanier Institute of the Family, 2010). The majority of women between 20 and 29 years of age will have had at least one cohabiting partner. Indeed, the 2001 Census reported that for the 20- to 29-year age group, cohabitation was the norm. It is interesting that in 1970 cohabitation was certainly not the norm, but within 30 years it has become the norm. In Canada, people in their twenties who do not cohabit are now the minority. Even among those over 50 years of age, cohabitation is increasing as a post-divorce alternative to marriage (Vanier Institute of the Family, 2010).

As Gwartney-Gibbs (1986) originally suggested, many people use cohabitation as a new stage in mate selection. This stage allows couples to have a "trial marriage" to see if there is role compatibility in the context of living together. As Chapter 4 suggested, not all cohabitations are so focused. Some cohabitation results from haphazard "sliders" while others do not intend to move from cohabitation to marriage. For example, it is reported that 70 percent of women in Quebec will cohabit and that more than 34 percent of children under 15 years of age in Quebec reside in a common-law union (Statistics Canada, 2006c). The conclusion seems to be that common-law relationships are used by some as an alternative to marriage, by others as a prelude to marriage, and by still others (sliders) as a living arrangement without longer-term goals.

Marriage

There is little doubt that marriage rates in both Canada and the United States are declining (Lee & Payne, 2010). In 1981, about 65 percent married at least once by middle age (50 years), whereas in 2006 only about 45 percent could expect to get married. Rates of decline continue to be sharp among the most recent age cohorts (Vanier Institute of the Family, 2010). Even though same-sex couples may now marry, only about 16 percent do so (Statistics Canada, 2006c).

Some of the decline in marriage rates is due to changes in timing. In 1981 the average female married around 23 years of age, whereas in 2004 she married at 28.5 years of age (Vanier Institute of the Family, 2010). This change in age at marriage explains some of the decline in marriage, because the age cohort in its twenties is delaying marriage. Another factor that explains the decline in marriage rates is that the alternative of cohabitation is no longer socially deviant and for many represents a viable alternative to marriage. Finally, some women may decide to remain childless (voluntary childlessness) and therefore may feel less compelled to marry, since today there are more alternative lifestyle satisfactions for single, never-married women than in previous periods.

Births

As we saw in Chapter 6, fertility rates in Canada and much of the developed world are below replacement level. The decline in Canada began in 1971 and has continued since then. Women are having children at older ages, with age-specific fertility increasing among women between 30 and 39 years of age. Women are increasingly less likely to be married when they have their first child, with almost 60 percent of first births in Quebec and an average of 26 percent of first births in Canada being to single, never-married women (Vanier Institute of the Family, 2010). Of course, some of these single, never-married females are in cohabiting relationships. Recall, however, that 18 percent of children under 15 years of age live in lone-parent families.

So, although we still have traditional families, lower birth rates and lower marriage rates coupled with more lifestyle alternatives (cohabitation and single, never-married) have created greater diversity in families, and the married, two-parent couple with children is no longer the majority family structure in Canada.

Parenting

One hundred years ago, the average family had two adults and slightly more than two children. Today, the average family has 3.1 persons. About 44 percent of families are two-person families, 22 percent are in three-person families, 21 percent are four-person families, and the remaining 13 percent have five or more persons. Therefore, the majority of families (66 percent) are one parent–one child, one parent–two children, or two parents–one child families. Only 21 percent of families resemble the two parents–two children families of the 1950s (Vanier Institute of the Family, 2010).

With smaller numbers of children and alternative family structures come new challenges for parents. Lone-parent families with one child certainly involve an intensified parental role for the lone parent, but the role of the only child is intensified as well. Only children lack not only the ready-made playmate of a sibling but also the buffering effect that multiple targets of parental attention afford children with siblings. However, smaller family structures are not the sole reason for role intensification. Certainly, the menagerie of "family experts" has grown. Thirty years ago, doctors, nurses, and teachers provided advice to and placed pressure on parents. Since that time, our society has added such professions as early childhood educators and witnessed increasing politicization in areas such as child discipline and nutrition (obesity). Today's parents are pressured by varied and multiple concerned parties.

In addition to this intensification of parental roles, parents are likely to find that work role demands are more intense for today's family. Married or common-law males have close to 97 percent participation in the labour force. Women with children between the ages of 7 and 15 years have a 78.2 percent participation rate. The number of reported work hours has increased during the last decade, meaning that time for parenting is more constrained. Although most parents both work, this affords them a slightly better standard of living than 30 years ago (Vanier Institute of the Family, 2010). As we saw Chapter 6, these couples will reach the median family income about five years later than those in the 1970s.

Divorce and Repartnering

Divorce rates are no longer as high as they were in the 1970s, but they are still high. About 35 to 40 percent of Canadians marrying today can expect to divorce before their thirtieth year of marriage (Vanier Institute of the Family, 2010). Most of these divorces will occur during the early years of marriage, as discussed in Chapter 9. The great majority of divorced people will repartner either in another marriage or with a common-law partner. For example, the Vanier Institute of the Family (2010) reports that within five years after divorce, 36 percent of females and 51 percent of males have repartnered. As the marriage rate continues to decline, post-divorce cohabitation will continue to increase.

Leaving Home

In the 1960s, most young adult children quickly left the parental home and established their own residence. During the 1980s, delayed home leaving and the return of children to the parental home (**boomerang kids**) were on the rise (Mitchell, Wister, & Burch, 1989). Today, among adult children 20 to 24 years of age, 65 percent of males and 55 percent of females live in the parental home. Males tend to stay longer, with 30 percent between 25 and 29 years of age still residing with parents, versus 20 percent of females of the same age (Vanier Institute of the Family, 2010). Adult children live with their parents. The positive side of this is the higher level of social and economic support enjoyed by these adult children. However, on the other hand, some developmental theorists have suggested that these young adults are having truncated life experiences (Arnett, 2004) and others have questioned the effect on attaining financial independence and savings (Beaujot, 2004).

Aging Families

It has almost become a cliché to say that we are living in an aging population. Certainly, most of us recognize this. The details, however, are more interesting. Members of the postwar baby boom (those born in 1943 to 1960) are now entering retirement. Even though Canada no longer has a mandatory retirement age, 65 years remains the anchor point for many considering retirement. Those born in the first year of the postwar baby boom turned 65 in 2008, but the median age for retirement is considerably below 65 years (around 61 years).

Every society is concerned that its dependency ratio (number of individuals under 16 years plus the number of individuals 65 years and older, divided by the number of individuals 16 to 64 years of age) not be imbalanced. Yet with the baby boom generation, we can expect up to 25 percent of Canadians to be out of the labour force and this will increase the tax burden on those still in the labour force. One way this could change is for more of those individuals over 65 years to remain in the labour force.

As couples and individuals age, they are increasingly likely to live alone. By the time people are 75 years or older, almost 19 percent of the men and more than 40 percent of the women are living alone (Vanier Institute of the Family, 2010). Between 1976 and 2007, the elderly living alone on average have seen increases in economic well-being, a 40 percent increase for males and a 71 percent increase for females (Vanier Institute of

the Family, 2010). The increases in economic well-being for females are especially significant due to their greater life expectancy and the income penalties for time spent out of the labour force while raising children.

CHANGING CANADIAN SOCIO-CULTURAL CONTEXT

The family in Canada is changing, but so are the cultural, social, and economic contexts in which families find themselves. These are dynamic relationships in which the family is affected by broader social changes but also can be seen to cause some of these changes. For example, women's labour force participation and pursuit of higher education undoubtedly created delays in the timing of marriage that led, in part, to lowered fertility rates. In turn, the lowered fertility rate affects the labour force and the need for immigration. Understanding this shifting Canadian socio-cultural context is necessary to recognizing some of the changes that families are experiencing.

Women in the Labour Force

Without a doubt, one of the most significant changes that Canada and, indeed, the world witnessed in the last 50 years is the massive increase in women participating in the labour force. Women's participation rate in 1976 was 45.7 percent; in 2006, it had shifted to 62.6 percent. It must be kept in mind that these statistics are point-in-time estimates and do not include women who have taken time away from the labour force to raise children. Men's participation rates during the same time interval declined from a high of 77.7 percent to 72.0 percent. Clearly, there is a convergence in participation rates over time (Statistics Canada, 2006c).

There are several ramifications of women's increased participation rates for Canadian society. First, to gain increased access to jobs and career mobility, higher levels of education are needed. As a result, women's attendance at post-secondary institutions has increased. A second effect of the increase in women's labour force participation rates is that women have delayed marriage because of both prolonged education and early career commitments.

Probably the single most discussed effect of women's increased labour force participation rates is the changing exchange patterns in couples and families. Certainly, Scanzoni (1975) and Oppenheimer (1997) have discussed the altered exchanges in couples. The old exchange pattern was that women traded their affectionate services and household labour for access to men's salaries and status. However, as women gained their own salaries and status from their own labour force participation, the exchange pattern was disrupted since men's salaries and status are now worth less to women. As a result, women are positioned to negotiate a new exchange pattern.

The principal focus of these negotiations has been the division of household labour. For example, in 1989 Hochschild and Machung described women as performing "a second shift" of housework after coming home from work. In 2006, Marshall showed that the total number of hours that men and women work (including both paid and unpaid domestic labour) is the same (8.8 hours per day). Men, however, spend more hours per day in paid work (5.3 hours) than do women (3.7 hours). Women spend more hours per day doing housework (2.4 hTours) than do men (1.4 hours). Women also spend more time shopping (0.9 hours) and on child care (1 hour) compared to men (0.6 and 0.5 hours, respectively). Marshall's data suggest that neither gender works longer hours than the other (both 8.8 hours), but clearly more of women's daily hours are spent on domestic affairs.

Immigration and Ethnic Diversity

Today, Canada has one of the highest immigration rates in the world, taking in between 240 000 and 265 000 immigrants per year. Although Canada may lead the world when immigration is measured relative to population size, other countries have higher raw numbers of immigrants, especially those in Europe. Most immigration is driven by a country's need to address labour shortage, low birth rates, and capital. This is reflected in Canada's immigration by category of immigrant. In 2009, Canada accepted 65 204 *family class* immigrants, 153 491 *economic class* immigrants, and 22 848 *refugee class* immigrants (Citizen and Immigration Canada, 2010). The largest category of immigrants, the economic class, includes skilled workers needed by Canada and those immigrants who can invest a minimum amount of money in Canada ($800 000). All immigrants, regardless of their class of immigration, compensate for the shortfalls in natural fertility (see Figure 12.2).

Canada's high immigration rates are changing the country's distribution of ethnic diversity. For example, in the early 1900s most Canadian immigration was from European nations. By the late 1900s, the major source of immigrants had shifted to Asia (Figure 12.3). In addition, the Canadian Multiculturalism Act of 1985 established not only tolerance of but also governmental support for cultural and ethnic diversity.

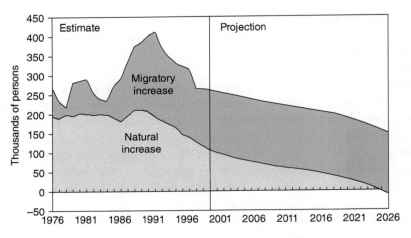

Figure 12.2 Immigration and Population Growth in Canada

Note: The projection is based on medium assumptions: fertility rates at 1.5; immigration at 225 000 new immigrants per year, a gradual increase in life expectancy from 77 to 80 years for men and 83 to 85 for women.

Source: Statistics Canada, Chart 3. Immigration is an important part of population growth in Canada, http://www.statcan.gc.ca/kits-trousses/issues-enjeux/c-g/edu01c_0002c-eng.htm

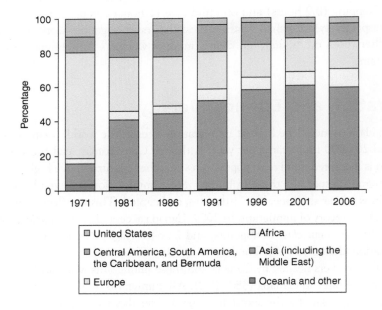

Figure 12.3 Region of Birth of Recent Immigrants to Canada, 1971 to 2006

Note: *Recent immigrants* refers to landed immigrants who arrived in Canada within five years prior to a given census. *Other* includes Greenland, Saint-Pierre and Miquelon, the category "other country," as well as a small number of immigrants born in Canada.

Source: Statistics Canada, censuses of population, 1971 to 2006.

Although source of immigration is one way to examine diversity, another way is to study ethnic identity in the total population. For example, the 2006 Census reports that of Canada's 31 241 030 people, 35.5 percent self-identified British Isles as their ethnic origin, 15.8 percent self-identified as French, 4.3 percent self-identified as Chinese, 4.2 percent self-identified as South Asian, and 7.1 percent self-identified as East and Southeast Asian. So, although Canada is changing, its European and British ethnicity remains the dominate majority. In urban areas of Canada, the impact of immigration is more noticeable because of self-identified visible minority groups. For example, visible minorities comprise about 23 percent of Ontario's population, about 25 percent of British Columbia's population, and about only 9 percent of Quebec's population (Statistics Canada, 2006c).

Changing Age Distribution

One of the most profound ongoing changes in Canadian society is the aging of our population. As discussed in Chapters 1 and 10, the Canadian population is getting older and the number of people who are not in the labour force is increasing. The ideal population perhaps approximates a pyramid, with many children and fewer aged. Canada, like many countries that experienced a postwar baby boom, is currently experiencing a population bulge that is just beginning to enter retirement age. As a result, we expect to see increasing dependency ratios representing fewer people in the labour force. The projections through 2050 (www.statcan.gc.ca/ads-annonces/91-520-x/pyra-eng.htm) support the perspective that it will be a very long time (if ever) before Canada's population returns to a pyramid shape (see Figure 12.4). Indeed, Canada's lower fertility rate promises to be a long-term trend.

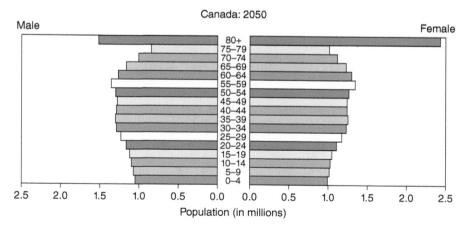

Figure 12.4 Projected Population Pyramid for Canada, 2050

Source: U.S. Census Bureau, International Data Base, http://instruct.uwo.ca/economics/317b-570/Population%20Pyramid%20Summary%20for%20Canada.htm

DYNAMICS FOR LIFE COURSE TRAJECTORIES

The discussion and data earlier in this chapter are largely static, but life course analysis also maintains a more dynamic perspective. In a dynamic perspective of families and individuals, many of the macro-level socio-cultural shifts are conceptualized as products of the historical period (period effects) or as products unique to a particular age cohort (cohort effects). It is important to understand how the numerous macro-level changes affect the life course of individuals.

Imagine that your life is a branching process wherein you make choices at various junctures of the process (Figure 12.5). Each choice has a timing component such as your age and the corollary duration of time spent in the previous stage. If you traverse the life course in the same way as the majority in your age cohort (blue lines in Figure 12.5), your life course may be normative for your age cohort but different from those of other age cohorts. This would be a generational difference. In your grandparents' generation there was very low probability that they would transition from single at Time 1 (age 20) to cohabiting at Time 2 (age 25), but in your generation the probability is about 0.30. Your grandparents would have had their first child by Time 2 (age 25) but your generation generally waits until Time 3 (age 30). Each normative life course (blue lines) represents what the majority in an age cohort does, but it fails to capture the degree of adherence to

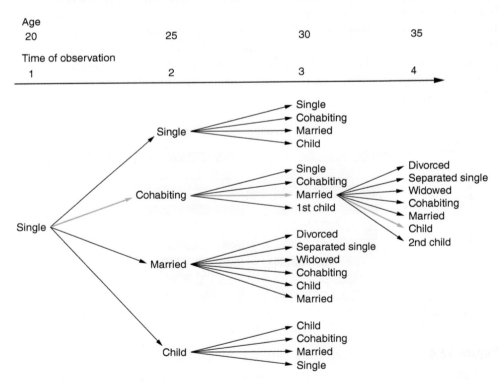

Figure 12.5 Branching Process of the Life Course

or variation from that life course. As discussed, the current 20- to 29-year-old age cohort has a great deal of variation from the modal line of the life course.

Each generation (age cohort) is guided through this process by the norms of their age cohort and the more general Canadian norms in the particular period of history. The general cultural norms are tied to the social organizations within each institutional sector. For example, the institution of the family carries timing and sequencing norms, such as "get married before you have a child," that each generational age cohort may be influenced by but also may ignore. In general, age cohorts ignore broader norms when those norms are not adaptive to the other institutional organizations surrounding them. For example, older Canadian cohorts might suggest that young Canadians "finish their education before they start their first full-time job." Such timing norms cross two institutional sectors: education and work. Older cohorts might also suggest that young Canadians "get a stable job before having children" (institutions of work and family). When timing norms are conjoined, there is an entire life course sequence, such as "finish your education, then start a full-time job, then get married, then establish job security, and then have a child." Indeed, life course norms involve a sequence of norms and events but they also take time, which is at least in part why these norms and events are also age graded (see Career Box 12.1).

Career Box 12.1

Maggie Learns about Institutional Age Grading

Maggie had always wished that she could attend university. She finished high school with good grades, but back in those days only a few people went on to university. After she retired, Maggie learned that the local university accepted "mature" students, and the best part was that the university did not charge tuition for students over 65 years of age. Maggie started reading some of the textbooks for the courses she wanted to take a year before enrolling. She knew it would be intimidating to be with all of those bright young minds in class and she feared she might be too old for all of this.

Despite her crisis of confidence, Maggie walked into her first university classroom in the fall. She looked for a place to sit and had to navigate a very narrow passage down a row of seats to an open seat. She had a hard time getting into the seat since it was so small and narrow. After the 50-minute lecture, everyone rose and started to leave but Maggie could barely get up because the desk top had wedged her into the seat. When she finally extricated herself, she felt students pressing behind her and wondered if she would be knocked down.

After successfully exiting the lecture hall, Maggie decided to get the additional course materials from the bookstore. She found a very long lineup just to get into the bookstore and through the store's windows she could see long lineups at the checkout. She asked one of the students how much time this might take and was told two hours. Maggie was already tired and she knew this long wait would mean missing the first lecture in her next class. She didn't know what to do.

One thing was evident: Universities are geared toward flexible young people who can stand in long lineups! Maggie thought that it might have been easier to be there when she was younger.

Table 12.1 Description of Cross-Institutional Sequences

Age	Education	Work	Family
0–6	Preschool		Sibling relationship
7–18	School	Temporary job	Dating
19–22	Post-secondary education	Temporary job	Dating → mate selection
23–25	Advanced training	Full-time job	Mate selection and cohabitation
26–29		Job changes	Cohabitation and marriage
30–35		Stable job	Children
36–45		Career investment	Full house or divorce
46–55		Stable job	Launching of children
56–65		Stable job	Children return
66–75		Retirement	Last child leaves

Clearly, there are normative careers or pathways that most Canadians traverse in work, family, and education. Several researchers (e.g., Donnelly, Burgess, Anderson, Davis, & Dillard, 2001; Hogan, 1978; White, 1987, 1991, 1999) have demonstrated that when careers become off time or out of sequence with the dominant normative path, individuals experience a lack of synchronization in other institutions. An obvious example is a teenage pregnancy and birth, which creates off-time events in terms of graduation from high school, dating, and being in the labour force. Researchers have documented more subtle effects for being off time and out of sequence, such as later time absent from labour force participation, illness, and divorce. The theoretical ramification has been the development of a proposition that being out of synchrony at one point in the life course makes it difficult to regain normative synchrony. Institutions are organized by age and sequential stages (see Table 12.1), so being out of synchrony has effects on one's life course events.

Every age cohort (generation) experiences different norms because social organizations are constantly adapting their norms to reflect changes in other social organizations. For example, the focus in the 1960s was on the structural and systemic exclusion of women from the labour force and education, but at the same time divorce rates started to climb. By 1970, it was obvious that barriers to work and education were falling and the divorce rate was soaring, so that post-secondary education for women was both possible and desirable. By extending the time spent in education and early work experience, women delayed marriage but not coupling. Indeed, the rise in cohabitation is tied to the changing timing of the life course. Cohabitation allows couples the freedom to live together without the formal social expectations of "husband and wife." Furthermore, young cohabiting couples are unlikely to have expectations for a first child until they marry, so cohabitation delays social expectations of parenthood. This is a complex example of the timing and sequencing norms of different institutions.

Micro and Macro Changes

We have already examined some of the macro-level changes affecting Canadian society, such as women's labour force participation, the age distribution, and immigration. These macro-level changes provide the unique historical period for Canada and affect the cohorts coming of age in Canada. However, it is important to understand how these factors affect individuals and families through Canadian social organizations and institutions.

Societies cannot have social institutions such as education, family, and work organized so that independent demands pile up or aggregate at a specific point in the life course. Imagine buying your first house, having your first child, getting married, graduating from university, and starting your first full-time job all at the same time. Experiencing these stressful events at the same time would be very difficult if not impossible. One benefit of relatively strong and clear social norms about sequencing and timing is that these events usually are not expected to occur all at once. On the other hand, societies that experience platykurtic distributions of norms may find that individuals are awash in role stress and have problems with time management.

One of the wonderful characteristics of Canada is that it is a free and tolerant society. As our society becomes more diverse, we reduce the overall clarity and specificity of norms. Sometimes this is simply a matter of social change and demands for fairness, such as the changing norms about division of labour in the home. On the other hand, there are other demands to accommodate very traditional ethnic norms about the roles of women and men. As the diversity in our society increases, we move to a point where couples and families need to talk about the norms for family roles, because these norms probably are no longer clear and well defined.

If norms about the roles we assume in family relationships are not clear, then the timing and sequencing norms are also probably unclear. However, there is a big difference in the sources of these norms. Whereas family roles can be negotiated and managed within the social group, timing and sequencing norms are more closely tied to social organizations within the institutional sector. For example, look around your classroom and see if the chairs, desks, and physical space are more conducive to those 18 to 22 years of age or to those over age 65. Social institutions such as education and family are usually age graded and sequentially organized. The social organization reflects this fact. Whereas family roles may be more negotiable, institutional timing and sequencing norms are more phlegmatic and slow to change.

Because of this slow adaptation, the social institutions of family, work, and education and the associated timing and sequencing of events may be somewhat detached from the fast-paced negotiations and changes noted by individuals and families. An example of dynamic sequencing of early life events is the change from "first comes love, then comes marriage, then comes Suzy with a baby carriage" to "first comes love, then comes cohabitation, then comes marriage . . . " In the late 1960s, premarital cohabitation was practised by few and considered more or less deviant. It could have been seen as a random variation to couple patterns. In the 1970s, as women entered the labour force in large numbers, they also increased their participation rates in post-secondary education to prepare for the labour force. As a result, sequencing norms such as "finish your education before you commit to a full-time job" and "get some work experience before marriage" led to a significant shift in age at marriage. For women, delaying marriage meant that role demands for being a "wife" and "mother" were delayed so that work roles could be established. The usual timing for marriage was delayed but coupling also shifted to cohabitation, which did not carry the roles of wife or mother. With the median age at marriage delayed to the late twenties, marriage was spread over an entire decade rather than being intensely focused in the early twenties. The spread meant that half of all available spouses were married by the median age. One way to not assume the marital role yet have a partner was to establish a cohabiting union. In many regards, the sequencing changes over this 40-year period were adaptations to the changing educational and labour force participation of women.

Today, the institutionalization of premarital cohabitation as a mate selection stage is all but complete, with the majority of young people cohabiting before marriage. We are also moving rapidly toward institutionalizing cohabitation as an alternative form to marriage. Some provinces such as British Columbia are rewriting their matrimonial property acts to stipulate the rights and responsibilities of cohabiting partners. Interestingly, these rights and responsibilities appear to be very similar to those for marriage partners. Indeed, as more cohabiting partners seek the same protections under law enjoyed by marital partners, it is likely that cohabitation will become increasingly institutionalized and similar to marriage.

Social Changes in Timing Norms

The rise in premarital cohabitation illustrates a more general proposition about social change. The adaptations of timing and sequencing within one institutional sector, such as work or education, require adaptations of timing and sequences in other institutions, such as the family and marriage. All institutional norms apply to the individuals participating in those institutions, but any one individual participates in several institutions (e.g., work, family, education, religion, polity). As long as the timing and sequencing within these various institutions align and are articulated with one another, there should be no "pileup" of role demands. Social change comes about because these various institutions are constantly adjusting to changes in the composition of populations and the environment. When social change is most rapid, the pileup of stressors on individuals may be enormous, and often the only recourse is some form of deviance regarding one or more sets of institutional norms. In the example of cohabitation, the changes in institutional expectations for work and education led to deviance concerning the norms about mate selection. Fifty years later, that "deviance" is now the norm. That new norm, however, requires adjustments in the labour force, since delayed marriage is associated with fewer

children and low fertility leads to labour force shortages, which in turn leads to the need for more immigration.

The Future for the Canadian Family and Family Policy Changes

We can imagine many different scenarios for the future of the Canadian family and probably none will be exactly correct. The best predictions are always made in hindsight. However, it is useful to apply our knowledge to project future scenarios. Such projections allow students to gain a better understanding of the limits of their knowledge. Projections also may assist in developing programs and policy to mitigate future trends such as population decline and a depleted labour force.

Certainly, one change we have documented in several chapters is the steady decline in the marriage rate. Some authors, such as Lee and Payne (2010), have argued that this is a pervasive and troubling decline. Coupled with the decline in marriage rates is the increase in cohabitation as a substitute for marriage. Although many young couples may consider cohabitation as a new stage of courtship (trial marriage) as they move toward marriage, many others are having families without feeling the need to marry. Indeed, about half of the children born in Quebec are born into a cohabiting relationship or have a single parent. The question arises: Is marriage simply an anachronistic institution that will soon be replaced by cohabitation?

We have seen that cohabitation has some additional problems. While cohabiting couples cannot get divorced because they are not married, the laws affecting divorce such as matrimonial property acts certainly protect the married person from exploitation. British Columbia is currently rewriting its matrimonial property act to extend its coverage to cohabitation. As governments try to protect individuals in cohabiting unions by making those unions more similar to institutionalized marriage, we may see a decline in the popularity of cohabitation and increased rates of marriage or we may see a decline in both cohabitation and marriage in favour of a less normatively governed and more flexible form of union.

In 1961, lone-parent families represented only 11 percent of all families with children; in 2004, lone-parent families represented 25 percent of all families with children (www.imfcanada.org/article_files/Single%20Parent%20Homes%20in%20Canada.pdf). This increase in lone-parent families is associated with declining marriage rates but not with increases in divorce. Divorce rates were relatively stable between 1994 and 2004 yet there was a 21 percent increase in lone-parent families in that period. Cohabitation is one possible evolving family form linked to declining marriage rates, but the lone-parent family is another. Scholars such as Therborn (2004) have traced the decline of patriarchy over the past century. From a feminist perspective, the family is seen as one of the bastions of patriarchy. If patriarchy is declining, we may ask if the traditional family is also declining. Indeed, the decline of marriage rates may be one salient indicator of this decline in patriarchy.

In Canada, probably the most important single trend concerns fertility. Since about 1970, Canadian fertility has been below replacement level. Immigrant groups have largely replicated the Canadian trend within two generations. Certainly, we all know that children are expensive in terms of both monetary costs and the costs of lost opportunities. Low fertility is a common and serious problem for most of the states in the Organisation for Economic Co-operation and Development (OECD). Most other OECD states have resorted either to **pronatalist policies**, such as extensive parental leave, taxation benefits, and universal child care, or to massive immigration to solve their labour shortages. Canada has thus far not developed a uniform policy on this issue.

What is more certain than the governmental response to low fertility is that young people faced with labour market uncertainty and instability will have problems attaining the money needed to finance having children. We have already seen that it takes much longer today to reach the median family income in Canada and that people are 30 years of age or more when they accomplish this (see Chapter 6, Figure 6.5). It is somewhat upsetting that in earlier periods of Canada's history (e.g., the 1970s) this median income was reached midway through one's twenties and often with only one breadwinner rather than the two now required. The lack of stable long-term employment and the increase in contract employment of relatively short duration do not suggest that young people will be able to cope with the economic strains associated with having children.

If the fertility problem is placed in the perspective of an aging population in which dependency ratios are increasing, the resulting economic burden on those in the labour force is daunting. As the baby boomers retire, we will have fewer skilled workers than we need to replace them. As a result, like every other nation in the OECD, Canada will be competing for skilled labour from the developing world. Of course, these developing countries will want to keep the workers they have trained and educated so that their own development can proceed. In some ways, Canada is well situated to compete for consumers in the global market. Canada is rich in natural resources and energy and therefore its productivity is less limited than many other developed economies by the need to import raw materials and energy. Furthermore, Canada has fairly well developed industrial, banking, and transportation infrastructures.

Immigrants will be essential to Canada's future well-being. Canada will be competing with the other developed countries for educated and skilled immigrants. Furthermore, Canada will be competing with the developing countries of origin that will seek to retain their educated labour force. Canada also needs the consumers in these developing countries to buy Canadian exports. To some extent, these export "sales" will be contingent on our knowledge of and sensitivity to the languages and cultures of these various developing countries. In turn, to some extent this sensitivity will depend on the knowledge of these cultures provided by our immigrants. Thus, Canada's economic success depends not only on immigrant labour but also on the cultural backgrounds of these immigrants.

Many potential immigrants will be faced with the opportunity to live and work in one of several countries. Most of these immigrants will come from societies that value family and have traditional and religious views that emphasize family. These immigrants are likely to consider where they may be better off not just economically but also in terms of social and family values. Keeping this in mind, is Canada competitive? On the family policy side, many other developed countries have much more to offer in terms of universal child care, parental leave from work, and even fertility bonuses. In 2008, France offered 40 weeks of close to replacement salary leave for mothers who have a third child, exceptional status for government housing, generous universal subsidies for child care, and tax benefits until the youngest child is 18 years of age (www.ehow.com/facts_7408703_france_s-pro-natalist-policies.html). Not only do other OECD countries offer substantial forms of family support, but many of the fastest developing nations offer more substantial forms of support than does Canada. For example, in 1987 Singapore gave a child care grant of $100 per month for all children under 6 years of age. By 2000, new initiatives included a $20 000 baby bonus for a third child (Wong & Yeoh, 2002). In comparison, Canada has some small taxation deductions for child care for employed mothers and offers some modest assistance for daycare. However, there is no universal daycare program or fertility incentive (with the exception of Quebec).

Canada has been slow to acknowledge its declining fertility rate publicly and, at this time, there are no policies aimed at attempting to increase natural fertility in the Canadian population. Furthermore, taxation policies, federal divorce and marriage acts, and provincial matrimonial property acts often contradict each other and work at cross purposes. For example, Revenue Canada decided to close the loophole allowing cohabiting couples two principal domiciles rather than the one domicile allowed to married couples. The admission on the income tax form of "cohabiting for a year or more" implies that each cohabiting couple is allowed only one principal residence. This loophole was closed without consideration of the possibility that this could encourage young people to remain single because marriage may be perceived as providing a net loss for two people.

Canada's low fertility coupled with its aging population will require pronatalist policies both to encourage increases in natural fertility and to appeal to prospective immigrants. As we have seen, Canada's social policy has a considerable distance to go relative to many other developed and developing nations. As immigrants from countries with strong values concerning families and family life examine the social policy of Canada in this regard, they may well be attracted to other more favourable countries. Although some scholars have suggested that pronatalist policies do not do much to increase native fertility, there is some evidence that they may work. In the end, Canada will be forced to compete with pronatalist policies as much because of perceptions of being a family-friendly environment for immigrants as because of natural fertility.

Between now and the time when we find ourselves in a Canada more favourable to children and families, we will continue to have a diversity of family types, including single-parent families, cohabiting families, stepfamilies, and married families. As our society becomes more dominated by immigration, we will see a return to more traditional family forms. In the short run, we expect to continue to see great diversity of family forms as Canada tries to adapt to global changes. Over the next 50 years, as Canada begins to develop immigration and natural fertility policies in a consistent and attuned manner, we expect family forms to become more traditional and nuclear. Thus, true to historian Laslett's (1972) warning, the shorter-term patterns of variation may be but minor perturbations to the long-term dominance of the nuclear family.

IS THE FAMILY DISAPPEARING?

The notion that the family is disappearing has a long and varied history in academic discussion. Naturally, this argument is somewhat dependent on how we define *family*; however, many of the arguments are so broad as to encompass most family forms so that the argument turns on almost any family form (single parent, cohabiting, or married) versus no families and state control of reproduction and socialization.

This subject started with the association of various family structures with types of economies. Blumberg and Winch (1972) argued that family complexity varied with the economic form of the society. In hunter-gatherer societies, mobility to follow game and resources dictated a small and mobile family, the nuclear family. Pastoral herders could have somewhat larger families, but the largest families were linked to agriculture and domestication of animals. In these societies, a stable home base could be maintained and the limit on agricultural productivity was often the number labourers. Labourers were supplied by fertility, so prosperous families were often large. With the Industrial Revolution, we once again needed small mobile families to go where jobs were to be found. Children were no longer economic assets but economic liabilities that required mandatory schooling. Thus, in these authors' view, we have returned to the small nuclear family.

On the other hand, the noted historian of the family, Laslett (1972), argued that unless there is strong and compelling evidence to suggest otherwise, family scholars should adopt the "null hypothesis" regarding family change. He suggested that most of the recent history of the family is simply the nuclear family form. Certainly, difficult economic times, wars, and pestilence all deflect family forms temporarily, but the overall dominance of the nuclear family form in history suggests that it is normative. As a result, Laslett's "null hypothesis" is that there is no change and that the nuclear family will continue to dominate with minor deflections.

Popenoe (1988) argue that the family has undergone defunctionalization and deinstitutionalization. The functions of the family have been claimed by professionals in such areas as daycare, nursing, and teaching so that the family has few functions other than economic support. Furthermore, Popenoe argues that the norms around family life have weakened so that, as an institution, there is more variation than conformity to a set of established norms about family behaviour and parenting.

Certainly, demographic transition theory has had several and diverse iterations. The original versions were concerned with the prediction of changes in fertility relative to mortality. The basic idea was that as societies moved from an agrarian balance between fertility and mortality to industrialized modern societies with advanced medical treatments, an imbalance would be created, with fewer deaths but high fertility. As developing countries increased modernization, balance eventually would be restored, with birth rates declining to match mortality. Therefore, societies that were developing would have an imbalance (high fertility and low mortality) until they were fully modern and would again become balanced by reducing fertility.

The problem with demographic transition theory is that it did not anticipate fertility below replacement level and the impending population decline across much of the developed world, including Canada. Some OECD countries have already slipped into population decline (they have more deaths than births) and that is far from balanced. Because of this anomaly, there has been some need to restate demographic transition theory. One recent hypothesis has been that the theory failed to measure and take into account the rate of social development (principally education and health) achieved by a country and the effect that social development has on fertility. For example, Myrskyla, Kohler, and Billani (2009) argued that when countries attain a very high level of social development, fertility will once again increase (with the notable exceptions of Canada and Japan). They see social development as a moderating influence between fertility and mortality. This very new theoretical modification has already met with objections from those reanalyzing the data. For example, Fumitaka (2009) failed to find the J-shaped curve hypothesized by Myrskyla et al. (2009).

Most of these theories have failed to come to terms with the notion of post-industrial society. Laslett (1972) and Blumberg and Winch (1972) could not anticipate the computer revolution nor the changes in communication technology. Popenoe (1988) and later demographic transition theorists (Myrskyla et al., 2009) do not incorporate the global nature of communication nor the fluidity of immigration (in which immigrants may hold citizenship in several countries). Most importantly, many of these arguments fail to consider the essential nature of post-industrial societies. Indeed, the change from production as the major limit to economic growth in industrial societies to the limits of consumption in post-industrial societies is critical. Post-industrial societies can automate industries but cannot prosper without consumers. Thus, the developing world contains the future consumers for most post-industrial economies, but in a competitive world, a country's natural fertility also ensures consumers.

Probably the biggest single factor suggesting the survival of the family is that governments would be hard pressed to take over what the family does to produce citizens and workers. The economic costs of raising a child to the age of 18 are shouldered mainly by parents. Most citizens' moral and ethical core is learned at an early age in their families. As well, the state or government would be hard pressed to replace the nurturance, attachment, and social, economic, and emotional support that families provide throughout the life course. As a social group and as an institution, the family must be considered a "building block" for any society. As we have discovered with the cases of isolated children, we are only persons because of the nurturance and socialization provided by family members. Even the renowned "rational choice" sociologist James Coleman (1990) argued that it is doubtful that a child's holistic interactions with parents and family members could be replaced by interactions with only specialized and segmental roles such as child-care worker and teacher without doing significant harm to the fabric of any society. We agree and believe that the Canadian family in some of its many forms is bound to survive in the twenty-first century.

SUMMARY OF KEY POINTS

- Changing families:
    - Family structure: Only 38.7 percent of couples with children are married. Lone-parent and cohabiting couples with children are increasing. Married couples still have more children (1.9) per family form.
    - Cohabitation: The majority of 20- to 29-year-olds cohabit at least once. Cohabitation is a new normative (expected) stage in mate selection.
    - Marriage: Less than half will marry by 50 years of age. Some of the decline in marriage rates is due to delayed age at marriage.
    - Births: Fertility in Canada has been below replacement level (2.1) since 1971. Twenty-six percent of births in Canada are to single, never-married women (almost 60 percent in Quebec).
    - Divorce and repartnering: Thirty-five to 40 percent of marriages can expect to end in divorce by the thirtieth year of marriage. Repartnering increasingly takes the form of cohabitation rather than remarriage.

- Leaving home: Sixty-five percent of males and 55 percent of females aged 20 to 24 years of age live in the parental home. Males stay longer, with 30 percent between ages 25 and 29 living in the parental home.
- Aging families: The number of those out of the labour force will increase as the baby boom generation retires. As people age, they are increasingly likely to live alone (40 percent of women 75 years and older).

- Socio-cultural changes:
  - Women's rate of labour force participation doubled from 1970 to 2006.
  - Associated with labour force changes, women increased their participation rates in post-secondary education.
  - Men and women do about the same amount of labour in household plus paid work (8.8 hours per day) but women do more household work and child care and men do more paid work.
  - Canada's immigrants help to replace the country's shortfalls in natural fertility and the labour force.
  - Population projections for 2050 suggest that Canada will be an inverted pyramid.

- Dynamics:
  - All of our statistics are based on statuses or on stages of family through which individuals pass.
  - Different life course paths have different consequences.
  - Non-normative paths tend to be poorly synchronized with institutional norms and produce individuals who are off time and out of sequence with one or more institutions.
  - Although age cohorts have some normative changes, timing and sequencing norms in all institutions (work, education, and family) are slow to change.

- Future families and policies:
  - Low fertility and labour force shortages will continue.
  - Immigration will increase.
  - Canada's policy of multiculturalism is an attraction for immigration.
  - Pronatalist policies will need to be competitive with other OECD nations to attract immigrants.
  - Pronatalist policies also need to be aimed at increasing natural fertility.
  - Family forms will continue to be diverse, including single-parent and cohabiting families as well as the traditional married couple family.
  - Future families will require support, but the disappearance of the family in some of its forms is unlikely because the institution of the family serves governments well in the nurturance and socialization of citizens and the labour force.

Critical Thinking Questions

1. Has marriage outlived its usefulness as a social institution? Is cohabitation the "new" marriage?

2. Do you think that the family is a basic building block for society? If the family is in decline, what does that imply about our society?

3. What government policies would you put into place to encourage fertility, families, and marital stability?

Glossary

boomerang kids Children who have been launched from their family homes but return home during their twenties or later.

LATs A term used by Trost (2010) to describe couples who are committed to one another but live separately (living apart together).

pronatalist policies Policies favourable to natural fertility and, in a broader sense, to children and child rearing.

Connections

http://usgovinfo.about.com/cs/censusstatistic/a/carsperhouse.htm
www12.statcan.ca/english/census01/products/analytic/companion/age/cda01pymd.cfm
www.statcan.gc.ca/ads-annonces/91-520-x/pyra-eng.htm
www.cic.gc.ca/english/resources/statistics/facts2010-preliminary/01.asp
www.imfcanada.org/article_files/Single%20Parent%20Homes%20in%20Canada.pdf
www.ehow.com/facts_7408703_france_s-pro_natalist-policies.html

Remember to log on to the Companion Website at **www.pearsoncanada.ca/white** to find self-graded quizzes and useful resource tools for further study. You can log on to the Companion Website using the Student Access Code that comes packaged with your copy of *Families Across the Life Course*.

References

Ackerman, D. (1994). *A natural history of love*. New York, NY: Random House.

Ahrons, C. R. (2007). Family ties after divorce: Long-term implications for children. *Family Process, 46*(1), 53–65.

Ainsworth, M., Blehar, M., Waters, E., & Wall, S. (1978). *Patterns of attachment*. Hillsdale, NJ: Erlbaum.

Ainsworth, M. D. (1967). *Infancy in Uganda*. Baltimore, MD: Johns Hopkins Press.

Aldous, J. (1999). *Family careers: Rethinking the developmental perspective*. Thousand Oaks, CA: Sage.

Allen, E. S., Baucom, D. H., Burnett, C. K., Epstein, N., & Rankin-Esquer, L. A. (2001). Decision-making power, autonomy, and communication in remarried spouses compared with first married spouses. *Family Relations, 50*(4), 326–334.

Allison, B. N., & Schultz, J. B. (2004). Parent–adolescent conflict in early adolescence. *Adolescence, 39*(153), 101–120.

Amato, P., Johnson, D., Booth, A., & Rogers, S. (2003). Continuity and change in marital quality between 1980 and 2000. *Journal of Marriage and Family, 65*(1), 1–22.

Amato, P. R. (1996). Explaining the intergenerational transmission of divorce. *Journal of Marriage and the Family, 58*(3), 628–640.

Amato, P. R. (2010). Research on divorce: Continuing trends and new developments. *Journal of Marriage and Family, 72*(3), 650–666.

Amato, P. R., Booth, A., Johnson, D. R., & Rogers, S. J. (2007). *Alone together*. Cambridge, MA: Harvard University Press.

Amato, P. R., & DeBoer, D. (2001). The transmission of divorce across generations: Relationship skills or commitment to marriage? *Journal of Marriage and Family, 63*, 1038–1051.

Amato, P. R., & Rogers, S. J. (1997). A longitudinal study of marital problems and subsequent divorce. *Journal of Marriage and the Family, 59*(3), 612–624.

Amato, P. R., & Sobolewski, J. M. (2001). The effects of divorce and marital discord on adult children's psychological well-being. *American Sociological Review, 66*(6), 900–921.

Ambert, A.-M. (2005). *Cohabitation and marriage: How are they related?* Ottawa, ON: Vanier Institute of the Family.

American Nurses Association. (1995). *Integrating an understanding of sleep knowledge into your practice*. Washington, DC: Author.

Anderson, S., Russell, C., & Schumm, W. (1983). Perceived marital quality and family life cycle categories. *Journal of Marriage and the Family, 45*, 127–139.

Angell, R. C. (1965/1936). *The family encounters the Depression*. New York: Scribner.

Ansara, D. L., & Hindin, M. J. (2009). Perpetration of intimate partner aggression by men and women in the Philippines. *Journal of Interpersonal Violence, 24*(9), 1579.

Antioch College. (2005). The Antioch College sexual offense prevention policy. Retrieved from http://antiochmedia.org/mirror/antiwarp/www.antioch-college.edu/Campus/sopp/index.html

Arnett, J. (2004). *Emerging adulthood: The winding road from late teens through adulthood*. New York, NY: Oxford University Press.

Arnett, J. J. (2000). Emerging adulthood: A theory of development from the late teens through the 20s. *American Psychologist, 55*(5), 469–480.

Arnett, J. J. (2001). Conceptions of the transition to adulthood: Perspectives from adolescence through midlife. *Journal of Adult Development, 8*, 133–143.

Aron, A., Steele, J. L., Kashdan, T. B., & Perez, M. (2006). When similar do not attract: Tests of a prediction from the self-expansion model. *Personal Relationships, 13*, 387–396.

Artis, J. E. (2007). Maternal cohabitation and child well-being among kindergarten children. *Journal of Marriage and Family, 69*(1), 222–236.

Atherton, J. (2010) *Learning and teaching: Piaget's developmental theory*. Retrieved from http://www.learningandteaching.info/learning/piaget.htm

Australian Bureau of Statistics. (2008). Marriages, Australia, 2007. Catalogue no. 3306.0.55.001 [electronic product]. Canberra, Australia: Author.

Axinn, W. G., & Barber, J. S. (1997). Living arrangements and family formation attitudes in early adulthood. *Journal of Marriage and Family, 59*, 595–611.

Axinn, W. G., & Thornton, A. (1992). The relationship between cohabitation and divorce: Selectivity or causal influence? *Demography, 29*, 357–374.

Babcock, J. C., Costa, D. M., Green, C. E., & Eckhardt, C. I. (2004). What situations induce intimate partner violence? A reliability and validity study of the proximal antecedents to violent episodes (PAVE) scale. *Journal of Family Psychology, 18*(3), 433–442.

Bäckman, L., Small, B. J., Wahlin, A., & Larsson, M. (2000). Cognitive functioning in very old age. In F. I. M. Craik and T. A. Salthouse (Eds.), *The handbook of aging and cognition* (2nd ed., pp. 499–558). Mahwah, NJ: Lawrence Erlbaum Associates.

Bailey, B. (1988). *From front porch to back seat: Courtship in twentieth-century America*. Baltimore, MD: Johns Hopkins University Press.

Baker, L., & Oswald, D. (2008, February). *Shyness and online social networking services*. Poster presented at the annual meeting of the Society for Personality and Social Psychology, Albuquerque, NM.

Balakrishnan, T. R., Rao, K. V., Lapierre-Adamcyk, E., & Krotki, K. J. (1987). A hazard model analysis of the covariates of marriage dissolution in Canada. *Demography, 24*(3), 395–406.

Baltes, P. B. (1987). Theoretical propositions of life-span developmental psychology: On the dynamics between growth and decline. *Developmental Psychology, 23*(5), 611–626.

Bandura, A. (1978). Social learning theory of aggression. *Journal of Communication, 28*(3), 12–29.

Barber, J., Axinn, W. G., and Thornton, A. (2002). The influence of attitudes on family formation processes. In R. Lesthaeghe (Ed.), *Meaning and choice* (pp. 45–96). Brussels, Belgium: NIDI/CBGS Publications.

Barczak, B., Miller, T. W., Veltkamp, L. J., Barczak, S., Hall, C., & Kraus, R. (2010). Transitioning the impact of divorce on children throughout the life cycle. In T. W. Miller (Ed.), *Handbook of stressful transitions across the lifespan* (pp. 185–215). New York, NY: Springer.

Barg, K., & Beblo, M. (2007). The male marital wage premium in Germany: Selection versus specialization. *Journal of Applied Social Sciences Studies, 127*(1), 59–73.

Barrett, A. E., & Turner, R. J. (2005). Family structure and mental health: The mediating effects of socioeconomic status, family process, and social stress. *Journal of Health and Social Behavior, 46*(2), 156.

Baumrind, D. (1967). Child care practices anteceding three patterns of preschool behavior. *Genetic Psychology Monographs, 75*, 43–88.

Baumrind, D. (1997). Necessary distinctions. *Psychological Inquiry, 8*(3), 176–182.

Baumrind, D., Larzelere, R. E., & Cowan, P. A. (2002). Ordinary physical punishment: Is it harmful? Comment on Gershoff (2002). *Psychological Bulletin, 128*, 580–589.

Beaujot, R. (2000). *Earning and caring in Canadian families*. Peterborough, ON: Broadview.

Beaujot, R. (2004). *Delayed life transitions: Trends and implications*. Ottawa, ON: Vanier Institute of the Family.

Beaujot, R., & Kerr, D. (2007). *Emerging youth transition patterns in Canada: Opportunities and risks*. Ottawa, ON: Policy Research Initiative.

Beaujot, R. P., & Andersen, R. (2008). Time-crunch: Impact of time spent in paid and unpaid work, and its division in families. *The Canadian Journal of Sociology, 32*, 295–315.

Beaulaurier, R. L., Seff, L. R., Newman, F. L., & Dunlop, B. (2007). External barriers to help seeking for older women who experience intimate partner violence. *Journal of Family Violence, 22*, 747–755.

Becker, G., & Tomes, N. (1979). An equilibrium theory of the distribution of income and intergenerational mobility. *Journal of Political Economy, 87*, 1153–1189.

Becker, G., & Tomes, N. (1986). Human capital and the rise and fall of families. *Journal of Labor Economics*, 43, S1–S39.

Becker, G. S. (1981). Altruism in the family and selfishness in the marketplace. *Economica*, 48(189), 1–15.

Becker, G. S. (1991). *A treatise on the family*. Cambridge, MA: Harvard University Press.

Bee, H. (1998). *Lifespan development* (2nd ed.). New York, NY: Longman.

Beeby, D. (2006). End polygamy ban, report urges Ottawa. *The Globe and Mail*, January 13. Retrieved from http://www.theglobeandmail .com/news/national/end-polygamy-ban-report-urges-ottawa/article143996/

Beeghley, L. (2004). *The structure of social stratification in the United States*. Boston, MA: Allyn & Bacon.

Belsky, J. (1984). The determinants of parenting: A process model. *Child Development*, 55, 83–96.

Belsky, J. (1988). The effects of infant daycare reconsidered. *Early Childhood Research Quarterly*, 3, 235–272.

Belsky, J. (2003–2005). Child care and its impact on young children (0–2). *Encyclopedia on Early Childhood Development*. Retrieved from http:// www.child-encyclopedia.com/documents/ BelskyANGxp_rev-Child_care.pdf

Belsky, J., & Eggebeen, D. (1991). Early and extensive maternal employment and young children's socioemotional development: Children of the National Longitudinal Survey of Youth. *Journal of Marriage and the Family*, 53, 1083–1110.

Belsky, J., Lang, M., & Rovine, M. (1985). Stability and change in marriage across the transition to parenthood: A second study. *Journal of Marriage and Family*, 47, 855–865.

Belsky, J., & Rovine, M. (1990). Patterns of marital change across the transition to parenthood: Pregnancy to three years postpartum. *Journal of Marriage the Family*, 52, 5–19.

Belsky, J., Spanier. G. B., & Rovine, M. (1983). Stability and change in marriage across the transition to parenthood. *Journal of Marriage and the Family*, 45, 567–577.

Belsky, J., & Steinberg, L. (1978). The effects of daycare: A critical review. *Child Development*, 49, 929–949.

Benjet, C., & Kazdin, A. E. (2003). Spanking children: The controversies, findings, and new directions. *Clinical Psychology Review*, 23, 197–224.

Benoit, C. M. (2000). *Women, work and social rights: Canada in historical and comparative perspective*. Scarborough, ON: Prentice Hall, Allyn and Bacon.

Benson, P. L., Donahue, M. J., & Erickson, J. A. (1993). The Faith Maturity Scale: Conceptualization, measurement, and empirical validation. *Research in the Social Scientific Study of Religion*, 5, 1–26.

Bernstein, B. (1971). *Class, codes and control: Theoretical studies toward a sociology of language*. London, UK: Routledge and Paul.

Bianchi, S. M., Robinson, J. P., & Milkie, M. A. (2006). *Changing rhythms of American family life*. New York, NY: Russell Sage Foundation.

Bibby, R. W. (2001). *Canadian teens: Today, yesterday, and tomorrow*. Toronto, ON: Stoddart.

Bibby, R. W. (2002). *Restless gods: The renaissance of religion in Canada*. Toronto, ON: Stoddart.

Bierman, A., Fazio, E. M., & Milkie, M. A. (2006). A multifaceted approach to the mental health advantage of the married. *Journal of Family Issues*, 27(4), 554.

Black, D. S., Sussman, S., & Unger, J. B. (2010). A further look at the intergenerational transmission of violence: Witnessing interparental violence in emerging adulthood. *Journal of Interpersonal Violence*, 25(6), 1022.

Blair-Loy, M. (1999). Career patterns of executive women in finance: An optimal matching analysis. *The American Journal of Sociology*, 104, 1346–1397.

Blood, R., & Wolfe, D. (1960). *Husbands and wives*. New York, NY: The Free Press.

Blossfeld, H.-P., De Rose, A., Hoem, J., & Rohwer, G. (1995). Education, modernization, and the risk of marriage disruption in Sweden, West Germany, and Italy. In K. O. Mason & A. M. Jensen (Eds.), *Gender and family change in industrialized countries* (pp. 200–222). Oxford, UK: Clarendon.

Blumberg, R., & Winch, R. (1972). Societal complexity and familial complexity: Evidence for the curvilinear hypothesis. *American Journal of Sociology*, 77, 898–920.

Blumenthal, J., Emery, C., Madden, D., Schniebolk, S., Walsh-Riddle, M., George, L., . . . Coleman, R. (1991). Long-term effects of exercise on psychological functioning in older men and women, *Journal of Gerontology, 46,* 352–361.

Blumstein, P., & Schwartz, P. (1983). *American couples: Money, work, and sex.* New York, NY: William Morrow and Company.

Bogle, K. A. (2007). The shift from dating to hooking up in college: What scholars have missed. *Sociology Compass, 1*(2), 775–788.

Booth, A., & Amato, P. R. (2001). Parental predivorce relations and offspring post-divorce well-being. *Journal of Marriage and Family, 63*(1), 197–212.

Booth, A., Johnson, D. R., White, L. K., & Edwards, J. N. (1986). Divorce and marital instability over the life course. *Journal of Family Issues, 7*(4), 421.

Borell, K., & Karlsson, S. G. (2002). Reconceptualising intimacy and aging: Living apart together. Paper presented at International Symposium, Reconceptualising Gender and Aging, Center for Research on Aging and Gender, University of Surrey, June 25–27.

Bourdieu, P. (1984). *Distinction: A social critique of the judgement of taste.* (R. Nice, Trans.). Cambridge, MA: Harvard University Press.

Bowlby, J. (1953). *Child care and the growth of love.* London, UK: Penguin Books.

Bowman, C. G. (2007). Social science and legal policy: The case of heterosexual cohabitation. *Journal of Law & Family Studies, 1,* 1–52.

Bramlett, M. D., Mosher, W. D., & Forente Stater National Center for Health. (2002). *Cohabitation, marriage, divorce, and remarriage in the United States* (Vol. 22). Washington, DC: National Center for Health Statistics.

Bratter, J. L., & King, R. B. (2008). "But will it last?": Marital instability among interracial and same race couples. *Family Relations, 57*(2), 160–171.

Brehm, S. S., & Brehm, J. W. (1981). *Psychological reactance: A theory of freedom and control.* New York, NY: Academic Press.

Bronfenbrenner, U. (1979). *The ecology of human development: Experiments by nature and design.* Cambridge, MA: Harvard University Press.

Brown, B. B. (1999). You're going out with who?: Peer group influences on adolescent romantic relationships. In W. Furman and B. B. Brown (Eds.), *The development of romantic relationships in adolescence* (pp. 291–329). New York, NY: Cambridge University Press.

Brown, S. L. (2004). Family structure and child well-being: The significance of parental cohabitation. *Journal of Marriage and Family, 66*(2), 351–367.

Brown, S. L. (2006). Family structure transitions and adolescent well-being. *Demography, 43*(3), 447–461.

Brown, S. L., & Bulanda, J. R. (2008). Relationship violence in young adulthood: A comparison of daters, cohabitors, and marrieds. *Social Science Research, 37*(1), 73–87.

Brown, S. L., & Kawamura, S. (2010). Relationship quality among cohabitors and marrieds in older adulthood. *Social Science Research, 39,* 777–786.

Brown, S. L., Lee, G. R., & Bulanda, J. R. (2006). Cohabitation among older adults: A national portrait. *The Journals of Gerontology Series B: Psychological Sciences and Social Sciences, 61,* S71–S79.

Brown, S. L., Sanchez, L. A., Nock, S. L., & Wright, J. D. (2006). Links between premarital cohabitation and subsequent marital quality, stability, and divorce: A comparison of covenant versus standard marriages. *Social Science Research, 35,* 454–470.

Brownridge, D. A. (2008). The elevated risk for violence against cohabiting women. *Violence Against Women, 14*(7), 809.

Buchmann, C., & Diprete, T. A. (2006). The growing female advantage in college completion: The role of family background and academic achievement. *American Sociological Review, 71*(4), 515–541.

Buck, D., & Plant, E. A. (2008, February). *Impression formation and sexual orientation: The role of timing of disclosure.* Poster presented at the meeting of the Society for Personality and Social Psychology, Albuquerque, NM.

Bulanda, R., & Manning, W. (2008). Parental cohabitation experiences and adolescent behavioral outcomes. *Population Research and Policy Review, 27,* 593–618.

Bulcroft, K. A., & Bulcroft, R. A. (1991). The timing of divorce. *Research on Aging, 13,* 226–243.

Bumpass, L., & Lu, H.-H. (2000). Trends in cohabitation and implications for children's family contexts in the United States. *Population Studies: A Journal of Demography, 54,* 29–41.

Bumpass, L., & Raley, K. (2007). Measuring separation and divorce. In S. L. Hofferth & L. M. Casper (Eds.), *Handbook of measurement issues in family research* (pp. 125–143). Mahwah, NJ: Lawrence Erlbaum.

Burlage, D. D. (1974). Judeo-Christian influences of female sexuality. In A. L. Hageman (Ed.), *Sexist religion and women in the church.* New York, NY: Association Press.

Buss, D. M. (1989). Sex differences in human mate preferences: Evolutionary hypotheses tested in 37 cultures. *Behavioral and Brain Sciences, 12,* 1–14.

Buss, D. M. (2003). *The evolution of desire: Strategies of human mating* (rev. ed.). New York, NY: Basic Books.

Buss, D. M., & Schmitt, D. P. (1993). Sexual strategies theory: An evolutionary perspective on human mating. *Psychological Review, 100*(2), 204–232.

Calasanti, T., & Kiecolt, K. J. (2007). Diversity among late-life couples. *Generations, 31,* 10–17.

Campbell, A., Converse, P., & Rogers, W. (1976). *The quality of American life.* New York, NY: Russell Sage Foundation.

Canary, D. J., & Stafford, L. (2001). Equity in the preservation of personal relationships. In J. H. Harvey & A. E. Wenzel (Eds.), *Close romantic relationships: Maintenance and enhancement* (pp. 133–151). Mahwah, NJ: Lawrence Erlbaum.

Carlson, D. S., Kacmar, K. M., Wayne, J. H., & Grzywacz, J. G. (2006). Measuring the positive side of the work–family interface: Development and validation of a work-family enrichment scale. *Journal of Vocational Behavior, 68,* 131–164.

Carlson, M., McLanahan, S., & England, P. (2004). Union formation in fragile families. *Demography, 41,* 237–261.

Caron Malenfant, E., & Belanger, A. (2006). The fertility of visible minority women in Canada. In *Report on the demographic situation in Canada, 2003 and 2004.* Catalogue no. 91-209-XIE. Ottawa, ON: Statistics Canada.

Carrere, S., & Gottman, J. M. (1999). Predicting divorce among newlyweds from the first three minutes of a marital conflict discussion. *Family Process, 38*(3), 293–301.

Cary, M. S. (1976). Talk? Do you want to talk? Negotiation for the initiation of conversation between the unacquainted. (Unpublished doctoral dissertation). University of Pennsylvania, Philadelphia, PA.

Casper, L., & Bianchi, S. (2002). *Continuity and change in the American family.* Thousand Oaks, CA: Sage Publications.

Castells, M. (2004). *The power of identity* (2nd ed.). Malden, MA: Blackwell.

Caughlin, J. P., & Huston, T. L. (2006). The affective structure of marriage. In A. L. Vangelisti & D. Perlman (Eds.), *The Cambridge handbook of personalrelationships* (pp. 131–155). New York, NY: Cambridge University Press.

Cavanagh, A. (2007). *Sociology in the age of the internet.* Buckingham, UK: Open University.

Cavanagh, K., Dobash, R. E., & Dobash, R. P. (2007). The murder of children by fathers in the context of child abuse. *Child Abuse & Neglect, 31*(7), 731–746.

Cavanagh, S. E., & Huston, A. C. (2006). Family instability and children's early problem behavior. *Social Forces, 85,* 551.

CBC News. (2004). Same-sex divorce. Retrieved from http://www.cbc.ca/news/background/samesexrights/samesexdivorce.html

CBC News (2009). Polygamy charges in Bountiful, B.C. thrown out. Retrieved from http://www.cbc.ca/canada/british-columbia/story/2009/09/23/bc-polygamy-charges-blackmore-oler-bountiful.html

CBC News. (2010). 4 in 10 1st marriages end in divorce: Report. Retrieved from http://www.cbc.ca/news/canada/story/2010/10/04/vanier-study004.html

Chappell, N., McDonald, L., & Stones, M. (2008). *Aging in contemporary Canada* (2nd ed). Toronto, ON: Pearson Education Canada.

Chatters, L. M., & Taylor, R. J. (2005). Religion and families. In V. Bengtson,

D. Klein, A. Acock, K. Allen, & P. Dilworth-Anderson (Eds.), *Sourcebook on family theories and methods*. Thousand Oaks, CA: Sage Publications.

Cherlin, A. (1978). Remarriage as an incomplete institution. *American Journal of Sociology, 84*(3), 634–650.

Cherlin, A. J. (2009). *The marriage-go-round: The state of marriage and the family in America today*. New York, NY: Knopf.

Cherlin, A. J., & Furstenberg, F. F., Jr. (1986). *The new American grandparent: A place in the family, a life apart*. New York, NY: Basic Books.

Chesler, P. (2009). Are honour killings simply domestic violence? *Middle East Quarterly,* Spring, 61–69. Retrieved from http://www.meforum.org/2067/are-honor-killings-simply-domesticviolence

Chevan, A. (1996). As cheaply as one: Cohabitation in the older population. *Journal of Marriage and Family, 58*, 656–667.

Citizen and Immigration Canada. (2010). Canada: Permanent residents by category, 2006–2010. Retrieved from http://www.cic.gc.ca/english/resources/statistics/facts2010-preliminary/01.asp

Clark, C. A., Worthington, E. L., & Danser, D. B. (1986). The transmission of Christian values from parents to early adolescent sons. Paper presented at the annual meeting of the American Psychological Association, Washington, DC.

Clark, W. (2007). Delayed transitions of young adults. *Canadian Social Trends, 84*, 14–22.

Coleman, J. (1990). *Foundations of social theory.* Cambridge, MA: Belknap Press of Harvard.

Collins, P. H. (1991). *Black feminist thought*. New York, NY: Routledge.

Collins, W. A., Hennighausen, K. C., Schmit, D. T., & Sroufe, L. A. (1997). Developmental precursors of romantic relationships: A longitudinal analysis. In S. Shulman and W. A. Collins (Eds.), *Romantic relationships in adolescence: Developmental perspectives*. San Francisco, CA: Jossey-Bass.

Connidis, I. A. (1989). *Family ties and aging.* Toronto, ON: Butterworths/Harcourt Brace.

Connolly, J., Furman, W., & Konarski, R. (2000). The role of peers in emergence of heterosexual romantic relationships in adolescence. *Child Development, 71*, 1395–1408.

Coontz, S. (1992). *The way we never were: American families and the nostalgia trap*. New York, NY: Basic Books.

Cooper, C., Selwood, A., & Livingston, G. (2008). The prevalence of elder abuse and neglect: A systematic review. *Age and Ageing, 37*(2), 151–160.

Cornell, C. P., & Gelles, R. J. (1985). *Intimate violence in families*. Thousand Oaks, CA: Sage Publications.

Cornwall, M. (1989). The determinants of religious behavior: A theoretical model and empirical test. *Social Forces, 68*, 572–592.

Coser, L. A. (1974). *Greedy institutions: Patterns of undivided commitment*. New York, NY: Free Press.

Cottrell, B. (2001). *Parent abuse: The abuse of parents by their teenage children*. Ottawa, ON: Health Canada.

Cottrell, B., & Finlayson, M. (1996). *Parent abuse: The abuse of parents by their teenage children*. Ottawa, ON: Health Canada.

Cottrell, B., & Monk, P. (2004). Adolescent-to-parent abuse. *Journal of Family Issues, 25*(8), 1072.

Cowan, C. P., & Cowan, P. A. (1999). *When partners become parents: The big life change for couples*: London, UK: Routledge.

Craig, M. E. (1990). Coercive sexuality in dating relationships. *Clinical Psychology Review, 10,* 395–423.

Cranswick, K., & Dosman, D. (2008). Eldercare: What we know today. *Canadian Social Trends* (Catalogue no. 11-008-X). Ottawa, ON: Statistics Canada.

Cristina d'Addio, A. (2007). Intergenerational transmission of disadvantage: Mobility or immobility across generations? A review of the evidence for OECD countries. Retrieved from http://www.oecd.org/dataoecd/27/28/38335410.pdf

Cristina d'Addio, A., & Mira d'Ercole, M. (2005). *Trends and determinants of fertility rates in OECD countries: The role of policies*. OECD Social, Employment, and Migration Working Papers No. 27. Organisation for Economic Co-operation and Development.

Cummins, H. A. (2005). Mommy tracking single women in academia when they are not mommies. *Women's Studies International Forum, 28*(2–3), 222–231.

Daly, M. (1974). Theology after the demise of God the Father: A call for the castration of sexist religion. In A. L. Hageman (Ed.), *Sexist religion and women in the church.* New York, NY: Association Press.

Damaske, S., & Gerson, K. (2008). Viewing 21st century motherhood through a work-family lens. In K. Korabik, D. S. Lero, & D. L. Whitehead (Eds.), *Handbook of work and family integration.* New York, NY: Elsevier.

Davis, K. (1947). Final note on a case of extreme isolation. *American Journal of Sociology, 52,* 432–437.

Day, R., Peterson, G., & McCracken, C. (1998). Predicting spanking of younger and older children by mothers and fathers. *Journal of Marriage and Family, 60,* 79–94.

De Vaus, D., Qu, L., & Weston, R (2005). The disappearing link between premarital cohabitation and subsequent marital stability, 1970–2001. *Journal of Population Research, 22,* 99–118.

Deater-Deckard, K., & Dodge, K. A. (1997). Externalizing behavior problems and discipline revisited: Nonlinear effects and variation by culture, context, and gender. *Psychological Inquiry, 8*(3), 161–175.

DeLeire, T., & Kalil, A. (2002). Good things come in threes: Single-parent multigenerational family structure and adolescent adjustment. *Demography, 39*(2), 393–413.

DeMaris, A., & Rao, V. (1992). Premarital cohabitation and subsequent marital stability in the United States: A reassessment. *Journal of Marriage and the Family, 54,* 178–190.

Demo, D. H., & Fine, M. A. (2009). *Beyond the average divorce.* Thousand Oaks, CA: Sage Publications.

deMunck, V. C., Korotayev, A., deMunck, J., & Khaltourina, D. (2011). Cross-cultural analysis of models of romantic love among U.S. residents, Russians, and Lithuanians. *Cross-Cultural Research,* 1–27. doi:10.1177/1069397110393313

Dew, J., & Wilcox, W. B. (2011). If Momma ain't happy: Explaining declines in marital satisfaction among new mothers. *Journal of Marriage and Family, 73*(1), 1–12.

Dixon, R. A. (2000). Concepts and mechanisms of gains in cognitive aging. In D. C. Park and N. Schwarz (Eds.), *Cognitive aging: A primer* (pp. 23–41). Philadelphia, PA: Taylor and Francis.

Donnelly, D., Burgess, E., Anderson, S., Davis, R. & Dillard, J. (2001). Involuntary celibacy: A life course perspective. *Journal of Sex Research, 38,* 159–169.

Dowling, G. (1995). Sleep problems in older adults. *The American Nurse,* April–May, 24–25.

Downs, K. J. M., Coleman, M., & Ganong, L. (2000). Divorced families over the life course. In S. J. Price, P. C. McKenry, & M. J. Murphy (Eds.), *Families across time: A life course perspective* (pp. 24–36). Los Angeles, CA: Roxbury Publishing Company.

Drobnic, S., Blossfeld, H., & Rohwer, G. (1999). Dynamics of women's employment patterns over the family life course: A comparison of the United States and Germany. *Journal of Marriage and Family, 61,* 133–146.

Duncan, R. D. (1999). Peer and sibling aggression. *Journal of Interpersonal Violence, 14*(8), 871.

DuRant, R., Champion, H., Wolfson, M., Omli, M., McCoy, T., D'Agostino, R. B., Jr., Wagoner, K., & Mitra, A. (2007). Date fighting experiences among college students: Are they associated with other health-risk behaviors? *Journal of American College Health, 55*(5), 291–296.

Durkheim, E. (1888). Suicide et natalité: étude de statistique morale. *Rev philosophique France l'étranger, 26,* 446–463.

Durkheim, E. (1893/1984). *The division of labor in society.* New York, NY: Free Press.

Durkheim, E. (1933). *The division of labor in society.* New York, NY: Macmillan.

Durrant, J. E., Trocmé, N., Fallon, B., Milne, C., & Black, T. (2009). Protection of children from physical maltreatment in Canada: An evaluation of the Supreme Court's definition of reasonable force. *Journal of Aggression, Maltreatment & Trauma, 18*(1), 64–87.

Dutton, D. G. (2007). *The abusive personality: Violence and control in intimate relationships.* New York, NY: Guilford Press.

Dutton, D. G. (2010). Anger in intimate relationships. In M. Potegal, G. Stemmler, & C. Speilberger (Eds.), *International Handbook of Anger* (pp. 535–544). New York, NY: Springer.

Duxbury, L., Higgins, C., & Coghill, D. (2003). *Voices of Canadians: Seeking work–life balance.* Ottawa, ON: Health Canada.

Dwyer, J. W., Lee, G. R., & Jankowske, T. B. (1994). Reciprocity, elder satisfaction, and caregiver stress and burden: The exchange of aid in the family caregiving relationships. *Journal of Marriage and Family, 56,* 35–43.

Ebbesen, E. B., Kjos, G. L., & Konecini, V. J. (1976). Spatial ecology: Its effects on the choice of friends and enemies. *Journal of Experimental Social Psychology, 12,* 505–518.

Ebersole, P., & Hess, P. (2004). *Toward healthy aging: Human needs and nursing response.* St. Louis, MO: Mosby.

Elder, G. (1974). *Children of the Great Depression.* Chicago, IL: University of Chicago Press.

Ellis, B. J., Simpson, J. A., & Campbell, L. (2002). Trait-specific dependence in romantic relationships. *Journal of Personality, 70,* 611–659.

Ellison, C. G., & Bradshaw, M. (2009). Religious beliefs, socio-political ideology, and attitudes toward corporal punishment. *Journal of Family Issues, 30*(3), 320–340.

Ellison, N., Heino, R., & Gibbs, J. (2006). Managing impressions online: Self-presentation processes in the online dating environment. *Journal of Computer Mediated Communication, 11*(2), 415–441.

Elze, D. E. (2002). Against all odds: The dating experiences of adolescent lesbian and bisexual women. *Journal of Lesbian Studies, 6,* 17–29.

Erikson, E. (1950). *Childhood and society.* New York, NY: Norton.

Erikson, E., & Erikson J. M. (1997/1982). *The life cycle completed.* New York, NY: Norton.

Eshleman, J. R., & Wilson, S. J. (2001). *The family* (3rd ed). Toronto, ON: Pearson.

Even, W. E., & Macpherson, D. A. (2001). Children's effects on women's labor market attachment and earnings. In S. Houseman & A. Nakamura (Eds.), *Working time in comparative perspective, Volume II: Life cycle working time and non-standard work* (pp. 99–127). Kalamazoo, MI: W. E. Upjohn Institute.

Feeney, J., Hohaus, L., Noller, P., & Alexander, R. (2001). *Becoming parents: Exploring the bonds between mothers, fathers, and their infants.* New York, NY: Cambridge University Press.

Felmlee, D. H. (1998). Fatal attractions: Contradictions in intimate relationships. In J. H. Harvey (Ed.), *Perspectives on loss: A sourcebook* (pp. 113–124). New York, NY: Routledge.

Festinger, L., Schachter, S., & Back, K. W. (1950). *Social pressures in informal groups: A study of human factors in housing.* New York: Harper & Brothers.

Fincham, F. D., Harold, G. T., & Gano-Phillips, S. (2000). The longitudinal association between attributions and marital satisfaction: Direction of effects and role of efficacy expectations. *Journal of Family Psychology, 14,* 267–285.

Fine, M. A., & Harvey, J. H. (2006). *Handbook of divorce and relationship dissolution.* New York, NY: Lawrence Erlbaum.

Finke, R., & Stark, R. (1992). *The churching of America: 1776–1990.* New Brunswick, NJ: Rutgers University Press.

Finkelhor, D. (1984). *Child sexual abuse: New theory and research.* New York, NY: Free Press.

Finkelhor, D., Ormrod, R., Turner, H., & Hamby, S. L. (2005). The victimization of children and youth: A comprehensive, national survey. *Child Maltreatment, 10*(1), 5.

Floyd, F. J., & Wasner, G. H. (1994). Social exchange, equity, and commitment: Structural equation modeling of dating relationships. *Journal of Family Psychology, 8*(1), 55–73.

Foshee, V. A. (1996). Gender differences in adolescent dating abuse prevalence, types and injuries. *Health Education Research, 11*(3), 275.

Foucault, M. (1976). *Histoire de la sexualité. Tome 1: La Volonté de savoir.* Paris, France: Gallimard.

Fox, M. (2000). Age and infertility: The biological clock: Fact or fiction? Retrieved from http://www.dcmsonline.org/jax-medicine/2000journals/may2000/ageinf.htm

Fozard, J. L., & Gordon-Salant, S. (2001). Sensory and perceptual changes with aging. In J. E. Virren & K. W. Schaie (Eds.), *Handbook of the psychology of aging* (5th ed.). San Diego, CA: Academic Press.

Freedman, R., & Whelpton, P. K. (1950). Social and psychological factors affecting fertility: Fertility planning and fertility rates by religious interest and denomination. *Milbank Memorial Fund Quarterly, 28,* 294–343.

Freud, S. (2000/1905). Three essays on the theory of sexuality. (J. Strachey, Trans.). New York, NY: Basic Books.

Friedan, B. (1981). *The second stage.* New York, NY: Summit.

Friedman, H. S. (1991). *The self-healing personality: Why some people achieve health and others succumb to illness.* New York, NY: Holt.

Friendly, M. (2008). Building a strong and equal partnership between childcare and early childhood education in Canada. *International Journal of Child Care and Education Policy, 2*(1), 36–52.

Frisco, M. L., Muller, C., & Frank, K. (2007). Parents' union dissolution and adolescents' school performance: Comparing methodological approaches. *Journal of Marriage and Family, 69*(3), 721–741.

Fu, H. S., & Goldman, N. (1996). Incorporating health into models of marriage choice: Demographic and sociological perspectives. *Journal of Marriage and the Family, 58,* 740–758.

Fuller, S. (2008). Job mobility and wage trajectories for men and women in the United States. *American Sociological Review, 73*(1), 158.

Fumitaka, F. (2009). Looking for a J-shaped development-fertility relationship: Do advances in development really reverse declines? *Economics Bulletin, 29,* 3067–3074.

Furseth, I., & Repstad, P. (2006). *An introduction to the sociology of religion.* Burlington, VT: Ashgate.

Galarneau, D., & Sturrock, J. (1997). Family income after separation. *Perspectives on Labour and Income, 9,* 18–28.

Gee, E. M., Mitchell, B. A., & Wister, A. V. (2001). Homeleaving trajectories in Canada: Exploring cultural and gendered dimensions. Paper presented at the annual meetings of the Canadian Sociology and Anthropology Association and the Canadian Population Society, Laval University, Quebec City, QC.

Gershoff, E. T. (2002). Corporal punishment by parents and associated child behaviors and experiences: A meta-analytic and theoretical review. *Psychological Bulletin, 128*(4), 539.

Gescheider, G. A. (1997). *Psychophysics: The fundamentals.* Mahwah, NJ: Erlbaum.

Girard, M. (2010). Effects of non-standard work on the work-family balance: A literature review. *McGill Sociological Review, 1,* 46–58.

Glenn, N., & Marquardt, E. (2001). *Hooking up, hanging out, and hoping for Mr. Right: College women on dating and mating today.* A report conducted by the Institute for American Values for the Independent Women's Forum.

Glenn, N. D. (1998). The course of marital success and failure in five American 10-year marriage cohorts. *Journal of Marriage and the Family, 60*(3), 569–576.

Goldscheider, C. (1971). Religion, minority group status, and fertility. In C. Goldscheider (Ed.), *Population, modernization, and social structure* (pp. 270–298). Boston, MA: Little, Brown.

Goldscheider, C. (2006). Religion, family and fertility: What do we know historically and comparatively? In R. Derosas & F. van Poppel (Eds.), *Religion and the decline of fertility in the Western world* (pp. 41–57). New York, NY: Springer.

Goldscheider, F., & Goldscheider, C. (1999). *The changing transition to adulthood: Leaving and returning home.* Thousand Oaks, CA: Sage.

González, L., & Viitanen, T. K. (2009). The effect of divorce laws on divorce rates in Europe. *European Economic Review, 53*(2), 127–138.

Goode, W. (1963). *World revolution and family patterns.* New York, NY: Free Press.

Goode, W. J. (1970). *World revolution and family patterns.* New York, NY: Free Press.

Goodwin, M. P., & Roscoe, B. (1990). Sibling violence and agonistic interactions among middle adolescents. *Adolescence, 25*(98), 451–467.

Gormly, A. (1997). *Lifespan human development* (6th ed.). Fort Worth, TX: Harcourt Brace College Publishers.

Gornick, J. C., & Meyers, M. K. (2003). Welfare regimes in relation to paid work and care. *Advances in Life Course Research, 8,* 45–67.

Gottman, J. M., & Levinson, R. W. (1992). Marital processes predictive of later dissolution: Behavior, physiology, and health. *Journal of Personality and Social Psychology, 63,* 221–233.

Gottman, J. M., Coan, J., Carrère, S., & Swanson, C. (1998). Predicting marital happiness and stability from newlywed interactions. *Journal of Marriage and the Family, 60,* 5–22.

Gottman, J. M., & Silver, N. (1994). *Why marriages succeed or fail: What you can learn from the breakthrough research to make your marriage last.* New York, NY: Simon & Schuster.

Gove, W. R. (1984). Gender differences in mental and physical illness: The effects of fixed roles and nurturant roles. *Social Science and Medicine, 19,* 77–84.

Greeff, A. P., & Du Toit, C. (2009). Resilience in remarried families. *The American Journal of Family Therapy, 37*(2), 114–126.

Greenhalgh, S. (1995). Anthropology theorizes reproduction: Integrating practice, political economic, and feminist perspectives. In S. Greenhalgh (Ed.), *Situating fertility: Anthropology and demographic inquiry.* Cambridge, UK: Cambridge University Press.

Grzywacz, J. G., Almeida, D. M., & McDonald, D. A. (2002). Work–family spillover and daily reports of work and family stress in the adult labor force. *Family Relations, 51,* 28–36.

Gubrium, J. F. (1975). Being single in old age. *International Journal of Aging and Human Development, 6,* 29–41.

Gunnoe, M. L., & Mariner, C. L. (1997). Toward a developmental-contextual model of the effects of parental spanking on children's aggression. *Archives of Pediatrics and Adolescent Medicine, 151*(8), 768.

Guttman, D. (1994). *Reclaimed powers: Men and women in later life* (2nd ed.). Evanston, IL: Northwestern University Press.

Guzzo, K. B. (2008). Marital intentions and the stability of first cohabitations. *Journal of Family Issues, 30*(2), 179–205.

Gwartney-Gibbs, P. (1986). The institutionalization of premarital cohabitation: Estimates from marriage license applications, 1970 and 1980. *Journal of Marriage and the Family, 48,* 423–434.

Hagestad, G., & Uhlenberg, P. (2005). The social separation of old and young: A root of ageism. *Journal of Social Issues, 61,* 343–360.

Haig-Brown, C. (1988). *Resistance and renewal: Surviving the Indian residential school.* Vancouver, BC: Arsenal Pulp Press.

Halford, K., Nicholson, J., & Sanders, M. (2007). Couple communication in stepfamilies. *Family Process, 46*(4), 471–483.

Hall, D. R., & Zhao, J. Z. (1995). Cohabitation and divorce in Canada: Testing the selectivity hypothesis. *Journal of Marriage and Family, 57,* 421–427.

Han, S.-K. & Moen, P. (1999). Work and family over time: A life course approach. *Annals of the American Academy of Political and Social Science, 562,* 98–110.

Hans, J., Ganong, L., & Coleman, M. (2009). Financial responsibilities toward older parents and stepparents following divorce and remarriage. *Journal of Family and Economic Issues, 30*(1), 55–66.

Härkönen, J., & Dronkers, J. (2006). Stability and change in the educational gradient of divorce: A comparison of seventeen countries. *European Sociological Review, 22*(5), 501–517.

Harris, M. (1997). *Culture, people, nature: An introduction to general anthropology* (7th ed.). New York, NY: Longman.

Hartup, W. W., French, D. C., Laursen, B., Johnston, M. K., & Ogawa, J. R. (1993). Conflict and friendship relations in middle childhood: Behavior in a closed field situation. *Child Development, 64*(2), 445–454.

Hartwick, C., Desmarais, S., & Hennig, K. (2007). Characteristics of male and female victims of sexual coercion. *The Canadian Journal of Human Sexuality, 16*(1–2), 31–44.

Hassan, R. (1995). Rights of women within Islamic communities. *Canadian Women Studies, 15*(2).

Hatch, R. G. (1995). *Aging and cohabitation.* New York, NY: Garland

Hatfield, E. (1983). Equity theory and research: An overview. In H. H. Blumberg, A. P. Hare, V. Kent, & M. Davies (Eds.), *Small groups and social interaction* (Vol. 2, pp. 401–412). Chichester, UK: Wiley.

Havighurst, R. (1948). *Developmental tasks and education.* Chicago, IL: University of Chicago Press.

Hayward, M., & Zhang, Z. (2001). Demography of aging: A century of global change, 1950–2050. In R. Binstock & L. George (Eds.), *Handbook of aging and the social sciences* (pp. 69–85). New York, NY: Academic Press.

Hazan, C., & Shaver, P. R. (1987). Romantic love conceptualized as an attachment process. *Journal of Personality and Social Psychology, 52*(3), 511–524.

Health Canada. (2003). *Healthy aging: Physical activity and older adults.* Catalogue no. H39-612/2002-4E. Ottawa, ON: Minister of Public Works and Government Services Canada.

Heaton, T. B., Albrecht, S. L., & Martin, T. K. (1985). The timing of divorce. *Journal of Marriage and the Family, 47*(3), 631–639.

Helmick, R. G., & Petersen, R. L. (2002). *Forgiveness and reconciliation: Religion, public policy and conflict transformation.* West Conshohocken, PA: Templeton Foundation Press.

Hendrick, C., & Hendrick, S. S. (2003). Romantic love: Measuring cupid's arrow. In S. J. Lopez & C. R. Snyder (Eds.), *Positive psychological assessment: A handbook of models and measures* (pp. 235–249). Washington, DC: American Psychological Association.

Heuveline, P., & Timberlake, J. M. (2004). The role of cohabitation in family formation: The United States in comparative perspective. *Journal of Marriage and Family, 66,* 1214–1230.

Hewitt, B., & De Vaus, D. (2009). Change in the association between premarital cohabitation and separation, Australia 1945–2000. *Journal of Marriage and Family, 71*(2), 353–361.

Hewitt, B., Western, M., & Baxter, J. (2006). Who decides? The social characteristics of who initiates marital separation. *Journal of Marriage & Family, 68,* 1165–1177.

Hickey, M. W. (2009). Estate planning for cohabitants. *Journal of American Academy of Matrimonial Law, 1,* 1–28.

Hildebrandt, A. (2009). Honour killings: Domestic abuse by another name? CBC News. Retrieved from http://www.cbc.ca/news/canada/story/2009/07/24/f-honour-killings.html

Hill, R. (1949). *Families under stress.* Westport, CT: Greenwood Press.

Hill, R., & Rodgers, R. (1964). The developmental approach. In H. Christianson (Ed.), *Handbook of marriage and the family* (pp. 171–211). Chicago, IL: Rand McNally.

Hilton, J. M., & Macari, D. P. (1997). Grandparent involvement following divorce: A comparison in single-mother and single-father families. *Journal of Divorce and Remarriage, 28,* 203–224.

Hochschild, A., & Machung, A. (1989). *The second shift: Working parents and the revolution at home.* New York, NY: Viking Press.

Hofferth, S. L. (2006). Residential father family type and child well-being: Investment versus selection. *Demography, 43*(1), 53–77.

Hoffman, K. L., Kiecolt, K. J., & Edwards, J. N. (2005). Physical violence between siblings a theoretical and empirical analysis. *Journal of Family Issues, 26*(8), 1103.

Hogan, D. (1978). The variable order of events in the life course. *American Sociological Review, 43,* 573–586.

Hogan, D. P., & Astone, N. M. (1986). The transition to adulthood. *Annual Review of Sociology, 12,* 109–130.

Hoge, D. R., Johnson, B., & Luidens, D. A. (1994). *Vanishing boundaries: The religion of mainline Protestant baby boomers.* Louisville, KY: Westminster Press.

Holmbeck, G. N., & Hill, J. P. (1991). Conflictive engagement, positive affect, and menarche in families with seventh grade girls. *Child Development, 62*(5), 1030–1048.

Holmes, T. H., & Rahe, R. H. (1967). The social readjustment rating scale. *Journal of Psychosomatic Research, 11,* 213–218.

Hospers, J. (1967). *An introduction to philosophical analysis* (2nd ed.). Englewood Cliffs, NJ: Prentice-Hall.

Howell, J. D. (1998). Gender role experimentation in new religious movements: Clarification of the Brahma Kumari case. *Journal for the Scientific Study of Religion, 37*(3), 453–461.

Hoyer, W. J., & Verhaeghen, P. (2006). Memory aging. In J. E. Birren & K. W. Schaie (Eds.), *Handbook of the psychology of aging* (6th ed., pp. 209–232). Burlington, MA: Elsevier Academic Press.

Huang, Q., El-Khouri, B. M., Johansson, G., Lindroth, S., & Sverke M. (2007).

Women's career patterns: A study of Swedish women born in the 1950s. *Journal of Occupational and Organizational Psychology, 80*, 387–412.

Hughes, M. E., & Waite, L. J. (2009). Marital biography and health at mid-life. *Journal of Health and Social Behavior, 50*(3), 344.

Huntington, S. (1996). *Clash of civilizations and the remaking of world order.* New York, NY: Simon & Schuster.

Huston, T. L., Caughlin, J. P., Houts, R. M., Smith, S. E., & George, L. J. (2001). The connubial crucible: Newlywed years as predictors of marital delight, distress, and divorce. *Journal of Personality and Social Psychology, 80*(2), 237–252.

Huxley, A. (1932). *Brave new world.* London, UK: Chatto and Windus.

Indian and Northern Affairs Canada. (1990). Impacts of the 1985 Amendments, Vol. 5, Summary Report, p. 11.

Inhelder, B., & Piaget, J. (1958). *The growth of logical thinking from childhood to adolescence.* New York, NY: Basic Books.

Ishwaran, K. (1983). *Marriage and divorce in Canada.* New York, NY: Taylor & Francis.

Jaakkola, R., Aromaa, K., & Cantell, I. (1984). The diffusion of consensual unions in Finland in the 1970s. In *Yearbook of population research in Finland* (pp. 15–25). Helsinki, Finland: Population Research Institute.

Jacobs, J. A., & Gerson, K. (2004). *The time divide: Work, family, and gender inequality.* Cambridge, MA: Harvard University Press.

Jagger, E. (1998). Marketing the self, buying an other: Dating in a post modern, consumer society. *Sociology, 32*(4), 795–814.

Jain, S. (2003). The right to family planning, contraception and abortion: The Hindu view. In D. C. Maguire (Ed.), *Sacred rights: The case for contraception and abortion in world religions.* New York, NY: Oxford University Press.

James, W. (1983/1890). *The principles of psychology.* Cambridge, MA: Harvard University Press.

Jepsen, L. K., & Jepsen, C. A. (2002). An empirical analysis of the matching patterns of same-sex and opposite-sex couples. *Demography, 39*, 435–453.

Jesser, C. J. (1978). Male responses to direct verbal sexual initiatives of females. *Journal of Sex Research, 14*, 118–128.

Johnson, M. P. (1999). Personal, moral, and structural commitment to relationships: Experiences of choice and constraint. In J. M. Adams & W. J. Jones (Eds.), *Handbook of interpersonal commitment and relationship stability* (pp. 73–87). New York, NY: Kluwer Academic/Plenum.

Johnson, M. P. (2008). *A typology of domestic violence: Intimate terrorism, violent resistance, and situational couple violence.* Boston, MA: Northeastern University Press.

Jose, A., O'Leary, K. D., & Moyer, A. (2010). Does premarital cohabitation predict subsequent marital stability and marital quality? A meta-analysis. *Journal of Marriage and Family, 72*, 105–116.

Kahlor, L., & Eastin, M. S. (2011). Television's role in the culture of violence toward women: A study of television viewing and the cultivation of rape myth acceptance in the United States. *Journal of Broadcasting & Electronic Media, 55*(2), 215–231.

Kahn, J. R., McGill, B. S., & Bianchi, S. M. (2011). Help to family and friends: Are there gender differences at older ages? *Journal of Marriage and Family, 73*(1), 77–92.

Kalache, A., Barreto, S. M., & Keller, I. (2005). Global aging: The demographic revolution in all cultures and societies. In M. Johnson (Ed.), *The Cambridge handbook of age and ageing* (pp. 30–46). New York, NY: Cambridge University Press.

Kalliath, T., & Brough, P. (2008). Work–life balance: A review of the meaning of the balance construct. *Journal of Management and Organization, 14*, 323–327.

Kalmijn, M. (2005). Attitude alignment in marriage and cohabitation: The case of sex-role attitudes. *Personal Relationships, 12*, 521–535.

Kalmijn, M., & Poortman, A. R. (2006). His or her divorce? The gendered nature of divorce and its determinants. *European Sociological Review, 22*(2), 201.

Kamp Dush, C. M., Cohan, C. L., & Amato, P. R. (2003). The relationship between cohabitation and marital quality and stability: Change across cohorts? *Journal of Marriage and Family, 65*, 539–549.

Karren, K. J., Hafen, B. Q., Smith, N. L., & Frandsen, K. J. (2006). *Mind–body health: The effects of attitudes, emotions, and relationships* (3rd ed.). San Francisco, CA: Pearson Benjamin Cummings.

Keith, P. M. (1985). Financial well-being of older divorced/separated men and women: Findings from a panel study. *Journal of Divorce, 9,* 61–72.

Kenrik, D. T., Trost, M. R., & Kelley, K. (1987). *Females, males, and sexuality: Theories and research.* Albany, NY: State University of New York Press.

Kerckhoff, A. C., & Davis, K. E. (1962). Value consensus and need complementarity in mate selection. *American Sociological Review, 27,* 295–303.

Kertzer, D. (1995). Political-economic and cultural explanations of demographic behavior. In S. Greenhalgh (Ed.), *Situating fertility* (pp. 29–53). Cambridge, UK: Cambridge University Press.

Kertzer, D. (1997). The proper role of culture in demographic explanation. In G. W. Jones (Ed.), *The continuing demographic transition.* Oxford, UK: Clarendon Press.

Kiecolt-Glaser, J. K., Malarkey, W. B., Chee, M., Newton, T., Cavioppo, J. T., Mao, H. Y., & Glaser, R. (1993). Negative behavior during marital conflict is associated with immunological down-regulation. *Psychosomatic Medicine, 55,* 395–409.

Kiecolt-Glaser, J. K., & Newton, T. L. (2001). Marriage and health: His and hers. *Psychological Bulletin, 127,* 472–503.

Kiernan, K. (2002). The state of European unions: An analysis of data on partnership formation and dissolution. In M. Macura & G. Beets (Eds.), *Dynamics of fertility and partnership in Europe: Insights and lessons from comparative research* (Vol. 1, pp. 57–76). New York and Geneva: United Nations.

King, R. B., & Harris, K. M. (2007). Romantic relationships among immigrant adolescents. *International Migration Review, 41*(2), 344–370.

King, U. (1993). *Women and spirituality.* Basingstoke, UK: Macmillan.

King, U. (1995). *Religion and gender.* Oxford, UK: Blackwell.

King, U. & Beattie, T. (2004). *Gender, religion and diversity.* London, UK: Continuum.

King, V., & Elder, G. H., Jr. (1997). The legacy of grandparenting: Childhood experiences with grandparents and current involvement with grandchildren. *Journal of Marriage and Family, 59,* 848–859.

King, V., & Scott, M. E. (2005). A comparison of cohabiting relationships among older and younger adults. *Journal of Marriage and Family, 67*(2), 271–285.

Kline, D. W., & Schaie, K. W. (Eds.). (1996). *Handbook of the psychology of aging* (4th ed.). San Diego, CA: Academic Press.

Kline, G. H., Stanley, S. M., Markman, H. J., Olmos-Gallo, P. A., St. Peters, M., Whitton, S. W., & Prado, L. M. (2004). Timing is everything: Pre-engagement cohabitation and increased risk for poor marital outcomes. *Journal of Family Psychology, 18*(2), 311–318.

Kneip, T., & Bauer, G. (2009). Did unilateral divorce laws raise divorce rates in Western Europe? *Journal of Marriage and Family, 71*(3), 592–607.

Knodel, J. (1974). *The decline of fertility in Germany, 1871–1939.* Princeton, NJ: Princeton University Press.

Kohlberg, L. (1971). From "is" to "ought": How to commit the naturalistic fallacy and get away with it in the study of moral development. In T. Mischel (Ed.), *Cognitive development and epistemology* (pp. 151–284). New York, NY: Academic Press.

Kohn, M. (1969). *Class and conformity: A study in values.* Homewood, IL: Dorsey Press.

Korabik, K., Lero, D. S., & Whitehead, D. L. (2008). *Handbook of work–family integration: Research, theory, and best practices.* New York, NY: Academic Press.

Kotre, J. N. (1984). *Outliving the self: Generativity and the interpretation of lives.* Baltimore, MD: Johns Hopkins University Press.

Kreider, R. M., & Bureau, U. S. C. (2008). *Living arrangements of children, 2004.* Washington, DC: U.S. Department of Commerce, Economics and Statistics Administration, U.S. Census Bureau.

Kübler-Ross, E. (1969). *On death and dying.* New York, NY: Macmillan.

Kunin, I., & Davis, J. (2009). Protecting children and the custodial rights of co-habitants.

Journal of American Academy of Matrimonial Law, 1, 29–54.

Lachs, M., & Pillemar, K. (2004). Elder abuse. *Lancet, 364*(9441), 1263–1272.

Lagerspetz, K. M. J., Bjorkqvist, K., & Peltonen, T. (1988). Is indirect aggression typical of females? Gender differences in aggressiveness in 11- to 12-year-old children. *Aggressive Behavior, 14*(6), 403–414.

Laner, M. R., & Ventrone, N. A. (1998). Egalitarian daters/traditionalist dates. *Journal of Family Issues, 19,* 468–477.

Langhamer, C. (2007). Love and courtship in mid-twentieth century England. *The Historical Journal, 50*(1), 173–196.

Lareau, A. (2003). *Unequal childhoods.* Berkeley, CA: University of California Press.

LaRossa, R., & LaRossa, M. (1981). *Transition to parenthood: How infants change families.* Beverly Hills, CA: Sage.

Larzelere, R., & Kuhn, B. (2005). Comparing child outcomes of physical punishment and alternative disciplinary tactics: A meta-analysis. *Clinical and Family Psychology Review, 8,* 1–37.

Larzelere, R. E., Sather, P. R., Schneider, W. N., Larson, D. B., & Pike, P. L. (1998). Punishment enhances reasoning's effectiveness as a disciplinary response to toddlers. *Journal of Marriage and the Family, 60,* 388–403.

Laslett, P. (Ed.). (1972). *Household and family in past time.* Cambridge, UK: Cambridge University Press.

Laursen, B., Coy, K. C., & Collins, W. A. (1998). Reconsidering changes in parent–child conflict across adolescence: A meta-analysis. *Child development, 69*(3), 817–832.

Lawrence, E., Rothman, A. D., Cobb, R. J., Rothman, M. T., & Bradbury, T. N. (2008). Marital satisfaction across the transition to parenthood. *Journal of Family Psychology, 22,* 41–50.

Le Bourdais, C., & Lapierre-Adamcyk, É. (2004). Changes in conjugal life in Canada: Is cohabitation progressively replacing marriage? *Journal of Marriage and Family, 66*(4), 929–942.

Lee, G. R., & Payne, K. (2010). Changing marriage patterns since 1970: What's going

on and why? *Journal of Comparative Family Studies, 41,* 537–556.

Lee, J. A. (1988). Love styles. In R. J. Sternberg & M. L. Barnes (Eds.), *The psychology of love.* New Haven, CT: Yale University Press.

Lee, M. (2009). A path analysis on elder abuse by family caregivers: Applying the ABCX model. *Journal of Family Violence, 24*(1), 1–9.

Lehrer, E. (2000). Religion as a determinant of entry into cohabitation and marriage. In L. J. Waite (Ed.), *The ties that bind: Perspectives on marriage and cohabitation* (pp. 227–252). Hawthorne, NY: Aldine De Gruyter.

Leisering, L. (2003). Government and the life course. In J. Mortimer & M. Shanahan (Eds.), *Handbook of the life course* (pp. 202–225). New York, NY: Kluwer Academic/Plenum Press.

Leisering, L., & Walker, R. (1998). *The dynamics of modem society: Poverty, policy and welfare.* Bristol, UK: The Policy Press.

Lester, D. (1972). *Why people kill themselves.* Springfield, IL: Charles C. Thomas Publishing.

Lesthaeghe, R. (1995). The second demographic transition in Western countries: An interpretation. In K. O. Mason & A. M. Jensen (Eds.), *Gender and family change in industrialized countries.* Oxford, UK: Clarendon Press.

Levin, I. (2004). Living apart together: A new family form. *Current Sociology, 52*(2), 223–240.

Levinger, G. (1965). Marital cohesiveness and dissolution: An integrative review. *Journal of Marriage and Family, 27*(1), 19–28.

Levinger, G. (1976). A social psychological perspective on marriage dissolution. *Journal of Social Issues, 32*(1), 21–47.

Levinger, G. (1999). Duty toward whom? Reconsidering attractions and barriers as determinants of commitment in a relationship. In J. M. Adams & W. H. Jones (Eds.), *Handbook of interpersonal commitment and relationship stability* (pp. 37–52). New York, NY: Kluwer Academic/Plenum Press.

Levi-Strauss, C. (1949/1969). *Les structures élémentaires de la parenté.* (R. Needham, Trans.). Boston, MA: Beacon Press.

Lewis, R. A., & Spanier, G. B. (1979). Theorizing about the quality and stability of marriage. In

W. R. Burr, R. Hill, F. I. Nye, & I. L. Reiss (Eds.), *Contemporary theories about the family* (Vol. 1, pp. 268–294). New York, NY: Free Press.

Lichter, D. T., & Qian, Z. (2008). Serial cohabitation and the marital life course. *Journal of Marriage & Family, 70,* 861–878.

Lichter, D. T., Qian, Z., & Mellott, L. (2006). Marriage or dissolution? Union transitions among poor cohabiting women. *Demography, 43,* 223–240.

Liefbroer, A. C., & Dourleijn, E. (2006). Unmarried cohabitation and union stability: Testing the role of diffusion using data from 16 European countries. *Demography, 43,* 203–221.

Lillard, L. A., Brien, M. J., & Waite, L. J. (1995). Pre-marital cohabitation and subsequent marital dissolution: A matter of self-selection? *Demography, 32,* 437–457.

Lin, I. (2008). Consequences of parental divorce for adult children's support of their frail parents. *Journal of Marriage and Family, 70,* 113–128.

Lindsay, J. M. (2000). An ambiguous commitment: Moving into a cohabiting relationship. *Journal of Family Studies, 6,* 120–134.

Ling, P. (1989). Sex and the automobile in the jazz age. *History Today, 39,* 18–24.

Locke, K. D., & Horowitz, L. M. (1990). Satisfaction in interpersonal interactions as a function of similarity in level of dysphoria. *Journal of Personality and Social Psychology, 58,* 823–831.

Loh, C., & Gidycz, C. A. (2006). A prospective analysis of the relationship between childhood sexual victimization and perpetration of dating violence and sexual assault in adulthood. *Journal of Interpersonal Violence, 21,* 732–749.

Lonardo, R., Giordano, P., Longmore, M., & Manning, W. (2009). Parents, friends, and romantic partners: Enmeshment in deviant networks and adolescent delinquency involvement. *Journal of Youth and Adolescence, 38,* 367–383.

Lorenz, F. O., Wickrama, K. A. S., Conger, R. D., & Elder, G. H. (2006). The short-term and decade-long effects of divorce on women's midlife health. *Journal of Health and Social Behavior, 47*(2), 111.

Lupri, E., & Frideres, J. (1981). The quality of marriage and the passage of time: Marital satisfaction over the family life cycle. *Canadian Journal of Sociology, 6,* 283–305.

Luster, T., Rhoades, K., & Hass, B. (1989). The relation between parental values and parenting behavior: A test of the Kohn hypothesis. *Journal of Marriage and the Family, 51,* 139–147.

Maccoby, E., & Martin, J. (1983). Socialization in the context of the family: Parent–child interaction. In E. Hetherington (Ed.), *Handbook of child psychology* (Vol. 4, pp. 1–101). New York, NY: Wiley.

Mackey, A. L., Fromuth, M. E., & Kelly, D. B. (2010). The association of sibling relationship and abuse with later psychological adjustment. *Journal of Interpersonal Violence, 25*(6), 955–968.

Main, M., & Solomon, J. (1986). Discovery of an insecure-disorganized/disoriented attachment pattern. In T. B. Brazelton & M. W. Yogman (Eds.), *Affective development in infancy.* Norwood, NJ: Ablex Publishing.

Manning, M., Wainwright, L., & Bennett, J. (2011). The double ABCX model of adaptation in racially diverse families with a school-age child with autism. *Journal of Autism and Developmental Disorders, 41*(3), 320–331.

Manning, W. D. (1993). Marriage and cohabitation following premarital conception. *Journal of Marriage and Family, 55,* 839–850.

Manning, W. D., Cohen, J. A., & Smock, P. J. (2011). The role of romantic partners, family, and peer networks in dating couples' views about cohabitation. *Journal of Adolescent Research, 26*(1), 115.

Manning, W. D., Giordano, P. C., & Longmore, M. A. (2006). Hooking up: The relationship context of "nonrelationship" sex. *Journal of Adolescent Research, 21*(5), 459–483.

Manning, W. D., & Lamb, K. A. (2003). Adolescent well-being in cohabiting, married, and single parent families. *Journal of Marriage and Family, 65*(4), 876–893.

Manning, W. D., Longmore, M. A., & Giordano, P. C. (2007). The changing institution of marriage: Adolescents' expectations to cohabit and to marry. *Journal of Marriage and Family, 69,* 559–575.

Manning, W. D., & Smock, P. J. (2002). First comes cohabitation and then comes marriage? *Journal of Family Issues, 23,* 1065–1087.

Manning, W. D., & Smock, P. J. (2005). Measuring and modeling cohabitation: New perspectives from qualitative data. *Journal of Marriage and Family, 67,* 989–1002.

Marshall, K. (2006). Converging gender roles. *Perspectives, 7*(7). Catalogue no. 75-001-XIE. Ottawa, ON: Statistics Canada.

Marston, A. (1997). Planning for love: The politics of prenuptial agreements. *Stanford Journal Law Review, 49*(4), 887–916.

Martens, A., Goldenberg, J. L., & Greenberg, J. (2005). A terror management perspective on ageism. *Journal of Social Issues, 61,* 223–239.

Martin, J. (1990). Motherhood and power: The production of a women's culture of politics in a Mexican community. *American Ethnologist, 17,* 470–490.

Martin, P., Schoon, I., & Ross, A. (2008). Beyond transitions: Applying optimal matching analysis to life course research. *International Journal of Social Research Methodology, 11,* 179–199.

Martin, T. C., & Bumpass, L. L. (1989). Recent trends in marital disruption. *Demography, 26*(1), 37–51.

Martin, T. F., White, J. M., & Perlman, D. (2001). Religious socialization: A test of the channeling hypothesis of parental influence on adolescent faith maturity. *Journal of Adolescent Research, 18,*169–187.

Martin-Matthews, A. (1991). *Widowhood in later life.* Toronto, ON: Butterworths/Harcourt.

Marx K., & Engels, F. (1965/1865). *The German ideology.* London, UK: Lawrence & Wishart.

Mathes, E. W., & Kozak, G. (2008). The exchange of physical attractiveness for resource potential and commitment. *Journal of Evolutionary Psychology, 6,* 43–56.

Matouschek, N., & Rasul, I. (2008). The economics of the marriage contract: Theories and evidence. *Journal of Law and Economics, 51*(1), 59–110.

Mattessich, P., & Hill, R. (1987). Life cycle and family development. In M. Sussman & S. Steinmetz (Eds.), *Handbook of marriage and the family.* New York, NY: Plenum Press.

Matthews, S. (2002). *Sisters and brothers/daughters and sons: Meeting the needs of old parents.* Bloomington, IN: Unlimited.

Mayer K. U. (2004). Whose lives? How history, societies and institutions define and shape life courses. *Research in Human Development, 1,* 161–187.

Mayer, K. U. (2009). New directions in life course research. *Annual Review of Sociology, 35,* 413–433.

McClelland, G. (1983). Family size desires as measures of demand. In R. Bulatao & R. Lee (Eds.), *Determinants of fertility: A summary of knowledge (part A)* (pp. 234–277). Washington, DC: National Academy Press.

McClintock, E. A. (2010). When does race matter? Race, sex, and dating at an elite university. *Journal of Marriage and Family, 72,* 45–72.

McCubbin, H. I., Sussman, M. B., & Patterson, J. M. (1983). *Social stress and the family: Advances and developments in family stress theory and research.* London, UK: Routledge.

McDill, T., Hall, S. K., & Turell, S. C. (2006). Aging and creating families: Never-married heterosexual women over forty. *Journal of Women and Aging, 18,* 37–50.

McDonald, L. (2002). *The invisible retirement of women.* SEDAP Research Paper no. 69. Hamilton, ON: McMaster University.

McFarland, P. I., & Sanders, S. (2003). A pilot study about the needs of older gays and lesbians: What social workers need to know. *Journal of Gerontological Social Work, 40*(3), 67–80.

McGoldrick, M. (1999). Becoming a couple. In B. Carter & M. McGoldrick (Eds.), *The expanded family life cycle: Individual, family, and social perspectives* (3rd ed., pp. 231–248). Boston, MA: Allyn & Bacon.

McGoldrick, M., & Gerson, R. (1985). *Genograms in family assessment.* New York, NY: W. W. Norton.

McGregor, M. J., Ericksen, J., Ronald, L. A., Janssen, P. A., Van Vliet, A., & Schulzer, M. (2004). Rising incidence of hospital-reported drug-facilitated sexual assault in a large urban community in Canada: Retrospective population-based study. *Canadian Journal of Public Health, 95,* 441–445.

McLanahan, S., & Bumpass, L. (1988). Intergenerational consequences of family disruption. *American Journal of Sociology, 94*(7), 130–152.

McNulty, J. K., & Fisher, T. D. (2008). Gender differences in response to sexual expectancies and changes in sexual frequency: A short-term longitudinal study of sexual satisfaction in newly married couples. *Archives of Sexual Behavior, 37*(2), 229–240.

McPherson, B. D., & Wister, A. (2008). *Aging as a social process: Canadian perspectives* (5th ed.). Toronto, ON: Oxford University Press.

McPherson, M., Smith-Lovin, L, & Cook, J. M. (2001). Birds of a feather: Homophily in social networks. *Annual Review of Sociology, 27*, 415–444.

McQuillan, K. (2004). When does religion influence fertility? *Population and Development Review, 30*, 25–56.

McQuillan, K., & Ravanera, Z. R. (Eds.). (2006). *Canada's changing families: Implications for individuals and society.* Toronto, ON: University of Toronto Press.

Mead, G. H. (1934). *Mind, self and society.* Chicago, IL: University of Chicago Press.

Mead, M. (1928). *Coming of age in Samoa.* New York, NY: Morrow.

Mead, M. (1930). *Growing up in New Guinea.* New York, NY: Blue Ribbon Books.

Mendenhall, T. J., & Berge, J. M. (2010). Family therapists in trauma-response teams: Bringing systems thinking into interdisciplinary fieldwork. *Journal of Family Therapy, 32*(1), 43–57.

Meston, C. M., Trapnell, P. D., & Gorzalka, B. B. (1996). Ethnic and gender differences in sexual behaviour between Asian and non-Asian university students. *Archives of Sexual Behavior, 25*, 33–72.

Miller, J. K., Todahl, J. L., & Platt, J. J. (2010). The core competency movement in marriage and family therapy: Key considerations from other disciplines. *Journal of Marital and Family Therapy, 36*(1), 59–70.

Miller, R. S., & Perlman, D. (2009). *Intimate relationships* (5th ed.). New York, NY: McGraw-Hill.

Miller, R. S., Perlman, D., & Brehm, S. S. (2007). *Intimate relationships.* Whitby, ON: McGraw-Hill Higher Education.

Miller, S. (2011). Social institutions. In E. N. Zalta (Ed.), *The Stanford encyclopedia of philosophy.* Stanford, CA: The Metaphysics Research Lab, Stanford University.

Miller, T. W. (2010). *Handbook of stressful transitions across the lifespan.* New York, NY: Springer Verlag.

Mills, R., Alati, R., O'Callaghan, M., Najman, J. M., Williams, G. M., Bor, W., & Strathearn, L. (2011). Child abuse and neglect and cognitive function at 14 years of age: Findings from a birth cohort. *Pediatrics, 127*(1), 4–10.

Mitchell, B., Wister, A., & Burch, T. (1989). The family environment and leaving the parental home. *Journal of Marriage and the Family, 51*, 605–613.

Mitchell, B. A. (2006). The boomerang age from childhood to adulthood: Emergent trends and issues for aging families. *Canadian Studies in Population, 33*, 155–178.

Mitchell, B. A. (2006). *The boomerang age: Transitions to adulthood in families.* New Brunswick, NJ: Aldine Transaction.

Mitchell, B. A. (2009). *Family matters: An introduction to family sociology in Canada.* Toronto, ON: Canadian Scholar's Press.

Mitchell, D., & Gray, E. (2007). Declining fertility: Intention, attitudes and aspirations. *Journal of Sociology, 43*, 23–44.

Moen, P. (2003). *It's about time: Couples and careers.* Ithaca, NY: Cornell University Press.

Moore, M., & Butler, D. (1989). Predictive aspects of nonverbal courtship behavior in women. *Semiotica, 3*, 205–215.

Moore, M. M. (2010). Human nonverbal courtship behavior: A brief historical review. *Journal of Sex Research, 47*(2–3), 171–180.

Morgan, M. Y. (1987). The impact of religion on gender-role attitudes. *Psychology of Women Quarterly, 11*, 301–310.

Morgan, S. P., Lye, D. N., & Condran, G. A. (1988). Sons, daughters, and the risk of marital disruption. *American Journal of Sociology, 94*(1), 110–129.

Morgan, S. P., & Rackin, H. (2010). A half century of fertility change. *Journal of Comparative Family Studies, 41*, 515–536.

Morton, S. (1992). The June bride as the working-class bride: Getting married in a Halifax working-class neighbourhood in the 1920s. In B. Bradbury (Ed.), *Canadian family history: Selected readings* (pp. 360–379). Toronto, ON: Copp Clark Pitman.

Moustgaard, H., & Martikainen, P. (2009). Nonmarital cohabitation among older Finnish men and women: Socioeconomic characteristics and forms of union dissolution. *The Journals of Gerontology Series B: Psychological Sciences and Social Sciences, 64B,* 507–516.

Muehlenhard, C. L., & Linton, M. A. (1987). Date rape and sexual aggression in dating situations: Incidence and risk factors. *Journal of Counseling Psychology, 34*(2), 186–196.

Mulder, C. H. (2003). The effects of singlehood and cohabitation on the transition to parenthood in the Netherlands. *Journal of Family Issues, 24,* 291–313.

Murray, R. B., Zentner, J. P., Pangman, V., & Pangman, C. (2006). *Health promotion strategies through the lifespan* (Canadian ed.). Toronto, ON: Pearson Prentice Hall.

Murstein, B. I. (1980). Mate selection in the 1970s. *Journal of Marriage and the Family, 42,* 777–792.

Murstein, B. I. (1986). *Paths to marriage.* Beverly Hills, CA: Sage.

Murstein, B. I. (1987). A clarification and extension of the SVR theory of dyadic pairing. *Journal of Marriage and the Family, 49,* 929–933.

Must, A., Spadano, J., Coakley, E. H., Field, A. E., Colditz, G., & Dietz, W. H. (1999). The disease burden associated with overweight and obesity. *Journal of the American Medical Association, 282,* 1523–1529.

Mustard, J. F. (2006). *Early child development and experience-based brain development: The scientific underpinnings of the importance of early child development in a globalized world.* Washington, DC: The Brookings Institution.

Myrskyla, M., Kohler, H., & Billani, F. (2009). Advances in development reverse fertility declines. *Nature, 460,* 741–743.

Natayanan, V. (1990). Hindu perceptions of auspiciousness and sexuality. In J. Becher (Ed.), *Women, religion, and sexuality: Studies on the impact of religious teachings on women.* Geneva, Switzerland: World Council of Churches Publications.

National Advisory Council on Aging. (2003–2004). Hidden harm: The abuse of seniors. *Expressions: Bulletin of the NACA, 17*(1). Ottawa, ON: Author.

National Advisory Council on Aging. (2004). The seniors of Canada's Far North. *Expressions: Bulletin of the NACA, 17*(2). Ottawa, ON: Author.

National Campaign to Prevent Teen and Unplanned Pregnancy. (2008). Retrieved from http://www.thenationalcampaign.org/sextech/PDF/SexTech_PressReleaseFIN.pdf

Nazio, T., & Blossfeld, H. (2003). The diffusion of cohabitation among young women in West Germany, East Germany and Italy. *European Journal of Population, 19,* 47–82.

Nelson, A., & Robinson, B. W. (2002). *Gender in Canada* (2nd ed). Toronto, ON: Pearson.

Nett, E. (1988). *Canadian families: Past and present.* Toronto, ON: Butterworths.

Newsome, J., & Schulz, R. (1996). Social support as a mediator in the relations between functional status and quality of life in older adults. *Psychology and Aging, 11,* 34–44.

Nock, S. L., Sanchez, L. A., & Wright, J. D. (2008). *Covenant marriage: The movement to reclaim tradition in America.* New Brunswick, NJ: Rutgers University Press.

Norris, S. (2001). *Reproductive infertility: Prevalence, causes, trends and treatments.* Ottawa, ON: Parliamentary Research Branch, Library of Parliament. Retrieved from http://dsp-psd.pwgsc.gc.ca/Collection-R/LoPBdP/EB-e/prb0032-e.pdf

Novak, M., & Campbell, L. (2010). *Aging and society: A Canadian perspective* (6th ed.). Toronto, ON: Nelson Education.

Nye, F. I. (1979). Choice, exchange, and the family. In W. R. Burr, R. Hill, F. I. Nye, & I. L. Reiss (Eds.), *Contemporary theories about the family: General theories/theoretical orientations, Volume II.* New York, NY: Free Press.

Oderkirk, J. (1994). Marriage in Canada: Changing beliefs and behaviours 1600–1990. *Canadian Social Trends, 33,* 2–7.

Ogburn, W. F. (1937). The influence of inventions on American social institutions in the future. *The American Journal of Sociology, 43,* 365–376.

O'Leary, K. D., Malone, J., & Tyree, A. (1994). Physical aggression in early marriage: Prerelationship and relationship effects. *Journal of Consulting and Clinical Psychology, 62*(3), 594–602.

Olson, D. H., Sprenkle, D. H., & Russell, C. S. (1979). Circumplex model of marital and family systems: I. Cohesion and adaptability dimensions, family types, and clinical applications. *Family Process, 18*(1), 3–28.

O'Neill, W. L. (1965). Divorce in the progressive era. *American Quarterly, 17*(2), 203–217.

Oppenheimer, V. (1997). Women's employment and the gain to marriage: The specialization and trading model. *Annual Review of Sociology, 23*, 431–453.

Oppenheimer, V. K. (1994). Women's rising employment and the future of the family in industrial societies. *Population and Development Review, 20*(2), 293–342.

Oppenheimer, V. K. (2003). Cohabiting and marriage during young men's career-development process. *Demography, 40*, 127–149.

Organisation for Economic Co-operation and Development. (2001). *Society at a glance 2001*. Paris, France: OECD Publishing.

Organisation for Economic Co-operation and Development. (2007). *Babies and bosses: Reconciling work and family life: A synthesis of findings for OECD countries*. Paris, France: OECD Publishing.

Ortmayr, N. (1997). Church, marriage, and legitimacy in the British West Indies (nineteenth and twentieth centuries). *The History of the Family, 2*(2), 141–170.

Ory, M. G., Hoffman, R. R., Yee, J. L., Tennstedt, S., & Schulz, R. (1999). Prevalence and impact of caregiving: A detailed comparison between dementia and nondementia caregivers. *The Gerontologist, 39*(2), 177.

O'Sullivan, L. P., & Allgeier, E. R. (1998). Feigning sexual desire: Consenting to unwanted sexual activity in heterosexual dating relationships. *Journal of Sex Research, 35*, 234–243.

Ozorak, E. W. (1996). The power, but not the glory: How women empower themselves through religion. *Journal for the Scientific Study of Religion, 1*, 17–29.

Pagani, L. S., Japel, C., Vaillancourt, T., & Tremblay, R. E. (2010). Links between middle-childhood trajectories of family dysfunction and indirect aggression. *Journal of Interpersonal Violence, 25*(12), 2175–2198.

Papademtriou, D. G., & Terrazas, A. (2009). *Immigrants and the current economic crisis: Research evidence, policy changes, and implications*. Washington, DC: Migration Policy Institute.

Parsons, T. (1954). The kinship system in the contemporary United States. In T. Parsons (Ed.), *Essays in sociological theory*. Glencoe, IL: Free Press.

Parsons, T., & Bales, R. F. (1955). *Family, socialization and interaction process*. Glencoe, IL: Free Press.

Patterson, C. J. (2006). Children of lesbian and gay parents. *Current Directions in Psychological Science, 15*(5), 241.

Paveza, G. J., Cohen, D., Eisdorfer, C., Freels, S., Semla, T., Ashford, J. W., . . . Levy, P. (1992). Severe family violence and Alzheimer's disease: Prevalence and risk factors. *The Gerontologist, 32*(4), 493.

Pearce, L. D. (2002). The influence of early life course religious exposure on young adults' dispositions toward childbearing. *Journal for the Scientific Study of Religion, 41*, 325–340.

Peek, C., Fisher, J., & Kidwell, J. (1985). Teenage violence towards parents: A neglected aspect of family violence. *Journal of Marriage and the Family, 47*, 1051–1058.

Peterson, D. R. (2002). Conflict. In H. H. Kelley, E. Berscheid, A. Christensen, J. H. Harvey, T. L. Huston, G. Levinger, . . . D. R. Peterson (Eds.), *Close relationships* (pp. 265–314). Clinton Corners, NY: Percheron Press.

Peterson, G. W., & Hann, D. (1999). Socializing children and parents in families. In M. Sussman, S. Steinmetz, & G. Peterson (Eds.), *Handbook of marriage and the family* (2nd ed., pp. 327–370). New York, NY: Plenum Publications.

Phelan, P. (1986). The process of incest: Biologic father and stepfather families. *Child Abuse & Neglect, 10*(4), 531–539.

Phillips, J. A., & Sweeney, M. M. (2005). Premarital cohabitation and marital disruption among white, black, and Mexican American women. *Journal of Marriage & Family, 67*, 296–314.

Phillips, R. (1991). *Untying the knot: A short history of divorce*. Cambridge, UK: Cambridge University Press.

Piaget, J. (1952/1936). *The origins of intelligence in children*. New York, NY: International University Press.

Pillemer, K., & Suitor, J. J. (1992). Violence and violent feelings: What causes them among family caregivers? *Journal of Gerontology*, 47(4), S165.

Plagnol, A., & Easterlin, R. (2008). Aspirations, attainments, and satisfaction: Life cycle differences between American women and men. *Journal of Happiness Studies*, 9(4), 601–619.

Pollock, G. (2007). Holistic trajectories: A study of combined employment, housing and family careers by using multiple-sequence analysis. *Journal of the Royal Statistical Society: Series A (Statistics in Society)*, 170, 167–183.

Popenoe, D. (1988). *Disturbing the nest: Family change and decline in modern societies*. New Brunswick, NJ: Transaction Publishers.

Popenoe, D. (2009). Cohabitation, marriage, and child well-being: A cross-national perspective. *Society*, 46(5), 429–436.

Proudfoot, S. (2010). Canada's families: The incredible shrinking family. *Vancouver Sun*, October 7.

Pudrovska, T., Scott, S., & Deborah, C. (2006). Strains of singlehood in later life: Do race and gender matter? *Journal of Gerontology*, 61B, S315–S322.

Puts, D. A. (2005). Mating context and menstrual phase affect women's preferences for male voice pitch. *Evolution and Human Behavior*, 26, 388–397.

Ranson, G. (1998). Education, work and family decision making: Finding the "right time" to have a baby. *Canadian Review of Sociology and Anthropology*, 35, 517–533.

Reiss, I. L. (1967). *The social context of premarital sexual permissiveness*. New York, NY: Holt, Rinehart and Winston.

Reiss, I. L., & Miller, B. C. (1979). Heterosexual permissiveness: A theoretical analysis. *Contemporary Theories about the Family*, 1, 57–100.

Rhodes, G. (2006). The evolutionary psychology of facial beauty. *Annual Review of Psychology*, 57, 199–226.

Rhyne, D. (1981). Bases of marital satisfaction among men and women. *Journal of Marriage and the Family*, 43, 941–955.

Richer, S. (1968). The economics of child rearing. *Journal of Marriage and the Family*, 30, 462–466.

Richmond-Abbott, M. (1983). *Masculine and feminine: Sex roles over the life cycle*. Reading, MA: Addison-Wesley.

Riessman, C. K., & Gerstel, N. (1985). Marital dissolution and health: Do males or females have greater risk? *Social Science and Medicine*, 20, 627–635.

Riley, M. W. (1998). A life course approach: Autobiographical notes. In J. Giele & G. H. Elder, Jr. (Eds.), *Methods of life course research: Qualitative and quantitative approaches*. Thousand Oaks, CA: Sage Publications.

Rindfuss, R., Choe, K., Bumpass, L., & Tsuya, N. (2004). Social networks and family change in Japan. *American Sociological Review*, 69, 838–861.

Ritchie, D. (1997). Parents' workplace experiences and family communication patterns. *Communications Research*, 24, 175–187.

Robles, T. F., & Kiecolt-Glaser, J. K. (2003). The physiology of marriage: Pathways to health. *Physiology & Behavior*, 79, 409–416.

Rodgers, R. H., & White, J. M. (1993). Family development theory. In P. Boss, W. Doherty, R. LaRossa, W. Schumm, & S. Steinmetz (Eds.), *Sourcebook of family theories and methods: A contextual approach* (pp. 225–254). New York, NY: Plenum.

Roehlkepartain, C., & Benson, P. L. (1993). *Youth in Protestant churches*. Minneapolis, MN: Search Institute.

Rogoff, B. (2003). *The culture nature of human development*. New York, NY: Oxford University Press.

Rollins, B., & Feldman, H. (1970). Marital satisfaction over the family life cycle. *Journal of Marriage and the Family*, 32, 20–27.

Ross, C. E., Mirowsky, J., & Goldsteen, K. (1990). The impact of family on health: The decade in review. *Journal of Marriage and the Family*, 52, 1059–1078.

Rossi, A. S. (1968). Transition to parenthood. *Journal of Marriage and the Family*, 30, 26–39.

Rotermann, M. (2008). Trends in teen sexual behaviour and condom use. *Health Reports*, 19(3).

Rothman, S. M. (1978). *Women's proper place: A history of changing ideals and practices: 1870 to the present*. New York, NY: Basic Books.

Rowe, J., & Kahn, R. (1997). Successful aging. *The Gerontologist*, 37(4), 433–440.

Ruan, F. F. (1991). *Sex in China: Studies in sexology in Chinese culture*. New York, NY: Plenum Press.

Rubinstein, R. L. (1987). Never married elderly as a social type: Re-evaluating some images. *The Gerontologist, 27*, 8–113.

Rubinstein, R. L., Alexander, B. B., Goodman, M., & Luborsky, M. (1991). Key relationships of never married, childless older women: A cultural analysis. *Journal of Gerontology, 46*, S270–S277.

Ruiz, S. A., & Silverstein, M. (2007). Relationships with grandparents and the emotional well-being of late adolescent and young adult grandchildren. *Journal of Social Issues, 63*(4), 793–808.

Russell, C. S. (1974). Transition to parenthood: Problems and gratifications. *Journal of Marriage and the Family, 36*, 294–302.

Russell, D. E. H. (1986). *The secret trauma: Incest in the lives of girls and women*. New York, NY: Basic Books.

Russell, G. (1986). Grandfathers: Making up for lost opportunities. In R. A. Lewis & R. E. Salt (Eds.), *Men in families* (pp. 233–259). Beverly Hills, CA: Sage.

Ryff, C. D. (1995). Psychological well-being in adult life. *Current Directions in Psychological Science, 4*(4), 99–104.

Ryff, C. D., & Singer, B. H. (2005). Social environments and the genetics of aging: Advancing knowledge of protective health mechanisms. *Journal of Gerontology: Series B, 60B*, 12–23.

Rymer, R. (1993). *Genie: A scientific tragedy*. New York, NY: HarperCollins.

Sabo, D. F., Gray, P. M., & Moore, L. A. (2000). Domestic violence and televised athletic events: It's a man thing. In J. McKay, M. A. Messner, & D. F. Sabo (Eds.), *Masculinities, gender relations, and sport* (pp. 127–146). Thousand Oaks, CA: Sage.

Sahlstein, E. M. (2006). The trouble with distance. In D. C. Kirkpatrick, S. Duck, & M. K. Foley (Eds.), *Relating difficulty: The processes of constructing and managing difficult interaction* (pp. 119–140). Mahwah, NJ: Erlbaum.

Sassler, S. (2004). The process of entering into cohabiting unions. *Journal of Marriage and Family, 66*(2), 491–505.

Sassler, S., Cunningham, A., & Lichter, D. T. (2009). Intergenerational patterns of union formation and relationship quality. *Journal of Family Issues, 30*(6), 757–786.

Scanzoni, J. (1975). *Sex roles, life styles, and child-bearing*. New York, NY: Free Press.

Schaie, K. W. (1990). The optimization of cognitive functioning in old age: Predictions based on cohort-sequential and longitudinal data. In P. B. Baltes & M. M. Baltes (Eds.), *Successful aging: Perspectives from the behavioral sciences* (pp. 94–117). Cambridge, UK: Cambridge University Press.

Scheflen, A. E. (1965). Quasi-courtship behavior in psychotherapy. *Psychiatry, 28*, 245–257.

Schellenberg, G., & Ostrovsky, Y. (2008). Retiring together, or not. *Perspectives on Labour and Income, 9*(4). Catalogue no. 75-001-X. Ottawa, ON: Statistics Canada.

Schoen, R. (1992). First unions and the stability of first marriages. *Journal of Marriage and Family, 54*, 281–284.

Schoen, R., Kim, Y., Nathanson, C., Fields, J., & Astone, N. M. (1997). Why do Americans want children? *Population and Development Review, 23*, 333–358.

Schoen, R., Rogers, S. J., & Amato, P. R. (2006). Wives' employment and spouses' marital happiness. *Journal of Family Issues, 27*(4), 506.

Schoen, R., Urton, W., Woodrow, K., & Baj, J. (1985). Marriage and divorce in twentieth century American cohorts. *Demography, 22*(1), 101–114.

Schoon, I., McCulloch, A., Joshi, H., Wiggins, R. D., & Bynner, J. (2001). Transitions from school to work in a changing social context. *Young, 9*, 4–22.

Schumacher, J. A., & Leonard, K. E. (2005). Husbands' and wives' marital adjustment, verbal aggression, and physical aggression as longitudinal predictors of physical aggression in early marriage. *Journal of Consulting and Clinical Psychology, 73*(1), 28–37.

Schusky, E. L. (1965). *Manual for kinship analysis*. New York, NY: Holt, Rinehart & Winston.

Seccombe, K., & Ishii-Kuntz, M. (1994). Gender and social relationships among the never-married. *Sex Roles, 30*, 585–603.

Seccombe, K., & Lee, G. R. (1987). Female status, wives' autonomy, and divorce: A cross-cultural study. *Family Perspective, 20,* 241–249.

Seiger, C. P., & Wiese, B. S. (2011). Social support, unfulfilled expectations, and affective well-being on return to employment. *Journal of Marriage and Family, 73*(2), 446–458.

Seltzer, J. A. (2004). Cohabitation in the United States and Britain: Demography, kinship and the future. *Journal of Marriage and Family, 66,* 921–928.

Simonelli, C. J., Mullis, T., Elliott, A. N., & Pierce, T. W. (2002). Abuse by siblings and subsequent experiences of violence within the dating relationship. *Journal of Interpersonal Violence, 17*(2), 103.

Simpson, J. A., Campbell, B., & Berscheid, E. (1986). The association between romantic love and marriage: Kephart (1967) twice revisited. *Personality and Social Psychology Bulletin, 12,* 363–372.

Singh, D. (2004). Mating strategies of young women: Role of physical attractiveness. *Journal of Sex Research, 41,* 43–54.

Skipper, J. K., Jr., & Nass, G. (1968). Dating behaviour: A framework for analysis and an illustration. In M. B. Sussman (Ed.), *Sourcebook in marriage and the family* (3rd ed., pp. 211–220). Boston, MA: Houghton Mifflin.

Slade, E., & Wissow, L. (2004). Spanking in early childhood and later behavior problems: A prospective study of infants and young toddlers. *Pediatrics, 113,* 1321–1330.

Sleebos, J. (2003). *Low fertility rates in OECD countries: Facts and policy responses.* Paris, France: OECD Employment, Labour and Social Affairs Committee.

Smetana, J. G., & Asquith, P. (1994). Adolescents' and parents' conceptions of parental authority and personal autonomy. *Child Development, 65*(4), 1147–1162.

Smock, P. J. (2000). Cohabitation in the United States: An appraisal of research themes, findings, and implications. *Annual Review of Sociology, 26,* 1–20.

Smock, P. J., Casper, L. M., & Wyse, J. (2008). *Non-marital cohabitation: Current knowledge and future directions for research.* Ann Arbor, MI: Population Studies Center, University of Michigan.

Snyder, A. R. (2006). Risky and casual sexual relationships among teens. In A. C. Crouter & A. Booth (Eds.), *Romance and sex in adolescence and emerging adulthood: Risks and opportunities* (pp. 161–170). Mahwah, NJ: Lawrence Erlbaum.

Soble, A. (2002). *Philosophy of sex* (4th ed.). Landham, MD: Rowman and Littlefield.

South, S. J., & Spitze, G. (1986). Determinants of divorce over the marital life course. *American Sociological Review, 51*(4), 583–590.

Spock, B. (1985/1946). *Baby and child care.* New York, NY: Pocket Books.

Sprecher, S., & Felmlee, D. (1992). The influence of parents and friends on the quality and stability of romantic relationships: A three wave attitudinal investigation. *Journal of Marriage and the Family, 54,* 888–900.

Stafford, L., Kline, S. L., & Rankin, C. T. (2004). Married individuals, cohabiters, and cohabiters who marry: A longitudinal study of relational and individual well-being. *Journal of Social and Personal Relationships, 21*(2), 231.

Stanley, S. M., Markman, H. J., & Whitton, S. W. (2002). Communication, conflict, and commitment: Insights on the foundations of relationship success from a national survey. *Family Process, 41*(4), 659–675.

Stanley, S. M., Rhoades, G. K., Amato, P. R., Markman, H. J., & Johnson, C. A. (2010). The timing of cohabitation and engagement: Impact on first and second marriages. *Journal of Marriage and Family, 72,* 906–918.

Stanley, S. M., Rhoades, G. K., & Markman, H. J. (2006). Sliding versus deciding: Inertia and the premarital cohabitation effect. *Family Relations, 55,* 499–509.

Stark, R., & Bainbridge, W. S. (1985). *The future of religion: Secularization, revival and cult formation.* Berkeley, CA: University of California Press.

Statistics Canada. (2001). *Living arrangements of seniors aged 65 and over by sex and age group, Canada.* Retrieved from http://www.statcan.gc.ca/pub/89-582-x/t/4152839-eng.htm

Statistics Canada. (2002). Vital statistics, birth and death databases: Estimates of population by age and sex for Canada, the provinces and the territories.

Statistics Canada. (2003a). Ethnic diversity survey. Retrieved from http://www.statcan.gc.ca/cgi-bin/imdb/p2SV.pl?Function=getSurvey&SDDS=4508&lang=en&db=imdb&adm=8&dis=2

Statistics Canada. (2003b). The retirement wave. *The Daily*, February 21. Retrieved from http://www.statcan.gc.ca/pub/75-001-x/00203/6449-eng.html

Statistics Canada. (2005a). Demography division, annual demographic statistics 2005. Catalogue no. 91-213-X and CANSIM table 051-0001.

Statistics Canada. (2005b). Early sexual intercourse, condom use and sexually transmitted diseases. *The Daily*, May 3. Retrieved from http://www.statcan.ca/Daily/English/050503/d050503a.htm

Statistics Canada. (2005c). *Projections of the Aboriginal populations, Canada, provinces and territories: 2001 to 2017*. Catalogue no. 91-547-XIE. Ottawa, ON: Minister of Industry.

Statistics Canada. (2006a). *Annual demographic statistics, 2005*. Catalogue no. 91-213. Ottawa, ON: Author.

Statistics Canada. (2006b). CANSIM 2006, live births by marital status of mother, Canada, provinces and territories, annual. Table 102-4506.

Statistics Canada. (2006c). *Census of population*. Catalogue no. 97-552-XCB2006007.

Statistics Canada. (2006d). *Census of population*. Catalogue no. 97-553-XCB2006025.

Statistics Canada. (2006e). Child care: An eight year profile. *The Daily*, April 5. Retrieved from http://www.statcan.gc.ca/daily-quotidien/060405/dq060405a-eng.htm

Statistics Canada. (2006f). *Child care in Canada*. Catalogue no. 89-599-MIE2006003. Retrieved from http://www.statcan.gc.ca/pub/89-599-m/89-599-m2006003-eng.pdf

Statistics Canada. (2006g). *The wealth of Canadians: An overview of the results of survey of financial security, 2005*. Catalogue no. 13F0026ME2006001. Ottawa, ON: Author.

Statistics Canada. (2007a). 2006 census: Families, marital status, households and dwelling characteristics. *The Daily*, September 12. Retrieved from http://www.statcan.gc.ca/daily-quotidien/070912/dq070912a-eng.htm

Statistics Canada. (2007b). *Leading causes of death in Canada*. Catalogue no. 84-215-XWE. Ottawa, ON: Minister of Industry.

Statistics Canada. (2007c). *Portrait of the Canadian population in 2006, by age and sex, 2006*. Catalogue no. 97-551XIE. Ottawa, ON: Author.

Statistics Canada. (2008). Aboriginal peoples in Canada in 2006: Inuit, Métis and First Nations, 2006 census. *The Daily*, January 15. Retrieved from http://www.statcan.gc.ca/daily-quotidien/080115/dq080115a-eng.htm

Statistics Canada. (2009). *Income trends in Canada 1976–2007*. Catalogue no. 13F0022XCB. Ottawa, ON: Author.

Statistics Canada. (2010). Canadian vital statistics, marriage database. CANSIM Tables 101-1011 and 101-1012.

Steinberg, L. (1990). Autonomy, conflict, and harmony in the family relationship. In S. S. Feldman & G. R. Elliott (Eds.), *At the threshold: The developing adolescent* (pp. 255–276). Cambridge, MA: Harvard University Press.

Steinmetz, S. (1979). Disciplinary techniques and their relationship to aggressiveness, dependency, and conscience. In W. Burr et al. (Eds.), *Contemporary theories about the family* (Vol. 1, pp. 405–438). New York, NY: The Free Press.

Stepan, C. (2003). Seniors are becoming moms and dads again. *Hamilton Spectator*, December 11.

Stets, J. (1992). Interactive process in dating aggression: A national study. *Journal of Marriage and the Family, 52*, 501–514.

Stevens, J. C., Cruz, A., Marks, L. E., & Lakatos, S. (1998). A multimodal assessment of sensory thresholds in aging. *Journals of Gerontology: Psychological Sciences, 53B*, 263–272.

Stewart, M., Burns, A., & Leonard, R. (2007). Negative side of the mothering role: Abuse of mothers by adolescent and adult children. *Sex Roles, 56*(3–4), 183–191.

Stolzenberg, R. M., Blair-Loy, M., & Waite, L. J. (1995). Religious participation in early adulthood: Age and family life cycle effects on church membership. *American Sociological Review, 60*, 84–103.

Stone, E. A., Shakelford, T. K., & Buss, D. M. (2007). Sex ratio and mate preferences: A cross-cultural investigation. *European Journal of Psychology, 37*, 288–296.

Straus, M. (1996). Spanking and the making of a violent society. *Pediatrics, 98*, 837–842.

Straus, M., & Donnelly, D. (2001). *Beating the devil out of them*. New Brunswick, NJ: Transaction Publishers.

Straus, M., & Paschall, M. (1999). Corporal punishment by mothers and child's cognitive development: A longitudinal study. In M. Straus (Ed.), *The primordial violence*. Walnut Creek, CA: Alta Mira Press.

Straus, M. A., Sugarman, D. B., & Giles-Sims, J. (1997). Spanking by parents and subsequent antisocial behavior of children. *Archives of Pediatrics and Adolescent Medicine, 151*(8), 761.

Strohschein, L. (2005). Parental divorce and child mental health trajectories. *Journal of Marriage and Family, 67*(5), 1286–1300.

Struckman-Johnson, C., & Struckman-Johnson, D. (1994). Men pressured and forced into sexual experience. *Archives of Sexual Behaviour, 23*, 93–114.

Stull, D. E., & Scarisbrick-Hauser, A. (1989). Never married elderly: A reassessment with implications for long-term care policy. *Research on Aging, 11*, 124–139.

Swami, V., Greven, C., & Furnham, A. (2007). More than just skin deep? A pilot study integrating physical and non-physical factors in the perception of physical attractiveness. *Personality and Individual Differences, 42*, 563–572.

Sweeney, M. M. (2010). Remarriage and step-families: Strategic sites for family scholarship in the 21st century. *Journal of Marriage and Family, 72*(3), 667–684.

Sweeney, M. M., & Phillips, J. A. (2004). Understanding racial differences in marital disruption: Recent trends and explanations. *Journal of Marriage and Family, 66*(3), 639–650.

Swenson, D. (2008). *Religion and family links*. New York, NY: Springer.

Symons, D. (1979). *The evolution of human sexuality*. New York, NY: Oxford University Press.

Talbott, M. M. (1998). Older widows' attitudes towards men and remarriage. *Journal of Aging Studies, 12*, 429–449.

Teachman, J. D. (1983). Early marriage, premarital fertility, and marital dissolution. *Journal of Family Issues, 4*(1), 105.

Teachman, J. D. (2002). Stability across cohorts in divorce risk factors. *Demography, 39*(2), 331–351.

Teachman, J. D. (2003). Premarital sex, premarital cohabitation, and the risk of subsequent marital dissolution among women. *Journal of Marriage and Family, 65*, 444–455.

Teachman, J. D. (2008). Complex life course patterns and the risk of divorce in second marriages. *Journal of Marriage & Family, 70*, 294–305.

Teachman, J. D., & Polonko, K. A. (1990). Cohabitation and marital stability in the United States. *Social Forces, 69*, 207–220.

Ternikar, F. B. (2004). Revisioning the ethnic family: An analysis of marriage patterns among Hindu, Muslim, and Christian South Asian immigrants. *Dissertation Abstracts International, 65*(8), 3176A–3177A.

Testa, M., & Dermen, K. H. (1999). The differential correlates of sexual coercion and rape. *Journal of Interpersonal Violence, 14*, 548–561.

Therborn, G. (2004). *Between sex and power: Family in the world, 1900–2000*. London, UK: Routledge.

Thibaut, J. W., & Kelley, H. H. (1959). *The social psychology of groups*. New York, NY: Wiley.

Thomas, A., & Chess, S. (1968). *Temperament and behavior disorders in children*. New York, NY: New York University Press.

Thornton, A., Axinn, W. G., & Xie, Y. (2007). *Marriage and cohabitation*. Chicago, IL: University of Chicago Press.

Tremblay, H., & Capon, P. (1988). *Families of the world: Family life at the close of the twentieth century*. New York, NY: Farrar, Straus and Giroux.

Trocmé, N., Fallon, B., MacLaurin, B., Daciuk, J., Felstiner, C., Black, T., . . . Cloutier, R. (2005). *Canadian incidence study of reported child abuse and neglect—2003: Major findings*. Ottawa, ON: Minister of Public Works and Government Services Canada.

Troll, L. E. (1985). The contingencies of grandparenting. In V. L. Bengston & J. F. Robertson (Eds.), *Grandparenthood* (pp. 63–74). Beverly Hills, CA: Sage.

Trost, J. (2010). The social institution of marriage. *Journal of Comparative Family Studies, 41*, 507–513.

Trovato, F. (1988). A macrosociological analysis of change in the marriage rate: Canadian women, 1921–25 to 1981–85. *Journal of Marriage and the Family, 50,* 507–521.

Tucker, M. B., & Mitchell-Kernan, C. (1995). *The decline in marriage among African Americans: Causes, consequences, and policy implications.* New York, NY: Russell Sage Foundation.

Turner, H. A., & Finkelhor, D. (1996). Corporal punishment as a stressor among youth. *Journal of Marriage and the Family, 58*(1), 155–166.

Tversky, A., & Kahneman, D. (1988). Rational choice and the framing of decisions. In D. E. Bell, H. Raiffa, & A. Tversky (Eds.), *Decision making: Descriptive, normative and prescriptive interactions* (pp. 167–192). Cambridge, UK: Cambridge University Press.

Twenge, J., Campbell, W., & Foster, C. (2003). Parenthood and marital satisfaction: A meta-analytic review. *Journal of Marriage and Family, 65*(3), 574–583.

Uhlenberg, P. (2004). Historical forces shaping grandparent–grandchild relationships: Demography and beyond. *Annual Review of Gerontology and Geriatrics, 24,* 77–97.

Uhlenberg, P., & Mueller, M. (2004). Family context and individual well-being. In J. T. Mortimer & M. J. Shanahan (Eds.), *Handbook of the life course* (pp. 123–148). New York, NY: Springer.

Uller, T., & Johansson, C. (2003). Human mate choice and the wedding ring effect: Are married men more attractive? *Human Nature, 14*(3), 267–276.

Umberson, D. (1987). Family status and health behaviors: Social control as a dimension of social integration. *Journal of Health and Social Behavior, 28,* 306–319.

United Nations General Assembly. (2006). *In-depth study on all forms of violence against women.* Retrieved from http://daccessdds.un.org/doc/UNDOC/GEN/N06/419/74/PDF/N0641974.pdf?OpenElement

Valiant, C., & Valiant, G. (1993). Is the U-curve of marital satisfaction an illusion? A 40-year study of marriage. *Journal of Marriage and the Family, 55,* 230–239.

van den Berghe, P. (1979). *Human family systems.* New York, NY: Elsevier North-Holland.

Van Poppel, F., & Derosas, R. (Eds.). (2006). *Religion and the decline of fertility in the Western world.* New York, NY: Springer.

Vanderbilt, H. (1992). Incest: A chilling report. *Lear's, 29,* 49–64.

Vanier Institute of the Family. (2010). *Families count: Profiling Canada's families IV.* Ottawa, ON: Author.

Ventura, S. J., & Bachrach, C. A. (2000). Nonmarital childbearing in the United States, 1940–1999 (National Vital Statistics Reports, Vol. 48, No. 16). Washington, DC: National Center for Health Statistics.

Vosko, L., Zukewich, N., & Cranford, C. (2003). Precarious jobs: A new typology of employment. *Perspectives on Labour and Income, 15,* 39–49.

Voydanoff, P. (1987). *Work and family life.* Beverly Hills, CA: Sage.

Voydanoff, P. (2007). *Work, family, and community: Exploring interconnections.* Mahwah, NJ: Lawrence Erlbaum Associates.

Vygotsky, L. S. (1978). *Mind and society: The development of higher mental processes.* Cambridge, MA: Harvard University Press.

Waaldijk, K. (Ed.). (2004). *More or less together: Levels of legal consequences of marriage, cohabitation and registered partnerships for different-sex and same-sex partners.* Paris, France: Institut National d'Etudes Demographiques.

Waite, L. J., Luo, Y., & Lewin, A. C. (2009). Marital happiness and marital stability: Consequences for psychological well-being. *Social Science Research, 38*(1), 201–212.

Wallace, H., & Roberson, C. (2010). *Family violence: Legal, medical, and social perspectives.* Upper Saddle River, NJ: Prentice Hall PTR.

Walster, E. H., Walster, G. W., & Berscheid, E. (1978). *Equity: Theory and research.* Upper Saddle River, NJ: Allyn & Bacon.

Wardle, L. D. (2004). Withering away of marriage: Some lessons from the Bolshevik family law reforms in Russia, 1917–1926. *Georgetown Journal of Law & Public Policy, 2,* 469–522.

Warner, W. L., Meeker, M., & Eells, K. (1949). *Social class in America: A manual of procedure for the measurement of social status.* Oxford, UK: Science Research Associates.

Waters, E. (1995). The Bolsheviks and the family. *Contemporary European History, 4*, 275–291.

Wechsler, D. (1939). *The measurement of adult intelligence*. Baltimore, MD: Williams & Wilkins.

Weiss, Y., & Willis, R. J. (1997). Match quality, new information, and marital dissolution. *Journal of Labor Economics, 15*(1), 293–329.

Weiten, W., & McCann, D. (2007). *Psychology: Themes & variations* (1st Canadian ed.). Toronto, ON: Nelson Education.

Welden, B. A. (2010). Restoring lost "honor": Retrieving face and identity, removing shame, and controlling the familial cultural environment through "honor murder." *Journal of Alternative Perspectives in Social Sciences, 2*(1), 380–398.

Westhuis, D. J., Fafara, R. J., & Ouellette, P. (2006). Does ethnicity affect the coping of military spouses? *Armed Forces & Society, 32*(4), 584–603.

White, G. L., & Mullen, P. E. (1989). *Jealousy: Theory, research, and clinical strategies*. New York, NY: Guilford Press.

White, J. M. (1987). Premarital cohabitation and marital stability in Canada. *Journal of Marriage and the Family, 49*(3), 641–647.

White, J. M. (1991). *Dynamics of family development*. New York, NY: Guilford Press.

White, J. M. (1999). Work–family stage and satisfaction with work–family balance. *Journal of Comparative Family Studies, 30*, 163–175.

White, J. M. (2004). *Advancing family theories*. Thousand Oaks, CA: Sage Publications.

White, J. M., & Klein, D. M. (2008). *Family theories* (3rd ed.). Thousand Oaks, CA: Sage Publications.

White, J. M., Larson, L. E., Goltz, J. W., & Munro, B. E. (2005). *Families in Canada: Social contexts, continuities, and changes* (3rd ed.). Toronto, ON: Pearson Education Canada.

White, L. K. (1990). Determinants of divorce: A review of research in the eighties. *Journal of Marriage and the Family, 52*(4), 904–912.

White, L. K., & Booth, A. (1985). The quality and stability of remarriages: The role of stepchildren. *American Sociological Review, 50*(5), 689–698.

White, L. K., & Brinkerhoff, D. B. (1981). Children's work in the family: Its significance and meaning. *Journal of Marriage and the Family, 43*(4), 789–798.

White, P., & Mick, H. (2007). Teen death highlights cultural tensions. *The Globe and Mail*, December 12. Retrieved from http://www.theglobeandmail.com/life/article138753.ece

Whitehead, B. D. (1997). *The divorce culture*. New York, NY: Knopf.

Whitehead, B. D., & Popenoe, D. (2000). *Sex without strings, relationships without rings: Today's young singles talk about mating and dating*. New Brunswick, NJ: The National Marriage Project.

Whitehead, B. D., & Popenoe, D. (2006). The state of our unions: The social health of marriage in America. The National Marriage Project. Retrieved from http://www.stateofourunions.org/2010/SOOU2010.php

Whitson, S., & El-Sheikh, M. (2003). Marital conflict and health: Processes and protective factors. *Aggression and Violent Behavior, 8*, 283–312.

Wiik, K. A. (2008). "You'd better wait!"— Socio-economic background and timing of first marriage versus first cohabitation. *European Sociological Review, 25*(2) 139–153.

Wilken, C. S. (2002). *Myths and realities of aging*. Gainesville, FL: University of Florida Cooperative Extension Service, Institute of Food and Agricultural Sciences, EDIS. Retrieved from http://edis.ifas.ufl.edu

Williams, J. (2000). *Unbending gender: Why work and family conflict and what to do about it*. Oxford, UK: Oxford University Press.

Williams, K., & Umberson, D. (2004). Marital status, marital transitions, and health: A gendered life course perspective. *Journal of Health and Social Behavior, 45*(1), 81.

Wilson, B., & Smallwood, S. (2008). The proportion of marriages ending in divorce. *Population Trends, 131*, 28–36.

Wilson, J., & Sherkat, D. (1994). Returning to the fold. *Journal for the Scientific Study of Religion, 33*, 148–161.

Wilson, M., & Daly, M. (1998). Lethal and nonlethal violence against wives and the

evolutionary psychology of male sexual pro-
prietariness. *Sage Series on Violence Against
Women, 9*, 199–230.

Winch, R. F. (1955). The theory of complementary needs in mate-selection: A test of
one kind of complementariness. *American
Sociological Review, 20*(1), 52–56.

Wineberg, H. (1988). Duration between marriage and first birth and marital instability.
Biodemography and Social Biology, 35, 91–102.

Wolfers, J. (2006). Did unilateral divorce laws
raise divorce rates? A reconciliation and
new results. *The American Economic Review,
96*(5), 1802–1820.

Wolfinger, N. H., Kowaleski-Jones, L., & Smith,
K. R. (2003). Double impact: What sibling
data can tell us about the long-term negative
effects of parental divorce. *Biodemography and
Social Biology, 50*(1), 58–76.

Wong, T., & Yeoh, B. (2002). Fertility and the
family: An overview of pro-natalist policies
in Singapore. Research paper series #12,
Asian MetaCenter, National University of
Singapore, Singapore. Retrieved from http://
www.populationasia.org/Publications/
ResearchPaper/AMCRP12.pdf

Woods, L. N., & Emery, R. E. (2002). The
cohabitation effect on divorce: Causation or
selection? *Journal of Divorce & Remarriage,
37*, 101–122.

Woolsey, T. D. (1882). *Divorce and divorce legislation: Especially in the United States*. New York,
NY: Scribner's Sons.

Wright, S., & Martin, A. (2010). Were toddlers in
the boot drugged with Nytol before mother

"asphyxiated them"? *Daily Mail*, January 27.
Retrieved from http://www.dailymail.co.uk/
news/article-1246546/Mother-Fiona-
Donnison-kills-children-leaves-bodies-car-
boot.html#ixzz1AgINL3cC

Yodanis, C. (2004). Gender inequality, violence
against women, and fear: A cross-national
test of the feminist theory of violence against
women. *Journal of Interpersonal Violence, 19*,
655–675.

Yodanis, C. (2005). Divorce culture and marital
gender equality. *Gender & Society, 19*(5), 644.

Young, K. (2009). Understanding online gaming
addiction and treatment issues for adolescents. *The American Journal of Family
Therapy, 37*(5), 355–372.

Zajonc, R. B. (2001). Mere exposure: A gateway
to the subliminal. *Current Directions in
Psychological Science, 10*, 224–228.

Zhang, S. (2009). Can I make my own decision?
A cross-cultural study of perceived social
network influence in mate selection. *Journal
of Cross Cultural Psychology, 40*(1), 3–23.

Zhang, Z., & Hayward, M. D. (2006). Gender, the
marital life course, and cardiovascular disease
in late midlife. *Journal of Marriage and Family,
68*(3), 639–657.

Zhao, J. K. (2009). Social security, differential
fertility and the dynamics of the earnings distribution. Paper 3, Department of Economics,
University of Western Ontario, London,
ON. Retrieved from http://publish.uwo
.ca/~kzhao5/SSandDF.pdf

Zimmerman, C. C. (1947). *Family and civilization*.
New York, NY: Harper.

Credits

Literary Credits

Pages 4–5 Adapted from Statistics Canada publication *The Daily*, September 12, 2007, http://www.statcan. gc.ca/daily-quotidien/070912/dq070912a-eng.htm. **9** © Government of Yukon 2011. Department of Community Services, Government of Yukon, email: employmentstandards@gov.yk.ca. **44** Clara H. Mulder, *Journal of Family Issues* (April 2003, Vol. 24, no. 3), pp. 291–313, copyright © 2003 by SAGE Publications. Reprinted by Permission of SAGE Publications. **64** Hartwick, C., Desmarais, S., & Hennig, K. (2007). Characteristics of male and female victims of sexual coercion. *The Canadian Journal of Human Sexuality*, 16(1–2), 31–44. Reprinted by permission of *The Canadian Journal of Human Sexuality*. **69** Reprinted with permission of Pearson Canada. **71** Adapted from Statistics Canada Website, http://www40.statcan.gc.ca/l01/ cst01/demo10a-eng.htm (Accessed Feb 20, 2011). **86** Liefbroer, A. C., & Dourleijn, E. (2006). Unmarried Cohabitation and Union Stability: Testing the Role of Diffusion Using Data from 16 European Countries. *Demography, 43*, 203–221. Figure 1 page 213. Reprinted with permission of Population Association of America. **87** With kind permission from Springer Science+Business Media: *Society*, "Cohabitation, Marriage, and Child Wellbeing: A Cross-National Perspective", volume 46, issue 5, 2009, pp. 429–436, Popenoe, D., Table 1 page 431. **89** Source: Liefbroer, A. C., & Dourleijn, E. (2006). Unmarried Cohabitation and Union Stability: Testing the Role of Diffusion Using Data from 16 European Countries. *Demography, 43*, 203–221. Figure 2 page 217. Reprinted with permission of Population Association of America. **91** Based on Statistics Canada 2001 and 1991 Census (Public Use Microdata Files) data. **97** From Canada Revenue Agency, Marital status, URL: http://www.cra-arc.gc.ca/tx/ndvdls/tpcs/ncm-tx/rtrn/cmpltng/prsnl-nf/mrtl-eng. html. Reproduced with permission of the Minister of Public Works and Government Services Canada, 2011. **98** Thornton, A., Axinn, W. G., & Xie, Y. (2007). *Marriage and Cohabitation*. Chicago: The University of Chicago Press. Reprinted with permission. **103** Heuveline, P., & Timberlake, J. M. (2004). The role of cohabitation in family formation: The United States in comparative perspective. *Journal of Marriage and Family*, 66, 1214–1230. Table 1 page 1219. Reprinted by permission of John Wiley and Sons, Inc. **106** Alissa Goodman and Ellen Greaves, 'Cohabitation, marriage and child outcomes', © Institute for Fiscal Studies 2010. **107** Alissa Goodman and Ellen Greaves, 'Cohabitation, marriage and child outcomes', © Institute for Fiscal Studies 2010. **117 (top)** Based on Statistics Canada 2006 to 1981 Census of Population data, Catalogue no. 97-554-XCB2006011. **117 (bottom)** Based on Statistics Canada, 2006 Census of Population, Statistics Canada catalogue no. 97-552-XCB2006007 (Canada, Code01). **118** Based on Statistics Canada CANSIM Database, Tables 101-1011 and 101-1012. **119** Statistics Canada, Annual Demographic Statistics, 91-213-XIB2005000, April 2006; http://www.statcan.gc.ca/bsolc/olc-cel/olccel?catno=91-213-XIB&lang=eng# olcinfopanel and the Statistics Canada CANSIM database http://cansim2.statcan.gc.ca, Figure 5.2, April 5, 2011. **120** Based on Statistics Canada CANSIM Database, Tables 101-1011 and 101-1012. **131** Adapted from Caughlin, J. P., & Huston, T. L. (2006). The affective structure of marriage. In Anita Vangelisti and Daniel Perlman (Eds). *Cambridge Handbook of Personal Relationships*. New York: Cambridge Univeristy Press, p. 132. Reprinted with the permission of Cambridge University Press. **133** Adapted from Miller and Perlman, Miller, R., & Perlman, D. (2009). *Intimate Relationships*, 5e, McGraw-Hill Companies, Inc. Reprinted with the permission of The McGraw-Hill Companies, Inc. **134** Reprinted from *Handbook of Interpersonal Commitment and Relationship Stability*, J. M Adams and W. H. Jones (Eds), 1999, page 77, Personal, moral and structural commitment to relationships: Experiences of Choice and Constraint, Johnson, M., Figure 4.1 "The General Commitment Model", New York: Plenum Press, with kind permission from Springer Science+Business Media B.V. **148** Changing Fertility Patterns: Trends and Implications. *Health Policy Research Bulletin*, Issue 10, May 2005. Public Health Agency of Canada, 2005. Reproduced with the permission of the Minister of Health, 2011. **150** Changing Fertility Patterns: Trends and Implications. *Health Policy Research Bulletin*, Issue 10, May 2005. Public Health Agency of Canada, 2005. Reproduced with the permission of the Minister of Health, 2011. **151** Changing Fertility Patterns: Trends and Implications. *Health Policy Research Bulletin*, Issue 10, May 2005. Public Health Agency of Canada, 2005. Reproduced with the permission of the Minister of Health, 2011. **152** Changing Fertility Patterns: Trends and Implications. *Health Policy Research Bulletin*, Issue 10, May 2005. Public Health Agency of Canada, 2005. Reproduced with the permission of the Minister of Health, 2011. **153 (top)** Changing Fertility Patterns: Trends and Implications. *Health Policy Research Bulletin*, Issue 10, May 2005. Public Health Agency of Canada, 2005. Reproduced with the permission of the Minister of Health, 2011. **153 (bottom)** Adapted from Statistics Canada website, http://www40.statcan.gc.ca/l01/cst01/health103a-eng.htm. **154** Adapted from Statistics Canada publication *The Daily*, Tuesday, Jan. 15, 2008, http://www.statcan.gc.ca/dailyquotidien/080115/dq080115a-eng.htm. **155** Reprinted with permission—Figure 1, page 517, by Morgan, S.P., & Rackin, H. (2010). A Half Century of Fertility Change. *Journal of Comparative Family Studies*, Vol. 41, No. 4, 40th Anniversary edition, pp. 515–535. **161** From Table 1. Belsky, J., and Rovine, M. (1990). Patterns of Marital Change across the Transition to Parenthood: Pregnancy to Three Years Postpartum. *Journal of Marriage and Family*, Vol. 52, No. 1 (Feb. 1990), pp. 5–19. Reproduced with permission of Blackwell Publishing Ltd. **183** http://www.canadiancrc.com/child_abandonment.aspx. Reprinted with permission. **186** From Figure 1, page 84 Belsky, J. © 1984. The determinants of parenting: A process model. *Child Development*. 55, 83–96. Reproduced with permission of Blackwell Publishing Ltd. **201** Miller, Seumas, "Social Institutions", *The Stanford Encyclopedia of Philosophy* (Spring 2011 Edition), Edward N. Zalta (ed.), URL = http://plato.stanford.edu/archives/spr2011/entries/social-institutions/. **203** Methods of life course research: qualitative and quantitative approaches by GIELE, JANET Z. Copyright 1998 Reproduced with permission of SAGE PUBLICATIONS INC BOOKS in the format Textbook via Copyright Clearance Center. **211** Buchmann, C., Diprete, T.A., *American Sociological Review* (Volume 71 and Issue Number 4) pp. 515–541, copyright © 2003 by SAGE Publications. Reprinted by Permission of SAGE Publications. **214–215** Martin, T.F., White, J.M., & Perlman, D., *Journal of Adolescent Research* (Volume 18 and Issue Number 2), pp. 169–187, copyright © 2003 by SAGE Publications. Reprinted by Permission of SAGE Publications. **223** Leisering, L., and Walker, R. (1998). *The Dynamics of Modern Society: Poverty, Policy and Welfare*. Bristol: The Policy Press. p. 10. Reprinted with permission of Policy Press. **225** Adapted from Statistics Canada publication *Healthy People, Healthy Places*, Catalogue 82-229-XWE2009000, http://www.statcan.gc.ca/bsolc/olc-cel/olc-cel?catno=82-229-x&lang=eng. **238** Reproduced with permission of Sage Publications, from Beyond the average divorce, David Demo and Mark Fine, Figure 2.1, page 49, © 2009; permission conveyed through Copyright Clearance Center, Inc. **240** OECD (2001), *Society at a Glance 2001: OECD Social Indicators*, figure (Chart G6.2.), OECD Publishing, ISBN: 013-214813-7, http://dx.doi.org/10.1787/soc_glance-2001-en. Reprinted with permission of OECD. **245** *Families Count 2010*, p. 45. Reprinted with permission of The Vanier Institute of the Family. **245–246** CBC.CA http://www.cbc.ca/news/canada/story/2010/10/04/vanier-study004.html. **250** Reprinted from *Handbook of Stressful Transitions Across the Lifespan*, 2010, page 213, Transitioning the impact of divorce on children throughout the life cycle, Barczak, B., Miller, T. W., Veltkamp, L. J., Barczak, S., Hall, C., & Kraus, R., with kind permission from Springer Science+Business Media B.V. **252** *Families Count 2010*, p. 47. Reprinted with permission of The Vanier Institute of the Family. **254** Fig 1; Kreider, R. M., & Bureau, U. S. C. (2008). Living arrangements of children, 2004: U. S. Dept. of Commerce, Economics and Statistics Administration, U. S. Census Bureau. **263** Adapted from Statistics Canada publication *Age and Sex, 2006 Census*, Catalogue 97-551-XWE2006001, http://www12.statcan.gc.ca/census-recensement/2006/as-sa/97-551/figures/c7-eng.cfm. **264** Adapted from Statistics Canada publication *A Portrait of Seniors in Canada*, 2006, Catalogue 89-519XIE2006001, http://www.statcan.gc.ca/pub/89-519-x/89-519-x2006001-eng.pdf. **265 (top)** Adapted from Statistics Canada publication *A Portrait of Seniors in Canada*, 2006, Catalogue 89-519XIE2006001, http://www.statcan.gc.ca/pub/89-519-x/89-519-x2006001-eng.pdf. **265 (bottom)** Adapted from Statistics Canada publication *A Portrait of Seniors in Canada*, 2006, Catalogue 89-519XIE2006001, http://www.statcan.gc.ca/pub/89-519-x/89-519-x2006001-eng.pdf. **266** Adapted from Statistics Canada publication *Health Reports*, Catalogue 82-003-XIE 2005001, Vol. 17, No. 1, page 45, http://www.statcan.gc.ca/pub/82-003-x/2005001/article/8709-eng.pdf. **275** Based on Statistics Canada Data, Catalogue 97-552-XCB2006007. **277** Based on Statistics Canada 2006 Census, Catalogue No. 97-554-XWE2006054; Statistics Canada, 2006 Census of Canada, Catalogue No. 97-553-XCB2006018. **280** Based on Statistics Canada publication *Perspectives on Labour and Income*, Catalogue 75-001-XIE2008104, Vol. 9, no. 4, April 2008, http://www.statcan.gc.ca/pub/75-001-x/75-001-x2008104-eng.htm. **281 (top)** Based on Statistics Canada, *Income Trends in Canada 1976–2007*, Catalogue no. 13F0022XCB. **281 (bottom)** Based on Statistics Canada, Raj Chawla (2008), "Changes in Family Wealth," *Perspective on Labour and Income*, Statistics Canada, Catalogue no. 75-001-X. **282** Adapted from Statistics Canada publication *Canadian Social Trends*, catalogue 11-008-XIE2008002, http://www.statcan.gc.ca/pub/11-008-x/2008002/article/10689-eng.pdf. **285** John W. Rowe, Robert L. Kahn, Successful Aging, *The Gerontologist*, 1997, Vol. 37, No. 4, Figure 6.1, by permission of Oxford University Press. Copyright © 1997, The Gerontological Society of America. **294** Adapted from Statistics Canada publication *Family Violence in Canada: A Statistical Profile*, Catalogue 85-224-XWE2009000, http://www.statcan.gc.ca/pub/85-224-x/2009000/ct014-eng.htm. **296** Reprinted with permission from Inside Higher Ed, article found at: http://app3.insidehighered.com/layout/set/popup/news/2011/06/24/qt. **300** Social stress and the family: advances and developments in family stress theory and research by MCCUBBIN, HAMILTON I. Copyright 1983 Reproduced with permission of HAWORTH PRESS/TAYLOR & FRANCIS–BOOKS in the format Textbook and Other book via Copyright Clearance Center. **301** Olson, D. H., Sprenkle, D. H., & Russell, C. S. (1979). Circumplex model of marital and family systems: I. Cohesion and adaptability dimensions, family types, and clinical applications. *Family Process*, 18(1), 3–28. Figure 1 page 7. Reprinted by permission of John Wiley & Sons, Inc. **305** McGregor MJ, Ericksen J, Ronald LA, et al. Rising incidence of hospital-reported drug-facilitated sexual assault in a large urban community in Canada. Retrospective population-based study. *Can J Public Health*2004;95:441–5. pg 442. Reprinted by permission of the Canadian Public Health Association. **309** Canadian Incidence Study of Reported Child Abuse and Neglect 2003—Major Findings. Public Health Agency of Canada, 2003. Reproduced with the permission of the Minister of Health, 2011. **310** Reprinted by permission from Sun Media Corporation. **314** David S. Black, Steve Sussman, and Jennifer B. Unger, *Journal of Interpersonal Violence*, vol. 25, issue 6. pp. 1022–1042, copyright © 2010 by Sage Publications. Reprinted by Permission of SAGE Publications. **320** Source: Statistics Canada, 2006 census, Cat. 97-553-XCB2006007. **326 (top)** Chart 3: "Immigration is an increasingly important component of population growth in Canada", adapted from Statistics Canada website, http://www.statcan.gc.ca/kits-trousses/issues-enjeux/c-g/edu01c_0002c-eng. **326 (bottom)** Figure 2: "Region of birth of recent immigrants to Canada, 1971 to 2006": adapted from Statistics Canada publication *Immigration and citizenship*, 2006 Census, Catalogue 97-557-XIE2006001, http://www.statcan.gc.ca/bsolc/olc-cel/olc-cel?catno=97-557-XIE2006001&lang=eng.

Photo Credits

Page 1 © Monkey Business Images/Shutterstock. 7 © AISPIX by Image Source/Shutterstock. 21 © William Perugini/Shutterstock. 27 © SVLuma/Shutterstock. 33 © Tatiana Morozova/Shutterstock. 41 © iStockphoto.com/oneclearvision. 49 © Maridav/Shutterstock. 55 © Yuri Arcurs/Shutterstock. 63 ©iStockphoto.com/elkor. 78©Frontpage/Shutterstock. 81 ©mangostock/Shutterstock. 100©GoodMood Photo/Shutterstock. 114 © Anatoliy Samara/Shutterstock. 121 © Jose AS Reyes/Shutterstock. 128 ©Brocreative/Shutterstock. 141©Websubstance/Dreamstime.com. 145©Szczepko / Dreamstime.com. 157 © Monkeybusinessimages/Dreamstime.com. 168 © Pavla/Dreamstime.com. 186 © Jordache/Shutterstock. 190 © Mangroove/Dreamstime.com. 199 © Morgan Lane Photography/Shutterstock. 206 © oliveromg/Shutterstock. 212 © Matt Apps/Shutterstock. 230 © Stavchansky Yakov/Shutterstock. 234 © Zimmytws/Dreamstime.com. 253 © Fleyeing/Dreamstime.com. 259 © AISPIX by Image Source. 267 © ejwhite/Shutterstock. 279 © Andresr/Shutterstock. 292 © wavebreakmedia ltd/Shutterstock. 303 © Monkey Business Images/Shutterstock. 313 © Alexraths/Dreamstime.com. 318 © iStockphoto.com/Karin Lau. 324 © Andrew Lever/Shutterstock. 333 © Jaren Jai Wicklund/Shutterstock.

Index

married and unmarried couples comparisons in, 95*t*
married-couple families in, 4
median family income in, 334
miscarriage rates in, 153*f*
multiculturalism in, 21–22, 156
number of marriages and divorces in, 252*f*
polygamy in, 121
population aging in, 327, 327*f*
population by sex and age group, 71*f*
population growth in, 325
premarital sexual rates in, 54
same-sex couples in, 4
same-sex marriage in, 8
spanking of children in, 186
stepfamilies in, 254
total fertility rate in, 147–148, 152–154
unmarried people in, 5
women in workforce in, 203
young adults in parental home, 30, 323
Capon, Pat, 89
caregiving, 282–283, 282*t*
Caron Malenfant, É, 156, 218
Carrère, S., 132, 307
Cary, M. S., 54
Casper, Lynne Marie, 102, 108, 202
Castells, Manuel, 53–54
Catherine of Aragon, 232
Caughlin, John P., 131
Cavanagh, Kate, 306
Cavanagh, Shannon E., 249
CBC News, 62, 122, 246
CBR. *See* crude birth rate (CBR)
Changing Rhythms of American Family Life, 207
Charter of Rights and Freedoms, 8
Chatters, Linda M., 216, 217
Cherlin, Andrew J., 233, 251
child abuse, 293, 308–310
    fathers in, 306
    gender and, 293
child achievement, 184
child care,
    OECD countries and, 210
    state policies toward, 223
child compliance, 184
child custody, 93

cohabitation and, 94–95
grandparents and, 278
child development
    (theories of), 171
    attachment theory of, 180
    ecological theoretical model of, 179–180
    invariant ordering, 176
    nature-nurture debate, 173, 174
    ontogenetic, 175, 176
    Piaget's stages of, 177, 178*t*
    psychoanalytic theories of, 176–177
    psychological theories of, 177–178, 178*t*
    sociogenic, 175–176
    sociological theories of, 178–180
    time frame, 176
Child Development, 186
child neglect, 308–309
    internet addiction and, 310
child temperament, 171
child-to-parent unidirectional model, 171
childbirth, 142–143
    conformity as factor in wanting, 144
    life experience as factor in wanting, 144
    lower rates of, 321–322
    old age security as factor in wanting, 144
    premarital as factor in divorce, 235
    reasons for wanting, 143, 144, 146–147
    recent rates in Canada, 153–153*t*, 154
    social capital factor in wanting, 144
childhood, 36
    state's policies and, 223
Children of the Great Depression, 44
children,
    socialization of, 170–171, 173
China,
    cohabitation rates in, 94
    one-child policy, 222–223
Chomsky, Noam, 171
Chopin, Frédéric, 191
Christianity, 213–214
    family life and, 218–219

gender roles in, 217
    sexuality in, 218
chronic jealousy, 303
chronological age, 264, 270
Church of England, 232
Church of Jesus Christ of Latter-Day Saints, 122
circumplex model of family functions, 300–302, 301*f*
Civil Marriage Act (2005), 120, 220
civil unions, 93
Clark, Cynthia A., 214
Clark, Warren, 101
cluttered nest, 277
co-guardianship, 94
Coan, J., 132
cognition, 171
cognitive dissonance, 38
cohabitation, 39, 44
    Aboriginal peoples and, 90
    African rates of, 89
    asset protection and, 93–94
    changes in, 320–321
    channelling acceptance of, 99–100
    child custody and, 93, 94–95
    common-law marriage and, 90–92
    courtship patterns, 101–104
    cross-cultural studies on, 86–87
    cross-national government policies on, 90
    definitions of, 90–92
    deliberateness of entering, 102–104
    differences after separation between common-law and marriage, 96
    divorce and, 235, 236–237
    Eastern European rates of, 88
    education and, 211–212
    effects of legislation on, 92
    effects on adolescents of, 105–107
    effects on children across life course, 105, 107
    effects on children of intergenerational, 99
    effects on later marital quality of, 107–109
    egalitarian roles in, 161–162
    elderly and, 109–111

dynamics and, 16, 17
equivalence form of, 6
family, 336
forms of, 6
genus and species, 6
history of family, 5–7
ideological component of, 3
importance of, 3–5
kinship systems, 19, 22
legal, 8
marriage, 120
normative, 8, 10
of family, 3
research, 8, 11–12, 15–16
research and, 2–3
social institutions, 201
social norms and, 9–10
theoretical, 10, 11
types of, 8
Demo, David, 237, 238
demographic transition theory,
    147, 337
    divorce and, 235
    fertility and, 216
    problems with, 337
demography, 261
deoxyribonucleic acid (DNA), 173
dependency ratio, 225, 323, 334
Derosas, Renzo, 215, 216
descent,
    matrilineal, 19, 20
    unilineal, 19, 20
Desmarais, Serge, 59
developmental fallacy, 269–270
Developmental Psychology, 268
developmental tasks, 42
developmental theory, 31
deviance, 39
DFSA. *See* drug-facilitated sexual
    assault (DFSA)
Dhaka University, 296
*Diagnostic and Statistical Manual of
    Mental Disorders*, 4th edition
    (DSM-IV), 180
Dionysius, 232
DiPrete, Thomas A., 211
disillusionment model, 131
divorce, 8
    adolescents and, 249–250
    adult children and, 250
    as reconstruction of family, 247
    calculating rates of, 244

children in, 237, 248, 250
cohabitation as factor in, 235
current trends, 236
definitions, 231
demographic factors in, 235
determinants of, 234–235
diversity in Europe of, 239
diversity of, 237, 238–239
education and, 212
effects of, 247–248
elderly and, 274–275
family process as cause of, 235
fertility as factor in, 235
health problems and, 248
historical context, 232–234
in North America, 232–233
life course causes of, 235
macro-structural causes of, 234
potential causes of, 240–243,
    244
premarital childbirth as factor
    in, 235
premarital pregnancy as factor
    in, 235
process, 237
rates, 323
reasons for, 246
reducing risk of, 236
rise in rates of, 81
Roman law and, 232
same-sex marriage and, 120
state involvement in, 224
see also individual divorce rate
    calculating methods
Divorce Act of 1968, 233, 239
Divorce Act, 1985, 233, 239
Divorce Culture, The, 231
divorce variation and fluidity model
    (DVFM), 237, 238, 238f
DNA. *See* deoxyribonucleic acid
    (DNA)
domestic family, 202
domestic partnership legislation, 90
domination, 133
Donahue, M. J., 214
Donnelly, Denise A., 30
Dosman, Donna, 282
double ABC-X model of family
    stress theory, 299
double standard, 54
Dourleijn, E., 86, 88, 89
Drobnic, Sonia, 204

Dronkers, Jaap, 212
drug-facilitated sexual assault
    (DFSA), 305t
DuRant, Robert, 305
Durkheim, Emile, 151, 201, 202, 206
Durrant, J.-E., 308
Dutton, Donald G., 296
Duxbury, J., 207
DVFM. *See* divorce variation and
    fluidity model (DVFM)
dyad, 172–173, 179–180
    divorce and, 238
dynamic theory, 16
    life course and, 33–34

E

Easterlin, Richard A., 129
ecological correlates of divorce,
    240, 241t
ecological theoretical model of
    development, 179–180
education,
    cohabitation and, 211–212
    as social institution, 200, 329,
        331–332
    childhood care and, 210
    divorce and, 212
    family and, 209–210
    marriage and, 211–212
    separation and, 212
    women in, 325
educational norms, 44
Eells, Kenneth, 189–190
Eggebeen, David J., 181
egocentric bias, 69
elder abuse, 283
    adult children and, 312–313
    preventing, 284
    risk factors for, 283
Elder, Glen H., Jr., 44
elderly,
    cohabitation and, 109–111
Elliott, Ann N., 312
Ellison, Christopher G., 308
Ellison, Nicole B., 56
Elze, Diane E., 53
empiricism, 170
Employment Insurance Act, 9
Employment Standards Act
    (Yukon), 9
empty nest stage, 276–277
endogamy, 70

enduring dynamics model, 131
episodic memory, 272
equity theory (of mate selection),
    68, 69
Erickson, J. A., 214
Erikson, Erik, 177, 267
eros, 62
Ethnic Diversity Study, 156
ethnic diversity, 327
Euthyphro, 6
evolutionary psychology, 294–295
evolutionary theory, 32, 294–295
exogamy, 70
experimental design of research,
    186
expressive divorce, 233
expressive role, 206
external locus of control, 274
extraneous factors, 14

F

Fallon, B., 308
Families Count, 154
*Families: Changing Trends
    in Canada*, 252
family development theory,
    298–299
    propositions of, 298–299
family dysfunction,
    child abuse and, 309–310
    circumplex model as
        explanation for, 300–302,
        301f
    evolutionary psychological
        explanations for, 295–296
    family development theory as
        explanation for, 298–299
    family stress theory as
        explanation for, 298, 299, 300
    intergenerational transmission
        of, 314
    incest and, 310–311
    intergenerational issues, 313
    macro sociological explanations
        for, 297
    micro sociological explanations
        for, 297–298
    parental abuse by adolescents,
        312
    psychological explanations for,
        296–297
    sibling violence, 312

sociobiological explanations for,
    294–295
theory of patriarchy as
    explanation for, 297
family of orientation, 19
family of procreation, 19
family stress theory, 298, 299
    ABC-X model of, 299, 300
family(ies),
    aging of, 323
    as social institution, 331–332
    biological constraints and, 35
    common-law couple, 4
    compositional changes in, 205
    definitions of, 3, 5–9
    disappearance of, 336–338
    diversity in, 322
    dynamic work interaction, 204
    dysfunction, 295
    dysfunction of work
        interaction, 204
    economics and, 336
    education and, 210
    feminist perspective of, 202
    functions, 337
    future for Canadian, 333–336
    gender inequality in, 205
    government legislation on, 8
    history of definitions of, 5–7
    institutional influences on, 201
    interaction with other social
        institutions, 202
    kinship definition of, 22
    kinship systems and, 19
    legal definitions of, 8
    life course and, 203, 302
    life course of, 17–18
    lone parent, 4, 319–320,
        322, 334
    married couple, 4
    normative definitions of, 10
    one-person households, 4–5
    policy changes affecting,
        333–336
    religion and, 212
    research contexts for, 12
    rites of passage and, 212–213
    role intensification in, 322
    same-sex couples, 4
    social class influence on,
        191–192
    social construction of, 8

socio-cultural context, 324
state's role in, 220–222
state's role in labour force and,
    223–224
structural changes in, 34
structures, 41–42
theoretical analyses of, 30–31
theoretical definition of, 10
transitions, 211–212
work and, 203–205, 322
family-workplace interaction,
    dynamics of, 207–208
    feminist perspective on,
        205, 206
    functionalist approach to,
        205–206
    historical context, 205–207
    life course and, 203–204
    rapid changes in, 207
    recent trends in, 207–209
Faulks, Tara, 60
Feeney, S., 159
Feldman, H., 159
Felmlee, Diane H., 59, 304
feminist theories, 30, 81
    family, 202
    family-workplace interaction,
        205, 206–207
    gender and religion, 217
    patriarchy, 334
    theory of patriarchy, 297
fertility, 143
    actual, 145
    age-specific rates of, 147
    as factor in divorce, 235
    below replacement rate in
        Canada, 334
    current trends in Canada, 153
    delaying, 151
    desired (intended), 145
    desired family size and, 146
    economic factors in, 151–152,
        152f
    education as factor in, 151, 151f
    gender roles and, 220
    involuntary, 157
    lower rates of, 321–322
    measurement, 147
    processes of, 146
    religion and, 215–216
    timing, 148–149
    worldwide rates, 155, 155f, 156

Festinger, Leon, 55
filter model (of mate selection),
    69–70, 69f
    sex ratio as, 70, 72
    social group, 70
financial exploitation, 283
Finch, Jennifer, 310
Fine, Mark, 237, 238, 240
Finland,
    cohabitation rates in, 80
Finlayson, M., 312
Firebaugh, G., 215
First Nations peoples. *See*
    Aboriginal (First Nations)
    peoples; Inuit peoples; Métis
    peoples
Fisher, T. D., 307
Floyd, Frank J., 69
Foshee, Vangie A., 305, 314
Foster, C. A., 127–128
Foucault, Michel, 218
France,
    cohabitation legislation in, 92
    cohabitation rates in, 80, 85
    parental leave in, 335
    pro-natalist policies in, 156
Freedman, R., 216
Freud, Anna, 177
Freud, Sigmund, 176, 177
Friedan, Betty, 144
Fromuth, Mary Ellen, 312
Fumitaka, F., 337
functional age, 264
functional theories, 30
    family-workplace interaction,
    205–206
Furseth, Inger, 219

G

Gecas, V., 192
Gelles, Richard J., 312
gender equality, 209
gender inequity, 205
gender roles,
    fertility and, 220
    religion and, 217–219
general marriage rate, 116
General Social Survey 2004, 297
generational stake hypothesis, 283
generativity, 267
genetics, 173
genogram analysis, 18

Germany,
    pro-natalist policies in, 156
Gerson, Kathleen, 206–207
Gibbs, Jennifer L., 56
Giddens, Anthony, 201
Gidycz, Christine, 59
Giordano, Peggy C., 51
Glenn, Norval, 51
Globe and Mail, The, 296
Goldscheider, Calvin, 216, 220
Goldsteen, Karen, 126
González, Libertad, 239
Goode, William J., 147, 320
Gornick, Janet C., 223
Gottman, J. M., 131, 132, 307
grandparenthood, 278
    as prime caretakers, 277, 277f
    child custody and, 278
    teens and, 278
    types of, 278
Gray, E., 146, 147, 151, 152
Great Depression (1929-1938), 43,
    44, 268
Greenhaigh, Susan, 216
Growing Up in New Guinea, 179
Grzywacz, J. G., 204
Guaranteed Income
    Supplement, 264
Guinness World Records, 266
Gwartney-Gibbs, Patricia A., 321

H

habitus, 191, 192
Haig-Brown, Celia, 206, 210
Hall, Clay, 249
Han, Shin-Kap, 207
*Handbook of Stressful Transitions
    Across the Lifespan*, 249
Härkönen, Juho, 212
Harley, B., 215
Harris, Kathleen, 52
Hartwick, Cailey, 59
Harvey, John H., 240–243
Hassan, Y., 219
Hatch, R. G., 109
Havighurst, Robert J., 42
Hays, S., 182
Hazan, Cindy, 180
Health Canada, 148, 150, 151,
    152, 153
health,
    marriage and, 125–127

Heino, Rebecca D., 56
Hennig, Karl, 59
Henry VIII, King of England, 232
heterogamy, 70
Heuveline, Patrick, 85, 102
Hickey, Margaret, 94
higher-order marriages, 236
Hill, Reuben, 42, 298, 299
Hippocrates, 171
historical dialectics, 32
Hochschild, Arlie, 325
Hoffman, III, R. R., 313
Hogan, Dennis P., 40
Hogan, W. H., 204
Hoge, Dean R., 214, 215
Holmes, Thomas, 36
homicide, 293
    spousal, 294f, 303
homogamy, 57, 70
    age, 118–119
honour killings, 61–62
hooking up, 51
housework, 325
Huston, Aletha C., 249
Huston, T. L., 131
Huxley, Aldous, 220–222
hypothesis, 13
    conceptual, 13–13f
    measurement, 13–13f, 14

I

IADL scale. *See* instrumental
    activities of daily living
    (IADL) scale
IGT. *See* intergenerational
    transmission (IGT)
illegitimate demands, 132
immigration, 2, 21–22, 325
    classes, 325
    ethnic diversity and, 325
    law, 8
Immigration and Refugee
    Protection Act, 2
implicit memory, 272
incest, 21–293, 310–311
    see also Marriage (Prohibited
    Degrees) Act (1990)
Indian Act (1985), 221
individual aging, 263
    challenge and/or opportunity,
    267
individualism, 234

Industrial Revolution, 82, 206
  family composition and, 205
infancy, 36
infanticide, 293
infertility, 152–153
Inhelder, B., 178
institutional norms, 39–40
  definition of, 39
  viewpoints on, 39
instrumental activities of daily
    living (IADL) scale, 272
instrumental role, 206
integrative agreement, 133
integrity, 267
intelligence quotient (IQ), 187
  aging and, 268–270
intergenerational transmission
    (IGT) of family dysfunction,
    314
intergenerational transmission
    (IGT) of marital aggression,
    314
intergenerational transmission
    (IGT) of social class,
    189–190, 191
  theoretical model for, 191,
    192, 192f
intergenerational transmission
    (IGT) of violence theory, 314
internal locus of control, 274
International Code of Marketing
    of Breast-milk Substitutes,
    163
Intimate Relationships, 133
intimate terrorism, 297
Inuit peoples, 154
involuntary childlessness, 146
involved grandparents, 278
Ishwaran, Karigoudar, 83
Islam, 214
  family life and, 219
  fertility rates, 216
  gender roles in, 217

J

Jagger, Elizabeth, 56
James, William, 176
Japan,
  cohabitation rates in, 88
Jesus Christ, 218
Johansson, L. C., 65
Johnson, Benton, 214

Johnson, David, 128
Johnson, Michael P., 134, 297
Johnson, Shannon, 310
Jose, A., 109
Journal of Marriage and Family, 296
Judaism, 213–214
  fertility rates, 216
  gender roles in, 217

K

Kahn, Joan, 208
Kalliath, Thomas, 207
Kalmijn, Matthijs, 238
Kamamura, Sayaka, 109
Kelley, Harold H., 65
Kelley, Kathryn, 63
Kelly, David B., 312
Kenrick, Douglas T., 63
Kerckhoff, A. C., 69, 73
Kerr, Don, 90
Kertzer, David I., 216
Khaltourina, D., 63
Kiernan, K., 88
King, Rosalind, 52
King, Ursula, 217
King, Valerie, 109
kinkeepers, 275
kinship analysis, 18, 19, 20f
kinship systems, 19
  definitions in, 19
  incest and, 21
  inheritance and, 20
  meanings of, 20–21
  structure of, 20–21
kitchen-sinking, 133
Klein, David M., 298
knowledge (theories of), 171
Kohlberg, Lawrence, 177
Kohler, H., 337
Kohn, Melvin, 191, 192
Korotayev, A., 63
Kotre, John, 267
Kraus, Robert, 249
Kreider, Rose M., 254
Kübler-Ross, Elisabeth, 284
Kunin, Israel L., 94

L

labour (work),
  as social institution, 319, 329,
    331–332
  household, 325

women participating in,
    324–325
Laner, Mary Rieger, 51
Lang, Mary E., 160
Lareau, Annette, 191
LaRossa, Maureen Mulligan, 160
LaRossa, Ralph, 160
Larson, D. B., 188
Larzelere, R. E., 188
Laslett, Peter, 336, 337
launching (children leaving
    home), 276–277, 323
learning, 170–171
Leave It to Beaver (television
    show), 206
Lee, Gary R., 333
Lee, Minhong, 299
Leisering, Lutz, 222, 223
Leonard, Rosemary, 312
leptokurtotic, 38, 151
Lester, D., 311
levels of analysis, 38, 38t
  individual, 38–39
Levinger, George, 130
Levinson, Robert W., 131
Lewis, Robert A., 129
Lichter, Daniel T., 104, 313
Lietbroer, A. C., 86, 88, 89
life course theory, 17, 31
  Aboriginal peoples and, 37
  age, period, and cohort matrix,
    43–44, 43t
  anticipatory socialization, 44
  branching process, 328–328f
  divorce, 235
  duration, 42
  dynamic perspective, 328
  events, 35, 41–42, 41f
  family and, 203
  family and workforce, 203–204
  first pregnancy and, 158–159
  generativity, 267
  government in, 220
  institutional norms, 39–40
  levels of analysis, 38, 38t
  marital satisfaction, 129
  normative theory and, 31, 39–40
  off time, 40
  out of sequence, 40, 330
  pathways, 37–37f
  research, 44
  retirement, 224–225, 226

social dynamics and, 33–34
stages in, 36–42, 41f
transitions, 36, 42–43
life events, 35, 41–42, 41f
transition, 36
life expectancy, 266, 266f
life stages, 35–36
lifetime stability theory, 269
Lindsay, J. M., 102
Ling, Peter, 82
Linton, M. A., 60
living apart together (LAT)
marriage, 122, 319
Livingston, Gill, 312
Locke, John, 171
Lockhead, Clarence, 246
Loh, Catherine, 59
Longmore, Monica A., 51
love,
meaning of, 63
types, 62–63
ludus, 62
Luidens, Donald A., 214
Luther, Martin, 232
Lye, Diane N., 235

M
Maccoby, Eleanor, 185
Machung, Anne, 325
Mackey, Amber L., 312
macro-historical theories, 32
criticism of, 32
magnetic resonance imaging
(MRI), 226
Main, M., 180, 181
male selection,
biosocial theory of, 63–65
social exchange theory of, 65–66
mania, 63
Manning, Wendy D., 51, 99, 102,
105–107, 300
marital commitment,
types, 134–135
marital satisfaction, 127
factors in, 129
first pregnancy and, 159–160
interaction patterns, 131, 132
life course and, 128f, 129
marital stability and, 129
premarital factors, 131
research, 127–128, 159–160
U-shaped curve of, 159–160

marital stability,
cohabitation and, 84, 88
marriage satisfaction and, 129
Markman, Howard J., 102
Marquardt, Elizabeth, 51
marriage,
adjustment, 307
age at, 118–119, 120f
anxiety of newly married, 306
arranged, 52
as economic necessity, 81–82
conflict resolution within, 124
conflict, 307
covenant, 135–136
decline in during parenthood,
160–161
decline in rates, 321, 333
definitions of, 5–120
definitions of by Canada
Revenue Agency, 97
division of labour within, 124,
162–164
divorces per, 245
education and, 211–212
emotional climate of, 124–125
expectations, 307
first pregnancy and, 159
gay and lesbian, 10
health and, 125–127
historical context, 116
impact of children on, 307–308
interracial, 52–53
legal definitions of, 8
living apart together (LAT),
122, 319
marital tasks, 123–124
moral commitment to, 134
mother's role in, 162
personal commitment to, 134
quality of, 127
rates, 116, 118
reasons for, 115–116, 246
same-sex, 8, 118–321
satisfaction, 127–129
state definition of, 220
state involvement in, 224
structural commitment to, 135
theoretical definition of, 10
traditions, 121–122
transition to, 122–124
types, 129f, 131–132, 131f
Marriage and Cohabitation, 98

Marriage (Prohibited Degrees) Act
(1990), 22
marriage squeeze, 70
Marriage-Go-Round, The, 232
Marshall, Katherine, 325
Marston, Allison A., 123
Martin, John, 185
Martin, T. Castro, 235
Martin, T., 215
Marx, Karl, 201
mate selection, 62
cohabitation and, 320–321
equity theory of, 68, 69
filter model of, 69–70, 69f
sex ratio and, 69, 72
theories, 63–65, 66, 68, 69
mating gradient, 70
Matouschek, Niko, 115–116
matrilineal descent, 19, 20, 22
matrilocality, 20, 21–22
maturation (physical), 175
McDonald, D., 204
McGill, Brittany S., 208
McGregor, M., 304–305
McNulty, J. K., 307
McQuillan, Kevin, 216, 217, 219
Mead, George Herbert, 176,
178, 179
Mead, Margaret, 101, 179
measurement, 11
fertility, 147
hypothesis, 13–14
marriage rate, 116, 118
Meeker, Marchia, 190
Meno, 170
menopause, 270
Merkel, Angela, 156
Metaphysics, 6
Métis peoples, 154
Mexico,
cohabitation rates in, 80
Meyers, Marcia K., 223
Mick, H., 62
middle age, 36
Millennium Cohort Study, 105,
106, 107
Miller, R., 133
Miller, Rowland S., 60, 243
Miller, Thomas, 249
Mills, Ryan, 309
Milne, C., 308
Mind, Self and Society, 179

retirement, 224–225, 226, 279, 323
  patterns of, 279–280
  state's involvement in, 225–226
Rhoades, Galena Kline, 102
ribonucleic acid (RNA), 173
Richer, S., 171
Riggs, D. S., 314
Riley, Sarah, 203
rites of passage, 212
  family and, 212–213
RNA. *See* ribonucleic acid (RNA)
Rodgers, Roy H., 42, 298
Roehlkepartain, Eugene C., 214
Rogers, Stacy J., 129
Rogers, Willard L., 159
Rohwer, G., 204
role overload, 207
Rollins, B., 159
Roman Catholic Church, 232
Roman Empire, 202
romantic jealousy, 303
Romulus, 232
Roosevelt, Theodore, 233
Ross, Catherine E., 126
Rossi, A., 160
Rotermann, Michelle, 54
Rothman, S., 205
Rovine, Michael, 160, 161
Russell, Bertrand, 101
Russell, C., 301
Russell, C. S., 160
Russia,
  cohabitation rates in, 89
Ryff, Carol D., 273

S

same-sex couples,
  definition of, 3
  divorce, 120
  in Canada, 4
Sanchez, L. A., 135
sandwich generation, 282
Saskatchewan,
  young adults in parental homes
    in, 5
Sassler, Sharron, 313
Sather, P. R., 188
Scanzoni, John H., 219, 325
Schachter, Stanley, 55
Scheflen, Albert, 54
Schellenberg, G., 280
Schimmele, Christoph, 252

Schmitt, David P., 295
Schneider, W. N., 188
Schoen, Robert, 129, 234
Schultz, J. B., 311
Schulz, R., 313
Scott, Mindy E., 109
Second Stage, The, 144
second-parent adoption, 94
secularization of society, 81
selection effect, 105
  cohabitation and, 108
selection hypothesis (on marriage
    and health), 125
selective attention, 273
self-neglect, 283
self-summarizing, 133
Selwood, Amber, 312
semantic memory, 272
separation, 133
  education and, 212
  reasons for, 246
sequencing norm, 39–40, 332
  breakdown of, 40
SES. *See* socio-economic status
    (SES)
sex ratio, 69
  by country or culture, 72*t*
  imbalances in, 70, 275
  mate selection and, 72
sexting, 82, 83
sexual abuse, 283
sexual assault, 61, 305*t*
sexual coercion, 59–60, 304
  gender differences in, 59–60, 64*f*
  see also date rape; rape
sexual harassment, 61
sexual imposition, 61
sexual revolution, 81
sexual script, 124
sexual standards, 53–54
Shackelford, Todd K., 72
Shakespeare, William, 303
Shaver, Phillip, 180
Sherkat, D. E., 214
sibling violence, 22–312
similarity theory (of attraction), 57
Simonelli, Catherine J., 312
singlehood, 44
situational couple violence, 297
Skipper, James, Jr., 53
Slade, Eric P., 187
sliding (into relationship), 102, 321

Smock, Pamela, 97, 102, 108
Soble, Alan, 218
social aging, 270
social capital, 144
social class, 189
  categories of, 189–190
  cultural capital and, 190–191
  influence on family of, 191–192
  speech patterns and, 191
social dynamics, 33–34
social exchange theory, 30, 171
  comparison level concept of, 66
  formal propositions of, 66–67
  mate selection, 65–66
  reward concept of, 66
  salience concept of, 66
social expectations, 31
social institutions, 200
  definition, 201
  education, 200, 210, 329
  family and influences of,
    200–203
  government, 200, 220
  influences, 201
  labour, 200–201, 329
  more than unidirectional
    influences of, 203
  religion, 200
social mobility, 189
social norms, 3, 31
  age-graded, 31
  breakdown of, 40
  formal, 31
  informal, 31
  legal definitions and, 9–10
  sexuality and, 82
  women in workforce, 203, 204
social strain hypothesis (on
    marriage and health), 127
social support hypothesis, 126
social theories, 10–11
socialization (theories of),
    175–176, 178
  religious, 213–214, 215
society,
  Canada as free and tolerant, 331
  individualization of, 202
socio-cultural context, 324
socio-economic status (SES), 190
sociobiology, 295
sociogenic development, 175–176
sociological theories, 178–180

game stage of, 179
play stage of, 179
Socrates, 171
Solomon, J., 180, 181
South, Scott J., 235, 236
Spanier, Graham B., 129, 184
spanking (of children), 186
  compared to other disciplinary
    measures, 188
  effects of, 187–188
  research, 187–188
  unresolved debate on, 188–189
Spitze, Glenna, 235, 236
Spock, Dr. Benjamin, 174
Sprecher, Susan, 59
Sprenkle, D. H., 301
stages of family development,
  41–43, 41f
Stanley, Scott M., 102, 104
Statistics Canada, 3, 4, 91, 117,
  119, 120, 153, 154, 225, 263,
  265, 275, 277, 281, 294, 326
  2006 Census, 4
  divorce, 233
  divorce rates, 246
  family structures, 320
  life expectancy, 266
  population pyramids, 262
  widowhood, 274
  women in workforce, 203
Steinberg, L., 181
Steinmetz, Suzanne K., 187, 188
stepfamilies, 253–254, 255
  effects on children, 255
  roles within, 255
Stets, Jan, 61
Stewart, Michel, 312
stimulus-value-role (SVR) theory
  (of attraction), 57–58, 69
  sex ratio and, 70
  stages of, 58
Stolzenberg, Ross M., 215
Stone, Emily A., 72
storge, 62
Straus, Murray A., 30, 187
Strengths and Difficulties
  Questionnaire (SDQ), 105
stress buffering hypothesis (on
  marriage and health), 127
stress tests, 36
Stromberg-Stein, Sunni, 122
Struckman-Johnson, Cindy, 59

Struckman-Johnson, David, 59
structural improvement, 133
Supreme Court of Canada, 308
Survey of Income and Program
  Participation (2004, U.S.),
  254
Sussman, S., 314
sustained attention, 273
Suzuki method (of music
  teaching), 175, 178
Suzuki, Shinichi, 175
Swanson, C., 132
Sweden,
  cohabitation legislation in, 92
  cohabitation rates in, 85
Sweeney, Megan M., 253, 255
Swenson, Don, 219
symbolic interaction theories, 30
system theories, 30

T
tabula rasa (blank slate), 171, 173
Taylor, Robert Joseph, 216, 217
Teachman, J., 236
technical generativity, 267
teen pregnancy, 40, 149
Tennstedt, S., 313
TFR. See total fertility rate (TFR)
theoretical analysis, 28–29
  families and, 30–31
theoretical assumptions, 29, 32
  types of, 29–32
theory, 10
  social science, 10
Therborn, Goran, 88, 89, 334
Thibaut, John W., 65
Third World development, 36
Thornton, Arland, 81, 82, 97, 98,
  102, 108
Timberlake, Jeffrey M., 85, 102
Time Divide, The, 207
timing norm, 39, 143, 151
  social changes and, 332
Toope, Stephen J., 296
Toronto,
  young adults in parental
    homes in, 5
total dependency ratio, 261–262
total fertility rate (TFR), 147
  in Canada, 147–148
  worldwide, 155, 155f
transition event, 36, 44

childbirth, 142–143
cohabitation, 306
first pregnancy, 158–159
parenthood, 156–157
relationship formation, 302–303
transition point, 143
transitions, 36
Tremblay, Hélène, 89
Trocmé, Nico, 308, 309
Trost, Melanie R., 63, 319
trustee family, 202
Tucker, M. Belinda, 52
Twenge, J. M., 128

U
U.S. Census Bureau, 327
Uhlenberg, P., 203
Uller, T., 65
Unger, J., 314
UNICEF. See United Nations
  Children's Fund (UNICEF)
unilineal descent, 19, 20
union formation,
  effects of legislation on, 92
United Kingdom,
  cohabitation legislation in, 92
United Nations Children's Fund
  (UNICEF), 162, 163
United Nations General
  Assembly, 62
United Nations Study on Violence
  against Children, 186
United States (U.S.),
  cohabitation legislation in,
    92, 93
  cohabitation rates in, 80, 85, 87
  decline in marriage rates in, 321
  divorce rates in, 233
  intended fertility in, 145
  no-fault divorce in, 239
  remarriage rates in, 251–252
  spanking of children in, 186
  stepfamilies in, 254
universal taboo, 293
University of Amsterdam, 44
University of British Columbia,
  296
Urton, William, 234

V
Valiant, C. O., 159
Valiant, G. E., 159